D1065192

CHICAGO PUBLIC LIBRARY

R00970 13010

SOCIAL SCIENCES DIVISION
CHICAGO PUBLIC LIBRARY
400 SOUTH STATE STREET
CHICAGO, IL 60605

Studies in the Zohar

SUNY Series in Judaica:
Hermeneutics, Mysticism, and Religion

Michael Fishbane, Robert Goldenberg, and Arthur Green, Editors

Studies in the Zohar

Yehuda Liebes

Translated from the Hebrew
by
Arnold Schwartz, Stephanie Nakache, Penina Peli

STATE UNIVERSITY OF NEW YORK PRESS

97013010

Production by Ruth Fisher
Marketing by Theresa A. Swierzowski

Published by
State University of New York Press, Albany

© 1993   State University of New York

All rights reserved

Printed in the United States of America

No part of this book may be used or reproduced
in any manner whatsoever without written permission
except in the case of brief quotations embodied in
critical articles and reviews.

For information, address the State University of New York Press,
State University Plaza, Albany, NY 12246

Library of Congress Cataloging-in-Publication Data

Liebes, Yehuda.
    Studies in the Zohar / Yehuda Liebes ; translated from the Hebrew
by Arnold Schwartz, Stephanie Nakache, Penina Peli.
       p.   cm. — (SUNY series in Judaica)
    Includes bibliographical references and index.
    ISBN 0-7914-1189-3. — ISBN 0-7914-1190-7 (pbk.)
    1. Zohar.   2. Cabala—History.   3. Messiah—Judaism—History of
doctrines—Middle Ages, 600-1500.   4. Cabala and Christianity.
    I. Title.   II. Series
BM525.A59L54   1993
296.1'6—dc20   91-36469
                                                                           CIP

10 9 8 7 6 5 4 3 1

BM
525
.A59
.L54
1993

R00970 13010

SOCIAL SCIENCES DIVISION
CHICAGO PUBLIC LIBRARY
400 SOUTH STATE STREET
CHICAGO, IL 60605

Contents

ROGAN BRIEN
CHICAGO
400 SOUTH
CHICAGO

Preface

Sefer ha-Zohar, "The Book of Splendour," the fundamental book of Kabbala and a world-renowned masterpiece, has been subject to a great deal of investigation. As a student I fell in love with the Zohar on first sight, and I was sure that I would not let go of it for many years to come. But, convinced that the major problems concerning this book had already been solved, I decided, with the advice and guidance of the late Professor Gershom Scholem, to delve into details of the Zohar, the product of which was my doctoral dissertation "Sections of the Zohar's Lexicon." As I was working on this, I started to have the feeling, which grew stronger and stronger, that the hitherto completed research had missed much of the essential nature of the Zohar and failed to explain what was behind its magic. The research had concentrated on theoretical questions, neglecting other aspects, precisely those which gave Kabbala its special character.[1]

Therefore, I wrote the long article "The Messiah of the Zohar,"[2] which deals with the figure of the hero of the book, R. Simeon b. Yohai. In this piece I strove to demonstrate that the "literary framework" of the Zohar, previously dealt with only for proving its unhistoricity, is essential for understanding the "content" of the book and is inseparably interwoven with it. I also contend that through the figure of R. Simeon the author of the Zohar tells us a great deal about himself and his self-consciousness. A decade afterwards I advanced further in this direction and wrote the article "How the Zohar was Written,"[3] in which I proved, contrary to prior scholarly opinion, that the Zohar was not written by a single person. It was, rather, the product of a whole mystical circle, not unlike the circle R. Simeon described in it. This largely accounts for the special character of the book.

This text contains these two articles as well as a third, "Christian Influences on the Zohar."[4] Some chapters from "The

Messiah of the Zohar" are omitted here, namely those dealing with
ancient sources for the Zohar, and a chapter dealing with the way
later Kabbalists grasped the Idra parts of the Zohar and the figure
of R. Simeon b. Yohai. These Kabbalists, with whom the omitted
chapter deals, are R. Moses Cordovero, R. Isaac Luria (Ha-Ari), R.
Moses Luzzato, and R. Nahman of Bratslav.

All the articles were written, and originally published, in
Hebrew. The Hebrew versions include more philological and linguistic
details, which I found to be unnecessary for the non-reader of Hebrew,
for whom this volume is intended. "The Messiah of the Zohar" was
translated by the late Mr. Arnold Schwarz, for an intended volume
of the Israel Academy of Science and Humanities. Mrs. Devora
Gamelieli worked on the English version of this article. "How the
Zohar Was Written" was translated by Mrs. Stephanie Nakache.
"Christian Influences" was translated, in an abridged form, by Mrs.
Penina Peli, and was published, in this form, elsewhere.[5] For this
volume this translation was completed by Mrs. Nakache. The index
was prepared by Mr. Haggay Rosmarin.

1

The Messiah of the Zohar:
On R. Simeon bar Yohai as a Messianic Figure

Gershom Scholem maintains that the history of the Kabbala ought to be divided into two periods, each distinguished by a different attitude toward the idea of redemption.[1] In the first period, up to the expulsion from Spain, historical and national redemption was not in the forefront of Kabbalistic concerns. "The medieval Kabbalists," Scholem writes, believed more in "a personal, mystical redemption which signified the individual's escape from history to a time before history" than in a messianic hope focused on the end of days.[2] The Lurianic Kabbala, on the other hand, is concerned primarily with cosmic *tikkun* (restoration, perfection), and consequently also with national *tikkun*, a process that is to culminate at the end of days.[3] According to Scholem, the *Zohar*'s approach does not differ in this regard from that of the medieval Kabbalists.[4] He also maintains that the Messiah in classical Kabbala—though this would not be true of Shabbateanism—has no active role to play in effecting the *tikkun*, but merely symbolizes by his advent the end of a process that took place before his arrival.[5]

Scholem's distinctions are basically correct. In this chapter, however, I wish to show that their validity must be restricted to only part of the literature of classical Kabbala. It has become apparent to me after further study that the *Zohar* contains two strata which must, for our purposes, be distinguished from one another: that comprising the majority of the Zoharic material, and that of the *Idrot*.[6] Scholem's assertions hold for the former; I maintain, however, that the concern of the latter is primarily messianic. I shall try to prove that the messianic element within the *Idrot* already bears within itself the seeds of later Kabbalistic thought: we find in it an interesting and unique amalgam of mystical redemption and cosmic *tikkun* which signifies not the return of the world to what it once had been, but a messianic process establishing an unprecedented state. I shall also try to show that the *Idra* presents a messianic figure who is actively engaged in the process of the world's *tikkun*. While he is not the

1

Messiah himself—the latter will come only after the *tikkun*—it is he who paves the way for redemption and makes it possible. This figure is the literary persona of R. Simeon bar Yohai.

Accordingly, two strata of ideas must be distinguished in the *Zohar*: the *Idra* literature—the more profound stratum—and the rest of the book (I won't deal in this chapter with the *Ra'aya Meheimana* and the *Tikkunei Zohar*, which are later additions to the *Zohar*). This disparity in profoundness is not merely a matter of my own assessment; the text itself announces it explicitly and with great emphasis in its ceremonious description of the convening of *Idra Rabba*, the "great assembly" (*Zohar*, III, 127b–128a). The earlier disclosures, elsewhere in the *Zohar*, are referred to here as being of a lower grade. The text speaks of a need for warnings about the preservation of secrecy; for proper understanding, solemn oaths, and careful selection of the participants involved; and of much hesitation before disclosing the secrets of the *Idra*. None of this is to be found in other parts of the *Zohar*.

The Messiah in the Main Body of the Zohar

The Messiah is richly and variously described in the main body of the *Zohar*, as well as in the *Idrot*. The spirit of apocalypse hovers over most of those passages. The author of the *Zohar* made use of the Jewish apocalyptical literature, casting it in his own style, developing it in his own unique way, and bringing it into line with events of his day. This can be seen, for example, in the long passage on the Torah portion of *Shemot* (II, 7b–10a) and in many other places as well.[7] While these passages did not spring from a specifically Kabbalistic interest, this did not prevent the Kabbalist from interweaving them with matter of mystical concern, as, for example, in the passage in the *Zohar Hadash* on the Torah portion of *Balak* (55b–56c). Sometimes Kabbalistic material is used as a basis for calculating the advent of the End of Days.[8] However, the details of the *Zohar*'s apocalyptic teachings are beyond the scope of this essay.

The Kabbalistic-messianic idea most common in the main body of the *Zohar* is that of the harmony that will prevail among the *sefirot* after the coming of the Messiah, and especially that of the unification and coupling that will take place between the *sefirot* of *Tif'eret* and *Malkhut*. This unification, it should be stressed, is really a reunification, a return to what had been the normal situation before its disruption by the destruction of the sanctuary and the exile of the people, and it shall in no way be viewed as a culmination of the cosmic process of Creation. Furthermore, this ideal situation does not differ in essence from what is attainable even in exile through observance of the *Torah*'s injunctions. While it may be argued that the cosmic erotic union that is to take place with the advent of redemption will be fuller or more complete than that which can be achieved in exile, it would nevertheless appear that the object of the erotic unions achieved by the performance of such *mitsvot* as the recitation of *Shema'*, putting on phylacteries and marital relations on the Sabbath eve is not merely to hasten the advent of the Messiah. In the passages of the *Zohar* that deal with the *mitsvot*, the author seems to regard them as being of intrinsic worth.

The Messiah himself has no part in the Kabbalistic *tikkun*. As we have noted, his advent merely symbolizes the accomplishment of the *tikkun*. Kabbalistic symbolism is sometimes attached to him, but here, too, it is his passivity that is emphasized. The Messiah (i.e., the son of David) is identified primarily with the *sefira* of *Malkhut*, to which he bears a resemblance precisely on account of his humble status, as described by the prophet Zechariah (IV:9): "Humble, riding on an ass"; for *Malkhut*, too, is humble and "has nothing of its own" (*Zohar*, I, 238a). Even when the *Zohar* ascribes to the Messiah attributes of the *sefira* of *Yesod*, which is more active, it stresses their passive aspect: The Messiah is indeed righteous, an attribute associated with *Yesod*, but he is redeemed rather than redeemer, in accord with a reading of that same verse in Zechariah: "righteous and saved is he."[9]

Another element related to the figure of the Messiah in the main body of the *Zohar* is that of the new Torah and the profound mode of understanding that is to be revealed through him. This is described extensively in III, 164b, where it is developed on the basis of the *Otiot de-Rabbi Akiva*.[10] This mode of understanding is sometimes described as a feature of the Kabbalistic-ontological harmony (I, 103b), which takes on a different meaning in the *Idra*. The idea that the messianic era is one of mystical comprehension is quite common in medieval Jewish thought and has clear connections with Christianity. This idea does not exclude national-historical redemption but often relegates it to an instrumental level, where it is seen as a means for achieving the mystical-cognitive objective.[11] The *Zohar*, however, appears to view these various elements as different aspects of the same thing, and so, given the great diversity inherent in the *Zohar*'s symbolic mode of thought, a hierarchical ranking of this kind would be inapplicable.

The Idra as a Messianic Composition and R. Simeon bar Yohai as a Messianic Figure

Since the *Idra* is explicitly concerned with theosophy, the mystery of the Godhead, an attempt to read the work as a messianic text requires some justification. Although the ultimate justification of the attempt is its success, which I leave to the reader to judge, I believe that the *Idra* itself contains explicit indications of its messianic character. The convening of the *Idra* is viewed in the *Zohar* as a singular event, greater even than the assembly of the Israelites at Mt. Sinai for the giving of the Torah, an event the like of which will not occur again until the coming of the Messiah.[12] The messianic character of the occasion is so evident to R. Simeon that he even expresses his astonishment at the absence of the prophet Elijah, after which Elijah does appear and offers an apology (III, 144b).

His astonishment makes sense only if the *Idra* is taken as an event presaging the coming of the Messiah, for Elijah's role in that stage of the nation's history has been celebrated in Jewish literature ever since it was first announced by the prophet Malachi (iii:23). At the same time, it is also evident that what is described here is not the coming of the Messiah himself, but only a stage preparatory to his advent. R. Simeon, the messianic figure here, certainly cannot be confused with the Messiah himself; he merely proclaims the latter's coming and sustains the world until his arrival. This becomes more clear if we bear in mind that R. Simeon died more than a thousand years before the *Zohar* was written, so that its author could not have attributed any more to him than the sustenance of the nation in exile. Even his casting in the role of herald of the redemption was no simple matter. We must recall, however, that in the consciousness of the author of the *Zohar*, the historical period of R. Simeon's actual lifetime merged without a break into the period of the book's composition (or its "disclosure at the end of days"). The only way to make sense of the merger of these two eras so separated by time is to conclude that the author of the *Zohar* regarded his own activity as messianic and that he identified fully with his R. Simeon. It may be that it is the messianic nature of his activity that accounts for his choice of R. Simeon as the hero of the *Zohar*, even though he is not among the Talmud's more mystical personalities. It is precisely in the Jewish apocalyptical literature that R. Simeon, the zealot known for his rebellion against Rome, his scathing denunciations of the gentile nations, and his forthright statements concerning the redemption of Israel,[13] *became a central figure.*[14]

Another reason for the *Zohar*'s selection of precisely this tannaitic figure was his suitability for portrayal as the righteous man, who maintains the world (with this conception we shall deal below). In the rabbinic literature R. Simeon speaks of himself as being a unique figure,[15] the single-handed protector of his contemporaries, able, together with his son Eleazar and Jotham ben Uzziah, to "bring about the exemption of the whole world from judgement . . . from the day of Creation until the world's end."[16] Another version found in the Midrash speaks specifically of the advent of the "King Messiah," and not simply the "world's end," as delimiting the time until which R. Simeon can effectively intercede with heaven.[17] What rabbinical literature had described R. Simeon as being able to do is elaborated in the *Zohar* and brought to fruition, it appears, in the pre-Messiah event which is *Idra Rabba*. At this gathering, R. Simeon actualizes his ability and becomes a truly messianic figure, thereby turning the *Idra* into a messianic event and a messianic composition.

These statements by the rabbis about R. Simeon are developed differently elsewhere in the *Zohar*, in another clearly messianic passage (I, 4a–b). There R. Simeon, Ahiah of Shiloh and Hezekiah King of Judea (who appears in Sanhedrin 99a as a messianic personage) are described as heads of academies (yeshivas) of learning in the world to come. R. Simeon is concerned there with the mystery of redemption and the Messiah. God himself attends these three academies, and even lesser academies to learn that teaching, and by virtue of this study the Messiah is "crowned and adorned."

Here is another passage that explains the messianic character of the *Idra*:

> Mark now, in future generations the Torah will be forgotten, the wise of heart will assemble in the holy *Idra*, and there will be none to close and open.[18] Alas for that generation! There will be no generation like the present until the Messiah comes and knowledge will be diffused throughout the world, as it is written: "For all of them, from the least of them to the greatest, shall heed me." [Jer. xxxi:34] (III, 58a)

This passage, I believe, reflects the negative opinion that the author of the *Zohar* had of his own generation (a view expressed frequently in the *Zohar*). At the same time, however, he regards the *Idra*, which he perhaps identifies with his own activity and that of his circle, as a turning point. Henceforth, until the generation of the Messiah, there will not be another generation as bad as his own, as bad, that is, as the generation that preceded the gathering of sages which is the *Idra*. The whole passage is clearly influenced by a passage from the Talmud, whose exposition here resembles that of the statements around which the image of R. Simeon coalesced; that is, statements by the rabbis referring to the generation that came after the destruction of the Temple are read as though they referred to the last generation of the *Zohar*'s composition—and given messianic significance. The passage in question occurs in Tractate Shabbat (138b):

> Our Rabbis taught: When our Masters entered the vineyard at Javneh they said: The Torah is destined to be forgotten in Israel. . .A woman is destined to take a loaf of *truma* (heave-offering) and go about in the synagogues and academies to know whether it is ritually unclean or clean and none will know. . .R. Simeon bar Yohai said: "Heaven forbid that the Torah be forgotten in Israel, for it is said: "for it shall not be forgotten out of the mouths of their seed." [Deut. xxxi:21]

The meeting of the Sanhedrin at the vineyard in Yavne, at which the rabbis foresaw the woes that were in store for Israel (the "birth-pangs of the Messiah"), was thus transformed in the *Zohar* into the convention of the "holy *Idra*," whose purpose is to remedy that situation.[19] The meeting of the Sanhedrin took place shortly after the destruction of the Temple, while that in the *Zohar* takes place in the generation before the redemption—that of the *Zohar*'s own composition. That this did not prevent the *Zohar* from naming R. Simeon and his companions as the conveners of the gathering is an indication of the depth of its author's identification with his literary hero. A similar reference of the Sanhedrin's Yavne session to an eschatological vision is already to be found in the Midrash:

> The Holy One blessed be He will sit with the righteous sitting before Him as on a threshing floor, like that of Ahab: "The king of Israel and King Jehoshaphat of Judah were seated on their thrones, arrayed in their robes, in the threshing floor" [I Kings xxii:10]. Were they then sitting in a threshing floor? Surely what is intended is as we have learned in a Mishnah (Sanhedrin iv:3): "The Sanhedrin were seated in the formation of a semi-circular threshing floor." (Leviticus Rabba xi:8)

It is quite conceivable that the *Zohar*'s author was also influenced by this Midrash. The choice of the term "*idra*" may well allude to the Sanhedrin and its seating arrangement, for the word means "threshing floor,"[20] and it appears in the sources in reference to the Sanhedrin.[21] Its very sound calls up possible associations with the word *sanhedrin*. The use of the designation "kerem" (vineyard) for the Sanhedrin's session at Yavne (*kerem d'Yavne*) may also have had some small part in determining the choice, for "idra"—threshing floor—belongs to the same semantic realm. It is apparently to this vineyard that the beginning of *Idra Rabba* refers in its statement that "the reapers of the field are few, and only at the edge of the vineyard" (III, 127b). The entire opening of *Idra Rabba*, with its rueful description of the state of the times which sets the context for the gathering, parallels the passage I have analyzed here. It should be recalled, too, that Maimonides viewed the convening of the Sanhedrin as a precondition for redemption.

A similar complaint about the degenerate state of the people in the period of exile is attributed by Midrash ha-Ne'elam (*Zohar Hadash*, 6a) to none other than R. Akiva. It is his pupils, as we shall see below, who represent the state of *yir'a*, of worshipping God out of fear and respect, which R. Simeon seeks to remedy by the *Idra*. While in the Talmud R. Simeon is both actually and spiritually R. Akiva's pupil, in the *Zohar* he is, as it were, the reformer.

At the end of *Idra Rabba* there is a similar reverse parallelism between the R. Simeon of the Talmud and the messianic R. Simeon of the *Idra*. After the participants at the *Idra* leave the gathering, a fine aroma arises wherever they look, regarding which R. Simeon says: "The world is being blessed because of us" (III, 144b). This suggests a comparison with the talmudic description of the emergence of R. Simeon and his son from the cave, after which, it is related, "whatever they cast their eyes upon was immediately burned up. Thereupon a Heavenly Echo came forth and said to them: 'Have you come out to destroy My world? Get back to your cave!' " (*Shabbat* 33b; the session of the Sanhedrin at Yavne is mentioned on the same page). That, it would seem, is the difference between the period marking the beginning of the exile and the massianic End of Days.

The messianic significance of the *Idra* is also suggested by another passage in the *Zohar*. This passage is of great importance for establishing the messianic character of the *Idra* both because it comes from a section in the *Zohar* which is expressly and openly messianic and because it may be considered an early version of *Idra Rabba*. The idea of the *Idra* is much simpler here than in its final development in the *Idra Rabba*; with the realization that this is an earlier version of the same work, however, it will be easier to identify the messianic elements that are more subtly present in the later version. The passage (II, 9a–9b), which is part of a larger eschatological discourse,

appears after an exposition of the verse: "I adjure you, O maidens of
Jerusalem, by gazelles or by hinds of the field: Do not wake or rouse
love until it pleases" (Song of Songs ii:7). In the *Zohar*'s interpretation,
"Love" is *Hesed*, God's love with which he will redeem Knesset Israel.
This attribute will only awaken in a generation worthy of it, and the
adjuration in the verse is a warning against trying to hasten the end,
which would be to awaken love—and redemption—prematurely.[22] The
Zohar concludes its commentary with the words: "Happy is he who
will be worthy to be of that generation, happy is he in this world and
happy is he in the world to come." It is at this point that the passage
which I take to be an early version of *Idra Rabba* begins: "R. Simeon
lifted up his hands in prayer to the Holy One blessed be He and prayed.
When he had finished his prayer, R. Eleazar his son and R. Abba came
and seated themselves before him."

 The *Zohar* then relates how the three sages see lightning strike
the waters of the Sea of Tiberias. They interpret this, following the
myth recounted in the Talmud (Berakhot 59a), as tears shed by God
out of sorrow for his children who are in exile. Then, says the *Zohar*,
"R. Simeon wept, and his companions too." After that R. Simeon
commences to speak:

 "We have been awakened in the secrets of the letters of the Holy
Name,[23] in the mystery of His awakening to His sons,[24] but now
I must disclose what no one else has been allowed to disclose.
I may do this because the merit of this generation upholds the
world until the Messiah shall come." R. Simeon then said to R.
Eleazar his son and to R. Abba: "Rise in your places!" R. Eleazar
and R. Abba rose. R. Simeon wept once again and said: "Who
can bear what I have seen? The Exile will be protracted. Who
will be able to endure?" Then he too rose and said: "O Lord our
God! Lords other than You possessed us, but only Your name shall
we utter" (Isaiah xxvi:13). This verse has already been
interpreted,[25] but it contains the supreme mystery of faith [i.e.,
about the world of the divine *sefirot*]. This "O Lord our God" is
the beginning of supernal mysteries,[26] a place[27] [i.e., a spiritual
entity] whence emanate all the shining lights. . ."

 R. Simeon then begins to expound at length on the mystery of
the Godhead and on the situation of the *sefirot* during the history and
exiles of the Jewish people, and finally, from an examination of the
letters of the Tetragrammaton in combination with other calculations,
determines the date of the End of Days (II, 9a–10b). The End would
occur in several stages. The first, according to my calculations, was

to come in 1334.[28] But a generation or two before the beginning of redemption, in 1286, "distress will befall Israel." The *Zohar*'s composition began in that year, or shortly thereafter.[29] The period of distress coincides remarkably with the description in the passage cited above (III, 28a) of the wicked "last generation" during which the sages come together in the holy *Idra* to sustain the world until the advent of the Messiah. This definitely confirms the conception of the *Idra* as an event of messianic significance, as well as the identification of the gathering with the activity of the author of the *Zohar* himself.

Let us now compare this passage (II, 9) with *Idra Rabba* to prove my contention that it constitutes an early version of the latter. First of all, it should be noted that the description here is of a solemn event laden with pathos. This alone calls to mind *Idra Rabba*, though in *Idra Rabba* the aspect of ceremony is of course much more elaborate, just as all the elements found here are developed further there. In the earlier passages the occasion begins with a prayer and an oath: "R. Simeon lifted up his hands in prayer to the Holy One blessed be He." At the opening of *Idra Rabba*, too, we find that "R. Simeon prayed. . ." (III, 127b), while the oath is expanded considerably and dramatically described, with all the participants taking part. A statement similar to the first quoted above serves as the solemn opening of another passage, it too is one of the most profound in the *Zohar*, as well: "R. Simeon said: I raise up my hands in prayer [swearing that] that when the Most High Supreme Will. . . ." This passage appears in several places in the *Zohar*,[30] but should be regarded as part of the *Idra*, as evidenced by the fact that Kabbalists who lived before the invention of printing referred to it by the name "*Idra*."[31] As used in the *Zohar*, this opening statement expresses on the one hand an obligation to reveal the loftiest secrets and the great importance of doing so, and on the other a sense of abasement and modesty and an awareness of the prohibition against such a disclosure.[32] The ambivalence present in this passage is highly developed in the *Idra*, charging it with intensity. Further on in the passage R. Simeon weeps, as he also does at the opening of the *Idra*, and announces that he will disclose something whose revelation had hitherto been forbidden. This motif is, again, expanded in the *Idra*, where R. Simeon is portrayed as hesitating even at the very moment of his disclosure of the mysteries.

The greatest similarity, however, has to do with the gathering itself. To be sure, this passage has only three participants while the *Idra* has ten, but R. Simeon singles out three of those ten, whom he describes as "the sum of all" (III, 128a). The three are the very same who come together in the "early version," namely R. Simeon himself,

R. Eleazar, his son, and R. Abba. The description in *Idra Rabba* is clearly an expansion of that found here. What is more, the meeting of these three figures is in and of itself, I believe, of messianic significance. We have seen that the *Zohar* "actualizes" the pronouncements made by R. Simeon in various *midrashim*, where he appears as a figure capable of absolving the world of judgment until the advent of the Messiah—if he is joined by two others, one of whom is R. Eleazar, his son, and the other a biblical personality such as King Jotham ben Uzziah or Abraham. But even the author of the *Zohar* with his deficient chronological sense could not bring such a figure together with R. Simeon and his son and so brought in R. Abba instead.[33]

Furthermore, at the opening of the *Idra* R. Simeon declares concerning the trio (himself, his son, and R. Abba): "As for us—the matter depends on love." I will consider the meaning of this statement in a later section; here it will suffice to note that R. Simeon is alluding to several statements immediately preceding our early version that express the idea that the messianic era will be a time of the awakening of love. Not only does this indicate the link between the versions, but it also says something directly about the *Idra's* conception of itself as messianic. It should be noted that the *Zohar* also has these same three sages meeting in a cave in Lydda, where they converse on the mystery of the love between God and Knesset Israel (I, 244b–245b). Another passage, too (I, 20a–20b; also mentioned in I, 9a), describes an event related to these three. There R. Eleazar and R. Abba achieve a special status and are granted the title Peniel—i.e., those who have seen the countenance of the Shekhina—by R. Simeon because they have received a vision of R. Hamnuna Sava who descended from the World of Truth to reveal the secrets of the Torah to them. This event, however, is linked to *yir'a*, the fear of God, and not to love, and R. Simeon alludes to it at the opening of the *Idra* by way of contrast, saying: "There it was right to fear." In the *Idra* he associates this with the verse on which he had expounded at length in the previous passage (I, 7b): "O Lord, I have heard the report of You and am afraid" (Habakkuk 3:2).

Special status is also attributed to these same three at the beginning of *Idra Zuta* (III, 287b): they alone are inside, while the others remain outside for fear of the raging fire. R. Eleazar and R. Abba alone participate in *Idra Raza de-Razin* (II, 123b) as well, asking questions in a dream of R. Simeon, who is already in the World of Truth. Only these three, moreover, are deemed worthy to delve into the "Account of the Chariot," as R. Simeon tells them at the beginning of the commentary on the chariot of Ezekiel's vision (*Zohar Hadash*, 37c).

In the early version it is stated that "By the merit of this generation the world will exist until the advent of the Messiah." This notion is a development of one stated several times elsewhere in the *Zohar*—that there will not be a generation like this one until the generation of the Messiah (e.g., II, 147a; III, 149a). Those statements do not necessarily mean that the present generation has a messianic task. It is often asserted, in fact, that after R. Simeon's death things reverted to their earlier dreadful state: the Torah that had been disclosed was once again forgotten (III, 23a). Shortly before his death, R. Simeon proposes a strategem for maintaining the world after his decease which involves bringing a Torah scroll to the cemetery (I, 222a). The notion that it is the task of R. Simeon and his circle to uphold the world through the evil times that precede the coming of the Messiah—the period of the "birth-pangs of the Messiah"—is only one step away from the idea that his generation must take measures to induce the Messiah's coming. That step appears even smaller when we bear in mind that the disclosure in the earlier version is a description of the stages of redemption and an explanation of them in terms of processes taking place within the Godhead. This idea was further developed in the final version of the *Idra*, where the very description of the *tikkun* within the Godhead is bound up with the actual *tikkun* itself. So too with redemption. Although the messianic theme is much more subdued in the *Idra* and is incorporated within its theosophical element, which is developed at greater length there, and although the *Idra* contains neither apocalyptic descriptions nor calculations of the time of the End, close examination establishes the fundamental structural parallels between the two compositions (this is also observable in the theosophic descriptions, which in both works proceed downwards from above to below). The difference between the two works may be explained as resulting from a deepening and refinement that took place in the author's thought during the time that passed between the composition of the former and that of the latter. It would surely be incorrect to try to reverse their order and argue that the more primitive work was composed after *Idra Rabba*, a contention that makes no psychological sense.[34]

The existence of several versions of *Idra Rabba* is not so extraordinary, for in fact we find an early version of *Idra Zuta* as well. It appears in *Zohar Hadash* (18d–19a) and again in Tosefet (III, 309a–309b), and is part of *Midrash ha-Ne'elam* to the Torah portion of *Bereshit*. Like *Idra Zuta*, this passage too describes a gathering of R. Simeon's disciples with their master, who is about to die. In both versions, R. Simeon speaks with joy and enthusiasm to his disciples about the fate awaiting him in the world to come. In both *Idra Zuta* and in the early version, R. Simeon also lectures them on the deep mysteries of the Godhead, though in *Idra Zuta*, as I shall try to show below, this subject is closely bound up with the departure of R. Simeon's soul, an event which itself plays a crucial role in the *tikkun* of the upper worlds.

The earlier "draft" is referred to explicitly at the beginning of *Idra Zuta* (III, 287b). R. Simeon relates that after the scene recounted there his life was extended, and that is why he is still alive; only now has his time come to depart from the world. The author of the *Zohar* most likely inserted this comment into the more developed version of *Idra Zuta* in order to escape the contradiction arising from the existence in his work of two different accounts of R. Simeon's death (no such contradiction arises in the case of *Idra Rabba*, the two versions of which can be viewed as depicting different events). It seems that the author either did not want to excise the first version or was unable to do so, since the *Zohar*, as we know, was issued as separate tracts,[35] and the tract containing the first version may already have been published. Whatever the case, the reference to the first version is a clear indication that *Idra Zuta* was a later composition and should be regarded as a more profound reworking of the more primitive version. I wish to establish the same type of relationship with respect to the two "versions" of *Idra Rabba*. These examples of the author of the *Zohar* returning to earlier sections and reworking them on a deeper level sheds light on his method of working, yielding an insight that might fruitfully be brought to bear on other parts of the *Zohar* as well—but that would take us beyond the scope of this chapter.

Analysis of the Idra

In this section I shall describe the messianic significance of the *Idra* and analyze several key passages in which it is demonstrated, devoting special attention to the opening of the work (III, 127b–128a).

Idra Rabba opens with the following words: "R. Simeon said to his companions, 'Until when will we dwell in the place (or status, situation, reality, existence, world or foundation) of one pillar?'" His inquiry might also be translated thus: "Until when will we dwell where only one pillar is our support?" These words express a complaint about the state of things on the eve of the *Idra*, which its convening is meant to remedy. A precise understanding of this sentence is therefore necessary for an understanding of the *Idra*; and, conversely, we shall need to analyze the *Zohar*'s description of what is achieved in the course of the *Idra*, in order to understand its opening statement, devoting special attention to passages bearing linguistic allusions to it. It must also be borne in mind that precisely because of the poverty of its vocabulary, the language of the *Zohar* is richly laden with meanings, nuances and associations, as artificial languages generally are.[36] For this reason just one interpretation of the opening statement will not suffice, because there is a wealth of ideas here whose association with one another in the consciousness of the author of the *Zohar* reflects a depth of thought worthy of investigation.

What is this one pillar that has been the support of R. Simeon and his companions until *Idra Rabba*, whose exclusive support is the fault the *Idra* intends to remedy? Our analysis will show that this pillar has two aspects: on the one hand it is R. Simeon himself, but on the other it is also a divine force, which is essentially the attribute of divine judgement (*middat ha-din*). There are a number of dimensions to the fault of which R. Simeon complains. On the plane of human existence, first of all, there was only one righteous man in the world, namely R. Simeon, and the existence of the entire world was dependent on him alone. Second, on the same plane, love and friendship did not prevail among the sages as it should have. Third, on the epistemological plane, only very few people had knowledge of the Kabbala, and in fact only one person was really privy to its secrets, namely R. Simeon himself. Fourth, on the same plane, the secrets of the Kabbala that were known were of a low level; fifth, also on that plane, their apprehension was merely discursive and did not come as an intuitive grasp of a profusion descending from above. Sixth, on the ontological plane, the structure of the upper worlds lacked harmony, and the various divine attributes could not be divided into male and female and therefore could not maintain their existence. The supreme emanated configuration, the *Arikh Anpin*, had not undergone its requisite *tikkun*, and its light therefore did not shine on the lower configuration, *Ze'er Anpin*—and when the latter was by itself it poured forth stern and wrathful judgment. The seventh aspect of the fault of which R. Simeon complains is related to the previous one—since the upper and lower configurations were not in a continuous, intimate relationship to one another, full mystical *devekut* (cleaving, or communion) with the Godhead was not possible. Eighth, on the personal plane, R. Simeon was alone in the world and also apparently did not have the appropriate type of sexual relations with a female. Ninth, also on that plane, love did not prevail among R. Simeon's companions as it should have. Tenth, on the national-historical plane, Israel was in exile, without a sovereign of its own and subject to the rule of the gentiles (mainly "Edom," meaning the Christians), and Jerusalem and the Temple lay waste.

The dual nature of the pillar, as both terrestrial person and cosmic force, becomes clearer when we realize that behind the phrase in R. Simeon's statement lies the verse *ve-tsaddik yesod 'olam* (Proverbs x:25)—"the righteous is an everlasting foundation," or "the righteous is the foundation of the world"—and the meanings that have been attached to it in rabbinic and Kabbalistic literature.[37] Especially relevant here is the talmudic statement, "[The world] rests on one pillar, and its name is 'Righteous,' for it is said, 'Righteous is the foundation of the world'" (*Hagiga* 12a). It is difficult even in the rabbinical statements to determine whether what is meant is a cosmic pillar, which is called "Righteous," or a righteous person who is likened to a pillar. The context and formulation of the statement in Tractate Hagiga would seem to indicate a real pillar, but in other places a righteous person is undoubtedly intended; for example: "Even for the sake of a single righteous man does the world endure, as it is said, 'But the righteous is the foundation of the world'" (*Yoma* 38b). There are several persons to whom, by their description in rabbinic literature, this description would be applicable; R. Simeon is the most outstanding among them, but there are others.[38]

In Kabbalistic literature, this pillar is regarded as one of the *sefirot*, and it is called *Yesod* (Foundation). It serves as the foundation mainly of the world of the *sefira* of *Malkhut* (Kingdom), and sometimes also of *Netsah* (Endurance) and *Hod* (Majesty) (II, 123a). This, however, did not dispel the ambiguity presented by the verse, and the conception of "the righteous, the everlasting foundation" as both pillar and terrestrial person persisted. This can be seen, for example, in a passage from *Sefer ha-Bahir* (120) which, citing two opposing talmudic statements, begins with a pillar and concludes with a righteous person:

> There is one pillar from the earth to the firmament and Righteous is its name, after the righteous ones, and when there are righteous persons in the world it gains strength, and when there are not it is weakened, and it bears the burden of all the world, as it is written, "Righteous is the foundation of the world," and if it is weak the world cannot exist. Therefore even if there is only one righteous man in the world, he upholds the world.

Here the pillar is a cosmic entity, but its existence depends on the terrestrial righteous person, whose merit is greater than its own (the pillar's very name is derived from him). In *Sefer ha-Bahir* this pillar is identified with the cosmic tree, and here too for the first time in Jewish literature it also comes to symbolize the male organ, thus opening the way for the linkage in the mystical literature between the righteous man's virtue and the sexual realm.[39] This dual appreciation of "righteous" as referring to both person and cosmic entity is also found in the *Zohar*. Generally, however, the treatment is symbolic: the righteous man on earth is like the righteous above, and his relations with his terrestrial wife resemble those of the *sefira* of *Yesod* (or *Tiferet*) with the *Shekhina*. At times the *Zohar's* descriptions depart from the symbolic level and enter that of portraying direct sexual contact between the righteous individual and the *Shekhina*. It is also said that the *Shekhina* cohabits with scholars who spend all of the week studying the Torah and refrain from relations with their wives, on the condition, however, that they return to their wives on the Sabbath and on that day have relations with the *Shekhina* in symbolic fashion (I, 49b).[40] The righteous man is thus between two females, just as the *Shekhina* is between two "Righteous" entities, the one divine and the other earthly.[41] While this is true of righteous individuals in general, however, there are two exceptional individuals from whom the symbolic element is totally lacking, who are mythically "Righteous" in the fullest sense. One is Moses—the other R. Simeon.

As we noted above, R. Simeon as he is portrayed in rabbinic literature was befitting of the title "Righteous, foundation of the world." It is also said of him that no rainbow appeared in his lifetime, for he protected the world in its stead (*Ketubot* 77b). In the *Zohar* we find him proclaiming: "I am the sign that protects the world" (I, 225a). The rainbow (*keshet*) alludes to the *sefira* of *Yesod* (I, 18a), and the same word in its rabbinic usage, moreover, refers both to the male organ (*Sanhedrin* 92a) and to the glory of God (*Hagiga* 16a, based on Ezekiel i:28). R. Simeon's identification with the rainbow may also have messianic significance, for according to the *Zohar* (e.g., I, 62b), the rainbow will appear on the eve of the Messiah's coming (although there the rainbow would seem to represent the *sefira* of *Malkhut*, not *Yesod*).

At the beginning of the early version of *Idra Zuta* (*Zohar Hadash* 18d), R. Simeon is called "the pillar of the world." He fulfills this role by his teaching, constituting, as it were, a living Torah scroll, and in fact a Torah scroll will fulfill his function after his death (I, 225a). He is also likened to a candle who kindles all his pupils with the light of his teaching (II, 86b).[42] In another passage (II, 34b), the description of him upholding the entire world by virtue of his teaching is linked to his knowledge of matters concerning the *sitra ahra* (the power of evil, literally: the other side):

R. Simeon said: "The companions study the story of Creation
(*ma'ase bereshit*) and have knowledge of it, but only few know
how to interpret it in connection with the great sea monster, and
as we have learned, the entire world hangs from its fins. (II, 34b)

The story of Creation with which the companions are acquainted
is no doubt the Kabbalistic description of the emanation of the *sefirot*
which was called *ma'ase bereshit* and was studied widely at the time
of the *Zohar*'s composition.[43] But the mystery of the great sea monster,
as R. Simeon's discourse subsequently makes clear, concerns the *sefirot*
of *sitra ahra*.[44] This was known by very few—indeed, it was apparently
known by only one person, and it is therefore he alone who upholds
the world. It was to him, then, that the rabbis alluded in saying that
the whole world is supported on the fins of the Leviathan (*Pirqei de-
Rabbi Eliezer*; this is the "sea monster" of the *Zohar*). They did not
mean the actual fins of the Leviathan, but were referring figuratively
to the person who understands this matter (there is some ambiguity
here, however, for the actual Leviathan, through whose mystery the
ma'aseh may be apprehended, is also intended). That person is none
other than R. Simeon himself, who will later expound the mysteries
of the Leviathan in a mythic and surprising way unknown anywhere
else in our literature; the same R. Simeon who is referred to elsewhere
as "Righteous, the foundation of the world." R. Simeon's words,
beginning with "Few [who] know" and ending with only one who
knows, are reminiscent of an utterance of his in the Talmud: "I saw
the sons of heaven, and they are few, . . . and if they are two, they are
myself and my son" (Sukka 45b). They also bring to mind a statement
of his in *Pesikta de-Rav Kahana* about the thirty righteous men in
each generation who resemble Abraham, which concludes, "And if
there is one, I am he."[45]

The correctness of this interpretation is proven by parallel
passages I have found in the literature of the so-called "Gnostic
Kabbalists," a circle with which the author of the *Zohar* was closely
connected.[46] The source of the passage in the *Zohar* is to be found,
I believe, in the opening words of *Sefer Ammud ha-Semali* (the Left
Pillar) by R. Moses of Burgos: "The secrets of the left emanation . . . are
unknown to most of those with knowledge . . . transmitted to select
individuals."[47] Such boasts of particular knowledge of the mysteries
of the *sitra ahra*, which placed the members of their circle on a higher
rung than the Kabbalists who knew only the holy mysteries, are quite
common in the literature of the "Gnostic Kabbalists."[48] The connection
with this particular book lies in the phrase "only few know," which
is clearly echoed in the Aramaic of the above passage. The difference

between these Kabbalistic groups was also known to R. Isaac of Acre, who observed that the Kabbalists of Castile had merited "receiving the Kabbala of the outer rungs," while the sages of Catalonia (Gerona) had a Kabbala which was "correct in the ten *sefirot* of *belima*."[49] The *Zohar* is closer to the Castilian scholars both geographically and in content.[50]

That the "Righteous, the foundation of the world" should take the form of the Leviathan and be related to the forces of defilement is itself very interesting. On the one hand, the Leviathan is a fitting symbol for the foundation of the world, for "Leviathan" is one of the designations of the *sefira* of *Yesod* (in "Gnostic" circles as well).[51] However, the use of this symbol in the context of the forces of evil, which are called sea monsters, puts the notion of the righteous one who is the foundation of the world in a new light. It suggests that he upholds the world by fighting the evil forces, which is why there is a resemblance between him and them (compare II, 27b: the evil sea monsters are ruled over by superior monsters which have been blessed and no doubt are the holy *sefirot*). In this too R. Simeon resembles Moses, who, according to the beginning of the passage quoted above (II, 34a), was able to overcome the great monster—Pharaoh, King of Egypt—because he first of all entered him "room by room" and came to know him well. In this way his merit was greater than that of Job, for the latter, since he turned from evil (Job i:8), had no part in the *Sitra Ahra* and so awakened its envy.

This notion also originates among the "Gnostic Kabbalists," who relate it to the figure of the Messiah. In his *Ta'amei ha-Te'amim*, R. Isaac ha-Kohen writes: "When shall we be avenged? When our righteous Messiah shall come, who is likened to a serpent:[52] a serpent will come and take his revenge of a serpent." The same idea was subsequently taken up by the Shabbateans.[53] As we have noted, members of the "Gnostic" circle regarded themselves as superior to other Kabbalists because of their knowledge of the left emanation. In one place R. Isaac ha-Kohen's acclaim for the "few who know" is far-reaching indeed: "On this path have tread but 'two or three, berries on the topmost branch' [Isaiah xvii:6], and they are the ancient sages of Castile who ministered in the palace of *Sama'el* (the Prince of evil)."[54] The last phrase expresses the idea that black magic is the glory of the best Kabbalists. Elsewhere R. Isaac says: "We acquired this knowledge from the ancient elders of the Kabbala, from the sages of Castile, rabbi from rabbi, elder from elder, *ga'on* from *ga'on*. They all practiced the lesser magic of demons, which leads to the great holy magic, whereby one ascends the ladder of prophecy and acquires its power."[55] Here black magic is presented as a way to white magic and even to prophecy.[56]

Another passage from the writings of this circle is of great importance to our understanding of the nature of the *Zohar*'s Messiah. I refer to the ending of *Sefer Ammud ha-Semali*, whose opening we have seen echoed in the *Zohar*. Here, in the place where one would expect to find a wish for the advent of the Messiah like that with which Jewish books—including those by members of this circle—frequently closed, R. Moses of Burgos writes:

> Until God shall look down and see from the heavens: may He lighten from upon us the burden of the distress of our time and ready for us the support of *a lasting pillar* straight and faithful *by virtue of a righteous one, foundation of the world*, to rest against, that he [perhaps it should read: we] may be capable of drawing divine favor by fear of the Lord and by His worship, through instruction in the secrets of our flawless Torah. We shall then rejoice and be glad, and sorrow and sighing shall flee.[57]

This description of the redeemer who it is hoped would come is precisely how R. Simeon is described in the *Zohar* (a pillar who has the attribute of foundation—*Yesod*—and who redeems through study of the secrets of the Torah). Though it is possible chronologically for R. Moses to have seen the *Zohar* in his old age, it is most unlikely that he borrowed from it in this case, for he uses it nowhere else.[58] It is quite likely, on the other hand, that Moses de Leon fashioned R. Simeon bar Yohai as a messianic figure in light of expectations prevailing in his circle. It is also possible that its members had identified such a figure among themselves—perhaps even Moses de Leon himself.

The Messiah's symbolic rung, according to this Kabbalistic circle, was the *sefira* of *Yesod*.[59] Especially relevant in this context is a statement by Todros Abulafia: "None of the commentators I have seen say what is the name of the Messiah [who is mentioned in the Talmud among the things that were created before the creation of the world], but I tell you by the true way [i.e., Kabbala] that his name is Righteous (Zaddik), for it is written: 'He is righteous and redeemed' (Zech. ix:9); 'Righteous, foundation of the world'; and 'The righteous shall live by his faith' (Hab. ii:4)."[60] R. Todros is not claiming that the Messiah's name had not been stated explicitly before him, for several names—Menahem, for example—are mentioned in the Midrash, and several others were added in R. Todros' Kabbalistic circle. We even find the name Righteous in the Midrash as a name of the Messiah.[61] What had not been stated explicitly before R. Todros was able to do so on the basis of Kabbala is the name of the Messiah who was created before the world. The implication here—and it is not merely on a symbolic level, for he is speaking, as we shall see, of total identity—is that the Messiah is an incarnation of the *sefira* of *Yesod*. A similar apprehension, I believe, characterizes the *Zohar*'s view of R. Simeon, to whom the name Righteous is certainly applicable. It would appear, then, that the *Zohar*'s unique conception of the Messiah has its source among the "Gnostic Kabbalists." This circle also seems already to have taken up the custom of holding a night-long *tikkun* on the festival of Shavuot, a practice of messianic significance. It should also be noted that in its descriptions both of the Messiah and of R. Simeon the *Zohar* refers to the same verses as those used by R. Todros.

Let us return now to the literal interpretation of the expression *kaima dehad samkha* occurring at the beginning of *Idra Rabba*, which we have translated as "the place of one pillar." *Kaima* is both pillar and foundation.[62] It also means covenant,[63] and as such is related both to the *sefira* of *Yesod* and to R. Simeon's role of protecting the world, like the rainbow. *Kiyuma* means that which upholds the world and is the essence of the world. *Samkha* may mean foundation of the world. All of these refer to R. Simeon, who like Judah is called "the mainstay, the support of all supports" (I, 156a).

The Significance of the Gathering

As we have interpreted it, R. Simeon is here complaining about his loneliness in his role as foundation of the world. While the term "pillar" also attests to the strength of the one to whom this appellation is ascribed, even the strongest pillar cannot support the world as could several of them together, and certainly the personal fate of such a pillar is loneliness and suffering (like that of Atlas in the Greek legend). This is solved at the opening of the *Idra* by the assembly of nine of R. Simeon's disciples; and by the end of this passage, indeed, R. Simeon can already adopt the first person plural: "We are the pillars of the world."

The expression "pillars of the world" also has an intellectual meaning: just as R. Simeon has protected the world with his teachings, they too can protect it by virtue of the wisdom R. Simeon is teaching them. Compare this with another statement in II, 15b: "The 'wise and intelligent' are the pillars and sockets, since they ponder with understanding all things needful for upholding the palanquin"—the Kabbalists (the "wise and intelligent") know by their teachings how to uphold the upper world. While these "wise and intelligent" are also the upper *sefirot*, which support the *sefira* of *Malkhut* or *Yesod* from above, they are at the same time the terrestrial righteous persons who sustain those *sefirot*.

As used in the *Idra*, the expression "pillars of the world" has a similar dual meaning. The ten companions symbolize the ten *sefirot* that sustain the world. When they are appointed as such and come together in the *Idra*, a marked improvement occurs in the cosmic situation as well: while the world had rested on one pillar, it now rests on ten—a situation that is undoubtedly more stable. After the participants are seated in their places, then, R. Simeon can declare: "Now we have completed the arrangement of the pillars on which the world rests." (Later in the *Idra* these pillars are equated with the supports of the marital canopy of the upper world, which is revealed to the participants [III, 135a].) This declaration by R. Simeon should be compared with its parallel in *Midrash ha-Ne'elam*, which is itself a sort of *Idra Rabba*. It is related there that the *Shekhina* did not want to enter the room where the participants were seated, for the pillars had not yet been put in their proper order (II, 14a). This was remedied once R. Hiyya had found his place.

The precise seating arrangement of the participants at *Idra Rabba* is also of symbolic significance. This is reflected, among other things, in the way R. Simeon calls on the participants to deliver their discourse. To each of them in turn he says: "Rise in your place," which apparently also means: "Assume a particular attribute or *sefira*," or "In your discourse, which concerns a particular *sefira* (or one of the *tikkunim* [locks] of the Beard), perform a *tikkun* upon that place or *sefira*."[64] That this is how this form of address is to be understood is especially evident after the second *tikkun* of the Beard of Arikh Anpin (III, 132b). This *tikkun* was performed by R. Hezekiah, and R. Simeon praised him for it at length, describing what had occurred in the upper worlds as a consequence. As a sign of his appreciation, he intended to allow R. Hezekiah to perform the third *tikkun* as well, and he called upon him with the words: "Rise, R. Hezekiah, a second time." In protest, a heavenly voice declared: "One angel (messenger) does not perform two missions" (from Genesis Rabba 50:2, where the reference is in fact to an angel). Upon hearing this, R. Simeon "became agitated and said: 'Of course, each one in his place, and I and R. Eleazar my son and R. Abba complete the sublime wholeness.'" "In his place" means "in the place among the *sefirot* appropriate to him," which is the same "place" as that referred to by the words "Rise in your place" (in your *kiyuma*). The statement about R. Simeon, R. Eleazar, and R. Abba, who, according to the opening passage, constitute the other participants in the *Idra*, attests to this symbolic significance of the word "place." R. Simeon is of course persuaded by the heavenly voice and calls on another participant, R. Hiyya, to perform the third *tikkun*, which apparently is his "place." This understanding gains additional confirmation in the passage in *Midrash ha-Ne'elam* cited above: "He said to him, 'Rise in your place; because of you the upper world will be sustained.'"

The symbolism is especially prominent at the beginning of *Idra Rabba* with respect to three people. Of the ten participants, R. Simeon chooses two—R. Eleazar and R. Abba—seats them on either side of him and says: "We are the sum of all," that is to say, the ten *sefirot* are included in three. The idea and the language in which it is cast are taken, I believe, from *Pirkei de-Rabbi Eliezer* (chap. 3): "The world was created by ten sayings, and they are included in three." This is also the key to understanding the precise symbolic "place" of these three sages.[65] In this context the word "pillar" (*kaima*) also signifies existence—the existence or state of the world, how it is sustained, and that which sets it upon its foundation.[66]

The full text of R. Simeon's earlier declaration provides an indication of the cosmic status of the companions participating in the *Idra*: "I do not ask the heavens to give ear, nor the earth to hear, *for we are the pillars of the world.*" This is a direct allusion to Moses' exclamation at the beginning of chapter 32 of Deuteronomy, and by it R. Simeon is in effect saying that he and his companions enjoy a higher status than Moses in his time: he need not ask the heavens to give ear and the earth to hear, for he and his companions are themselves cosmic foundations. In this context, the expression "pillars of the world" also has the significance of "everlasting," the quality possessed by heaven and earth on account of which Moses called on them to serve as witnesses. According to Rashi, "Moses said, 'I am flesh and blood and tomorrow shall die,' and therefore he called upon heaven and earth to serve as witnesses, for they are everlasting." The parallel with Rashi's interpretation reinforces the impression that the participants at the *Idra* acquired a superhuman nature.[67]

The armor borne by the participants is also of cosmic and symbolic significance. R. Simeon invites his companions saying:

> Assemble, friends, at the threshing house (the *Idra*), clad in armor and bearing swords and spears; gird your weapons: counsel, wisdom, intellect, knowledge, vision, the power of hands and feet.

The scholars of the *beit midrash* are often described in rabbinical literature as heroes engaged in "the battle of the Torah" (e.g., Shabbat 63a), and this image occurs frequently in the *Zohar* as well (e.g., II,

111b; III, 191a; *Zohar Hadash* 14a). Here, however, the description
of the arms approximates the order of the *sefirot*, which are also
divided into two kinds—those whose symbols are spiritual, often
characterized as intellect and knowledge, and those that are
symbolized by bodily organs such as hands and feet. A similar duality
of meaning is present in the phrase "gird your weapons."[68] The
Aramaic word for "weapon," *tikkun*, also means "restoration" and in
the *Zohar* generally refers to the restoration of the upper worlds, or
to the restored worlds themselves.[69] It is well to note, moreover, that
the righteous are one day to take the Messiah in his arms, which are
forged of the letters of the Holy Name (II, 8b).

R. Simeon's invitation to the participants continues: "Enthrone
as king Him who has the power of life and death." While such
"enthronement" would ordinarily signify acceptance of the yoke of
the kingdom of heaven, here it may also be understood as indicating
the participants' entry into a realm where they themselves symbolize
the attributes of God. (The words "Him who has the power of life and
death" would seem to allude to the fate of those participants who died
at the end of the *Idra*.) The very next phrase—"to decree words of
truth"—reinforces this understanding: the participants, by virtue of
their cosmic symbolic status, are granted the capacity to issue decrees
relating to matters of the world. This, too, shows that they have now
become "righteous men foundations of the world," like R. Simeon, for
one of the qualities of the righteous man is his ability to issue decrees
affecting the upper world,[70] and this, according to the *Zohar*, is R.
Simeon's singular virtue.[71]

At the beginning of the *Idra* (just like in *Midrash ha-Ne'elam*),
the "decrees" of the sages are merely Kabbalistic truths. The word
"decree" is nevertheless in order, for they not only discourse on the
upper worlds but also, by their decree, sustain them and bring
redemption nearer. The participants at the *Idra* are thus higher than
the angels, which is why the angels "listen to their voice and are
happy to hear them and know them," as the passage goes on to say.
The description of the angels assembling to hear the words of the
scholars recurs several times in *Idra Rabba*.[72] In *Idra Zuta*, by contrast,
the place of the angels is taken by the righteous from Paradise (II,
288a). The image of the angels listening to and surrounding the
mystics has its source in descriptions by the *Merkava* mystics of the
Talmudic period (e.g., Hagiga 14b). The fire surrounding the
expounders was taken over by the *Zohar* from the same source;
similarly, the wedding motif ("the entertainments of a bridegroom
and bride") was developed extensively in the *Idra*.[73] Idra Zuta in its
entirety is described as a wedding, a point to be discussed in greater
detail later.

The Companions' Pledge

The cosmic importance of the *Idra* (apart from its historical and spiritual importance) lends the word *kaima* in the opening sentence, which we have rendered as "place" ("in the *place* of one pillar"), yet another meaning: that of "occasion" or "festive event." In this sense it is used to refer to the *Idra Rabba* assembly itself, contrasting it with the extended "event," up to that time, during which R. Simeon was alone. *Idra Rabba* is called *kiyuma* in III, 132b, where the word would appear to be a translation of the Hebrew word *ma'amad*, in its medieval sense, bearing within it the associations carried over from the expression *ma'amad har Sinai*, the "event" of the revelation at Mt. Sinai.[74] The comparison with the moment of the giving of the Torah is explicit in the *Idra*, which is conceived as the most important theophanous event to take place between the revelation at Mt. Sinai and the Messianic era (the "quasi-*Idra*" described in II, 15a is also compared to the revelation at Sinai).

As befits an event of such standing, the *Idra* is conducted with great solemnity and ritual. The participants enter decked out in their spiritual armor. They each place their hands on their breasts and R. Simeon has them swear a grave and solemn oath: " 'Cursed be the man who makes a graven or molten image, a work craftsmanship, and sets it up in secret,' and they all answered and said 'Amen' " (based on Deut. xxvii:15). The meaning of this curse is uncertain; it may really have been directed against attributing corporeality and anthropomorphic features to God, as Kabbalists have always interpreted it, or it may have been meant to serve as a general disclaimer, as it were, clearing a way for the far-reaching descriptions of this sort that appear later in the *Idra*.[75]

It seems much more likely, however, that this curse had nothing to do with the problem of anthropomorphism. First of all, there is no other such warning against anthropomorphism anywhere else in the *Zohar*, though it is characteristic of the *Zohar* for its ideas to appear in a number of places, developed somewhat differently in each. It is quite unlikely that an idea as important as God's incorporeality and the avoidance of anthropomorphisms would appear only once, especially if this idea were regarded as so important by the *Zohar* as to be included in the solemn oath with which the *Idra* opens. Moreover, the *Zohar* is in fact replete with anthropomorphisms. The author personifies the divinity on countless occasions, referring to God or his various aspects by such expressions as "the human face" or "the holy body." Secondly, the appearance of this subject here would disrupt the thematic development around which the opening of the

Idra, beginning with the "place of one pillar" and ending with the "pillars of the world," is constructed.

I therefore propose an interpretation of the curse that not only has many parallels in the *Zohar* but also seems to accord with the ideas presented at the opening of the *Idra*. As I understand this oath, R. Simeon has the participants swear by it that they will not study the secrets of the Torah on their own, but will speak only of what they receive through him (which includes not only what they hear from him directly, but also what they come to understand as a result of his inspiration and presence), and his warning to them to observe the covenant scrupulously (i.e., to avoid transgressions of a sexual nature, both in thought and in action is also bound up with this oath).

The idea of a relationship between the prohibition in the Decalogue against making graven and molten images and that against speaking words of Torah not heard from one's teacher appears elsewhere in the *Zohar* as well (II, 87a). The latter prohibition itself appears in the Talmud (Berakhot 27b), but there one who infringes it is not called an idolator; it is said of him only that "he causes the Divine Presence to depart from Israel." The reason for the prohibition in the *Zohar* is that a person who speaks words of Torah that he did not receive from his teacher is propounding false and artificial "secrets." The Godhead whose "secrets" he elucidates is his own invention, like a graven image made by his own hands. Later in the same discourse (II, 87b) the ban against graven images is also related to sexual sins, which mar the holy covenant and the *sefira* of *Yesod*. The verse "Suffer not thy mouth to bring thy flesh into guilt" (Eccl. v:5) is adduced in support of both parts of this exegesis. The very same verse is used later on in the opening of the *Idra* in connection with the requirement that the participants, who are "pillars of the world," guard the secrets.

The connection often reiterated in the *Zohar* between the evil inclination that arouses illicit sexual desires and the inclination towards idolatry appears in the rabbinic texts;[76] it is stronger in the *Zohar*, however, for there it is based on an ontological unity and related to error in the study of the Torah as well.[77] The verse from Ecclesiastes is often adduced by the *Zohar* in relation to the ban against thinking about a woman during the day so as not to be defiled by a nocturnal emission.[78] However, it is also applicable to one who does not treat the secrets of the Torah properly, for it was the verse cited in reference to Elisha B. Avuyah after he entered the Garden (*pardes*) and "mutilated the shoots" (Hagiga 15a). One who does not observe its instruction is certainly not fit to bear the title "foundation of the world," for "retribution is exacted of him and of all the world"

(Shevu'ot 39a). While this statement in Shevu'ot refers to one who utters God's name in vain rather than to one who discloses secrets, the *Zohar* conflates the two. In the passage mentioned above (II, 87b), it speaks of one who infringes the covenant through sexual transgression as "one who takes God's name in vain" (covenant=*Yesod*=God's name), and so too is one who discloses secrets, for the Torah is called the Name of God.[79] What both transgressions have in common is that they blemish the *sefira* of *Yesod*. It is quite possible, moreover, that in choosing this curse in particular ("Cursed be the man who makes a graven or molten image") the *Zohar* also took into account the rest of the similar curses in Deuteronomy 27, many of which concern "*gillui 'arayot*"—the "uncovering of nakedness," in proscribed sexual relations. The *Zohar* draws a connection between this "uncovering" and the prohibition against "*gillui sodot ha-Torah*"—disclosing the secrets of the Torah (III, 79a)—and this in the very place in the *Idra* where it is said in praise of R. Simeon and his companions that in their days alone was it permitted to speak openly, while since R. Simeon's death one must heed the same verse from Ecclesiastes cited above; that is, "Suffer not thy mouth to bring thy flesh into guilt."[80]

The oath administered by R. Simeon is thus really a pledge by the participants to learn the secrets of the Torah exclusively from him. The disciples of Isaac Luria took a similar oath, and it occurs in the document of their pledge to Luria's disciple, R. Hayyim Vital.[81] The *Zohar* alludes to the administration of this oath, which is meant to emphasize that no one other than R. Simeon bar Yohai is permitted to interpret the mysteries of the Torah, in other places as well (III, 159a; 179b). Permission to teach the secrets is elsewhere extended to R. Simeon's disciples as well, but only as long as he is alive (e.g., III, 106a). R. Simeon even gives his companions an explicit warning in this regard:

> I beseech you not to let fall from your mouth any word of the Torah of which you are not certain and which you have not learnt correctly from a "great tree," so that you not be the cause of *Hata'a* (sin) slaying multitudes of men. (I, 5a)

These words also help illuminate the meaning of the oath taken at the beginning of the *Idra*, for they were uttered in a similar context, before a description of the *Tikkun Leil Shavu'ot* (which bears a resemblance to the *Idra*) and after a description of the firmaments that will be created from the words of Torah spoken at these gatherings. "Worthless firmaments" are created from the teaching of secrets that do not come from a "great tree." *Hata'a*, the feminine form of *sitra ahra*, flies in those firmaments, and she can destroy the world. This mythical explanation can be related to R. Simeon's suspicion that the death of several of his companions at the end of *Idra Rabba* was attributable to the sin of disclosing the secrets. Elsewhere (II, 86b) the *Zohar* asserts that whoever separates himself from R. Simeon separates himself from life (this was later to become a common Hasidic saying).

To understand what is meant here and to appreciate the relationship between the prohibition against revealing secrets and sexual matters, we must consider another meaning of *kiyyumei 'almin* ("pillars of the world"), the designation applied to the participants in the *Idra* by the end of the opening section. This meaning adds another dimension to the image of R. Simeon as "Righteous, foundation of the world." The expression *kiyyumei 'almin* denotes not only "pillars of the world," but also "guardians of the secret." As explained at the opening of the *Idra*, a guardian of the secret is a "faithful spirit" (*ruha de-kiyyuma*), an appellation derived from the verse: "A base fellow gives away secrets, but a faithful spirit (*ne'eman ruah*) keeps a confidence" (Prov. xi:13).[82] The translation of the expression *ne'eman ruah* as *ruha de-kiyyuma* is based on an understanding of the word *ne'eman*, "faithful," as meaning "fixed firmly in place," as in the verse, "I will fasten him as a peg in a firm place (*makom ne'eman*)" (Isa. 22:23). The spirit of a guardian of the secret is fixed and remains in its place, as opposed to the spirit of one who tends to disclose secrets, which swirls around "like bran in water" (an expression derived from Bava Metzi'a 60b) and has no rest until it goes out. He who stays firmly in place is like a pillar and an everlasting foundation: it is he who is "Righteous, foundation of the world," whose trait is to guard the secret without disclosing it. This, then, is another reason why R. Simeon's companions are called *kiyyumei 'almin*, for they are fit to receive the secrets, and there is no fear that they will disclose them to others. Moreover, the expression "guardian of the secret" also denotes a person who hears the secrets only from a "faithful" source.

Disclosure versus Concealment

But there is more to the matter than this. The secret is part of the very essence of "Righteous, foundation of the world"; not only does he not reveal secrets, but he himself is called a secret and is guarded in secrecy. This emerges from the introduction to the *Idra*. In his explanation of *ruha de-kiyyuma* and *kiyyumei 'almin*, R. Simeon declares that the world exists by virtue of the secret. As is clear from the context, that of the response of the opening passage of the *Idra* to the complaint of being in a place of one pillar, the word *raza* (secret) here is a name for "Righteous, foundation of the world," the support of the world. As we saw above, the word "righteous" has a dual meaning, referring to both the supernal *sefira* and a terrestrial person. Using parallels from elsewhere in the *Zohar*, we shall now examine why the supernal "Righteous" is called "secret." This will enable us to draw conclusions regarding the features of the terrestrial righteous one, who is in the image and mold of the supernal "Righteous."

It is often said in the *Zohar* that the Godhead has both a revealed and a concealed aspect. The revealed aspect is the *sefira* of *Malkhut*, whose primary quality is *din*, judgment, while the concealed aspect is the *sefira* of *Yesod*, the spiritual source, or "place," of all blessings (II, 227b). The *Zohar* bases this on the rabbinic saying, "A blessing is found only in what is hidden from the eye" (e.g., Bava Metzi'a 42a). The rabbis meant only that whatever is counted, measured, and open to sight is liable to fall prey to the evil eye, but the *Zohar*, in developing this idea, added an ontological explanation: the source of blessings, which sustains the visible world, is the *sefira* which by its nature is hidden. He who reveals what is not meant for disclosure gives dominion to the evil eye (which is here transformed into the cosmic entity called *Sitra Ahra*) over the *sefira* of *Yesod*, the supernal source of blessings, as well.[83]

Now, just as God is both revealed and concealed, so too is his name (the tetragrammaton, which is not to be uttered and is pronounced as the name *Adonai*) and his *Torah*, which is also considered as his name.[84] The disclosed aspect of the Torah, consisting of the *mitsvot* and the narratives, parallels *Malkhut*, while its concealed aspect, the Kabbala, parallels *Yesod*.[85] Both the conception of *Yesod* as the hidden source of blessing and its conception as the source of the Kabbala are related to the principal symbol of this *sefira*, the male phallus; and this in turn is bound up with the secrets of the *Torah*: "The supreme secret of the *Torah* is the sign of the holy covenant [i.e., circumcision], which is called the secret of God, a holy covenant" (I, 236b).[86] Elsewhere (II, 166b–167a), the semen that issues from the male organ (i.e., the *sefira* of *Yesod*) is described as light, the light of the *Tora* and its hidden mysteries.[87]

The description of the *sefira* of *Yesod* as the source of blessing that is kept from sight is also applicable to the male organ. In the *Zohar* both the male organ and the *sefira* of *Yesod* are called the glory of the body, *hiddura de-gufa* (II, 186b). What the *Zohar* says, more precisely, is that although this organ should be kept from sight, the glory of the body depends on it, for if one's sexual organs are defective his glory as a whole is flawed. A eunuch has no beard and so lacks "hadrat panim," the glory of the face (as the beard, following Shabbat 152a is called),[88] nor does he have the voice or power of a man.[89] Thus, the foundation (*yesod*) that sustains and glorifies the entire body and the whole world must itself be kept from sight.

Such modesty is appropriate to all sexual matters, and whoever behaves otherwise will be harmed by the evil eye and fall under the influence of the evil inclination, which of course is lodged most intensely in this organ. (The evil inclination also has a cosmic source, the *Sitra Ahra*, enemy of the quality of *Yesod*; see I, 202a.) Accordingly, concealment befits *Yesod*, which is called "Righteous." That is why the letter *tsadi* is not the first letter of the Tora, even though it would have been fitting to create the world by its means. As the *Zohar* relates: "The letter *tsadi* entered. She said to Him: May it be your will, Master of the worlds, to create the world through me, for the righteous *tsaddikim* stamped with my soul, and You, who are called Righteous, are indicated in me [i.e., the letter *yod*, which stands for the name of God, is a component of the letter *tsadi*]. . . He said to her: *tsadi*, you are *tsadi* and you are *tsaddik* (righteous), but you must be concealed; you may not be so exposed" (I, 2b).[90]

The last sentence also applies to the terrestrial righteous man. Like his model among the *sefirot*, he too is a phallic symbol who is entrusted with the secrets of the *Torah*, and he too ought to be concealed.[91] Thus, at the beginning of the *Idra*, R. Simeon is seized by qualms about disclosing the secrets to his companions, for "the world's existence depends upon the secret," by which he undoubtedly is referring to himself, and therefore he should best remain removed from sight. If the author of the *Zohar* identified with his hero, R. Simeon, then this may be another reason for the world's pseudepigraphic character: the author also wanted to conceal himself, for he too is, as it were, "Righteous, foundation of the world," and so ought to be kept concealed.[92] Here may be found the origin of the Hasidic notion of the hidden righteous who sustains the world.[93]

An appreciation of R. Simeon's status can help to elucidate this problematic dialectic between disclosure and concealment. As the foundation of the world he has, by nature, to remain concealed, but that same nature requires that he reveal the mysteries of the *Torah*, for he is the power which begets and fructifies, and the revelation of secrets is his very task. Psychologically, too, he would appear unable to keep his secrets to himself, a dilemma that typifies men of the spirit in every age, and is already to be seen in Jeremiah (Jer. xx:9). However, in many places in the *Zohar* and especially in the *Idra,* R. Simeon and his generation are given special permission to speak openly about the secrets of the *Torah,* setting them apart from all other generations until the coming of the Messiah. As the *Zohar* says:

> In R. Simeon's generation, all are pious righteous men fearful of sin, and the *Shekhina* abides among them as in no other generation. Therefore the words [of *Torah* in R. Simeon's time] are stated openly and are not concealed. That is not so in other generations, and they [the wise] cannot disclose the supernal mystery, and those who know it fear [to reveal it]. (III, 79a)

Later on in the passage it is explained that the verse "With him do I speak mouth to mouth even manifestly, and not in dark speeches" (Num. xii:8) refers to R. Simeon's generation, a statement that also implies a direct equivalence between R. Simeon and Moses. One of the participants at the *Idra,* R. Yisa, was sentenced to death for concealing his words of wisdom in a metaphor (a parable of a bird laying an egg), and was indeed one of those who died at the end of *Idra Rabba.* Oblique speech of this kind was understood as an affront as diminishing R. Simeon's honor and merit. The author goes on to relate that in R. Simeon's time people used to say to each other: "Open your mouth and let your words spread light" (Berakhot 22a, though there the phrase has no connection with R. Simeon), while after his death they said: "Suffer not your mouth to bring your flesh into guilt" (Eccl. 5:5), the verse that appears at the beginning of *Idra Rabba.*

This special merit of R. Simeon and his generation is mentioned often in the *Zohar.* In his time secrets of wisdom were uttered even by children (I, 92b; III, 171a), by birds in the skies and by asses in the wilderness, and all the more so, of course, by the wise men who stood before R. Simeon (III, 22b). R. Simeon himself was greatest of all, for he was "Righteous, foundation of the world" and the things revealed to him had not been revealed even to the angels (III, 142a). Moreover, he imparted openly what had been revealed to him by heaven in a whisper (II, 190b). This is an implicit contrast with the practice of the rabbis when engaging in the mysteries of Creation: "As you hear it in a whisper, so must you say it in a whisper" (Genesis Rabba 3:4).

Nevertheless, R. Simeon is not spared vexation or anguish about whether or not to reveal the secrets. On the contrary, the opening of *Idra Rabba* is concerned with R. Simeon's qualms and apologies about just that. His first complaint, "Until when will we reside in the place of one pillar," is also a complaint about the degeneracy of his generation, as subsequent lines make clear. It is a generation that does not understand the mysteries, and that is the reason for all the other faults of the time. Disclosure, then, is the way to remedy the situation. That is its justification. But R. Simeon nonetheless resorts to the drastic measure of the oath, cautions the participants sternly to be guardians of the secret, and does not begin to disclose the secrets until he is persuaded that the companions really are *kiyyumei 'almin* in this sense as well. Even then he is still not at ease and at the end of the *Idra*, when three of the participants die in a state of devotional ecstasy (*devekut*), he fears that their death was caused by his sin of disclosing things that had been revealed only once in the past—to Moses at Sinai. His anxiety was calmed only by a heavenly voice. As we read at the beginning of the *Idra*, right after the participants enter: "R. Simeon sat down and wept,[94] and said: 'Woe if I reveal, and woe if I do not reveal.' "[95]

This dilemma about disclosing the secrets of the Torah is already present in the Mishna (Hagiga ii:1), but typifies in particular the medieval period. Maimonides' apprehensions in this regard are well known, and it was they that led him to adopt an esoteric style in writing the *Guide of the Perplexed* (see the introduction to that work). The problem was especially acute among the early Kabbalists, as can be seen, for example, by the laconic style used by Nachmanides whenever he presented a Kabbalistic interpretation in his commentary to the *Torah*. It is expressed with particular clarity in a letter by Isaac the Blind to the Kabbalists of Gerona, which was largely a complaint against the excessive disclosure of Kabbalistic secrets.[96] There is, moreover, an antinomian aspect to disclosure, and the problem relates to the essence of the *sefirot* as well.

As we shall see below, full disclosure of the secrets is among the marks of the Messianic era, and R. Simeon's ambivalent stand on this issue accords with his semi-messianic status. It should be noted that according to the *Zohar* the Messianic era will also eliminate the need for modesty in sexual matters, and we have already pointed out the relationship between the two realms. The openness to be practiced in sexual matters is explained by the fact that the origin of the need for sexual modesty was fear of the *Sitra Ahra* (indeed, even according to the plain meaning of the *Torah* the need for it arose only because of Adam's sin). This is expounded at length in the *Zohar*[97] in relation to the requirement that the words "Blessed be the name of the glory of His Kingdom forever,"—in the *Zohar*, the *tikkun* of the bride—be said in a whisper (except on *Yom Kippur*). The *Zohar* concludes there: "In the future these words will stand before *Attik Yomin* (the Ancient of Days) without shame." The period of *Attik Yomin*, the configuration that undergoes *tikkun* in the *Idra*, is the Messianic era.

R. Simeon's Generation

This dual wish, both to reveal and to conceal, is paralleled by the *Zohar*'s twofold assessment of R. Simeon's generation. Side by side with the enthusiastically positive evaluation described above appears another quite opposite evaluation. One passage expressing a decidedly negative assessment was cited above; another is the beginning of *Idra Rabba*.

R. Simeon opens his apology about the need to disclose the secrets with a complaint about the existing situation. After stating his general dissatisfaction ("Until when will we dwell in the place of one pillar?"), he declares: "It is time to act for the Lord, for they have violated Your *Torah*" (Ps. cxix:126). That is to say, the occasion for the vigorous activity of *Idra Rabba* was the generation's violation of the *Torah*. The *Zohar* at this point coins a phrase to describe the generation: "The days are short, and the Creditor presses." This is a paraphrase of a saying in the *Mishna*: "The day is short...and the master of the house presses [*dohek*]" (Avot ii:15), which is about the need to engage in *Torah* study. The *Zohar*, however, has transformed the master of the house, God, into the "Creditor" of Avot iii:16, according to which "...the Shopkeeper gives credit...and everyone who wishes to borrow let him borrow: but the collectors...exact payment"; and it thus turns the expression into an allusion to the duress (*dohak*) of the exile. This may refer to *Ze'er Anpin* in its flawed form, which is severe judgment, and which rules in the exile; its rule, in fact, is the cause of the exile. The passage continues with the words "a herald daily proclaims," an allusion to Avot vi:2: "A heavenly voice daily goes forth from Mt. Horev to proclaim: 'Woe to mankind for their contempt of the Law.'" The content of the herald's proclamation in the *Zohar*[98] would seem to be identical with that of the heavenly voice in the *Mishna*.

The *Zohar* next states that "the reapers of the field"—those who study the *Torah* properly, that is, by way of the *Kabbala*[99]—"are few." If that is so, then R. Simeon's complaint, "Until when will we dwell in the place of one pillar," appears to be concerned with the *Kabbala* being too little studied. Comparing it with the statement in the *Zohar* about the sea serpent, however, its object would seem rather to be the low level of kabbalistic study theretofore. There are several parallels between the passages: the *Idra* speaks of "one pillar," the other passage of "one sea serpent upon whom the world rests"; here "the reapers of the field" are few, there—"few are they who know." They differ, to be sure, with regard to the subject of the mystical study with which they are concerned. In the passage on the sea serpent,

R. Simeon's companions knew the mystery of the *sefirot*, but not the secrets of the *sitra ahra*. Here, on the other hand, they know the ordinary kabbalistic method of the *Zohar*, but not the deeper secrets which R. Simeon is to reveal at the *Idra*. The two subjects, however, are related, for *Idra Rabba* is to deal with worlds that were destroyed and are in need of restoration, and these are the very forces of evil from which the *sitra ahra* gained its powers, the great rivers of the sea serpents. In fact, in the sea serpent passage we find an allusion to the very same worlds that are described in the *Idra* (such allusions occur very rarely in the *Zohar* outside the *Idrot*). It is said that the great sea serpent entered the first of the rivers of the *Sitra Ahra* and "extinguished sparks that had come together in those worlds that were destroyed in the Beginning." Whichever interpretation of R. Simeon's complaint is correct, however, it may be that what the *Zohar* means by it is this: Most of the world, which heretofore had been satisfied with the plain meaning of the *Torah*, will henceforth engage in *Kabbala*, but the disciples of R. Simeon will ascend a further rung.

R. Simeon continues with a description of the situation of the Kabbalists: "And they are at the edges [*beshulei*; or, alternatively, *beshurei*—in the rows] of the vineyard." The expression "the edges of the vineyard," which has no parallel anywhere else, is somewhat obscure. I think that here the variant reading, "rows," is to be preferred. It alludes more clearly to the gathering at Yavne referred to in the Talmud as the "vineyard of Yavne"; as noted elsewhere in the *Zohar*, it was the situation described there, namely, that "in the future the *Torah* will be forgotten in Israel," which the *Idra* was meant to remedy, and it was, indeed, precisely because "they have violated Your *Torah*," and "the reapers of the field are few," that the need to convene the *Idra* arose. The phrase "the rows of the vineyard" would thus allude to the explanation offered by the rabbis as to why the meeting of the Sanhedrin at Yavne was called the "vineyard of Yavne": "A 'vineyard': this is the Sanhedrin. . .For when we say "the vineyard of Yavne," we do not mean that they sat in a vineyard, but rather the Sanhedrin is so-called because it was arranged in rows like a vineyard."[100]

Here we find, then, that R. Simeon, in noting the evils that compelled him to hold the *Idra*, mentions the presence of the sages "in the rows of the vineyard," that is to say, in the difficult situation, the straits, described at Yavne. The reading "at the edges of the vineyard" may nonetheless be correct, however, for it too retains the allusion to Yavne, and by changing "rows" to "edges" the author may have sought to make other allusions as well. The "vineyard," its significance influenced by that attached to the word *pardes*,[101] the "garden" of mystical knowledge, may also represent for him the wisdom of the *Kabbala*, with the transformation of "rows" to "edges" meant to suggest that the participants are still at the margins of Kabbalistic wisdom and have not yet gotten to the heart of it; this they will accomplish at the *Idra*.

The vineyard may also allude to the Garden of Eden in the sense of Paradise (*pardes*). The expression would then mean that the sages have not yet achieved the merit that would assure them a good place in paradise: their place is still at the edges. This meaning can also be maintained with the variant "rows," for there are three walls (Aramaic: *shurin*) around the Garden of Eden on which rest the souls of those who are not given to enter (III, 196b).[102] The fate of the individual soul is inextricably linked in the *Zohar* with the fate of the nation and of the world as a whole. R. Simeon's primary topic in *Idra Zuta* (III, 288a), and even more so in its early version, is the ascertainment of his place in Paradise. This interpretation accords well with his subsequent complaint against his companions at the opening of the *Idra*: "They do not watch as they should and do not know the place to which they are going." Moreover, the word "place" (*atar*) is used by R. Simeon in the early version of *Idra Zuta* to refer to his "place" in Paradise. However, the vineyard may also denote Israel (As in the prophecy of Isaiah: "For the vineyard of the Lord of Hosts is the House of Israel" [Isa. v:7]; the image was reiterated by the rabbis in their statement that "The vineyard of the Holy One blessed be He is Israel" [*Midrash Rabba*, Lev. xxxii:1], and so became the source of such expressions as "let the owner of the vineyard Himself rid it of thorns" [*Baba Metsi'a* 83b], and, analogously, the *Shekhina*, which is identified in the *Kabbala* with *Knesset Israel* (the Congregation of Israel).[103] In this context, the complaint against the sages "at the edges of the vineyard" would be that they did not concern themselves with the fate of Israel and of the *Shekhina* in exile. This, together with the other flaws we have noted, is precisely what will be their concern during *Idra Rabba*. The "place" which they previously had not known how to approach as they should is the *tikkun* and the advent of the Messiah—the *tikkun*, that is, of the entire world, for "the world and everything in it is fashioned like a vineyard."[104]

As we have seen, then, R. Simeon decided to disclose the secrets—although not without much hesitation—because of the serious faults he had observed in his generation. But the state of his times also heightened his fears, for it is forbidden to disclose the secrets of the *Torah* to evil men. Their souls are not from the Godhead, and disclosing the secrets to them is comparable to engaging in illicit sexual relations. It is permitted to disclose the secrets only to one "whose soul is from the body of the Holy King," and so can be trusted not to prattle and reveal them. One who reveals the secrets is viewed as though he had spilled blood, practiced idolatry (III, 294b), and engaged in illicit sexual relations (III, 79a); that is to say, as though he had broken all three commandments subject to the rabbinic injunction, "suffer death rather than transgress" (*Sanhedrin* 74a). One who keeps the secret, on the other hand, has a special sign in his ear; it curves in such a way as to spill the words inward without letting them out again, like the ear of God himself (III, 294b).

Fear of God

This dilemma explains why R. Simeon wept at the opening of the *Idra Rabba* and said, "Woe if I reveal and woe if I do not reveal." The *Zohar* reports that all of those present remained silent. It would seem that they did not have the courage to say of themselves that they were worthy of hearing the disclosure of the secrets. Then R. Abba, who was senior among the participants, rose and entreated:

> May it be the will of the master to reveal, for it is written: "The secret of the Lord is for those who fear Him" (Psalms xxv:14), and these companions are God-fearing. They have already entered the *Idra* of the Dwelling (*Idra de-Vei Mashkena*). Some have entered and some have emerged.

As we see, R. Abba regarded fear of God as the sign of a person to whom secrets can be disclosed. This idea is discussed several times in the *Zohar*, and always in connection with the verse from Psalms quoted here.[105]

What is the relationship between fear of God and guarding a secret? It may be said first of all that fear of God is a prerequisite for entrance into the world of the *Kabbala*, and as such parallels the *sefira* of *Malkhut*, which is the gateway from the lower world to the upper. This follows from the verse: "The fear of the Lord is the beginning of wisdom" (Ps. cxi:10).[106] But fear of God is related to mysticism in another way as well, and it is this that apparently is intended in the opening passage of the *Idra*. It is in this connection that R. Simeon further on quotes the verse from Habakkuk, "O Lord, I have heard the report of Thee and am afraid" (iii:2), referring by it to the level of God-fearing achieved by the companions prior to the *Idra*. This same verse is expounded at length in *Sefer ha-Bahir*[107] to explain the mystical character of the prophet Habakkuk, who apparently is regarded as the paradigmatic Jewish mystic.[108] In *Sefer ha-Bahir* (71) Habakkuk's fear of God is described as an intrinsic feature of the highest form of mystical apprehension. The mystic knows that the Holy One blessed be He explicitly commanded that he remain hidden and that no one come before him or seek him out ("One does not expound on the Chariot"); the mystic who nonetheless enters is therefore fearful "lest the King know that he is violating His command." On the other hand, it is clear that *Sefer ha-Bahir* views the mystic as having achieved an unparalleled height. There is thus an ambivalence here that is subtly, profoundly, and self-consciously antinomian, like that apparent in the story of Honi the Circle Drawer. This kind of God-fearing also calls to mind the medieval philosophical concept of the "fear of Majesty" which is also related to contemplation of the universe and of the greatness of the Creator, although not in a mystical sense. Fear of Majesty can dissuade one from disclosing the secrets, and R. Simeon's behavior at the opening of the *Idra* indicates that he had that fear.

As proof that the assembled companions fear God, R. Abba notes that they have already been to *Idra de-Vei Mashkena*. This is undoubtedly described in a work of that name, in the spirit of the *Idrot*, which dealt with the secrets of the Sanctuary (*mishkan*). The statement: "The companions have already expounded all the secrets of the Sanctuary at the Holy Assembly (*Idra kaddisha*)" (II, 214a) would also seem to refer to this work, which apparently has been lost.[109] R. Abba says that some entered *Idra de-Vei Mashkena* and some emerged. The expression "entered and did not emerge" refers to an ecstatic death. (No such thing would seem to have happened at *Idra de-Vei Mashkena*, since even those who are said not to have emerged attended *Idra Rabba*, their souls departing from them only at its conclusion; however, some kind of event resembling death did take place.) It is derived from an account of R. Akiva in the Talmud, where he is mentioned as one of the four sages who entered the mystical Garden (*pardes*), and the only one to enter and emerge unharmed.[110] The author of the *Zohar* apparently viewed the *Idra* as resembling the *pardes* of the rabbis. The motif of not emerging—that is, of the departure of the soul at the *Idra*—recurs in most of the works in this category (*Idra Rabba*, *Idra Zuta*, and *Idra de-Vei Mashkena*). The *Zohar* takes a very harsh view of those who enter and do not emerge, declaring that it would have been better had they not come into the world (III, 141a),[111] though without applying this judgment to those who died in *Idra Rabba*, or of course in *Idra Zuta* (III, 144a–b).

The deaths that occur in the *Idrot* would also be a reason for the sense of fear that characterizes these gatherings. That is why the

Idrot sometimes open with the verse "O Lord, I have heard the report of Thee and am afraid."[112] The verse is appropriate to this occasion, both because it is stated at the beginning of the mystical prayer of the prophet Habakkuk and because it was uttered by the prophet at the time when he saw his own death (I, 7b)[113]—the time of the soul's departure being the most fitting moment for mystical disclosures.[114] R. Simeon cites this verse in *Idra Rabba*, which ends with the departure of the souls of three of the participants, and in so doing apparently alludes to a similar citation of it at the beginning of *Idra de-Vei Mashkena* (in which it also happened that some sages entered and did not emerge). He says: "There [i.e., in *Idra de-Vei Mashkena*] it was right to be afraid [but] for us [in *Idra Rabba*] the matter depends on love." Even though some of the participants die in *Idra Rabba*, fear is inappropriate, for their souls depart in love; they die by a divine kiss. Such a death is not blameworthy, but deserving of praise.

The statement "There it was right to be afraid" and the concluding phrase "for us the matter depends on love" also have an interpretation bearing on the ontological realm, one mentioned explicitly later on in the *Idra*. After R. Simeon explains the *tikkunim* of *Ze'er Anpin*, the lowest divine configuration whose essence is judgment, he says:

> "O Lord I have heard the report of Thee and am afraid"—When the holy prophet (Habakkuk) had heard and looked and apprehended and understood these *tikkunim* (of *Ze'er Anpin*), he said, as is written, "I am afraid." There it was right to fear and be heartbroken before Him, for this was said in connection with *Ze'er Anpin*. (III, 138b)

It thus emerges that the word "there" refers not only to *Idra de-Vei Mashkena* but also to "a place," an aspect of the Godhead, namely *Ze'er Anpin*. Later in the passage this is contrasted with *Arikh Anpin*, which is there called: "the supreme grace of Attika de-Attikin, by which mercy for all is awakened."

The phrase "for us the matter depends on love" thus refers to *Arikh Anpin*, while "there it was right to be afraid" refers to *Ze'er Anpin*, paralleling the two *Idrot*—*Idra Rabba* and *Idra de-Vei Mashkena*. This also accords with the content of the *Idrot*. *Idra Rabba* begins with the *tikkun* of *Arikh Anpin*, and only when this is completed does it proceed to the *tikkun* of *Ze'er Anpin*; *Idra de-Vei Mashkena*, on the other hand, apparently dealt with *Ze'er Anpin* alone, resembling *Idra Raza de-Razin* (ll, 122b–123b) in this respect. Its opening passage in fact relates that the whole world depends on judgment, while in *Idra Rabba*, by contrast, "the matter depends on love," and a parallel statement relates that "the world is maintained only by the secret [*raza*]."

Love

This gives the *Idra* messianic significance as well. The complete *tikkun*, which begins with *Arikh Anpin*, is that of the entire cosmos; it is the messianic *tikkun* (see below). So, too, the awakening of the attribute of Divine Love (*Hesed*) takes place in the messianic period, and is not possible in exile ("Do not wake or rouse love until it please." [Song of Sol. ii:7]). Thus, *Idra de-Vei Mashkena*, which is concerned with Judgment (*Din*), perhaps parallels the meeting of the *Sanhedrin* at Yavne at which the exile, which *Idra Rabba* was meant to rectify, was described. "There," however, may also refer to another event that was also characterized essentially by Judgment.

"For us the matter depends on love" has a social, human meaning as well, for it refers to the love amongst the participants at the *Idra*, which is also of messianic significance. Love was part of the pledge to R. Simeon taken by the Companions.[115] In this too, it seems, *Idra Rabba* differs from *Idra de-Vei Mashkena*, in a way that relates to the fear of death which prevailed at the *Idra*, for the death of the participants at *Idra de-Vei Mashkena* was caused by hatred among them. The state of the relations among the companions also relates to their status as symbols of the *sefirot*, for hatred among them represents division among the *sefirot* and a flaw in the supernal world, while love among them is a condition for the disclosure of the secrets of the *Torah*. All these notions come together in the following passage:

> When the Companions came before R. Simeon, he saw a sign in their faces [that there was love among them], and he said: Come my holy children, come beloved of the King, come my cherished ones who love one another. For as R. Abba once said: All those companions who do not love one another pass from the world before their time. All the Companions in the days of R. Simeon loved one another in soul and spirit. That is why [the secrets of the *Torah*] were disclosed in R. Simeon's generation. As R. Simeon was wont to say: all the Companions who do not love one another divert from the straight path, and cause blemish to the *Torah*, for the *Torah* is love, brotherhood and truth. Abraham loves Isaac and Isaac loves Abraham, and they embrace one another—and they both hold Jacob in love and brotherhood,

giving their spirit to one another [i.e., by a kiss]. The Companions
must follow this example and not blemish [the *Torah*]. (II, 190b)

In speaking of the *Torah*, R. Simeon is also referring to the divine
entity symbolized by it (at the beginning of the *Idra* he had complained
about the nullification of the heavenly *Torah*; see below). His mention
of the Patriarchs is clearly a reference to the three central *sefirot:
Hesed* (Love), *Gevura* (Power), and *Tiferet* (Beauty). What was said
at the opening of the *Idra* of the three central participants can also
be said of these three *sefirot*: "We are the sum of all." These *sefirot*
are always symbolized by the Patriarchs, with *Tiferet*, which is Jacob,
situated between the two others and holding fast to both sides. In the
Zohar, the word *dugma*, "example," means symbol,[116] one which not
only represents but also influences the upper worlds. The Companions
must follow the example of the loving Patriarchs in the supernal world,
for if they do not they will be the cause of a defective situation on
high, and love among the *sefirot* themselves will cease.

The love amongst the participants at *Idra Rabba*, which follows
a period without love ("There it was right to be afraid") calls to mind
a similar incident in which messianic expectations also apparently
played a role. According to a story in the *Talmud (Yevamot* 62b), the
disciples of R. Akiva behaved disrespectfully towards each other, and
for that reason they all died in one season, between Passover and
Shavuot. R. Akiva subsequently took on new disciples who apparently
related to one another with love. One of them was R. Simeon. It may
well be that the death of the first group of R. Akiva's disciples
resurfaced in the account of those "who entered and did not emerge"
in *Idra de-Vei Mashkena* (where "it was right to be afraid"). The
talmudic story (in Hagiga 14b) about the four sages who entered the
Garden also concerns R. Akiva and his disciples: the three who did
not emerge safely from the Garden were pupils of his. It seems that
in the *Zohar* the two motifs were fused: the failure of the three to exit
safely from the Garden was conflated with the death of those who
failed to act respectfully towards their fellows. The ordination of R.
Akiva's five new disciples apparently was associated with the uprising
against Rome and so had messianic implications. This emerges from
a parallel account in the *Talmud* of the ordination of the same five
sages *(Sanhedrin* 13b) who are listed in both places by name. The event
is described there as an act of defiance against the Roman regime,
which had banned ordination. It was an act of rescue, for had it not
been performed "the laws concerning acts punishable by penalty fees
(dinei kenasot). . ."—which can be adjudicated only by authorized
individuals—"would have become inoperable."

The messianic implications of ordination were clear enough to the rabbis of sixteenth-century Safed, headed by R. Jacob Berab, who struggled to renew the institution in their own time. Paralleling the account in *Sanhedrin* of the salvage of a whole category of law, a passage in tractate *Yevamot* says of the five loving disciples of R. Akiva that "It was they who revived the *Torah* at that time."[117] This also calls to mind the opening of *Idra Rabba*, and R. Simeon's proclamation that "It is a time to act for the Lord; they have violated Your *Torah*." He proceeds to complain that the supernal *Torah* is being nullified; the concern of the *Idra* is to revive it. For the author of the *Zohar* this is also related to the world's very existence, for when R. Akiva's first disciples died "the world was desolate." It is therefore quite possible that the author of the *Zohar* identified the *Idra* with the ordination of R. Akiva's disciples, R. Simeon taking R. Akiva's place on the strength of the many associations linking the two.[118] Thus, R. Simeon is elevated in rank from being merely one of the five disciples and made the leader of the group, in place of R. Akiva.

The messianic nature of *Idra Rabba* will become more evident when viewed in light of the story of R. Akiva's disciples. The death of the former group, like the ordination of the new, was undoubtedly related to the Bar-Kokhba revolt, on which R. Akiva had pinned great hopes. As many have noted,[119] he was also one of its leaders. Furthermore, it could be that the *Zohar*'s author associated Bar-Kokhba's first name, Simeon, with that of his hero and consequently endowed Bar Yohai with some of Bar-Kokhba's characteristics. To be sure, R. Simeon and his companions in the *Zohar* were not warriors like Bar-Kokhba and his men, but their association with the latter may well have been among the reasons for the metaphorical description of the participants at the *Idra* bearing weapons and decked in armor.

The association between the participants at the *Idra* and R. Akiva's pupils is not explicit in the *Zohar*. The similarity between the two was pointed out, however, by Isaac Luria, who greatly elaborated it. While tradition may have it that he received his mystical knowledge from the prophet Elijah, it is known that Luria was also an intensive student of the *Zohar*. Hayyim Vital reports that "Sometimes he would spend the nights of all six weekdays alone in the study of only one problem in the *Zohar*."[120] Examination of his teaching most definitely confirms Vital's testimony. At times Luria's statements seem remote from anything that had been known theretofore, but close inspection of the *Zohar* reveals that the seeds of ideas he developed are to be found there.[121] This would seem to be the case in the present instance.

In Luria's view, *Idra Rabba* was held on *Lag Ba-'Omer*, a date to which no particular significance is attached in the *Zohar*. It is possible that the author of the *Zohar* knew of the tradition associated with it, since it is first mentioned by Menahem Meiri, who was his contemporary.[122] More likely, though, he was unfamiliar with this tradition, and in fact assigned *Idra Rabba* to *Shavuot*. In light of what we said above, however, Luria's *Lag Ba-'Omer* date is most appropriate, for tradition holds it to be the day on which death ceased striking down R. Akiva's pupils, and so also that on which his new disciples were ordained. The tradition about Lag Ba-'Omer is cited, moreover, as a source for the ruling that the mourning customs practiced during the *Omer* period in memory of the deaths of R. Akiva's disciples be stopped on that day. Though Luria, for subtle Kabbalistic reasons, did not accept this ruling, he did give a reason for it. As he saw it, the *tikkun* of the worlds is a process carried out through the course of world history and repeated annually on a small scale through the ritual of the holidays.

The *Omer* period is the time for the *tikkun* of the "brains" of *Ze'er Anpin*. Between Passover and *Lag Ba'Omer*, that is, "brains" enter into *Ze'er Anpin*. The substance of this "brains" is harsh rulings (*dinim kashim*). They are also R. Akiva's first disciples, those who, as Luria put it, "denounce and hate each other." From *Lag Ba-'Omer* onward, however, the "brains" are compassion (*Rahamim*). It is also the five disciples of R. Akiva, including R. Simeon, who loved one another. These, to be sure, do not represent full compassion, but they are the "powers of maturity" (*gevurot de-gadlut*), which is compassion in comparison with the first group. Accordingly, the earlier disciples died because they "were struck down by the attribute of judgment (*din*)."[123] As we have seen, the idea of a relationship between the love among the companions and the divine entities is present in the *Zohar* as well (though in a much simpler form), but here, in *Lurianic Kabbala*, it is greatly elaborated. An important question that presents itself at this juncture is that of whether the association of the sages with the divine attributes is symbolic here, as in the *Zohar*, or whether their souls are regarded as truly identical with those attributes.

The idea that love must prevail among the companions was not confined by *Lurianic Kabbala* to the theoretical, speculative realm, and it did not apply only to R. Akiva's disciples. Luria himself took pains to ensure that love would prevail among the members of his group. Before worshipping in the synagogue, an individual had to commit himself to the *mitsva* of loving one's fellow,[124] so that all of the prayers of Israel would be combined together. Especially important, writes Hayyim Vital, was "the love of companions who study *Torah* together; each of them must regard himself as though he were one part of the body of the group of his companions, especially if he has the knowledge and understanding to know his fellow's soul. . . . And my teacher cautioned me greatly about the need for love to prevail among the companions in our group." The source of this requirement for love in connection with prayer is the mystical conception of the *minyan* of ten worshippers in the synagogue as one body, symbolizing the *sefirot* or the bodily parts of the *Shekhina*.[125] It is related to Israel's designation as "the bodily parts of the Matron" (III, 231b).[126] The importance of knowing the soul of one's fellow, as mentioned in the passage above, is also related to this, for the roots of the soul originate in the various parts of the Godhead, and knowledge of these sources enables the latter to be joined into a "whole body."

Love within Luria's group was not only requisite for the disclosure of the mysteries; it was also a means for facilitating the messianic end—just as in *Idra Rabba*. In *Sefer Toledot ha-Ari* (ed. Benayau, pp. 201–2) it is related that Luria did not want to disclose certain mysteries. The companions, after much pleading, persuaded him to consent, but he then saw in a vision that his death was sealed for having done so. Some time later a quarrel broke out within the group (among the wives, who incited their husbands). Luria told them that the time of the decree's implementation had now arrived, for it was their mutual love that had deferred the judgment. He indeed died shortly thereafter. It is also related (p. 199) that after his death his disciples discovered that he was the messiah of the house of Joseph. The disclosure of the secrets followed by a breach of love thus caused a disaster in the messianic realm. This idea had its roots in a passage in the *Zohar* (I, 76b) which states that when love prevails among the companions, the attribute of judgment (*din*) can have no dominion over them, even if they rebel against the Holy One blessed be he; those who contend with one another, however, will not survive.[127]

The notion of obligatory love among the companions of a messianic circle calls to mind early Christianity. There Jesus instructed his disciples: "A new commandment I give unto you, That ye love one another; as I have loved you, that ye also love one another. By this shall all men know that ye are my disciples, if ye have love one to another" (John xiii: 34–35).

Let us now return to the *Zohar* and examine a passage which, since it occurs in one of the earlier versions of the *Idra* and elaborates in particular on the theme of love,[128] may help shed light on the meaning of love in *Idra Rabba*. Here love among the companions restores everything in need of *tikkun* and is employed by R. Simeon in the fulfillment of his role. He orders his group:

And you companions that are here, as you have loved before, do not part yourselves from one another from now on until the Holy One, blessed be He, be glad with you and call peace upon you, and may there be peace in the world on your account, as it is written: "For my brethren and companions' sake, I will now say, Peace be within you" (Ps. cxxii:8) [III, 59b].

What R. Simeon says here about the love that had prevailed in the past among the companions contradicts his statement in *Idra Rabba* that "there it was right to be afraid." The present statement is based by way of contrast on the rabbinic statement that those who engage in *Torah* study are initially antagonistic towards their companions but later come to love each other (*Kiddushin* 30b), another association which the author of the *Zohar* may have had in mind at the beginning of *Idra Rabba*. The request of them not to part in the future is also made in *Idra Rabba*, but it is presented there from a different perspective: there it is not love that is primary, but rather the guarding of the secrets and the bond with R. Simeon. The companions thus all remain together in R. Simeon's house in order that they, and no one else, will hear the secrets.

The love amongst the companions makes their master, who is "righteous, foundation of the world," wholly perfect and enables him to perform his role. This understanding receives additional confirmation from the theoretical discussion of love in I, 11b–12a, which develops the idea that "perfect love" must embrace two sides; it will then not be dependent upon anything and persist through good and ill. Love that embraces both sides is a love that also includes fear. On the supernal level it encompasses all of the *sefirot* and it is concentrated at the level of *Yesod*, which is at the center.[129] The companions, who are both Godfearing and perfect in their love (and thus embrace both sides), not only contribute to the symbolic *tikkun* that this state of affairs itself brings about, but also assist their master, who is on the level of *Yesod*, to achieve the fullness of love—that is, the *tikkun* of the world—by sexual union with the *Shekhina* (see below). That is why they are called upon to be both capable of guarding the secrets and sexually complete. R. Simeon and his disciples are thus transformed into a messianic team prepared to engage in theurgic messianic activity, which is what they later do at the *Idra*. We find, then, that R. Simeon's loneliness ("the place of one pillar") had negative consequences for the cosmic realm as well, which would be remedied by the love of his companions.

The messianic quality ascribed by R. Simeon to the love prevailing at the *Idra* is also reflected in the verses he cites. At the beginning he claims that "For us the matter depends on love," adding "as it is written, 'And you shall love the Lord your God' (Deut. vi:5), and it is written, 'Because the Lord loved you' (Deut. vii:8) and it is written, 'I have loved you, said the Lord' (Mal. i:2)." The first verse he cites speaks of the companions' obligation to love, while the latter two are about the reward of that love, which in both is clearly messianic. The verse in Deuteronomy (vii:8) speaks of the redemption from Egypt as having come about on account of God's love for his people. The context of noting the citation from Malachi is also significant: "I have loved you, said the Lord. Yet you say: 'Wherein hast Thou loved us?' Was not Esau Jacob's brother? says the Lord; yet I loved Jacob, but Esau I hated, and made his mountains a desolation and gave his heritage to the jackals of the wilderness." The destruction of Edom (i.e., the end of Christian rule) is the messianic aspiration of the *Zohar*'s author. As we shall see below, the accomplishment of this destruction and the enthronement of a king over Israel are the goals of *Idra Rabba*.

The Torah

It has already been noted that the *tikkun* in *Idra Rabba* is also that of the *Torah*, which had been violated.[130] Let us now examine in greater detail the flaw that was said to have blemished the *Torah* before the *Idra*, how it was remedied in the course of the *Idra*, and the messianic nature of that *tikkun*. The verse in Habakkuk reflecting the earlier, defective situation of fear ("O Lord, I have heard the report of You and am afraid") contains an element that may help us to understand how the defective state indicated by the expression "the place of one pillar" may be related to the *Torah* as well. Until the *Idra*, as we have seen, the world was supported by a single pillar, which was R. Simeon and was called "righteous, foundation of the world." The *Torah* may well have been in a similar situation, in which all its *mitsvot* were included in one. As the rabbis said: "Six hundred and thirteen precepts were told unto Moses. . .the two hundred and forty-eight positive precepts corresponding to the number of the members of man's body. . .but then came Habakkuk and set them all on one (principle), as it is written, 'The righteous shall live by his faith' (Hab. ii:4)" (Makkot 23b–24a). There is an evident similarity between the world supported by one pillar ("righteous, foundation of the world") and the *Torah* supported by one principle ("the righteous shall live by his faith"). R. Simeon may have been alluding to this similarity by his choice, at the opening of the *Idra*, of another verse from the same book of Habakkuk to indicate the fear that had prevailed prior to the *Idra* ("O Lord, I have heard the report of You and am afraid"). Now let us consider the verse "The righteous shall live by his faith," as interpreted by the Sages in Makkot. In the context of the opening of the *Idra* (assuming that it indeed alludes to this verse), there arises from it a sense of the tremendous loneliness of the righteous one, who, after the *Torah* has been nullified, must sustain it on his own and restore it to its proper status, on the strength of his personal faith alone. This sense accords with the complaint expressed by R. Simeon at the opening of the *Idra* which induced him to assemble his companions and bind them together with love, thereby both remedying his personal situation and bringing about the *tikkun* of the cosmos, the *Torah* and the nation.[131]

Even if there is no allusion here to the one precept upon which Habakkuk sets the entire *Torah*, there still is a relationship between the state of the cosmos and the state of the *Torah*, as R. Simeon proclaims at the opening of the *Idra*:

> Why is it "time to act for the Lord"? Because "they have violated Your *Torah*." What is meant by "they have violated Your *Torah*"? [It refers to] the supernal *Torah*, which is nullified if the *tikkun* of this Name is not performed. This is said to *Attik Yomin* (the Ancient of Days).

The use of the expression "the supernal *Torah*" makes it clear that the passage refers to the supernal source of the *Torah*. (The expression is found in *Sefer ha-Bahir* [196], where the "supernal *Torah*" is identified with the *Shekhina*, and its *tikkun* comes about when it joins with the Holy One blessed be he; this resembles its *tikkun* in the *Zohar*, which comes about when it joins with *Attika Kaddisha*, the Ancient Holy One.) The source of this *Torah* is *Ze'er Anpin* (or, elsewhere in the *Zohar*, the *sefira* of *Tif'eret*), which is called by the Ineffable Name. The nullification of the *Torah* blemishes this countenance (*partsuf*). Action must therefore be taken for its sake, and *tikkunim* must be performed on behalf of this Name—the Ineffable Name, which is *Ze'er Anpin*. That is why the verse reads "It is time to act for the Lord"—that is, for YHVH. The call is addressed to *Attik Yomin* (who is *Arikh Anpin*), for it is he who can bring about the *tikkun* of *Ze'er Anpin* (though for this to happen *Arikh Anpin* itself must first undergo *tikkun*). Following Tishby's interpretation, it is also possible that the expression "Your *Torah*" refers to *Arikh Anpin*, for *Ze'er Anpin* is "His *Torah*." The derivation of the idea that Israel's abandonment of the *Torah* weakens the Holy One blessed be He from the verse "It is time to act for the Lord, they have violated Your *Torah*" is found in several other places in the *Zohar* as well (e.g., II, 155b).

Arikh Anpin can restore *Ze'er Anpin*'s *Torah* by means of a connecting flow of illumination. Through the middle of *Arikh Anpin*'s hair runs a part, which—when things are as they should be—is linked to a similar part on the head of *Ze'er Anpin*; and from the latter branch out 613 pathways that are the sources of the 613 *mitsvot* in the *Torah*, as explained later on in the *Idra* (III, 129a; 136a).[132] This is typical of how the *tikkun* of every part of *Ze'er Anpin* is brought about: *Arikh Anpin*, when restored to perfection, shines its light upon *Ze'er Anpin*, and this softens the harsh judgment characteristic of the latter when it is parted from *Arikh Anpin*. Another example of this kind of *tikkun* is to be found in the *Zohar*'s discussion of *Ze'er Anpin*'s brow (III, 136b). On its own, this is the insolent "harlot's brow" of Jeremiah iii:3, and it is tempered only when it receives illumination from the brow of *Attika Kaddisha*, which is called the brow of favor or of providence. In the same way, the judgment in the enraged red eyes of *Ze'er Anpin* is tempered by the milk that flows from the calm white eye of *Attika*. The same principle applies to the other features of the face, such as the nose.

It seems, then, that the defect in the *Torah* before the *Idra* was that of untempered judgment. We have considered the source of this defect in the Godhead, but it must also find expression in the essence of the *Torah* itself, as it is actualized in history. Kabbalistic symbols are not mere names that have lost all connection with their plain meaning because of the symbolic meanings they have taken on. The symbolic meaning supplements and deepens the plain meaning, but does not replace it. This is explained in another passage in the *Zohar* (III, 152a) that distinguishes between several different layers in the *Torah* and draws parallels between them and the supernal essences (and even locates their sources in those essences). The lowest level is the *Torah*'s outer garments, which are the stories of the *Torah* in their plain sense; their supernal source lies not in the *sefirot* but in the heavens and their hosts (the stars, spheres, or angels). The stratum beneath the garments is the body, comprising the *mitsvot*, which are called *gufei Torah*, the "bodies of the *Torah*";[133] their source is the *Shekhina*. Beneath the body is the soul, which is the true essence of the *Torah* and has its origin in *Tif'eret*. The fourth stratum is the "soul of the soul"[134] of the *Torah*, and it originates in *Attika Kaddisha*.[135]

The *Zohar* does not say explicitly what the exact natures of the two most sublime layers are. It does disclose, however, that "the really wise, the servants of the supreme King, those who stood on Mt. Sinai," are able to see the soul of the *Torah*, that is, that derived from *Tiferet*, but they will see the "soul of the soul" only in the world to come. As we saw above, however, in *Idra Rabba* the *tikkun* of the *Torah* is brought about by the illumination of *Attika Kaddisha*; that is to say, *Idra Rabba* achieves the vision of the *Torah* pertaining to the world to come, that of the "soul of the soul" of the *Torah*! (The *Torah* of *Attika Kaddisha* is actualized only by the illumination and *tikkun* of the *Torah* of *Ze'er Anpin*, but according to this same passage, III, 152a, each more sublime stratum requires the one below it for its revelation.) Another indication that this passage may allude to *Idra Rabba* is its comparison between this revelation of the "soul of the soul" with what was seen by those who stood on Mt. Sinai. The *Idra*, too, compares itself to the giving of the *Torah* at Sinai and sees itself as a more sublime event, representing a stage between the giving of the *Torah* and the coming of the Messiah. The relationship between the *Idra* and the highest of the four possible apprehensions of the *Torah* is perhaps also hinted in II, 99a, where the highest stage is called seeing the *Torah* face to face, and seeing face to face (*anpin b'anpin*) is the object of the *Idra*. In this passage, too, the phrase has erotic overtones.[136]

How, then, is the *Torah* apprehended at the level of its soul (*Tiferet*)? We learned above from the *Idra* that the *Torah* of *Ze'er Anpin* (which is equivalent to *Tiferet*) has 613 mitsvot. It would seem, then, that these *mitsvot* are of the level of the *Torah* of *Ze'er Anpin*. If that is so, how is it that in the above passage (III, 152a) the "bodies of the *Torah*" (i.e., the *mitsvot*) are of the level of *Shekhina*, not *Tiferet*? In fact, however, there is no contradiction here. The *mitsvot* of the *Torah* are of two levels, one originating in *Malkhut* and the other in *Tiferet*. The level originating in *Malkhut* is that of observance of the practical *mitsvot*, whereas that originating in *Tiferet* is that of their theoretical study. *Malkhut*, in other words,[137] is the oral *Torah*, while *Tiferet* is the written *Torah* (this is generally true throughout the *Kabbala*; see, for example, III, 160a); and the 613 *mitsvot* are, indeed, recorded in the written *Torah*.

It turns out, then, that the *Torah* of *Ze'er Anpin*, which is stern judgment, and which *Attika Kaddisha* is to temper, consists of the *mitsvot* of the *Torah*. These can be tempered, as will become clear later, by engaging in the *Kabbala* of *Idra Rabba*, which is the *Torah* of *Attika Kaddisha*. This view of the *mitsvot* as an aspect of stern judgment that requires *tikkun* reflects an antinomian strain that calls to mind the ancient Gnostic attitude to the *Torah*. Nevertheless, the *Zohar* is not speaking here of supplanting the *Torah* with another, as is perhaps the case in *Ra'aya Meheimana* and *Tikkunei Zohar*; it speaks, rather, of deepening the *Torah* we possess and tempering it by means of a profound mystical vision.

An antinomian spirit may also inform the selection of the verse "It is time to act for the Lord, for they have violated Your *Torah*." This verse had been applied already in the *Talmud* to cases wherein it was necessary to violate certain *mitsvot* for the sake of heaven: " 'They have violated Your *Torah*'. Why? Because 'it is time to act for the Lord' " (Berakhot 63a). Rashi comments: "An example is that of Elijah on Mt. Carmel, who sacrificed on a high place even though this is forbidden, for he sought to restrain Israel for the sake of the Holy One, blessed be He." According to this interpretation, the word *heferu*, "they violated," should be read *haferu*, in the imperative voice, and not in the past tense as in the Masoretic text. The choice of words in the *Idra*'s opening passage may also allude to another rabbinic saying: "There are times when the abrogation of the *Torah* is its foundation" (Menahot 99a–b). However, it appears that the author of the *Zohar* is not alluding to a general abrogation of the *mitsvot*, but only to the disclosure of the secrets of the *Torah*, a transgression that besmirches, as it were, the honor of God. Qualms about this are a major concern at the opening of the *Idra*, as I explained at length above. Todros Abulafia used the same verse in a similar sense: "One may not expound concerning the Chariot. . .although it is time to act for the Lord, but one may mark these texts with fine dots as hints."[138] The transgression to which the talmudic statement refers (following the previous Mishna) is the precedent set by Boaz of greeting a friend with the Name. To do so is similar to disclosing the secrets of the Holy One blessed be He.

R. Simeon announces that the *Torah* on its level prior to *Idra Rabba* will be nullified if it does not undergo *tikkun*. Apart from its kabbalistic significance (relating to the kings who died and were "nullified"), this statement also relates to the historical situation of the *Torah*. The *Zohar*'s view would seem to be that concern with the *mitsvot* alone, to the exclusion of their profound mysteries, would lead to the nullification of the *Torah*. This was also one of the major impulses for the appearance of the *Kabbala*: the feeling that an exclusive concern with the *Torah* as such would become meaningless and ultimately repugnant, and this would lead to the *Torah* quite literally being nullified. Still, it is not at all clear whether the author of the *Zohar*, in speaking of the *Torah* of *Ze'er Anpin*, was referring only to talmudic-rabbinical study and activity. He may also have included in it the ordinary level of Kabbalistic teachings found in most parts of the *Zohar*, apart from the *Idrot*, for this doctrine was also concerned with the interpretation of the *Torah* and the *mitsvot*.

As we have seen above, R. Simeon considers the Kabbala of the main body of the *Zohar* insufficient (it is the "place of one pillar") and views that of the *Idra* as a much higher level.

The Apprehension of the Torah in the Messianic Era

The "soul of the soul" of the *Torah*, the highest level of kabbalistic wisdom, is revealed at *Idra Rabba* and is the *Torah* of *Attik Yomin* (i.e., the *Torah* that has its source in *Attik Yomin* and the teaching concerned with that configuration). The choice of this name to designate the highest stage in the disclosure of the secrets of the *Kabbala* would seem to me to contain an allusion to a rabbinic statement in Pesahim 119a: "What is *mekhasse attik* [in Isaiah xxiii:18]? It refers to him who conceals [*mekhasse*] the things which *Attik Yomin* concealed. And what are these? The secrets of the *Torah*." Rashi comments that the secrets of the *Torah* are *ma'ase bereshit* (the account of Creation) and *ma'ase merkava* (the account of the supernal Chariot). At the time of the *Idra* these secrets, that is, the *Torah* of *Attik Yomin*, are disclosed, and this involves the *tikkun* of that *Torah* and of the entire world. This relationship between the *tikkun* of the *Torah* and that of the world is present in earlier literature as well. For example: "The world is to exist for six thousand years—two thousand of chaos (*tohu*), two thousand of *Torah* and two thousand of the Messianic era" (Sanhedrin 97a).[139] Here the years of *Torah* are the years between *tohu* and the Messianic period. The author of the *Zohar* would seem to have built upon this statement, seeing himself as standing at the boundary marking the end of the years of *Torah* and the beginning of those of the Messianic era. The *Torah* at this point stood in danger of nullification, which would have meant the return of the days of *tohu*. However, R. Simeon (or the author of the *Zohar* himself) intervened to restore the *Torah* of *Attik Yomin*, which is the *Torah* of the Messianic era.

Nonetheless, the *Idra* itself does not belong to the Messianic era. It is said explicitly to constitute an intermediate stage between the revelation at Sinai and the Messianic era. Nor is its teaching the actual *Torah* of the Messiah, for the *Idra* refers to this *Torah* in the future tense (III, 130b) and even then usually characterizes it as originating in *Attika*. We find, then, that the *Torah* of *Attik Yomin* has two aspects, one that comes to expression in *Idra Rabba* and another that will be revealed in the time of the Messiah.

How do these *Torah*s differ? Not in content, it would seem, for both have the same source. The difference between them lies, rather, in how they are apprehended. In the *Idra* the *Torah* is apprehended in a discursive fashion, while in the Messianic era it will be apprehended intuitively. In the *Idra* apprehension comes about as a result of an "awakening from below" to rectify the defect on high and of discourse among the companions; in the time of the Messiah after all defects have been rectified, however, knowledge will pour forth from above all at once, without any effort on the part of those below. This is the picture that emerges from the description of the Messianic era in the *Idra* (III, 130b). Spirit goes forth from the two nostrils of *Arikh Anpin*,[140] from the one to *Ze'er Anpin* and from the other to the Messiah, the Son of David (note that both are in the same category!). In the Messianic era the world will be whole and harmonious, and the Messiah will be not only of the six *sefirot* of *Ze'er Anpin*, which are included in three spirits, but also of the seventh level, which is the spirit of *Arikh Anpin* and comprehends them all. This accords with the verse describing the Messiah in Isaiah xi:1-2: "And there shall come forth a shoot out of the stock of Jesse, and a twig shall grow forth out of his roots. And the spirit of the Lord shall rest upon him, the spirit of wisdom and understanding, the spirit of counsel and might, the spirit of knowledge and of fear of the Lord."

The three spirits mentioned in the verse comprise six rungs (wisdom and understanding, counsel and might, knowledge and fear of the Lord—virtues that R. Simeon's disciples are credited with possessing at the beginning of the *Idra*) but the first, "the spirit of the Lord," comprehends them all and originates in *Arikh Anpin*. The Messiah is thus higher than King Solomon, who "sat on the throne of the Lord" (I Chronicles xxix:23), for Solomon's throne had only six steps leading up to it (according to I Kings x:19), while that on which the Messiah is to sit will have seven.[141] This cosmic wholeness will be expressed in the Messianic era in that perfect apprehension, intuitive rather than discursive, of which we spoke above; as the *Zohar* puts it: "In the days of the Messiah people will not say to one another, 'Instruct me in wisdom,' for it is written: 'No longer will they need to teach one another and say to one another, 'Heed the Lord'; for all of them, from the least of them to the greatest, shall heed me' [Jer. xxxi:34]." (The verse in Jeremiah continues, "For I will forgive their iniquities," and the author of the *Zohar* may have related this, too, to the spirit that goes forth from the nostril of *Arikh Anpin*, which is called *Seliha*, Forgiveness.) The passage continues: "In the days of the Messiah they will not have to teach one another, for their spirit, which includes all the spirits, knows all." That spirit, which includes the three spirits of *Ze'er Anpin*, is the spirit of *Arikh Anpin* and is here identified with the spirit of the people living at that time; it resembles the philosophers' notion of the active intellect in which every intellect participates. The knowledge it has is known a priori and does not require sensory data or thought processes for its acquisition—which is how Maimonides distinguished God's knowledge from that of man (*Guide of the Perplexed* III, 21).

The idea that the advent of the Messiah involved a new kind of intellectual and mystical cognition was widespread in the medieval period. It seems to me, in this connection, that the sharp distinction customarily made between the "spiritual" messianism of Christianity and Jewish Messianism, which is said to be "historical," is incorrect. Just as Christianity, itself is an offshoot of Judaism, so too did Christian Messianism, develop by elaborating certain ideas of Jewish origin. The spiritual aspect of messianism never ceased to exist among Jews, just as the historical messianic hope persisted in certain Christian circles. Moreover, the two religions continued to influence one another in this respect. The *Zohar's* spiritual portrayal of the Messiah is based, on the one hand, on rabbinic statements to the effect that the Messiah will reveal a new *Torah*h, and on the other hand on this link between messianism and mysticism, which drew its inspiration from the prophecy of Joel iii:1–2 regarding the day of the Lord: "After that I will pour out My spirit on all flesh; your sons and daughters shall prophesy; your old men shall dream dreams and your young men shall see visions" (in the medieval period the identification of prophecy with the highest level of mysticism was viewed as self-evident). In the Middle Ages this relationship between messianism and mysticism took a variety of forms. Maimonides, for example, saw the Messiah as a terrestrial political Redeemer, but regarded his advent and the redemption he was to effect as no more than a condition and means for the attainment of that intellectual (and frequently mystical) apprehension which is the end and purpose of man. As he wrote in a kind of coda to the *Mishne Torah*:

> The Sages and Prophets did not long for the days of the Messiah that Israel might exercise dominion over the world . . . but that Israel be free to devote itself to the Law and its wisdom, with no one to oppress or disturb them, so that they thus be worthy of life in the world to come, as we explained in Laws Concerning Repentance. In that era there will be neither famine nor war . . . and the one preoccupation of the world will be to know the Lord. Hence Israel will be very wise, they will know the things that are now concealed and will attain an understanding of their Creator to the utmost capacity of the human mind, as it is written: "For the earth shall be full of the knowledge of the Lord, as the waters cover the sea" (Isa. xi:9).[142]

In "Laws Concerning Repentence" the "world to come" is described as the soul's attainment of true ideas after the death of the body. In another place Maimonides repeats his view that the days of the Messiah are merely a condition and means for achieving the level of cognition that characterizes the life of the world to come, but adds that the Messiah must possess wisdom and prophecy of the highest level, and one of his tasks, perhaps the most important of them, is to disseminate that wisdom:

> For in those days, knowledge, wisdom and truth will increase. . . .
> Because the king who will arise from the seed of David will possess more wisdom than Solomon, and will be a great prophet, approaching Moses our teacher, he will teach the whole of the Jewish people and instruct them in the way of God; and all nations will come to hear him. (Hilchot Teshuva ix:2)[143]

This motif of the wisdom and *devekut* that characterize the Messiah reached its furthest development in the thinking of R. Abraham Abulafia, who saw himself as a Messiah and prophet.[144] His messianic activity consisted primarily of efforts to bring about the attachment of the intellect of the "Messiah" to the active intellect and the domination of the material element by the spiritual. He later applied the name Messiah to both the active intellect and the individual human intellect that redeems man from his corporeality. The historical redemption of Israel comes about in a natural way alongside these messianic activities, but without any real connection with them. Abulafia's concern seems to have been essentially spiritual, so that in his case the historical redemption was "neutralized."

Ideas of this sort, which originated with Abulafia and his circle, seem to have penetrated the messianic doctrines of the "Gnostic Kabbalists,"[145] and from there found their way into the *Zohar*. In the *Zohar*, however, it is impossible to determine whether the spiritual or the historical element takes precedence; both are symbolic aspects of one reality—the *tikkun* of the upper worlds.

As we have indicated, the *Idra* does not represent the actual advent of the Messiah, but is only a stage preparatory to it. The participants at the *Idra* therefore do not achieve permanent *devekut* while they are still alive; at the end of the *Idra* (III, 144b), however, the souls of three of them depart by a divine kiss, which is the most perfect *devekut* possible in this world.[146] This *devekut* is not death, but true life, and a heavenly voice thus declares as their souls depart: "But you that did cleave to the Lord your God are all of you alive today"

(Deut. iv:4).[147] The place in Paradise of the three—R. Yose, R. Hezekiah, and R. Jesse[148]—was assured, and they were borne there by the holy angels.

Devekut (Mystical Union) and Tikkun (Amendment)

Apart from benefiting their own souls, the death of these three sages also brought about a *tikkun* of the world. This we see from R. Simeon's comment on their death: "For it is written: 'With the loss of his first-born he shall lay its foundation, and with the loss of his youngest son shall he set up its gates' [Josh. vi:26], and certainly their souls did cling with a great will in the moment they were taken" (III, 144a). R. Simeon here disregards the curse at the beginning of the verse— "Cursed be the man before the Lord, that riseth up and buildeth this city Jericho. . ."—and instead praises the act of rebuilding the city.[149] The death of the three is presented not only as a consequence of this act, but as the very way by which it is accomplished. What is more, Jericho here appears to symbolize the *Shekhina*,[150] which is "built" and restored by the deaths of the three sages. They are sons, as it were, of R. Simeon, who is the principal agent of the *Shekhina*'s restoration, and their deaths parallel that of R. Simeon at the end of *Idra Zuta* (as we have noted, in both instances the expiration of the soul is called "life"), which is a *tikkun* of the *Shekhina*. There, too, not only does his soul arrive in Paradise, which is the *Shekhina*,[151] but by his death and his *devekut* he effects its *tikkun*. Moreover, the *tikkun* brought about by the three sages in *Idra Rabba* is apparently also accomplished through a kind of erotic union, which is a development of the motif of "death by a kiss."

The surrender of the soul to the *sefira* of *Malkhut* is also mentioned in the *Zohar* as an explanation for the movement of prostration performed at the end of the *Amida* prayer (III, 120b–121a), to which the end of the *Idra* is possibly to be viewed as a parallel. The reason given there for the surrender of the soul is that it atones for man's spiritual sins in the same way as his actual death. But *Malkhut* also derives pleasure from the act, for otherwise this offering of the soul would not be accepted in lieu of its actual surrender in death. Not surprisingly, this *sefira* is there called the "Tree of Death,"[152] meaning that death is within its realm. It is explained in another passage that this act "causes pleasure to that side wherein death is present" (*Zohar Hadash, Teruma* 42a). This "side" is not the *Sitra Ahra* but the *sefira* of *Malkhut*,[153] and the surrender of the soul to it must be performed with the full devotion of the heart,[154] for only such *devekut* will properly satisfy the *Shekhina*. The highest form of such *devekut* is described at the end of *Idra Rabba*, when the three sages die. The phrase 'it causes pleasure" may also have a sexual connotation, for the word *naiha* (pleasure) often appears in the *Zohar* in a sexual context.[155] Other explanations for the movement of prostration at prayer also relate to the coupling of the *Shekhina* with *Tif'eret*.[156]

In another passage (I, 245b), the *Zohar* explains that the souls of the righteous ascending upon their death awaken the *Shekhina*'s passion for her husband, the Holy One blessed be he, and so are as the "feminine waters"[157] that the female (the *Shekhina*) brings forth, as opposed to the seed of the male (the *sefira* of *Tif'eret*). All Luria had to do, then, to produce a doctrine of the *kavvanot* called for when "prostrating oneself" in prayer was to formulate the ideas scattered throughout the *Zohar*, developing their implications into a unified system.[158] According to Luria, the worshiper must, in prostrating himself, seek to achieve the devotional attitude of giving himself up to death, an act that brings forth "feminine waters" and thereby assists the union of the masculine and feminine elements of the Godhead. In reciting the *Shema*, by contrast, he is to set his heart on death for the sanctification of the Name (martyrdom), thereby assisting the higher coupling of the configurations of the Father and the Mother (*Abba* and *Imma*).[159] But if the couplings are greatly flawed these *kavvanot* alone will not suffice, and under such circumstances actual death for the sanctification of the Name becomes necessary.

This relationship between the *devekut* of the soul and the *tikkun* of the world may seem surprising. Mysticism is generally viewed as an individual quest antithetical to efforts at improving the external world or rectifying the situation of the people from a national and historical point of view. Furthermore, the mystical ideal involves the abnegation of individual will within Being, and such selfabnegation would seem incompatible with an intention to act in this terrestrial world. These difficulties originate, however, in a misunderstanding of the special nature of the mysticism of the *Zohar* and of *Kabbala* in general. The mysticism of the *Zohar* does not involve the abnegation of individual will.[160] What is more, the soul, through *devekut*, is able to affect the terrestrial world by means of the supernal, or to influence the supernal world itself. This is also the *Zohar*'s explanation for the effectiveness of magic. The difference between black magic (which the *Zohar* absolutely forbids—in contrast to the "Gnostic Kabbalists")— and the theurgical way of the *Kabbala*, wherein the *tikkun* of this world comes about as a consequence of that of the upper worlds, is only in the forces that are activated: in the former they are the forces of defilement, while in the *Kabbala* they are the ten *sefirot*. The method, however, is similar, as the author of the *Zohar* points out more than once. The magician or wizard, negative counterpart of the Kabbalist, "clings to the spirit of defilement" and is "swept up" into it; he draws unto himself an impure soul and so fortifies the "other side." There is no contradiction between mysticism and theurgy or magic, for the principle is the same throughout: only by having one's soul cling (in relationship, not by way of fusion or absorption) to a supernal (or infernal) force is it possible to affect that force and work through it.[161]

Nor should it be maintained that the mystic is concerned only with his own soul, and not with the *tikkun* of the world or of his nation. Mystical matters are bound up with apocalyptic and eschatological concerns even in early *Merkava* mysticism.[162] It would appear, moreover, that the messianic idea was of central importance among the *Merkava* mystics; not by chance did R. Akiba, known for his support of Bar-Kokhba, become a key figure in that circle. It should be noted, too that charismatic figures in the period of the Sages did not hesitate to use their influence in the upper world for such terrestrial things as bringing rain, and the *Zohar*'s figure of R. Simeon is modeled upon them. These individuals' relationship with God is not, however, purely mystical. It also has a powerful mythic strain, expressed in their depiction as sons and servants in the palace of the King who loves them and fulfills their every wish. It is this mythic aspect that enables them to preserve their individual wills and personalities and to act in this world even when they are in a state of supreme *devekut*. The intermixture of mysticism and myth is also typical of the mystical descriptions in the *Zohar*, where it has a similar function. The *Zohar* describes the mystic as "A son clinging always to his Father, without any separation at all; there is none to stop him; he worships his Creator and brings about the *tikkun* of the world" (III, 112a). The mythic side of his personality enables him to bring about the *tikkun* of the world even as he clings to his father without any separation at all.[163]

Even where the mysticism is more technical and substantive, it not only serves the mystic's own soul but often also contributes to the *tikkun* of the world—the supernal and, through it, the terrestrial. This is what R. Azriel of Gerona says: "Therefore the first of the pious would elevate their thought to its source and make mention of the *mitsvot* and the [supreme] beings, and through such mention and thoughts of such great *devekut* the beings would be blessed and come together and be accepted from emptiness of thought, as when a man opens a pool of water and it spreads hither and thither."[164] The "beings" that would be blessed are the supernal *sefirot*, upon which the Kabbalist opens the pool by means of the *devekut* of his thought to its source, which is the highest *sefira* and is called "emptiness of thought." In the *Zohar* and in the Lurianic *Kabbala*, that *devekut* of the soul which has the quality of "feminine waters," involving the devotional surrender—in *kavvana* or in fact—of one's life also brings about the *tikkun* of the upper *sefirot*. Both the act and the *tikkun*, however, are far more mythical in character than those described by R. Azriel.[165]

The Tikkun

Idra Rabba is concerned with the *tikkun* of the worlds. The death of the three participants is the crowning moment of this *tikkun*, but much had already been accomplished beforehand. Two types of *tikkun* in fact take place here. One is that of the symbolic *tikkun* effected by the gathering itself which, as we have already discussed above, parallels a new and better array of the supernal world. But this alone is not enough. After they assemble, the companions must actively perform further *tikkunim*. This is their main concern in the course of the *Idra*, and it is accomplished through expounding the *Torah* and, ultimately, through the departure of the soul.

The possibility of effecting *tikkun* by means of profound Kabbalistic discourses on the *Torah* calls to mind the mystical *tikkun* discussed above, for the discourses are divinely inspired. They may be regarded as initially representing a lower level of mysticism, which rises during the *Idra* and culminates in the ecstatic death of the mystics. In addition, the very disclosure of the *Torah* of *Attika Kaddisha*, which is among the signs of the messianic era, is itself a *tikkun*. But beyond that, the discourses on the *Torah* are conceived as having the power to affect the supernal realm and to change the world, even creating a new heaven and earth.

God in the beginning created worlds by means of words alone, and that is also the way of the mystic (like the patriarch Abraham, according to the end of *Sefer Yetsira*). The same notion underlies all magic; the sorcerer, however, uses an existing mythical world and fixed combinations of words in a strictly unvarying way, while the theory of the author of the *Zohar* about words weaving now a heaven and now an earth is much freer. Above all, it seems to me, his theory matches his own mythopoeic inclinations. Indeed, it is its creation of myths that sets the *Zohar* apart in Jewish literature. The author of the *Zohar* was well aware that he was not describing an existing mythical world but creating one out of his own literary imagination and homiletic talents.[166] Under the terms of his theory, however, this didn't detract at all from the ontological status of the mythical world he had created, for in his understanding the inner world of man's imagination took precedence over the external world. The latter owed its very existence to the external projection of thought by means of words. This is especially evident if we see—as I do—a messianic intention in the writing of the *Zohar*. The author's purpose, from this point of view, was to change and redeem the external world by verbally creating an imaginary group of men (R. Simeon and his companions), brought back from more than a thousand years in the past, who themselves redeem the world by means merely of talk and words. Their imagination, which is itself a product of the imagination of the author, thus creates a genuine reality; and this, I believe, expresses a great triumph of spirit over matter.

The *Zohar* explains the theoretical basis for the possibility that *tikkun* and the creation of genuine entities might be accomplished by means of discourse on the *Torah* in another passage, a bit before the description of the *Tikkun Leil Shavu'ot*, that is, the ritual *tikkun* that takes place in the night of *Shavu'ot* festival (I, 4b–5a), and also in the course of that description, so strikingly parallel to *Idra Rabba*, as well (I, 8b–9a). The explanation is as follows:

> At the moment that a person utters a new word of *Torah* (i.e., states something about the *Torah* that was not previously known), that word ascends and stands before the Holy One blessed be He. . . . A newly created word of [Kabbalistic] wisdom ascends and alights on the head of the Everlasting (or, better, the living of the worlds) Righteous One, and flies from there and sails through seventy thousand worlds and ascends to *Attik Yomin*, and all the words of *Attik Yomin* are words of wisdom comprising subline, esoteric mysteries. And when that esoteric word of wisdom newly created here ascends and joins with the words of *Attik Yomin* and ascends and descends. . .at that moment *Attik Yomin* savors the word, and He is greatly pleased with it above all. . .That word flies, ascending and descending, and becomes a firmament, and so every word of [Kabbalistic] wisdom becomes a firmament standing fully existent before *Attik Yomin*. . .and all the other words of *Torah* [non Kabbalistic] stand before the Holy One blessed be He and ascend and become. . .a new earth.

We learn from this that words of *Torah* are real entities and bring about ontological *tikkunim*. We also learn of the realms in which they operate: It is concerned with the *tikkun* of the Holy One blessed be he (*Tif'eret*, heaven) and therefore words of Kabbalistic wisdom first ascend to the configuration above him, to *Attik Yomin*, which is able to accomplish the *tikkun* of the configuration beneath it, for the *Torah* of *Attik Yomin* is the *Kabbala*. Words pertaining to the revealed Torah, on the other hand, first ascend to the Holy One blessed be he, and then descend and become a new earth; that is, they bring about the *tikkun* of the *Shekhina*, which is called Earth.

This passage, as we have said, precedes a description of *Tikkun Leil Shavu'ot*. In the latter description, the ontological *tikkun* of the firmaments of the supernal bride-groom and of the "stages" (worlds) of the bride appear more powerfully. The discourses not only motivate the supernal powers to praise those who speak them,[167] but also (and this is the primary Kabbalistic innovation) bring about a real *tikkun* of these powers. Here is the description of the *tikkun* followed by a detailed exegesis of it:

> R. Simeon resumed: "And the firmament proclaims His handiwork" [Ps. xix:2]—["His handiwork—] these are the companions, who keep this bride company and are her partners in covenant. He "proclaims" and records each one of them. Who is this "firmament"? It is the one wherein are the sun, the moon, the stars and the constellations, namely, the Book of Remembrance. He "proclaims" and records that they are sons of the heavenly palace, and that their will is always to be done. "Day unto day expresses utterance" [Ps. xix:2]—each "day" is one of the sacred heavenly days of the King, which extol the companions and repeat what each one uttered to the others; "day unto day" expresses that same utterance and extols it. "And night unto night reveals knowledge" [ibid.]—the forces ruling in the night praise this "knowledge" of the companions to one another and become their devoted and beloved friends. "There is no utterance, there are no words" (Ps. xix:4)—this refers to mundane words, which are not uttered before the holy King, nor does he wish to hear them. But as for those words, "their line is gone out through all the earth" [Ps. xix:5]. Those words trace the measure of the celestial and the terrestrial habitations. Through those words the firmaments are made, and the earth through that praise. And if you say the words are in one place, we are told that they roam the world: "and their words to the end of the earth" [ibid.]. And if firmaments are made of them,

who inhabits them? It goes on to say: "He placed in them a tent
for the sun" [ibid.]—the sacred sun made its habitation in them
and is crowned by them. Inhabiting those firmaments and
crowned by them, "it is as a bridegroom coming forth from his
chamber" [Ps. xix:6], joyously coursing through those
firmaments, emerging from them and entering and hastening
to another tower in another place. (I, 8b–9a)

Let us comment on this passage: "And the firmament proclaims
His handiwork" [Ps. xix:2]—("His handiwork"). These are the
companions who keep this bride company and are her partners in
covenant (in a double sense: those who are of the level of the *sefira*
of *Yesod*, which is called *Brit* [Covenant], awaken its erotic union with
the *Shekhina*, as is explained in the passage that precedes this one[168]
and as in the beginning of *Idra Rabba*, where they are called "pillars
of the world"; furthermore, their *tikkun* requires that they do not
violate the covenant and that they guard the secret). He "proclaims"
and records each one of them (the companions). Who is this
"firmament" (*Rakia*)? It is that one wherein are the sun, the moon,
the stars, and the constellations (i.e., the *sefira* of *Yesod*; one of the
seven firmaments—that are called "*Rakia*"—is described in just these
words in Hagiga 12b; elsewhere in the *Zohar* [I, 34a] it is explained
that this firmament is the *sefira* of *Yesod*), namely, the Book of
Remembrance (the reference is to the *sefira* of *Yesod*, which is often
described thus in the *Zohar*, as for example in II, 70a; "the royal book
of remembrance [*zikkaron*]," which is *Yesod*, the male [*zachar*]. He
"proclaims" and records that they are sons of the heavenly palace,
and that their will is always done. "Day unto day expresses utterance"
(Ps. xix:3); each "day" is one of the sacred heavenly days of the King
(the King is the male element in the Godhead, the *sefira* of *Tif'eret*
or *Ze'er Anpin*, and the days are the six "male" *sefirot* related to it),
which extol the companions and repeat what each one (of the
companions) uttered to the others (i.e., the *sefirot* repeat the discourses
delivered by the companions during the *Tikkun Leil Shavu'ot*); "day
unto day" (i.e., *sefira* unto *sefira*) expresses that same utterance and
extols it (i.e., the *sefirot* praise the discourses). "And night unto night
reveals knowledge" (Ps. xix:3)—the forces ruling in the night (i.e., the
forces of the *sefira* of *Malkhut*, which rules in the night) praise this
"knowledge" of the companions to one another and become their
devoted and beloved friends.[169] "There is no utterance, there are no
words" (Ps. xix:4)—this refers to mundane words, which are not uttered
before the holy King, nor does he wish to hear them. But as for those
words, "their line is gone out through all the earth" (Ps. xix:4). (This

sentence has two possible meanings: it could be that the expression "mundane words" refers to profane talk; such words, then, are to be shunned during the *Tikkun Leil Shavu'ot*, for the King—the Godhead—does not wish to hear them. If that is the case, "those words" are not the same as the "mundane words"; rather, they are the words of *Torah* spoken during the *tikkun*. But it is also possible, and I believe more likely, that the "holy King" is the male, and the words he does not wish to hear are those that effect the *tikkun* of the female. That is to say, the words revealed by night unto night are the *tikkunim* of the female, which is why "their line is gone out through all the earth"; the earth, it should be recalled, is the *Shekhina*, while the firmament is the Holy One blessed be he. "Mundane words" would thus refer to esoteric matters, the study of which, according to the passage interpreted above, effects the *tikkun* of the female only.) These words trace the measure of the celestial and the terrestrial habitations. (The author of the *Zohar* understands "their line" to refer to the "line of measure" by which the world is built and the upper *sefirot* restored; a long section in Zohar Hadash [*Va-ethanan*] is devoted to this subject. The upper and lower habitations are the degrees of the male and the female. The author is thus once again speaking about the *Torah* in general, without distinguishing, as he did above, between those discourses that effect the *tikkun* of the male element and those that effect the *tikkun* of the female.) Through these words the firmaments are made (he returns to this distinction: the male firmaments are restored by Kabbalistic discourses), and the earth through that praise. (Here the *tikkunim* of the bride are effected not through discourses on the esoteric aspects of the *Torah* but through songs of praise, as the "Gnostic Kabbalists" would have it.[170]) And if you say the words are in one place (i.e., discourses upon the *Torah* can accomplish *tikkun* only in one spot) we are told that they roam the world; "and their words to the end of the earth." (This verse indicates the contrary, i.e., that the *tikkun* affects all of the worlds. Another possible interpretation is that there is no distinction between the types of words, for both restore the same objects.) And if firmaments are made of them (i.e., of words of *Torah*), who inhabits them? It goes on to say: 'He placed in them a tent for the sun" (Ps. xix:4)—the sacred sun (i.e., the male divine element) made its habitation in them and is crowned by them. Inhabiting those firmaments and crowned by them, "it is as a bridegroom coming forth from his chamber" (Ps. xix:6) joyously coursing through those firmaments, emerging from them and entering and hastening to another tower in another place. (The tower [*migdal*] is the *Shekhina*, and the description refers to the erotic union between the male and the female, which is their ultimate *tikkun*. The use of the word "tower"—a motif that does not occur elsewhere in this passage—and the motif of running into it are an obvious allusion to a verse from Proverbs (xviii:10): "The name of the Lord is a tower of strength, to which the righteous man runs and is set up on high." This verse is the subject of a discourse elsewhere in the *Zohar* (III, 164a–b) which states explicitly that the tower is the *Shekhina*. But the righteous one is not necessarily the *sefira* of *Yesod* itself, but rather "the synagogue cantor, the true righteous one"[171] and symbol of the supernal Righteous One" (i.e., the *sefira* of *Yesod*).[172] It is he who is sixth to be called to the reading of the *Torah*. The author then goes on to compare him to the Messiah, who will proclaim his new Torah from the tower [*migdal* is the term used by Sefardi Jews for the lectern on which the *Torah* is placed for reading].)

To complete the comparison with the *Idra* and to illuminate more fully the relationship between the various aspects of the *tikkun*, it should be emphasized that later, in the passage about the making of the firmaments (I, 5a), the *Zohar* finds another function for them, that of hiding the Godhead from the eye of the beholder. The very *tikkun* of the *sefirot*, with the consequent possibility of their disclosure, simultaneously acts to conceal them. This dual role is one often described in kabbalistic literature. It parallels the demand made at the beginning of the *Idra* and discussed at length above that the companions who bring about the *tikkun* of the *sefirot* also be guardians of the secret. The author of the *Zohar* then goes on to describe the firmaments of *sitra ahra*, which are woven from those who are not "faithful spirits"; such individuals destroy the world rather than effecting its *tikkun*.

Let us now summarize the stages of the *Tikkun Leil Shavu'ot* in Part I, in order to compare it with the *tikkun* in the *Idra*. In the first stage, the male and female elements are restored separately through discourses on the *Torah*. For the *tikkun* of the male element (*Ze'er Anpin*), these discourses must first ascend to and link up with *Attika Kaddisha*; the *tikkun* will be brought about by means of that link. For the *tikkun* of the female element, on the other hand, the discourses must first link up with the male element. Only after these two configurations, the male and the female, have been restored separately does the final *tikkun*, which is the union of the male and the female, take place. From a parallel passage (alluded to here by the motif of running within the tower), we learn that this coupling is not necessarily to be performed by the *sefira* of *Yesod* itself, but by a figure "in its likeness"—the terrestrial righteous one, or perhaps even the Messiah. (This possibility may well intentionally have been left implicit, since the matter is one that calls for modesty.) The idea that before their union can take place, the male and female elements in the Godhead must each be restored separately, through the incorporation of their respective degrees, recurs several times in the *Zohar*.[173]

All these stages of *tikkun* are also found in the *Idra*. The various configurations are first restored, and then comes the union, which is perfect redemption and the complete *tikkun* of the *Shekhina*. As we shall see further on, that element which performs the coupling appears in the image of a flesh-and-blood redeemer. The *tikkun* in the *Idra*, however, is much more developed. Instead of mythical-midrashic descriptions, there is one highly technical and detailed myth that combines all the various stages into one great *tikkun*. While this detracts from the myth as a "story," it brings its ideational element— and especially its messianic element—to the surface. The details of this *tikkun* are far beyond the scope of the present essay, though they are tremendously interesting and contribute to an understanding of the theosophy of the most profound portions of the *Zohar*. The messianic element, however, can be seen even from a cursory review of the stages of the *tikkun*.

The *tikkun* in the *Idra* is a single downward moving continuum. It begins with the highest configuration (*Attika Kaddisha*), continues to the male configuration of the Godhead (*Ze'er Anpin*), and culminates in the Shekhina. This order is necessary, for it is the absence of *tikkun* at a higher level that causes disturbance at the level below it, and it is the higher level, once it has undergone to *tikkun*, that brings about the *tikkun* of that below it. The *Idra* thus begins with the *tikkun* of *Attika Kaddisha* (i.e., *Arikh Anpin*):

> And all of them [the earlier worlds that had been destroyed, i.e., the kings of Edom] did not exist until the hoary head of the Ancient of Ancients was restored, and when it was restored it brought about all the *tikkunim* below, all the *tikkunim* of upper and lower [worlds]. From this we learn[174] that the leader of a people must himself first be properly arrayed if his people are to be so; if he is not, neither are they, while if he is, so are they all. (III, 135a)

We have already encountered the idea that a connection with *Attika Kaddisha* is required for the *tikkun* of *Ze'er Anpin* to proceed in the passage that precedes the description of *Tikkun Leil Shavu'ot* (I, 4b). In the *Idra*, this idea is developed to the effect that the *tikkun* of *Ze'er Anpin* requires that *Attika* itself undergo *tikkun*. What is more, the *tikkun* brought about by each of the participants, through discourse, is in fact a *tikkun* of *Attika*; and the *tikkun* of *Ze'er Anpin* is then described as though it were brought about by *Attika* himself. It is also possible, moreover, that the very description of this *tikkun* (by R. Simeon) assists in its implementation.[175]

The *tikkun* of *Attika* is brought about by the companions' discourses on his restored condition. We learned of the theoretical possibility of such a *tikkun* in the description of *Tikkun Leil Shavu'ot* in Part I; the description in the *Idra* actualizes that possibility. This can be seen from the way R. Simeon invites the companions to deliver their discourses, saying, for example, "Arise, Eleazar my son, and do that *tikkun*" (III, 134a). These *tikkunim* are the curls in *Arikh Anpin*'s beard (III, 131a) and engaging in them is a kind of barbering. It seems that the speakers even took hold of their beards in a symbolic way while delivering their discourses.[176] At first the participants did not know themselves what *tikkun* was being brought about by their discourses, and R. Simeon had to tell it to them. As he himself testifies, "When we began to speak, the companions did not know that all those holy *devarim* were being roused here" (III, 138b). The word "*devarim*" is used here in a double sense: it refers both to the participants' discourses on the *Torah* and to real "things," that is, to the ontological reality to which these discourses give rise. R. Simeon explains this to the companions as they begin to speak: "And when each of them (i.e., the *tikkunim* of the Beard) issue from your mouths, it ascends, and is restored, and are adorned and concealed in the secret of the holy beard" (III, 132b). In the same passage, to be sure, he also speaks of the symbolic *tikkun*, which is related to the order in which the participants speak and sit. But both types of *tikkun* are inseparably linked in the mind of the *Zohar*'s author. Though the above quotation might be read to mean that only the discourses of the companions are restored and adorned, R. Simeon's accompanying description of the marital canopy spread over them makes it clear that "supernal things" or essences are also undergoing *tikkun*. These *tikkunim* as standing up on the canopy awaiting the utterances of the companions, and as each is restored in turn, it leaves the canopy and ascends to its place. This portrayal was undoubtedly influenced by the description of the angels and the canopy in the discourses of the ancient *Merkava* mystics. That description is reinterpreted here in terms of the Kabbalistic idea of *tikkun*, even as the midrashic imagery is retained. In R. Simeon's own words:

> When this canopy that you see above us was spread out, I saw all the *tikkunim* descending onto it. . . . I saw the *tikkunim* illuminating it. They were awaiting our discourses, to be

adorned by them and to rise each to its place. . . . As one of us opened his mouth to do a certain *tikkun*, that *tikkun* was sitting and waiting for the word to come from your mouth, and then it rose to its place and was adorned (III, 134b–135a).

The Death of R. Simeon as a Tikkun

As we have indicated, the final stage of the *tikkun* is the coupling of *Ze'er Anpin* with the *Shekhina*. This is mentioned at the end of *Idra Rabba* as the ultimate *tikkun* and "sweetening" of the world:

> For the Matron sat with the King, and they were joined face to face. . . in which all was sweetened.[177] Therefore judgments were sweetened [mitigated], and the upper and lower worlds were restored. (III, 142b–143a)

Idra Rabba does not mention the role of the companions in these relations, but on the basis of parallel passages it may be assumed, as I showed above, that the souls of the three sages who expired at the end of the *Idra* functioned as "feminine waters" and so facilitated the coupling of the divine configurations.

This erotical union is described in greater detail in a parallel passage at the end of *Idra Zuta* (III, 296a–296b), where we discover something most surprising: the *sefira* of *Yesod*, which is the coupling male organ, is none other than R. Simeon himself. The description of the *tikkun* consists entirely of discourses by him. As in *Idra Rabba*, the description of the union is preceded by a description of the *tikkun* of the supernal male and female organs. The male organ is described as concentrating within itself, within a drop of its semen, the powers of all the supernal organs.[178] That drop of semen derives from *Hesed*, Divine Love, which is closely related to the *sefira* of *Yesod*.[179] R. Simeon then goes on to describe the female organ. Beginning with the external parts or aspects and continuing inward, he explains how these aspects are successively "sweetened." He then comes to the innermost part or aspect, where the seed, which is called Life, issues forth and separates from *Yesod*. As R. Simeon describes the departure of Life from *Yesod* and its entry into the female, his own life too departs, his soul expiring at the word "Life."

The author of the *Zohar* would seem to have viewed this passage in *Idra Zuta*, and the death of R. Simeon, as the climax of his book (which also apparently should end here; the three pages that follow seem to be out of place). It expresses some of the profoundest ideas of the *Zohar*, condensed into the synonymity of the idea of the soul's *devekut*—which is identified with sexual orgasm—with the *tikkun* of the worlds. It means also the historical *tikkun* of the Jewish people, and also the personal *tikkun* of the author, by which his being reaches fullest expression, R. Simeon, the book's hero, with whom the author of the *Zohar* felt such deep affinity. This *tikkun* brings all the worlds to perfection and turns them into one body (male without female is considered half a body; see below). Duality disappears from the world, and the entire cosmos becomes a pantheistic unity. This is the messianic restoration.

The departure of R. Simeon's soul at the moment of orgasm is the culmination of a process alluded to at the beginning of the *tikkun* in *Idra Zuta*. This *tikkun* is conducted entirely by R. Simeon, with the companions taking part only as spectators. The process may thus be regarded as his own personal *tikkun*. He is the *Yesod*, the basic element that brings about the *tikkun* and simultaneously, himself undergoes *tikkun*, and it is his coupling with the *Shekhina* that brings about its redemption. This is clearly a messianic role. As we shall see, this idea draws upon the messianic notions of "Gnostic Kabbalists," a circle to which the author of the *Zohar* belonged.

I find the link between this conception and that of the "Gnostics" in the use made of the verse spoken by R. Simeon at the height of the erotic union, which is the moment of his soul's departure: "For there the Lord commanded the blessing, even life forever" (Ps. cxxxiii:3). R. Simeon expounds the psalm concluded by this verse as a description of the descent of the divine Plenty (the *shefa*, which is the seed) from the head (i.e., the supreme *sefira*) through all the organs to the male organ (i.e., *Yesod*); and this final line thus describes the passage of the seed to the female in the act of coupling. The verse is consistently used in exactly the same sense in the writings of R. Isaac ha-Kohen,[180] where its relationship to the messianic idea is clear, particularly in light of the fact that one of the names of the Messiah, Kashtsiel, is derived from it. The first four letters of this name are an acronym of the Hebrew words *ki sham tsiva Adonai*: "for there the Lord commanded." Putting this together with that circle's other commonly used name for the Messiah, Righteous (*Tsaddik*), and with its portrayal of Righteous, so similar to the *Zohar*'s figure of R. Simeon, we shall be left with no doubt as to the source of the unique brand of messianic thought found in the *Zohar*.

R. Simeon did not complete the verse, for his soul departed as he uttered the word "Life." The significance of this is easily apparent. First of all, death for R. Simeon is generally true life, for "the righteous in their death are called living" (*Berakhot* 18a). This idea here acquired a special turn of significance: that of the linkage of his soul with the place of life. But it also has a general meaning: his death is life for the world restored by him. In writing that his soul expired at the word "Life," the author of the *Zohar* was undoubtedly influenced by the description of the death of R. Eliezer the Great, whose soul departed in purity as he uttered the word "pure"[181] and perhaps also by the story of R. Akiva, whose soul departed with the word "one" (*Berakhot* 61b). It is very likely that the influence of the latter association was in fact by way of contrast, for unlike the death of R. Akiva, the death of R. Simeon is described as a festive and joyous occasion of messianic significance.[182]

The Historical Tikkun

The messianic character of R. Simeon's *tikkun* through erotic union is made even more evident by the names of the parts of the female sexual organ which he "enters" and "sweetens": Zion, Jerusalem, and the Holy of Holies.[183] That is to say, the *tikkun* of the female is also that of the heavenly Jerusalem, and perhaps that of the terrestrial Jerusalem as well. Entering the Holy of Holies, R. Simeon is like the high priest who enters it on the Day of Atonement—which may in fact have been the day on which *Idra Zuta* was held.[184] R. Simeon's messianic personality thus also absorbs elements of the figure of the high priest. A similar fusion occurs in the self-conception of Abraham Abulafia, a contemporary of the author of the *Zohar*.[185] This image of the mystical high priest entering the Holy of Holies and so bringing about the *tikkun* of both the upper worlds and the situation of the Jewish people calls to mind the story related in the Talmud by Ishmael ben Elisha: "I once went to the innermost part (of the Sanctuary) to offer incense, and I saw Akatriel Ya, the Lord of Hosts, seated upon a high and exalted throne. He said to me: 'Ishmael my son, bless Me.' I replied: 'May it be Your will that Your mercy may suppress Your anger and Your mercy may prevail over Your other attributes so that You may deal with Your children according to the attribute of mercy and may on their behalf stop short of strict justice.' And he nodded to me with His head" (*Berakhot* 7a). R. Simeon's act also calls to mind the act of another figure of the same name, Simeon the Just.

The *tikkun*, then, is completed with that of Jerusalem and the Sanctuary. Moreover, the defect it rectifies, too, has a historical aspect. The discussion of this defect in the *Idrot* (III, 128a; 135a; 142a; 292a) is founded upon the verse: "And these are the kings that reigned in the land of Edom before there reigned any king over the children of

Israel" (Gen. xxxvi:31). Not for naught was precisely this verse singled
out, for the defective situation manifested itself in history in the exile
of the Jews; during that time the kings of Edom (who are identified
with the kings of Rome and the Christian lands) rule the world, and
the Jews, who still have no king of their own, are subject to them.
In such a situation the kings of Edom themselves are "flawed" and
destroyed, for their natural state is one of subordination to the King
of Israel,[186] the Messiah who is to come after the *tikkun*. On their own,
the kings of Edom function as the agents of harsh judgment (just as
the judgment of *Ze'er Anpin* is harsh when he is separated from *Arikh
Anpin*), and that is the reason for their severity towards the Jews.
To be sure, the kings of Edom are symbolic here of the worlds that
were destroyed before the Holy One created our world. It is in the
nature of the kabbalistic symbol, however, to allude to supernal worlds
while speaking of terrestrial (and perhaps the converse as well). This
is also the case in the *Idra*, which would seem to speak only of
catastrophes that occurred prior to the creation of the world, but in
fact simultaneously alludes to current historical disasters and how
they may be overcome. Indeed, there is a profound link between the
two realms: the *sitra ahra*, which has its origin in the heavenly kings
of Edom, is the source of the power of the terrestrial kings of Edom
(i.e., the Christians). When the heavenly kings are overcome—or
undergo *tikkun*—the earthly monarchs, too, will be defeated—or
undergo *tikkun*. This idea is heavily reminiscent of a rabbinic saying
to which the *Zohar* often alludes: "The Holy One blessed be He does
not strike down a nation before He strikes down its (heavenly)
prince."[187]

Elsewhere in the *Zohar*, the verse "And these are the kings. . ."
is expounded as referring both to the reign of the historical kings of
Edom and to the reign of the *Sitra Ahra*, as, for example, in I,
177a–177b. Basing himself also on the verse "Let my lord pass over
before his servant" (Gen. 33:4), which Jacob said to Esau, the author
of the *Zohar* shows that the kingdom of Esau precedes the kingdom
of Jacob, and that when Jacob's kingdom comes, Esau's kingdom will
fall. So too with the heavenly "princes" of both sides: Following the
advent of the kingdom of the Holy One blessed be he (who is King
over the children of Israel), the kingdom of the degrees of defilement
(i.e., the *Sitra Ahra*, the kings of Edom) will fall. This idea is also
developed, in relation to the same verse, in II, 111a–111b. In another
place, the nations of the world as opposed to Israel and, similarly, the
Sitra Ahra as opposed to the *Sitra di-Kdusha* (the Holy Side), are
compared as husk or shell to pulp or core.[188] Today, the *Zohar* declares,
the peel comes before the fruit and protects it, but that will not be

so in the messianic era. Moreover, "The heathen nations, which are the 'peel,' came before, as it is written: 'and these are the kings that reigned in the land of Edom before there reigned any king over the children of Israel.' But in the future the Holy One blessed be He will form the pulp first without any peel" (II, 108b).

The question remains as to why the author of the *Zohar* did not explicitly mention the historical implications of his discourses at the *Idra*. Why has it been necessary for us to derive these implications from the significance of the verses he cites and from study of parallels elsewhere in the *Zohar*? In other sections R. Simeon does deal extensively with this aspect of the discourses. Why does he depart from this practice in the *Idra*? Why does he dissemble, pretending that he is concerned only with the upper worlds? I would say in reply that the historical elements are more esoteric here precisely because the *Idra*, unlike other parts of the *Zohar* where the discussion is purely theoretical, is a description of a theurgic and messianic act. As indicated in our discussion of the problem of concealment and disclosure, this would be a matter better not proclaimed publicly. It is even possible—though I say this with some hesitation, for I am aware of the difficulties involved in such a conjecture—that the *Idra* was written in the wake of some specific messianic expectation related to a known historical event, namely, the defeat of the last Crusader strongholds in Palestine, the most important of which, in Acre, fell in 1291. It would have been virtually impossible for such an event in the history of the Land of Israel to pass without awakening messianic hopes. This accords with the *Idra*'s own words to the effect that the kings of Edom not only preceded the kings of Israel but were also destroyed and "nullified." The "kings," from this point of view, would be the Crusaders, whose reign over the Land of Israel had come to an end. The *Idra* is held shortly after their demise, with the intention of establishing a new kingdom—not of Edom, but of Israel. If this is indeed the case, the *Idra* would have been composed only in the nineties of the thirteenth century. We know that R. Moses de Leon moved to Avila during these years, and that the *Idra*'s composition is perhaps related to the messianic movement centered around the "prophet of Avila" that sprang up there in 1295.[189]

The Tikkun of Erotic Union

The last *tikkun* in the *Idra*, as we have said, is the coupling. Nor should this surprise us, considering that the defects rectified at the *Idra* are all contained in or can be described—in the *Zohar*'s view—as an

absence of union, or celibacy. This is the ontological flaw that led to
the death of the kings of Edom and the exile of the *Shekhina* and so
caused Israel's historical exile. It is also the epistemological flaw
involved in the mysteries of the *Torah* not being clearly understood;
and it is R. Simeon's personal defect, which is why the redemption
of the cosmos is also his personal redemption.

All of these meanings are contained in the opening sentence of
a section of the *Zohar* called *Sifra di-Tsni'uta* ("The Book of
Concealment"), consisting of a sort of terse, obscure mishna that is
explicated at length in *Idra Rabba*. It begins as follows: "The book
of concealment, the book weighed in a balance; and before there was
a balance there was no looking face-to-face, and the first kings died"
(II, 176b). This esoteric book can be revealed because it is "weighed
in a balance";[190] that is to say, it deals with the restored world in which
the male and female elements look upon each other face-to-face;
similarly, the mysteries of the *Torah* are revealed, as it were, face-to-
face. Before things were weighed in this balance, the first kings (i.e.,
the ancient worlds) died and the world and the *Torah* were in a
defective state.

What is this balance that characterizes the restored world? It
is a kind of cosmic scales whose function is to make sure that
everything created in the world will be harmonious, that is, male and
female. On these scales are weighed, on the one hand, the souls of
human beings—male and female—before they enter the world, and
those that balance each other are destined to marry, and on the other,
the worlds (or *sefirot*) in their perfected state, before their emanation.
The absence of such a balance is what caused the celibacy and death
of the kings of Edom. (None of the kings of Edom in the list in chapter
xxxvi of Genesis is the son of the king who preceded him; none but
the last is mentioned as having a wife; and it is said of each but the
last that "he died." The author of the *Zohar* concludes from this that
they were celibate and regards this as the cause of their death, while
the last king is viewed as the beginning of the world of *tikkun*.)

As we have said, balance is a universal principle used by God
in creating his world. It is part of a myth elaborated in the *Zohar* that
presents God the Creator as the one who weighs and measures (based
on an image in Isa. 40:12). The balance can thus be identified, at least
partially, with the "line of measure,"[191] which is not only an implement
wielded by the Holy One and used by him in emanating and creating
his world, but also an instrument in the hands of the mystic, who uses
it to learn and measure the dimensions of the Holy One. The mystic
does not perform this measurement only for his own edification, for
his use of the "line of measure" makes him a partner in God's work

of restoring the worlds. The author of the *Zohar* showers praise upon the Kabbalist who thus engages (Zohar Hadash, *Va'ethannan, Ma'amar Kav ha-Mida*, 57d), elaborating in accordance with his own ideas the praise offered at the beginning of *Sefer Shi'ur Koma*[192] to those who know the dimensions of the Creator. Just as the Kabbalist uses the "line of measure" for his measurement, so can he use a "balance" to weigh up the supernal *sefirot*; and he does this by concerning himself with the idea of the balancing and coupling of the *sefirot*. This idea, to which the words "the book weighed in a balance" alludes I believe, is related to the notion that *tikkun* may be accomplished through homiletic discourse, as we discussed above.

This *tikkun* also rectifies the historical situation of the Jewish people (for he who knows the dimensions of the Creator also knows the time of the End). As we have seen, the reason for the exile is the severance of the male divine element from the female element (i.e., the exile of the *Shekhina*). The opening words of the *Sifra di-Tsni'uta*, "there was no looking face-to-face," allude to this as well. The *Zohar* discusses this at length at the beginning of one of the early "versions" of the *Idra*, basing itself on the rabbinic description according to which the cherubs in the Sanctuary (who were male and female) ceased embracing each other face-to-face when Israel sinned. We find, then, that the Kabbalist, bringing the *sefirot* to erotic union above, also remedies Israel's situation below.

As we have said, mysticism and the disclosure of esoteric lore are signs of the Messianic era, and the phrase "face to face" is also used to describe disclosure of this kind. It was said of Moses that "there hath not arisen a prophet since in Israel like unto Moses, whom the Lord knew face to face" (Deut. 34:10); and R. Simeon, as we have seen, is likened to Moses. In the *Zohar* the "face-to-face" disclosure of the secrets of the *Torah* also has erotic overtones, for the *Torah* is likened to a veiled princess who gradually reveals herself to her beloved; and the last stage, in which the deepest secrets are revealed, is called "face-to-face" (II, 99a). It seems to me, therefore, that it was this renewed opportunity to "gaze face-to-face" that allowed *Sifra di-Tsni'uta* to be revealed.

The relationship between the union of male and female and the possibility of disclosing the secrets finds concrete, quasi-halakhic expression in the *Idrot* in a way that explicitly demonstrates its connection with the idea of "balance." R. Simeon twice repeats his instruction that the secrets of the *Torah* not be revealed to anyone who is unmarried. In the first version of *Idra Zuta*, when he cautions the companions not to reveal the esoteric lore to those unworthy to know it, he adds "and not to unmarried people"; and in *Idra Rabba* he says: "I must reveal all these *tikkunim* and all these words [only] to those who are weighed in the balance" (II, 141a)—that is, married people, as I shall presently establish (to be sure, R. Simeon may also be referring to the latter phrase to those who "weigh in the balance," that is, to Kabbalists who perform *tikkunim* by weighing; the one interpretation does not, however, exclude the other). No such restriction confining the disclosure of the secrets to married people appears in the *Talmud*, neither in *Kiddushin* 71a, which enumerates the requirements a person must meet in order to be told the forty-two-letter full name of God, nor in *Hagiga* 13a, which lists those who are worthy of receiving the mysteries of the *Torah*. It would thus seem to be an innovation of the author of the *Zohar* stemming from Kabbalistic considerations. This is stated explicitly at the beginning of the early version of the *Idra*, which as we have noted, deals with the defective state of the cherubs when they do not look upon each other face-to-face: "From this [the matter of the cherubs] we learned that in any place where male and female are not both present one may not see the face of the *Shekhina*" (III, 19b).

As we have said, the souls of human beings are also weighed in the balance before birth. In that weighing male is balanced against female and marriages are preordained. (This is the *Zohar*'s mythic interpretation of such rabbinic statements as: "Forty days before the creation of an embryo a heavenly voice comes forth and proclaims: 'the daughter of so-and-so is for so-and-so' " [Sota 2a].) Special angels are charged with this weighing, and they are described as follows:

> All of them are entrusted with the existence of the world [i.e., marriages and reproduction]. . . it is they who weigh males and females in the balance that they may be married to one another and they [those angels] are called *Moznaim* [balances]. . . . All those [yet unborn souls] which are in balance, that do not weigh one more than the other, ascend and join together, and that is the joining together of male and female [i.e., marriage] of which it is said: "placed on a scale[193] all together" [Ps. 62:10] (II, 255a,b).

We see, then, that there is a similarity between the emanation of the *sefirot* and the creation of human beings: both are created by means of a balancing of male and female. Both, furthermore, achieve *tikkun* in the same way, by the union of male and female. This similarity is underscored by another myth, also relating both to man and to the Godhead, which describes the creation of man as male and female and his subsequent sawing in two. This myth, whose source is a rabbinic midrash on the creation of Adam,[194] was interpreted by the *Kabbala* from its inception as describing the emanation of the *sefirot Tif'eret* and *Malkhut*.[195] The *Zohar* retains this explanation, but it also adds a meaning relating to terrestrial humanity. Man and wife descend from above as a single soul. Afterwards, however, their souls are separated and must be joined again through coupling.[196] That is why marriage is so important and has active, symbolic meaning— and why abstention from marriage, too, has symbolic meaning. The importance of marriage, however, is multiplied many times over because of the parallel here between man and the supernal *sefirot*. Man is not called "man" if he is not both male and female,[197] because he is fashioned in the image of the Godhead, and it is the Godhead that is first called "man." Moreover, even the Godhead is not called "man" unless it too is male and female,[198] for it is meant to be "one body." A person who does not marry impairs this trait and diminishes the supernal Image;[199] and as he causes this defect above, so he himself, too, is called a "half body."[200] In this he joins company with the demons, which have no body and are not called "man."[201] According to the *Zohar*, the sin of one who abstains from marrying and does not seek to reproduce is grave beyond measure. It is the only sin for which the *Zohar* specifies the punishment (or *tikkun*) of reincarnation,[202] for it mars the upper worlds; and by its remedy the entire cosmos undergoes *tikkun*.

R. Simeon's Tikkun Through Erotic Union

The gravity of the sin of celibacy puts R. Simeon's complaint at the beginning of *Idra Rabba* in a new light. As we saw above, his complaint refers both to the state of the world and to his own loneliness in his situation as "Righteous, foundation of the world." I would now add that the complaint also refers to a defective sexual situation, and this, too, must be remedied during the *Idra*. It is precisely he who is "Righteous, foundation of the world" who is affected by this flaw, because of the sexual significance implicit in that designation. The defect is even more serious with respect to R. Simeon, moreover, because he discloses the mysteries of the *Torah*, which one who is flawed by celibacy is forbidden to do.

An allusion to this sexual defect appears in the very wording of the complaint: "Until when will we dwell in the place of one pillar?" Our various explanations of this question have not yet considered the verb *netiv*, translated here as "dwell." Its meaning becomes clearer, however, when we look at it in relation to the underlying rabbinic remark "It is better to dwell with two bodies than to dwell in widowhood" (*Kiddushin* 41a). Viewed in this context R. Simeon's complaint concerns the fact that he presently dwells with one pillar (i.e., woman) rather than with two. R. Simeon's sexual isolation may also be hinted at in another passage. As we have indicated, he identifies himself with the "fin of the Leviathan on which the world stands." This Leviathan on whom alone the world is supported is described elsewhere in the *Zohar* (II, 108b) as being without a female, which is considered a deplorable state of affairs. In identifying himself with the Leviathan, R. Simeon (or more precisely, the medieval author of the *Zohar*) may have been alluding to its celibate condition.

Was R. Simeon celibate? He certainly was not. He had a son, R. Eleazar, and the *Talmud* also mentions his wife, though his relations with her were not always close, particularly during his twelve years of hiding in a cave.[203] Moreover, the very reason he fled to the cave was that he did not count on his wife's ability to stand up to the Romans' investigations and not give him away, for as he said, "Women are light of mind" (*Shabbat* 33b). It may well be that Moses de Leon, who is considered to be a principal author of the *Zohar*, who identified strongly with his hero, was also not very close to his wife. Just how remote she was from his world is attested by R. Isaac of Acre,[204] who reports that when she asked her husband why he did not write in his own name in order to gain honor for himself, he replied merely that by so doing he would be paid more for his book. We also know from the same source that de Leon, after he had become impoverished, left his wife and daughters penniless to set out on the wanderings in the course of which he met his death. In the *Zohar* (I, 50a) there is a discussion of the problem of a traveler who is distant from his wife. His *tikkun* is to to have an erotic union with the *Shekhina*, which is precisely R. Simeon's *tikkun* in the *Idra*.

Though there is no suggestion here that R. Simeon's (or Moses de Leon's) family life was defective, there is an allusion to sexual deficiency. According to the *Zohar*, one female is not sufficient for a righteous man; he must be "adorned by two females" (I, 50a): his wife and the *Shekhina*. It thus appears that R. Simeon's complaint at the beginning of the *Idra* is about his not having this union with the *Shekhina*, a situation that is remedied by the end of the *Idra*, as we explained above. This deficiency is also suggested by the wording of the phrase "until when will we dwell. . ." for the notion of two females is elsewhere discussed in the *Zohar* in terms of "dwelling" (or "sitting"): "The male above dwells (sits) between two females" (I, 153b).[205] R. Simeon's complaint is that he dwells with only one. In Moses de Leon's Hebrew books the situation of a male between two females is called "*amida*," standing. "Every married male in Israel stands with two females, the one concealed and the other revealed."[206] This term too may be echoed in R. Simeon's complaint, in the word "*kayema*," place, whose Hebrew equivalent is "*ma'amad*"—standing place. The use of the word "*samkha*"—"pillar" or "support"—to denote the female may well derive from her role of assisting the male, which God specified at her creation: "I shall make a *help meet* for him" (Gen. ii:18); the Aramaic Targum renders the word "*ezer*," "*help meet*," as "*semakh*," and the same rendering occurs also in the *Zohar* (I, 34b).

A comparison with Moses, the father of all prophets and mystics, obviously suggests itself here. He too, in receiving the *Torah*, separated himself from his wife and had an erotic union with the *Shekhina*, ultimately dying by a divine kiss. As we have already noted, such comparisons between R. Simeon and Moses occur frequently in the *Zohar*, especially in *Idra Rabba*.[207]

We find, then, that even as R. Simeon's union with the *Shekhina* brings about the redemption of the entire cosmos and of the Jewish people in particular, it is also his own personal and sexual redemption. He is both redeemer and redeemed, which is precisely how the *Zohar* portrays the Messiah,[208] basing itself on the description of the prophet Zechariah: "Righteous and saved is he" (Zech. ix:9). The *Zohar* emphasizes that the Messiah himself is saved more than all those he comes to deliver, for he finds his proper sexual partner—the *Shekhina*. His suffering in exile, without her, is greatest of all, whereof it is written, "The righteous man perishes" (Isa. lvii:1).[209] The *Zohar*'s allusion, to be sure, is to the *sefira* of *Yesod*, which suffers in its isolation and is redeemed through coupling. The use of the verse from Zechariah indicates, however, that the Messiah himself, who in the *Zohar* is a symbol (or perhaps even an incarnation) of *Yesod*, is also intended, for its plain meaning refers to him. The same view was held by the "Gnostic Kabbalists," who developed this symbolism and called the Messiah by the name Righteous. Additional emphasis for this idea may be garnered elsewhere in the *Zohar*. At the beginning of a discourse on the verses "righteous and saved" and "the righteous man perishes," R. Simeon weeps and says, "A king without a noble lady is no king" (III, 69a).[210] The allusion here is clearly to both the King of the world and the Messiah. Within the description of the redeemer who is himself redeemed through an act of coupling we may thus discover a very illuminating parallel between R. Simeon and the Messiah. R. Simeon of the *Zohar* is a messianic figure who embodies the fate of the entire cosmos, its flaw, and its redemption.

I believe that this chapter has also demonstrated something else: what the *Zohar* says about the *Torah* can be applied to the *Zohar* itself. In Part II (99a), the *Zohar* likens the *Torah* to a princess who reveals herself little by little to her beloved, gradually removing the coverings and veils that separate her from him, and finally allowing him to penetrate her deeper, hidden levels and arrive at her inner secrets. The *Zohar*, too, behaves this way with those who love it, revealing its secrets only as a reward of long and arduous study.

─────────── APPENDIX 1: When was Idra Rabba Held? ───────────

As we noted above, R. Isaac Luria stated that *Idra Rabba* took place on *Lag Ba-'Omer. Lag Ba-'Omer*, however, is not mentioned anywhere in the *Zohar*, and its author had very likely never heard of it. From the *Talmud* he knew that the deaths of R. Akiva's disciples took place "between Passover and *Atseret*," ceasing from the festival of *Shavu'ot*. On the basis of the same considerations that led Luria to determine that *Idra Rabba* was held on *Lag Ba-'Omer*, then the *Zohar* would set the time for it as *Shavu'ot*. But even setting aside these considerations, I believe it can be shown that the time of *Idra Rabba* in the *Zohar* is *Shavu'ot* and that the gathering is actually the *tikkun* of *Shavu'ot* night, *Tikkun Leil Shavu'ot*. First of all, *Idra Rabba* itself frequently compares the occasion it describes with that of the giving of the *Torah* on Mt. Sinai, which took place on *Shavu'ot*. At *Idra Rabba* a "new *Torah*" is given, as explained at the beginning of the *Idra*. The gathering was held because the heavenly *Torah* had been "nullified" and had to be renewed. In this respect, the *Idra* perhaps parallels the custom of reciting all the *mitsvot* of the *Torah* on the night of *Shavu'ot*.[1] Secondly, the verse cited at the beginning of the *Idra*, "O Lord, I have heard the report of You and am afraid" (Hab. iii:2), occurs at the beginning of the *haftara* recited on the second day of Shavu'ot. Another clue is to be found in the fact that *Idra Rabba* is inserted in the *Zohar* under the Torah portion of *Naso*. There is only the slightest relationship between the two, consisting of just one associative allusion to the hair of a *nazir*. It seems to me that the main reason for the *Idra*'s insertion there is that Naso is read around the time of *Shavu'ot*.

But the major proof that *Idra Rabba* was a *Tikkun Leil Shavu'ot* will be gained from analyzing the description of that *tikkun* in the *Zohar* and comparing it with *Idra Rabba*. *Tikkun Leil Shavu'ot* is described at length in Part I, 8a–9a. The passage describes a gathering of the companions with R. Simeon on the night of Shavu'ot with the object of *tikkun*, which also refers to the adornment of the bride (i.e., the *Shekhina*) in jewels for her marriage the following day. In the body of this chapter (in the section entitled *Tikkun*) I compared this passage in great detail with *Idra Rabba* and showed that the latter, both in its method of *tikkun* (discourses on the *Torah*) and in the sequence (by which it proceeds the *tikkun* of the higher configurations as a condition for the *tikkun* of the *Shekhina*) may be seen as an elaboration of what is described in the account of *Tikkun Leil Shavu'ot*.[2]

The description of *Idra Rabba* is also "technically" similar to the description of *Tikkun Leil Shavu'ot*. At *Idra Rabba* each of the participants rises in turn to perform the *tikkun* that "belongs" to him. In the *Tikkun Leil Shavu'ot*, too, each of the companions rises in turn and performs one *tikkun* of the bride (I, 10a). Another similarity between the two passages lies in the motif of the bridal canopy: at *Tikkun Leil Shavu'ot* the companions are called "bridal canopy attendants," while in *Idra Rabba* a heavenly bridal canopy is spread above them.

The two passages are also similar in that both represent the Holy One as "old." This motif is more pronounced in *Idra Rabba*, the first part of which is devoted to the *tikkun* of *Attika Kaddisha*, the Ancient Holy One. It is not absent, however, from the *Tikkun Leil Shavu'ot*, though *Attika Kaddisha* there is partially identified with a mortal figure, Rav Hamnuna Sava, who reveals the secrets of the *Torah*. This identification also occurs at the beginning of *Idra Zuta* (III, 288a), where *Attika Kaddisha* appears in human form, taking part in the discourse on the Torah just like one of the sages.[3]

These three motifs—the concern with the entire body of Scripture, the bridal canopy, and the Godhead as "old"—are also found in the mysticism of the talmudic era and even then seem to have been associated with *Shavu'ot*, as we shall presently see. The special status ascribed to R. Eleazar and R. Abba,[4] along with R. Simeon, provides a further parallel between *Idra Rabba* and *Tikkun Leil Shavu'ot*, where they are called Peniel (a reference to Gen. xxxii:30) because they have seen the face of the *Shekhina* (I, 7b; 9a). Both passages, furthermore, are prefaced with warnings to be bound exclusively to R. Simeon and to the secrets. Further, the other motifs appearing in both places are those of the love among the companions and between them and the supernal entities, and the assertion that the companions are of the level of *Yesod*.

The revelation at Sinai is often described in rabbinical literature as a wedding between *Knesset Israel* and the Holy One blessed be He.[5] The *Zohar* developed this into a historical, theological, and ritual myth (III, 97a–98b), which compares the sequence of Passover, the counting of the *Omer* and *Shavu'ot* to the purification of a woman after her menstruation, which is likened to the uncleanliness of Egypt; Passover is analogized to the day she becomes clean of her impurity and the counting of the seven weeks of the *Omer* to the counting of the seven clean days following menstruation after which sexual intercourse is permitted. The author of the *Zohar* bases himself here on a textual similarity between the formulation of the commandment to count the Omer: "And you shall count unto you" [Lev. xxiii:15] and that of the commandment to the woman: "She shall count unto herself" (Lev. xv:28). During the forty-nine days of the *Omer* one leaves behind the forty-nine gates of the uncleanliness of Egypt and enters into the forty-nine gates of understanding, which are included in the seven *sefirot* below *Bina*, each of which is itself comprised of seven *sefirot* (this is elaborated in great detail by Luria). The process reaches its climax at the time of the wedding and erotic union (*Shavu'ot*).

This myth, developed with almost endless ramifications in the Lurianic *Kabbala*, underlies the customs practiced by the Kabbalists at this time of year and especially at their *Tikkun Leil Shavu'ot*. This *tikkun* is described in the *Zohar* (Part I) as an existing custom. To be sure, we have no historical evidence indicating that it was practiced at or prior to the time of the *Zohar*'s composition, or even thereafter until we come to Safed of the sixteenth century, a generation before Isaac Luria.[6] Wilhelm holds that the custom was not practiced at the time of the *Zohar*, and that the *Zohar*'s attestation to its existence is a product of its author's imagination.[7]

However, Moses de Leon also left us another description of the *Tikkun Leil Shavu'ot*,[8] not in his pseudepigraphic writings but in a work in Hebrew signed by the author himself. There de Leon declares that this *tikkun* was known to "the ancients of blessed memory, pillars of the world." This is not in itself historical evidence, of course, for this designation undoubtedly refers to figures in his own pseudepigraphic *Zohar*, who are also called "pillars of the world." But he goes on to say: "Those individuals, remnants whom the Lord calls, fulfill the tradition [*Kabbala*] of their forebears." That is to say, de Leon states that the traditional practice of the ancients (who are the figures of the *Zohar*) was continued and was preserved in his time by a number of individuals. Was this too concocted by de Leon? But it was written in a Hebrew book under his own name. It is unlikely that he would do this with something he had made up, for someone might ask him to supply more details. It therefore seems to me that what he said was true, and there were people in his time who kept this custom. Who were those people? Moses de Leon calls them "individuals, remnants whom the Lord calls." This expression, derived from the book of Joel (iii:5), was used in his day by the "Gnostic

Kabbalists"—a circle to which, as we have seen, de Leon was close—
to refer to themselves. It occurs in their writings,[9] with the word
"individuals" usually appearing before the biblical phrase "remnants
whom the Lord calls." The use of this word, which does not appear
in the biblical verse, shows that the expression is no mere rhetorical
turn of a scriptural phrase but the designation of a specific group.
Its source is Maimonides' *Guide of the Perplexed*,[10] where the word
"individuals" is also used. Nor is it surprising that the members of
the "Gnostic" circle, who were so remote from the spirit of
Maimonides, should have designated themselves by an expression
taken from the *Guide* and used there to refer to the finest of the
philosophers. It was customary for the members of this circle to seek
great authorities for their ideas and to write pseudepigraphically[11]—
which tendency was of course shared by the author of the *Zohar*.

At the beginning of R. Isaac ha-Kohen's *Perush Merkevet Yehezkel*
the author calls himself and his followers pupils of Maimonides.[12] The
members of the circle tended in general to take glorious designations
for themselves, the most common of which was *ha-ma'amikim*
(profound thinkers).[13] It was in keeping with this tendency, then, that
they called themselves "individuals, remnants whom the Lord calls"
(apparently interpreting the word "remnants" to mean "exalted and
special," as in Nachmanides' interpretation of the verse from Joel).[14]
When Moses de Leon said that there were Kabbalists in his day who
performed *Tikkun Leil Shavu'ot,* it would thus seem to have been this
circle to which he was referring.

I have not found anything in the writings of the members of this
circle to indicate that they performed this ritual. Considering that
so few of their writings have come down to us, testimony to it may
well have been lost. It is also possible that the practice was never
mentioned in writing because it was so esoteric. I have, however, found
in their literary remains a reference to another myth-bound ritual
whose description closely resembles the spirit and language of the
Tikkun Leil Shavu'ot as described in the *Zohar*,[15] and this similarity
reinforces my supposition that they also practiced the *Tikkun Leil
Shavu'ot.* The author of the description, himself one of the "Gnostic
Kabbalists," presents it in the context of a discussion of the mysteries
of the morning prayer. According to him the object of this prayer is
the coupling of the Shekhina with the *sefira* of *Yesod* and its elevation
to "the Exalted One," after which blessing will prevail over all. The
author describes the prayer rite as an ongoing mythic process: at each
stage the Shekhina is advanced one step further in its coupling and
elevation, just as it is in the Zoharic myth centering around the three

holidays of Passover, *Lag Ba-'Omer*, and Shavuot. Indeed, this passage even contains an exact parallel to the *Tikkun Leil Shavu'ot* in the form of the psalms that are recited before the prayer. With these verses the worshiper "decorates the bride in her adornments" (the phrase is taken not from the *Zohar*, but from this text originating in the "Gnostic" circle!) in order to prepare her for the coupling that takes place during the central *Amida* prayer. As we have seen, that is precisely what the *Tikkun Leil Shavu'ot* is about. In the *Zohar*'s *Tikkun Leil Shavu'ot* too, moreover, the bride is adorned with "praise."[16] There is thus no reason to dismiss de Leon's testimony regarding the *Tikkun Leil Shavu'ot* out of hand, and it is quite possible that this ritual was indeed customarily practiced in the Kabbalistic circle to which he was close. If it was, it almost certainly had a mystical character, as would be appropriate to *Shavu'ot*, and it was almost certainly also messianic, given the powerful messianic sentiments shared by the members of the circle. And since many of the *Idra*'s ideas—including that of the worlds that had been destroyed, and the figure of the redeemer and restorer—originated in this circle, it is not unreasonable to suppose that the *tikkun* performed by its members on *Shavu'ot* resembled that described in *Idra Rabba*.

What is more, we have what may be direct testimony to the convening of gatherings at which, as in *Idra Rabba*, an elder expounded mysteries of the Torah to a group of ten venerable sages designated "individuals" (as the members of the "Gnostic" circle called themselves). Like *Idra Rabba* and *Idra Zuta* (see Appendix II), these gatherings took place on *Shavu'ot* and *Yom Kippur*. As in the opening of *Idra Rabba*, moreover, these individuals responded to the words of the elder with the word "Amen." The passage in which this testimony is found originates in a circle which had a great deal of influence upon the *Zohar*'s author and his own circle. It appears at the end of *Sefer Baddei ha-Aron* by R. Shem Tov Ibn Gaon and reads as follows: "There was an old man there whom no one saw save ten venerable individuals, and on the day of the giving of the *Torah* and on Yom Kippur, on which he would pray in the *minyan* of ten, he would speak wondrous wise words. Once he sat alone with ten elders extremely learned in all aspects of the Torah and spoke. . .and all the elders answered 'Amen.' " The author of the *Zohar* may have had this passage before him and been directly influenced by it in his description of *Idra Rabba* and *Idra Zuta*.

Several considerations lead me to hypothesize, moreover, that something like a *tikkun* may already have been practiced on *Shavu'ot* night among the early mystics of talmudic times. First, ancient texts explicitly and often mention the link between the giving of the *Torah* on Mt. Sinai, which took place on *Shavu'ot*, and the *Merkava* mysticism they expound.[17] It may readily be imagined that the mystics regarded the giving of the *Torah* as the paradigmatic mystical experience, and the many descriptions written in the spirit of *Merkava* mysticism of Moses' ascent to heaven to receive the *Torah* are evidence of this. Nor is it hard to understand why the mystics in their dreams saw themselves "reclining on fine couches in a grand reception room atop Mt. Sinai" (*Hagiga* 14b). Further evidence for the mystical character of *Shavu'ot* in ancient times is to be found in Philo's description of the sect of the Therapeutae,[18] and also in the New Testament (Acts 2). *Shavu'ot*—Pentecost—is the day on which the Holy Spirit came upon Jesus' apostles, and the mystic nature of the holiday is preserved in Christianity. It may have been mutual influences between Jews and Christians that determined the nature of *Tikkun Leil Shavu'ot*.

The *haftarot* that were fixed for the two days of *Shavu'ot* are themselves important indications of the mystical nature of the holiday. These *haftarot* include what the *Merkava* mystics regarded as the most mystical chapters in the Prophets, namely, the first chapter of Ezekiel, on the chariot, and the third chapter of Habbakuk. The only thing that links them to the occasion on which they are read is their mystical character. It should be noted that the passage from Ezekiel on the chariot is read on *Shavu'ot* in direct contravention of the *Mishna*, which stipulates that "The portion of the Chariot is not to be read as a *haftara*." The practice of reading it is supported only by the minority view of the single *tanna* (R. Judah) who permits it. Since it is unlikely that the custom was instituted after and in opposition to the *Mishna*'s ruling, we would do better to assume that it predated the *Mishna* and that the *Tannaim* sought unsuccessfully to counter it. This is an indication both of the antiquity of the mystical understanding of *Shavu'ot* and of its power.

It therefore seems to me not at all unreasonable to suppose that something like *Tikkun Leil Shavu'ot* was already practiced in the circles of *Merkava* mysticism. This impression is reinforced by the observation that the descriptions of *Tikkun Leil Shavu'ot* (and of *Idra Rabba*) in the *Zohar* are to a large extent elaborations of descriptions of mystical events in the *Merkava* texts. The author of the *Zohar* may have been in possession of a tradition linking these disclosures to *Shavu'ot*. An esoteric tradition of mystical activities on *Shavu'ot* night may have been preserved and developed by the "Gnostic" Kabbalists and elaborated further in the *Zohar*, through which it was disseminated openly to the larger Jewish public. The absence of direct evidence of the existence of such a tradition is not surprising if we

consider the esoteric nature of the practice, as of all the practices of
the early mystics (to which the *Mishna*, as we have seen, had already
voiced its opposition). Another reason for secrecy may have been that
the practice had a messianic character even in ancient times. This
possibility automatically presents itself when we recall that the
leading ancient spokesman for Jewish mysticism was R. Akiva, who
was a supporter of Bar-Kokhba. Most of the statements relating the
"account of the Chariot" to the revelation at Sinai and likening it
to a wedding originate with him.[19] If all this is so, then the author
of the *Zohar* had a tradition on which to base himself with respect
to the messianic orientation of the *Idra*. The *Zohar* diverged from its
predecessors, however, by publishing the esoteric practice openly. It
did so, I believe, because it regarded its generation as that preceding
the advent of the Messiah: at such a time disclosure of the secrets
is a means of facilitating the redemption.

In his description of *Tikkun Leil Shavu'ot*, the author of the
Zohar indeed bases himself on mystical practices from talmudic times.
We find something similar to the *Zohar*'s statements about the
passage from *Torah* to Prophets and from Prophets to Hagiographa
in the *Midrash*, where it is viewed as a mystical technique:

> The disciples told R. Akiva: "Ben 'Azzai is sitting and
> expounding Scripture and a flame is burning around him." He
> went to him and said: "Are you perhaps engaged in study of the
> Chariot?" He answered: "No I am joining the words of the Torah
> to the Prophets and the Prophets to the Hagiographa [i.e., finding
> parallels between them]; and the words of the Torah are joyful
> as on the day they were given at Sinai." (Leviticus Rabba xvi:4)

The comparison of this teaching with the moment of the giving
of the *Torah* raises the possibility that this midrashic event, too, took
place on *Shavu'ot*. The wedding canopy mentioned in *Tikkun Leil
Shavu'ot* and in *Idra Rabba* and the angels who come to the wedding
as guests originate in descriptions by the *Merkava* mystics. These
motifs were readily associated (perhaps even in talmudic times) with
the conception of the day of the giving of the *Torah* as a wedding day
(*Idra Zuta*, moreover, speaks of the "wedding" of R. Simeon's soul to
its source at its expiry, which is the *Hillula* of R. Simeon bar Yohai).
The *Idra* is primarily concerned with the highest configuration of the
Holy One, described as a wholly merciful old man. This notion is taken
from a description by the Sages of self-revelation at Sinai, where he
stood revealed as "an old man filled with mercy"; at the Red Sea, by
contrast, he revealed Himself as a warrior.[20] The association of

the "old man" with *Shavu'ot* is highly developed in the Lurianic Kabbala, where the holiday marks the climax of *Ze'er Anpin's* growth, at which it is transformed into an old man like the supreme configuration. These parallels give an indication of the extent to which the *Zohar* develops ideas found in the early literature, and may further reinforce our supposition that the practice of *Tikkun Leil Shavu'ot* also has its roots in the circles of the Merkava mystics. Moreover, the parallel between the description of the old man in the *Zohar* and that in the *midrashim* is further proof that *Idra Rabba* is in fact a *Tikkun Leil Shavu'ot*.

One may well ask why this relationship to Shavu'ot is not made explicit in *Idra Rabba*. But that is the way of the *Zohar*. Its intentions can be understood only by comparing diverse statements that complement and elucidate one another. This may be seen in our case from the comparison between the description of *Tikkun Leil Shavu'ot* in Part I and the *Idra*. Furthermore, even the passage in Part I that is universally recognized as a description of *Tikkun Leil Shavu'ot* does not mention the name of the holiday explicitly, referring to it only as "the night the bride is to be joined to her husband." That the passage is about *Shavu'ot* emerges only when it is compared with another elsewhere in the *Zohar* (III, 98a) which does make explicit mention of the occasion.

It is interesting to note that the relationship between *Idra Rabba* and *Tikkun Leil Shavu'ot* has been greatly emphasized by latter-day Kabbalists, who highlight it by their custom of making *Idra Rabba* the principal text to be read and studied at the *Tikkun Leil Shavu'ot*. In the *Zohar* the study material for *Shavu'ot* is specified as Torah, Prophets, Hagiographa, Midrash, and "secret wisdom," which undoubtedly refers to Kabbala. Luria stipulated which biblical verses were to be read, but regarding the Kabbalistic material said only: "And afterwards, for the rest of the night, secrets of the Torah and the Book of the *Zohar* according to your grasp."[21] Luria's disciples, however, were more specific. The *tikkun* practiced today is based on *Sefer Hemdat Yamim*,[22] which speaks explicitly of *Idra Rabba* as the material to be read, and it is in fact the text printed in prayer books that include *Tikkun Leil Shavu'ot*.[23] Another allusion to the prevalent sense of a connection between *Idra Rabba* and Shavu'ot is perhaps to be found in the words of the Kabbalist Natan Shapira, who referred to the festival of the giving of the Torah as "*Yoma De-Hillula Rabba*." The mystical character of the *Tikkun Leil Shavu'ot* in later generations needs no proof. Suffice it to mention an incident involving Joseph Karo, to whom, as his friend Solomon Alkabez reported, the *Shekhina*—the *Mishna*—revealed herself in the form of a *maggid* during *Tikkun Leil Shavu'ot*. It is worth mentioning here, however, that messianic significance was also ascribed to this *tikkun*, and that it was on one such occasion that Nathan of Gaza was overcome by the spirit of prophecy and declared Shabbatai Zevi to be Israel's Messiah.[24]

———————— APPENDIX 2: When Was Idra Zuta Held? ————————

It is my view that *Idra Zuta*, at which R. Simeon died, was held on Yom Kippur. The tradition that R. Simeon died on *Lag Ba-'Omer* does not appear in the *Zohar*, nor was it known to Isaac Luria, who believed that *Idra Rabba* was convened on that day. As we have seen, *Idra Rabba* took the form of a *Tikkun Leil Shavu'ot*. There is, in fact, a certain resemblance in the *Zohar* between *Shavu'ot* and Yom Kippur. On both the Holy One has an erotic union with the *Shekhina*. As on *Shavu'ot*, moreover, the purpose of the practice of the ritual immersion on the eve of Yom Kippur is to ready the bride for her wedding (III, 214b). On Yom Kippur copulation between men and women is of course prohibited, but spiritual coupling, like that which took place at R. Simeon's death, may be a different matter. The author of the *Zohar* may be alluding to this in noting that on *Shemini Atseret* there is "corporeal copulation"—in contrast, perhaps, to the spiritual union on Yom Kippur. Furthermore, Yom Kippur, like *Shavu'ot*, is related to the giving of the *Torah* on Mt. Sinai, for it was on that day that Moses descended from the mountain with the second set of tablets.[1] The day is thus suitable for mystical revelations like those of *Idra Zuta*. It is on that day, in fact, that Moses asked to see the glory of God and was granted a vision of him.[2] We also know that in Provence and Spain in the period before the *Zohar*'s composition mystical-magical ceremonies were held on Yom Kippur at which secrets of the *Torah* were disclosed.[3] The evidence for the existence of such a practice stems, in fact, from the "Gnostic Kabbalists," de Leon's circle.[4] *Idra Zuta* may be part of a similar tradition.

In *Sidrei De-Shimmusha Rabba* it is related that it was the practice at such Yom Kippur gatherings to trace a circle on the ground. An old man would stand inside the circle, with the others standing around him. They would then invoke various angels, and these would reveal secrets of the *Torah*.[5] This is very reminiscent of *Idra Rabba*, at which the disciples surround R. Simeon for a very similar purpose; and in *Idra Zuta* (III, 288a), too, R. Hamnuna Sava is described as surrounded by seventy righteous men. The circle drawn on the ground, which was taken over from a practice of early mystics such as Honi the Circle-Drawer and the prophet *Habbakuk*—both of whom served as models for the author of the *Zohar*—also have its echo in the *Zohar*, perhaps even the form of the *Idra*, round like a threshing floor. Furthermore, *Idra Zuta* appears in the *Zohar* under the heading of the *Torah* portion of *Ha'azinu*, though there is no apparent justification for its insertion there (apart from the author's desire to set R. Simeon's death at the end of the work). However, this is the *Torah* portion read on the Sabbath before *Yom Kippur*. As we have seen, *Idra Rabba* is similarly located in the section dealing with the *Torah* portion of *Naso*, which is read on the Sabbath before *Shavu'ot*.

Yom Kippur is a most appropriate time for the departure from this world of a soul like R. Simeon. The day is associated with the *sefira* of *Bina* (III, 102a; b; and parallels),[6] which the *Zohar* refers to as "the world to come." Yom Kippur is also described as the most spiritual day of the year, on which the people of Israel in its self-affliction "exists more in soul than in body" (II, 185b). It is therefore said of it that it "takes all souls." This idea of "taking" attests to a wholeness or perfection of soul; with respect to the soul of R. Simeon, however, it may also have been understood in a literal sense, which is why his soul departed on this day. Yom Kippur is also the "day of judgment" on which all the creatures of the world, righteous and wicked, are tried in the heavenly court. It may be that R. Simeon is contrasting his own situation to that of all other mortals specifically on this universal day of judgment when he says in the first version of *Idra Zuta* (*Zohar Hadash*, 18d) that his trial does not take place in the heavenly court; he is judged, rather, by the Holy One blessed be he himself. It should be noted in this context that R. Akiva, too, died on *Yom Kippur*,[7] and we have already seen other parallels between R. Simeon's death and his. The death of Aaron's sons "before God" is also mentioned in the *Torah* reading for the day.

The spiritual nature of Yom Kippur finds expression in that Israel's virtue on this day is likened to that of the angels (II, 185b).[8] This notion may also be reflected in *Idra Zuta*, which differs from *Idra Rabba* in that it is attended not by angels but by righteous men from paradise (as R. Simeon states at the beginning of *Idra Zuta*, III, 287b–288a). There may also be an allusion to Yom Kippur in a statement made by R. Simeon at the beginning of *Idra Zuta*: "Now is a time of favor, and I want to enter the world to come without shame" (III, 287b). The designation "a time of favor" (*et ratson*) may well refer to Yom Kippur, for it is called that in chapter xlvi of *Pirkei De-Rabbi Eliezer*, a midrashic work (and chapter) of which the *Zohar* makes intensive use. It may also be argued, however, that the 'time of favor" which the *Zohar* had in mind was that of the Sabbath afternoon prayer, for he thus describes it in the *Zohar* (II, 89a; III,

288b). What is more, this latter "time of favor" is mentioned in that place as the time of Moses' death "by a kiss," making it an appropriate hour for the death under similar circumstances of R. Simeon, who resembles Moses in so many other respects as well. Or shall we, perhaps, conclude that R. Simeon died on a Yom Kippur that fell on the Sabbath?

The main evidence that *Idra Zuta* was held on Yom Kippur is that it is on this day that the high priest enters the Holy of Holies, and in *Idra Zuta* R. Simeon is described as doing just that. This evidence becomes even more persuasive when we take into account the parallels with the stories of R. Ishmael and, especially, Simeon the Just. Nonetheless, it must be acknowledged that these arguments are not as convincing as those brought in Appendix I for fixing Shavuot as the date of *Idra Rabba*. *Idra Zuta* may even contain evidence to the contrary, for it states that R. Abba recorded R. Simeon's statements (III, 287b; 296b; cf. II, 123b), which of course would be forbidden on Yom Kippur. Still, a special permit could have been granted to allow this activity on the grounds that "It is time to act for the Lord, violation of Your *Torah* is permitted."

In any event, it became customary to read *Idra Zuta* on Yom Kippur night.

2

How the Zohar Was Written

Since the Zohar first appeared in the lifetime of Moses ben Shem Tov de Leon, the problem of its composition has constantly preoccupied scholars in every generation.[1] Even today, despite the existence of so many worthy scholars of the Zohar (as shown by the conference and its proceedings volume, in which this paper first appeared), the problem seems to have been shelved as if it has been solved in the main. This is due, undoubtedly, to the detailed studies of Gershom Scholem.[2] These studies certainly set the debate on a firm base and at the same time also opened the way to the comprehensive research that has been conducted since then on the Zohar and on related literature. I think that it is now time to use the knowledge that has been accrued in recent years for a renewed study of the old and fundamental problem, to indicate the difficulties that have arisen as regards Scholem's doctrine, and to suggest new lines towards a solution.

Certainly the cornerstone laid by Scholem must remain in its place, and the cornerstone is the close connection between Moses de Leon and the Zohar (or at least most of it). This connection is established by innumerable parallels between the Hebrew writings of Moses de Leon, written in his name, and the Zohar, and by identical linguistic usages and patterns of thought that cannot derive from influence only, but must stem from the identity of the author. Further, the letter of a contemporary, Isaac of Acre, also establishes a connection between Moses de Leon and the Zohar.[3] We certainly acknowledge this connection, but at the same time we contest the importance Scholem attributed to it. He sees the entire book, both its content and its "narrative framework," as the independent creation of Moses de Leon, a view that raises many difficulties.

Firstly, despite all the parallels, the literary and ideological force of the Zohar goes far beyond the writings of Moses de Leon. In contrast to the uniformity of the Hebrew writings, belonging to a genre prevalent in that period, the Zohar was a unique creation in the Middle Ages in its variety, its richness of expression, and the originality of thought and imagination. The Jewish nature of the book is not diminished thereby, its roots remaining fast in the soil of tradition in which it is incorporated as an integral part, preserving and reviving doctrines and myths of ancient times, which seem to have been lost to Medieval Jewry. The gap between the Zohar and the writings of Moses de Leon is also reflected in the historic success—while the former became the basic book of the Kabbala, most of the works of Moses de Leon were not even published by the Kabbalists.

Secondly, while Scholem maintains that Moses de Leon wrote his Hebrew books after the Zohar, Alexander Altmann has since proved that one of Moses de Leon's books was written prior to the Zohar,[4] and I. Tishby demonstrated sufficiently convincingly that most of the Zohar was written after Moses de Leon's Hebrew books, and after 1293.[5] This view was confirmed recently by Dr. Eliyahu Peretz, in a comparative study of the names of the *sefirot* in the Zohar and in related literature,[6] and it is this view that we will adopt in this article. We will contribute several proofs to it, and show that a great many Kabbalists who were thought to have been influenced by the Zohar were not yet familiar with it. The explanation that the Zohar was written concurrently with the Hebrew books is unacceptable, since it is difficult to imagine that anyone immersed in the tremendous psychological tension of composing a book such as the Zohar would be at leisure to write "conventional" books at the same time. Even the transition from writing Kabbalistic books such as the Hebrew writings to independent writing of the Zohar is not easily acceptable, unless the author had teachers and friends and assistance inspiring him with the correct spirit and even providing bricks and mortar.

Furthermore, the writings of Moses de Leon are not completely identical to the Zohar even in style and language, and there are differences as regards the imagination, too. At times Moses de Leon even seems to use expressions whose Zoharic source is not as their original correct form.[7] Why then should we consider only similarities and not differences? Certainly, other authors contemporary to Moses de Leon, and those in the succeeding generation, wrote in the language of the Zohar and at times even in Aramaic. Examples to be cited are the author of the *Ra'aya Meheimana* and the *Tikkunei Zohar*, Joseph of Hamadan, David ben Judah he-Hasid, or Joseph Angelet.[8] Each of these certainly had his own specific stylistic traits that are not in the Zohar. However, it is doubtful whether we have a clear criterion for measuring the stylistic similarities and differences.

If as regards the main body of the Zohar we have an impression (in the absence of criteria we must depend on impressions) of the great affinity to the books of Moses de Leon, this does not apply to other literary units making up the Zohar. I am referring essentially, apart from the *Idrot* to which most of the article will be devoted, to the *Midrash ha-Ne'elam*. This composition, which basically does not have the symbolical character of the Kabbala of the *sefirot* but presents an allegorical exegesis, has no parallel in the Hebrew writings of Moses de Leon. (*Or Zaru'a* was indeed written not in accordance with the Kabbala of the *sefirot* and has several parallels to the *Midrash ha-Ne'elam*,[9] but it does not contain allegorical homiletics). Such exegesis, combined with Kabbalistic symbolism, does exist in the writings of Joseph of Hamadan,[10] and indeed we have found material of his that was introduced into the Zohar,[11] like many addenda that were not written by the principal author.[12] Another difficulty in ascribing the *Midrash ha-Ne'elam* to R. Moses de Leon lies in the fact that Isaac ibn Sahula quoted passages from this work several years before Moses de Leon wrote his books and already attributed them to "Haggadas" or "our Rabbis" or "Yerushalmi," just as Moses de Leon later did. Isaac ibn Sahula was a contemporary and fellow townsman of Moses de Leon, who probably knew him personally. It is difficult, therefore, to believe that he would have ascribed the writings of Moses de Leon to the Torah sages, and even before Moses de Leon himself did.[13]

Further, I do not think that the main body of the Zohar and the *Midrash ha-Ne'elam* can be ascribed to one author, since the differences between them are as great as the differences between the Zohar and the writings of Joseph of Hamadan, for instance. Firstly, on the linguistic plane: while the main body of the Zohar is written in Aramaic, the *Midrash ha-Ne'elam* is written principally in Hebrew and contains many eccentricities that do not exist in the main body of the Zohar.[14] There is an even greater gap in the style; in contrast to the flow of the homiletics and the elaboration of the sources in the main body of the Zohar, the style of the *Midrash ha-Ne'elam* is fragmented. It has almost no "narrative framework," and it quotes the sources of the sages in their own style. There also seems to be a difference in the literary taste here—the *Midrash ha-Ne'elam* lacks the refined taste that gives the Zohar its tremendous force.[15] How could these two works be the fruit of a single hand? In addition the content differs: the *Midrash ha-Ne'elam* is, as I have said, allegorical, while the Zohar is symbolical. It should be noted that the Zohar at times gives symbolic interpretations of passages from the *Midrash ha-Ne'elam*,[16] that correspond to interpretations given in the ancient midrashim, and similarly to the aforementioned passage of Joseph of Hamadan.

In order to reconcile these difficulties as regards the authorship of Moses de Leon, I wish to shift the center of gravity of the problem under study. We should not ask only who wrote the Zohar, but also how the book was written. I wish to suggest the possibility that the Zohar is the work of a whole group that dealt together with the doctrine of the Kabbala, on the basis of a common heritage and ancient texts. This group commenced its activity prior to the writing of the Zohar, and its beginning must be identified with the mid-thirteenth-century circle of "Gnostic Kabbalists" in Castile. I base this theory on several facts, *inter alia*: the similitude between this circle and between the Zohar as regards the method of literary creation and its content;[17] the existence of identical texts (late pseudepigraphic "midrashim") adapted in the two circles;[18] the existence of Kabbalistic rituals apparently customary in this group and described at length in the Zohar and in the writings of Moses de Leon.[19] Above all R. Simeon b. Yohai, the hero of the Zohar, himself alludes to this group and sees in them the few partners to his secret knowledge, while they for their part described in their writings a leader like R. Simeon b. Yohai of the Zohar, as I have shown elsewhere.[20] The group of the Zohar sprang from them, and some of the group wrote their words, formulating in their own language the results of the group's studies, each developing it in accordance with his own inclination, since the freedom of mystical creation is part of the ideology of the Zohar[21] and of the other members of its circle.[22] All these scribes thus have a broad common denominator in content and style, with personal differences. The group did not cease activity after composition of the first manuscripts, and its members and their successors continued to create in the same spirit and to combine their creation in the publication of the words of the ancients. Among the writers in the group, Rabbi Moses de Leon played a major part, writing most of the Zohar, but not all of it, with greater or lesser degrees of participation in the various stages. The group commenced composition of *Midrash ha-Ne'elam* for instance, before Moses de Leon began his activity.[23] We can ascribe to Moses de Leon most of the interpretations of the main body of the Zohar, which are similar in nature to his Hebrew writings. In other parts his degree of involvement is lesser, and he only adapted and drafted and enhanced. Such is the case in *Sifrut ha-Idra*, which will be discussed below, and about which Scholem himself wrote: "Naturally, we cannot determine if he [Joseph Gikatilla] was acquainted with the *Idrot* themselves in their present literary form, and if anyone says that Moses de Leon wrote them on the basis of ancient traditions, we do not consider this impossible *a priori*, and only detailed research will be able to determine in this respect."[24] I am now undertaking this detailed research, even though Scholem has since reconsidered the aforesaid view.

Moses de Leon attests to this group in *Sefer Ha-Rimmon*, when he says: "And those who understood the Torah concealed themselves behind their words. . .and for this reason the Torah has been much forgotten by Israel, until the Holy One Blessed be He aroused another spirit and men took good counsel to return to the true knowledge of the Holy One Blessed be He and understood things in the words of our Sages of blessed memory in the little that they awakened."[25] This is clearly a reference to the Zohar, which was written, in contrast to the previous Kabbalistic tradition, without concealment of things. Men who took for themselves another spirit appear here as members of one group. And the Zohar itself (Part 3, 58a) speaks of the convening of its group against the "forgetting of the Torah," as I have shown elsewhere.[26] R. Simeon b. Yohai's group, described in the Zohar and which recounts his teachings, can also serve as evidence of the way in which the book was written, and of a real fact that was merely ascribed to an earlier period. Several scholars already conjectured that the mythical description of Simeon b. Yohai's companions points to a historical group in the period of Moses de Leon,[27] although they were as yet unable to identify the members of the group and bring parallels from their writings. The group theory can also suggest an answer to the problem of the Zoharic traditions and customs that originate in Ashkenaz,[28] since the Zoharic group could also include ashkenazim such as Joseph ha-Arokh and David b. Judah he-Hasid; although the ashkenazi lineage of the latter is not certain, he was in any event well acquainted with ashkenazi tradition.[29] Moreover, even without the proofs, the group idea better fits the innovation and creation of a mystical secret doctrine such as the Kabbala, which is a secret tradition of a community. Clear examples of this are the groups of Kabbalists in Gerona and Safed (headed by Rabbi Isaac Luria—Ha-Ari, and his disciples) and Moses Luzzato's group, and the Hasidic communities. Individuals can be responsible only for the summarizing and preserving of what exists, and not for such astonishing creation as figures in the Zohar.

The group theory indeed raises many historical and philological problems, for some of which I have no answer. Moreover, the answers that I will give for others will certainly raise further difficulties and some will prove to be in need of correction, to the extent that it will be justifiable to argue that my theory has added rather than removed difficulties. Scholem's solution is far more clear-cut: one man wrote the Zohar with his intelligence and imagination, and it was he who invented the "literary framework" without any historical background,

the special language used by no man, and the literature quoted in
the Zohar and in other places without any books.[30] In this way we will
solve all difficulties by transferring them to the psychological realm
and to the boundless spirit of man. This applies likewise to the parallel
literature: Scholem supposed that it is all influenced by the Zohar
and imitates it, and the psychological problems raised by such a
solution are psychological problems and no more. Our method, on the
contrary, does not rely on only the mysteries of the human mind, but
also searches for a real background to the literary facts, and there
are many hidden and complex elements here that cannot be ignored.
I think that this path, however thorny, should be trodden, and I hope
that in the wake of this first attempt, other scholars will come and
build upon it and correct its errors.

Bahya B. Asher

In a study of this kind we must go beyond the framework of the main
Sefer ha-Zohar. The "canonical" Zohar contains various sections,
which are developed in the writings of other Kabbalists contemporary
to Moses de Leon. It is precisely in the study of these writings that
several of the keys to the Zohar are likely to be found. Most of this
chapter will be devoted to such a study, and we will commence with
the famous Torah commentator and Kabbalist, R. Bahya b. Asher.
Ephraim Gottlieb has already dealt with Bahya's relation to the Zohar
in detail in his book, *Ha-Kabbalah be-Khitvei Rabbenu Bahya ben
Asher*,[31] and produced an accurate and instructive compilation of all
the parallels between the Zohar and the writings of R. Bahya, with
a meticulous description of their nature. This work greatly facilitates
the task of anyone who wishes to understand the relation between
the two authors. The impression received on viewing this material,
however, completely contradicts the conclusion reached by its compiler.
Gottlieb, who first wrote his book as his doctoral thesis under the
guidance of Gershom Scholem, and after the latter had already
affirmed his most recent opinion concerning the composition of the
Zohar, concluded that Bahya copied from the Zohar with which he
was already familiar. However, all the long parallels in R. Bahya's
writings are formulated in a simple, condensed Hebrew. There is no
trace or hint that he is copying or translating an Aramaic text, where
the content is far more complex, and appears at times in the form
of dialogues between sages. Anyone versed in translations of the Zohar
into Hebrew (cf. David's translation dealt with below), knows that it
is easy to identify the Zohar background behind the translations. Here,

however, R. Bahya did not "come to grief" even once, and if we were not aware of the Zohar parallel we would never have suspected its existence!

Furthermore, some of the parallels to the Zohar appear in R. Bahya's works in his own name, and some as the opinion of another with whom he disagrees; sometimes he does not consider them as Kabbalistic matters at all. The parallels never appear as the words of the sages of blessed memory (indeed, the true words of the sages of blessed memory within the parallels are introduced by the words "our sages of blessed memory expounded"), and there is no hint that they belong to a pseudepigraphic work with which he was familiar, except for the two quotations referred to as "the Midrash of R. Simeon b. Yohai." These are unique in nature and will be discussed below; they also prove by their very existence that R. Bahya was not familiar with the other parallels in the form of an ancient midrash, or he would have noted this explicitly. From all this we learn that R. Bahya saw these things or heard them spoken even before they received their Zoharic form. He himself may have written some of the articles and participated in the Zohar circle.

Gottlieb submitted two arguments refuting such a possibility: firstly, that the Zohar does not normally translate long passages from other authors—and we can refute this by citing, for instance, the parallels from Gikatilla's works that also seem to have been adapted in the Zohar from an ancient source. Secondly, according to Gottlieb, the fact that the parallels from the Zohar are concentrated in certain *parashiot* indicates that only certain tracts from the Zohar reached R. Bahya. This too is not a decisive argument: R. Bahya may have been under the influence of the Zohar circle precisely in the latter stages of the writing of his exegesis (the parallels are mainly in the latter *parashiot* of the Torah); the argument can also be reversed to sustain that only parts of R. Bahya's exegesis reached the editor of the Zohar. Moreover, we will see that in a major subject of study Bahya does not follow the Zoharic line as consolidated in its final version, but adopts the system of a member of his circle, Joseph of Hamadan, who represents another stage and another direction in the thought of the circle.[32]

Bahya indeed quotes the *Midrash de-Simeon b. Yohai* in two places, and this is considered absolute proof that he was already familiar with the Zohar. A study of these two quotations will, however, change the picture: the quotations that Bahya uses show that the *Midrash de-Simeon b. Yohai* that he was familiar with is not identical to the Zohar we have before us. The two quotations are in Hebrew, and deal with the subject of angels in a non-Kabbalistic manner. One of the quotations does not figure in the early editions of the Zohar, and was introduced only in later editions from Bahya's exegesis.[33] The second section has a parallel in the Zohar,[34] but it is clear that the Zohar is not Bahya's source; rather, the *Midrash de R. Simeon b. Yohai* quoted by Bahya is the source of the Zohar. As the reader will see from the versions that I will cite, the quotations in the Zohar are in Aramaic and as a controversy between two sages, while the words of the Midrash cited by Bahya appear only as the combined words of both sages. Thus, the Zohar version would seem to be a development of the simple Hebrew midrash quoted by Bahya, as an expansion of the "narrative framework"; it is only reasonable that the framework was perfected as elaboration of the Zohar continued, as already shown by Scholem in another example.[35] This does not mean that Bahya simplified the Midrash, since he presented it explicitly as a literal quotation:

> And in the *Midrash de-R. Simeon b. Yohai* I saw: "and birds" [Gen. i,20]—this is Michael, as it is written [Is. vi,6) "then flew... unto me"; "will fly" [Gen. ibid.]—this is Gabriel, as it is written [Dan. ix,21] "being caused to fly swiftly"; "upon the earth" [Gen. ibid.]—this is Raphael; "on the face of the firmament of the heaven"—this is Uriel.[36]

The parallel in the Zohar, Part I, 46b, reads:

> "And birds to fly above the earth." The form *yeofef* [to fly] is peculiar. R. Simeon said: There is here a mystical allusion. "Birds" refers to the angel Michael, of whom it is written: "Then flew one of the Seraphim unto me" [Is. vi, 6]. "To fly" refers to Gabriel, of whom it is written, "The man Gabriel whom I had seen at first in a vision being caused to fly quickly" [Dan. ix, 21]. "Upon the earth": R. Abba says, "This is Raphael [lit. healer of God], who is charged to heal upon the earth, and through whom also he heals of his maladies." "On the face of the firmament of the heaven": this is Uriel.

From this we learn that for R. Bahya the R. Simeon midrash was merely an angelological midrash with which the writers of the Zohar were familiar before the final drafting of the book. This midrash can be identified perhaps with *Midrash ha-Mal'akhim*, quotations of which were preserved, in a mixture of Hebrew and Aramaic, in literature known to the Zohar circle.[37] While the quotations are not attributed here to R, Simeon b. Yohai, one of the books cited is.[38] It is also possible that the Midrash was known by two names: one relating to its content, *Midrash ha-Mal'akhim*; and one relating to its author, Midrash of R. Simeon b. Yohai. The attribution of the midrash to R. Simeon b. Yohai might also reflect a further stage of its development and incorporation into Zoharic literature.

The elaboration of a pseudoepigraphic midrash within the work is a Zohar characteristic. Below, I shall discuss several other cases where the Zohar and members of the Zohar circle elaborate a common source. I have already demonstrated in the past the existence of such a midrash: that of Mehetabel, the daughter of Matred, where the Zohar and R. Todros Abulafia developed a common source.[39] The midrash cited by Bahya is indeed closer to the Zohar, being attributed to R. Simeon b. Yohai, while the protagonist of the Mehetabel midrash is R. Yohanan b. Zakkai; this midrash may also have influenced the literary form of the Zohar.[40] (We found in yet another book, related to R. Bahya's book, the *Ta'amei ha-Mitzvot* (second version), a relationship similar to R. Bahya's to the Zohar; it also contains a midrash that served as a source to the Zohar.[41])

Joseph Ben Shalom Ashkenazi Ha-Arokh

Another remnant of the Midrash of R. Simeon b. Yohai (which as already noted may be the same as the *Midrash ha-Mal'akhim* that was developed subsequently in the Zohar is to be found in R. Joseph ben Shalom Ashkenazi's commentary to the *Bereshit* section of the *Midrash Genesis Rabba*[42]: "And so the Holy Rabbi R. Simeon b. Yohai said: 'the souls of the wicked are the demons of the world.'" There is a similar passage in the Zohar, formulated in an Aramaic very similar to R. Joseph's citation: "R. Judah said: 'the souls of the wicked are the demons of this world.'"[43] This was not, however, in my opinion, R. Joseph's source, as may be proven by several factors: a) The Zoharic passage is attributed not to R. Simeon b. Yohai but to R. Judah. b) Other than this sentence, no explicit quotations from the Zohar or from R. Simeon b. Yohai appear in R. Joseph's writings. c) The sentence does not deal with Kabbala but with demonology, as do the quotations mentioned in the writings of R. Bahya. d) The same sentence also appears in the *Midrash ha-Ne'elam*, where it is formulated in Hebrew and attributed to an ancient source: "We have learnt: it is the souls of the wicked that are the demons in the world."[44] The *Midrash ha-Ne'elam* habitually uses the term "we have learnt" and similar terms when referring to real sources.[45] Furthermore, the same sentence, cited in Hebrew in *Ra'aya Meheimana* and in *Tikkunei Zohar*, is given as a quotation from "the Sages of Matnitin" (Mishna)—"As it is written by the Sages of Matnitin: The souls of the wicked are the demons in the world."[46] The author of *Ra'aya Meheimana* habitually uses the term "Sages of Matnitin" only for what he considers to be the words of the "traditional" sages and not Zoharic passages, which he refers to in other terms.[47]

On the other hand, several difficulties also arise: a) If R. Joseph took his quotation from the Hebrew version before it was elaborated in the Zohar, why is it written in Zoharic Aramaic? b) Why does he attribute the saying to R. Simeon b. Yohai, when it is not attributed to R. Simeon either in *Midrash ha-Ne'elam* or in *Ra'aya Meheimana* and *Tikkunei Zohar*? c) R. Joseph also deals with this subject elsewhere, but not in the same language, and he attributes it not to R. Simeon b. Yohai but to *Pirkei de-R. Eliezer*. For instance: "This is the explanation of the statement in *Pirkei de-R. Eliezer*, that the demons come from the soul of the wicked."[48] We have found no such passage in the *Midrash Pirkei de-R. Eliezer*, and the statement in Chapter 34 relates only to the generation of the Flood who became spirits, and thus their bodies could not rise for the Day of Judgment, as explicitly opposed to other wicked men.[49] How then are we to explain this?

A possible resolution of these problems lies in the assumption that R. Joseph was involved in the creation of the Zohar. The idea of the souls of the wicked as demons does not exist in the writings of the sages, but somehow penetrated to Medieval Jewry from Hellenistic Jewish literature (of Josephus Flavius and Philo of Alexandria, for instance) or from Christianity;[50] and reached the Hasidic circles of Ashkenaz (we have also found it in *Sefer Hasidim*[51]; from there, like many Hasidic-Ashkenazi works of Torah, it reached the Sephardi Kabbala. The Zohar circle found it incorporated in the collection of angelology known as the Midrash of R. Simeon b. Yohai, and coupled it with the aforesaid saying in *Pirkei de-R. Eliezer*. As scholars of the Zohar know, the Midrash of R. Eliezer is one of the most important sources of the Zohar, and its protagonist, R. Eliezer b. Hyrkanus, evolved in the Zohar into R. Simeon b. Yohai.[52] (Possibly the saying had its source with R. Eliezer and was attributed to R. Simeon b. Yohai only after the fusion of the two personalities, and this is not the same midrash as quoted by R. Bahya. As already noted, this midrash or a like midrash is called simply *Midrash ha-Mal'akhim*.) Subsequently the idea was translated into Aramaic, as were the other sayings of R. Simeon b. Yohai, and with the development of the Zohar's "narrative framework," it was attributed to one of the members of R. Simeon b. Yohai's circle, namely to

R. Judah. R. Joseph was familiar with the idea in both its stages, as the words of R. Eliezer and as those of R. Simeon b. Yohai. Both stages of the saying have been conserved in the Zohar: the Aramaic form attributed to R. Simeon b. Yohai (the author of *Tikkunei Zohar* also found it in this form), and the final Zoharic form. Since R. Joseph b. Shalom Ashkenazi was familiar with both these forms, we might assume that he was a member of the Zohar group and participated in its creation. This might also be concluded perhaps directly from the language of the quotation; R. Joseph does not cite any book or midrash, but what "the Holy R. Simeon b. Yohai" said, as if he had heard it from R. Simeon b. Yohai's mouth, or more precisely from the leader of the group whom they called R. Simeon b. Yohai. This might also be surmised from the use of the expression "the Holy Rabbi," since no one in Medieval Jewry referred to R. Simeon b. Yohai of the Mishnah in such terms.

R. Joseph's affinity with the Zohar group is further confirmed by his doctrine. He was obviously acquainted with many subjects dealt with in the Zohar, but gave them a different interpretation, colored by his own Kabbalistic doctrine, which is completely different in nature and tendency. This can be seen, for instance, in the descriptions of the brain, parallel to the *Idra*, in his commentary of the *Sefer Yetzira*,[53] and in the way he uses sources such as *Sefer ha-Bahir* and the writings of *Hug ha-Iyyun*.[54] In this context, R. Joseph's ties with R. David b. Judah he-Hasid should be noted. Certainly, this interesting and secret Kabbalist,[55] R. Joseph b. Shalom Ashkenazi, and his special relation to the Zohar, constitute an important subject that should be studied in far greater detail than the scope of this chapter allows.

The *Idrot*

One section of the Zohar that is particularly important in the context of our study is that of the *Idrot*. This section presents a specific Kabbalistic myth, with ancient sources,[56] that are still in the main an enigma. The Zohar itself also ascribes particular importance to the *Idrot*. It attributes to them the revelation of secrets that are more profound than its other parts,[57] as does the late Kabbala, and principally Lurianic Kabbala, which was based on this doctrine. This section would appear to be made up of an anonymous Mishnah, called *Sifra di-Tsni'uta* (Zohar, Part II, 176b—179a),[58] and of several Assemblies (*Idrot*),[59] in which R. Simeon b. Yohai and his friends interpret this Mishnah. Scholem maintains that the Zohar only gives the impression that the *Sifra di-Tsni'uta* and the *Idrot* belong to two different strata; in his opinion, both sections were in fact written by one author, R. Moses de Leon. This claim, which contradicts the assertion of the main body of the Zohar, requires proof. The existence of a stylistic similarity is not sufficient. To prove that the author is one and the same, it must be shown that the author of the *Idrot* is familiar with the secrets of *Sifra di-Tsni'uta*, and for positive identification, parallels must be found in the writings of R. Moses de Leon. In the research literature, I found no evidence even of an internal Zoharic examination (apparently, because of the view that the division between *Sifra di-Tsni'uta* and the *Idrot* is a literary fiction). To my mind, the findings indicate the complete reverse. The *Sifra di-Tsni'uta* remains obscure even after study of the *Idrot*. Most of the enigmatic mythical material is not discussed at all in the *Idrot*, and cannot be understood through a study of the *Idrot*.[60] The commentaries contained in the *Idrot* do not always seem to contain the true meaning (as will be seen); and in cases where the commentary and the original do coincide, the original core of the *Sifra di-Tsni'uta* has often been improved or reworded in accordance with the commentary of the *Idrot*.[61] Further, in many places, sentences indicated as citations from the *Sifra di-Tsni'uta* or from *Tseni'uta di-Sifra* are quoted in the Zohar, and above all in the *Idrot*. Some of these citations have absolutely no source in the *Sifra di-Tsni'uta* known to us,[62] and others appear there in completely different wording, adapted to meet the aims of the *Idra*,[63] and even in two different versions, in each of the *Idrot*;[64] in one case the text of the *Idra* is even based on a faulty reading of the text of *Sifra di-Tsni'uta*.[65] As regards the contents, the new version at times appears quite the reverse of what is written in *Sifra di-Tsni'uta*.[66] At other times the author of the *Idra* explicitly disagrees with the contents of *Sifra di-Tsni'uta*.[67]

The main body of the Zohar itself, in my opinion, intimates the possible existence of another commentary of *Sifra di-Tsni'uta*, which differs from that expounded in the *Idra*. The subject of *Sifra di-Tsni'uta* is explained in the paragraph preceding this section (Zohar, II, 176a—b), serving as a kind of preface:

Now what is this "Book of the Hidden Mystery"? said R. Simeon. It contains five sections which are included in a great palace, and fill the whole earth. Said R. Judah: If these are included, they are of more worth than any other tome. In truth, replied R. Simeon, this is true for one who has entered and come out of the courts of wisdom, but not for one who did not enter and come out. There is a parable for it: Once there was a man who dwelt amongst the mountains, and was a complete stranger to

the ways of townsfolk. He sowed wheat, but knew no better than
to consume it in its natural condition. One day he went down
into a city, and there was a loaf of good bread placed before him.
He asked what it was, and was informed that it was bread and
was meant to eat. He ate it and liked it. "What is it made of?"
he said. They told him "Wheat". Later, he was given fine cake
kneaded in oil. He tasted it, and again asked: "And this, of what
is it made?" The same reply was made as before: "Of wheat".
Finally he was treated to some royal confection[68] flavoured with
oil and honey. Once more he asked his question and obtained
the same reply. Then he said: "Certainly, I have all these at my
command, because I eat the essential constituent of all, namely
wheat". Thus, through his untutored taste he remained a
stranger to all these delicious flavors, and their enjoyment was
lost to him.

This parable contains a polemical note. There were certainly
those who maintained that the chapters of *Sifra di-Tsni'uta* in their
possession were "of more worth than any other." The Zohar maintains
that the *Sifra di-Tsni'uta* is the "essential constituent," but only for
those who "have entered and come out" and understand the correct
exegesis of these chapters. Those who waive these commentaries
resemble the man who waives the delicacies baked from wheat, and
eats the wheat as it grew (the Zohar does not advocate "natural food").
There is possibly also an implication here that, as the preparation
changes the form of the actual wheat, so the author of the Zohar
introduced his commentaries and refinements into the original text
of *Sifra di-Tsni'uta* in his possession. Basically, however, these
commentaries are an adaptation of the *Sifra di-Tsni'uta* within the
Idrot. This is implied also in the term "entering and coming out."
Perhaps more than an allusion to the perfect mystic such as R. Akiva,
who "entered in peace and came out in peace," it is an abbreviation
of "who entered and came out of *bei Idra* (Assembly Hall), for only
this is the true perfection in the eyes of the Zohar and the Zohar
group.[69] As will be seen below, in *Idra Rabba* itself various contending
commentaries were conserved, which also use their polemic
rhetorically, and censure those who "have never entered or come
out."[70] In any case from the polemic expressed in the above parable
we learn that there were people who contented themselves with the
Sifra di-Tsni'uta without the exegesis of the *Idra*.

The above arguments suffice to refute the claim that one author
wrote all the works, and the claim of the integral relationship between
the *Sifra di-Tsni'uta* and the *Idrot*. Let us examine the assertion that

Moses de Leon wrote this section of the Zohar. Textual proof is difficult
to find. While the doctrine of the *Idrot* is developed in many parallels
in the writings of other contemporary Kabbalists, there is absolutely
no trace of the doctrine of *Sifra di-Tsni'uta* or the *Idrot* in the Hebrew
writings of R. Moses de Leon.[71] Why, then, should the composition of
this section be attributed precisely to him? We might perhaps ignore
the methodical difficulty and assume that Moses de Leon was the
founder of the doctrine, even if it does not appear in his Hebrew
writings; possibly the other members of the group imitated his Zohar
writings. However, further study will show that the members of the
group were not familiar with the *Sifra di-Tsni'uta* and the *Idrot* as
they appear in the Zohar or as we know them, but with another text,
which they elaborated, just as R. Moses de Leon elaborated it in the
Zohar; the members of the group and the Zohar had equal status in
this respect. Let us look at these parallels.

Several Kabbalistic writings parallel to the *Idrot* were written
in the same period as the Zohar (in addition to the writings of Gikatilla
and Rabbi Joseph of Hamadan that will be dealt with below, I also
refer to the author of the *Sefer ha-Yihud*[72] and the author of *Sod ha-
Gevanim le-Mineihem*[73] and similar writings). However, while parallel,
but containing the typical general lines specific to each one of them,
these writings differ from the *Idrot* in several aspects common to them
all: a) None have any trace of the "narrative framework" relating to
R. Simeon b. Yohai and his companions. b) None contain the climate
of the mystical revelation and the Messianic meaning or the sense
of *Tikkun* characterizing the *Idra*.[74] c) All lack the dualistic element
of the *Idra*. It seems more likely, therefore, that these authors were
acquainted with the *Idra* (or *Sifra di-Tsni'uta*) in a form other than
we know it in the Zohar today. Whoever was responsible for the final
version of the *Idrot* (R. Moses de Leon?) would appear to have added
elements that it did not contain originally. Perhaps he wished to merge
the old version with another text dealing with dualism between the
almighty concealed God who is entirely mercy, and the God of
Righteousness, identified with the God of the Torah and known by
the Jewish sacred names, that is, a text whose first source is in the
ancient gnosis. In his elaboration, the author of the final version also
added the experiences of his companions, which he ascribed to the
companions of R. Simeon b. Yohai, and the feeling of redemption and
of *tikkun* present in their meetings. He even alluded to an actual
historic event.[75] This elaboration was a gradual process; throughout
the writing of the Zohar the original text was elaborated and
reelaborated, and each time other principles were underscored,
according to the moods prevailing in the circle.[76]

Rabbi Joseph Gikatilla

Scholem dealt extensively with this Kabbalist's relationship to R. Moses de Leon,[77] a relationship that increases in complexity as research continues (in fact R. Joseph is depicted as the dominant personality of the two!),[78] as does his relationship to the Zohar. (Recently Dr. Asi Farber identified long passages in Gikatilla's Hebrew writings that also exist in Aramaic in the Zohar.)[79] Such a connection, in a Kabbalist writer of Gikatilla's stature, make his writings a cornerstone of Zohar scholarship. We have chosen to study some of the salient and numerous parallels in Gikatilla's writings to the section of the *Idrot* in the Zohar.[80]

I shall commence with a famous example, which has not yet been examined exhaustively. In *Idra Rabba* (Zohar, II, 134a) we read: "Rabbi Eleazar rose and said: all things depend on fortune, even the Book of the Law in the Temple, this we have understood from the *Sifra di-Tsni'uta*." This saying does not exist in the *Sifra di-Tsni'uta* in our possession. The Hebrew, epigrammatic language employed proves that it is, nonetheless, a quotation. In R. Joseph Gikatilla's writings the epigram is attributed to the "Sages of blessed memory" (the rabbis of the talmudic era), and not once but three times![81] It is not, however, a saying of the sages of blessed memory, and only for the first part, "all things depend on fortune," have we found ancient sources[82] (there is a parallel to this part in the *Sifra di-Tsni'uta*).[83] Nor should it be thought that an ancient midrash was the source of the saying, since the word *hekhal* (temple) in the sense of the holy ark of the Torah is specific to the Sephardi communities[84] and dates from a later period. (The saying was apparently influenced by the well-known Latin adage: *habent sua fata libelli*). It is interesting that R. Moses de Leon, in his Hebrew writings, also alludes to this saying (although he does not attribute it to the sages of blessed memory);[85] it seems to me that he was influenced in his words precisely by Gikatilla, who also refers to the subject in other places, without explicitly noting the sages of blessed memory.[86] In the context of our study, we can see that Gikatilla's Kabbalist interpretation of the saying is far closer to the interpretation of the *Idra* than R. Moses de Leon's interpretation.[87] The expression "the sages of blessed memory" cannot be said to allude to the Zohar, because such is not a characteristic of Gikatilla's writings. (Only in one other place have we found that Gikatilla introduces a Zoharic homily apparently with the words "a saying of the sages of blessed memory";[88] most surprisingly R. Moses de Leon also quotes this homily in his Hebrew writings, with the attribution to the sages of blessed memory, precisely from R. Joseph Gikatilla's

Sha'arei Ora).[89] It may logically be assumed that Gikatilla and the Zohar both drew from a no longer extant Spanish pseudomidrashic text,[90] which can be identified with the first edition of *Sifra di-Tsni'uta*. We have already viewed such sources above and will study other such sources, which are common to the Zohar and to the Zohar circle.

Let us now look at one of Gikatilla's compositions which is parallel to the *Idra*, "The Secret of the Thirteen Attributes emanating from the Supreme Crown and which are called the Springs of Salvation".[91] I have chosen this composition because the parallel is lengthy and very close. In my study I wish merely to revert to Gershom Scholem's original opinion. Before he became convinced of R. Moses de Leon's authorship of the Zohar, he expressed the following opinion vis-à-vis the "Secret of the 13 Attributes:" "There is here a Hebrew source parallel to the words of the *Idra* and it is possible that it is not taken from the *Idra Rabba* but parallel to it, because it contains things that were dropped from our version of the *Idra* or which the editors of the *Idra* did not include in *Tikkunei D'ikena* (the locks of the beard) and which were known to the author of this passage."[92] Scholem did not return to this subject when he formulated his new opinion on the composition of the Zohar; in my opinion, however, his original statement has not lost its validity, and I wish to reinforce it.

The composition enumerates and describes the thirteen attributes of compassion as lights and springs emanating from the *sefira* of *Keter*. This description parallels those of *Sifra di-Tsni'uta* and *Idra Rabba*, but without the basic element contained in the Zoharic sources: the anthropomorphic principle, namely the parallelization of the thirteen attributes to the thirteen locks (*tikkunim*) of the beard of the "Large Countenance." Which composition has a more original character? In order to answer this question we will begin by comparing two passages from the two compositions. The first includes the eleventh and twelfth *Tikkunim*. Gikatilla's description contains many details not found in the *Idra* (Zohar, III, 134a–b), including technical names of the attribute, called here the "Well of Prophecy" and the "Foundation of the Kings." From this we conclude that Gikatilla had a more complete version, as already noted by Gershom Scholem.[93] It might also be shown, however, that it is not a question only of a more complete version of the Zohar, but of a third version, which was elaborated both by the Zohar and by Gikatilla. In this common version, the eleventh attribute was lacking, as shown by the fact that the Zohar and Gikatilla each completed it in their own way: the Zohar, in the eleventh *Tikkun* (attribute or beard lock), notes only: "And the eleventh, because one hair is not pre-eminent over another hair, with 'mercy unto Abraham.' In other words, it does not describe the attribute and its meaning as it does for the other *Tikkunim*, but merely notes the appropriate *Tikkun* of the beard from the *Sifra di-Tsni'uta*[94] and the appropriate attribute from the thirteen articles of Micah.[95] Gikatilla describes this attribute at length, but his description of the twelfth attribute is a continuation of the description of that attribute. Indeed his description of the eleventh attribute revolves around the "secret of the oath," connected to the twelfth of the articles of Micah—"which you swore unto our fathers." Gikatilla thus divided the twelfth attribute into two in order to make up the number.

Let us now study the second of the attributes of compassion, which is described as follows by Gikatilla:

> And from this Crown 325[96] kinds of lights emanate and all are called light of countenance,[97] and they include "pardons iniquity" [literally: lifting iniquity][98] when he appears on the judgements, and this is the secret of [Numbers vi, 25—26]: "May the Lord make his face to shine upon you, may the Lord lift up his countenance upon you," and the secret of [Exodus xxvii, 20]: "pure oil olive beaten for the lamp." And when these lights appear there will be full repentance and there is no darkness there and no judgement. And from this place "the skin of Moses' face shone" [Exodus xxxiv, 35], our teacher of blessed memory,[99] and the secret of [Samuel i, ii, 1], together with Isaiah lxi, 10): "my horn is exalted in the Lord," which was anointed with the horn of anointing, "and exalt the horn of his anointed" [Samuel i, ii, 10], all are alluded to here.[100]

In the *Idra Rabba*, (Zohar, III, 132b) this attribute is described as follows.

> Second lock. The hair expands from one end of the mouth to the other.[101] Arise R. Hizkiya and stand in your place[102] and declare the worthiness of this part of the holy beard. Rabbi Hizkiya arose and said [Song of Songs vii, 11]: I am my beloved's, and his desire is towards me. Who is the cause that I am my beloved's? Because his desire is toward me.[103] I have meditated, and behold,[104] I have beheld the most excellent light of the supernal lights. It shone forth, and ascended on three hundred and twenty-five sides. And in that light was a certain darkness[105] washed away, as when a man bathes in a deep river, whose divided waters flow around him on every side from that part which is above. And that light ascends to the shore of the deep superior sea, for all good

openings and dignities are disclosed in that opening. I asked of them, what is the interpretation of that which I beheld; and commencing, they replied: you have beheld iniquity being pardoned [noseh avon]. He said: This is my second lock, and sat down. R. Simeon said: Now is the universe united together [or mitigated]. Blessed are you, R. Hizkiya, of the Ancient of the Ancient Ones. R. Simeon said: All the lights, the companions who come under this holy seal, I bring as witnesses the highest heavens and the highest holy earth, because now I can see what man has not beheld from that time, when Moses for the second time ascended Mount Sinai. For I see that my countenance shines like the vehement splendor of the sun, which is about to issue forth for the healing of the universe. As it is written, [Mal. iii, 20]: "But to you who fear my name shall the sun of righteousness arise, and healing in its wings". Further, I know that my countenance shines; Moses neither knew nor perceived this. As it is written (Exodus xxxiv, 29): "And Moses did not know that the skin of his face shone". Further, I behold with my eyes those thirteen attributes engraved before me, and like flaming light they shine. And when anyone of these is explained by your mouth, that same at once is raised, and adorned, and crowned, and concealed in the concealment of the locks of the beard. . . .Come, my holy companions, for surely there will not be such an event[106] until the King the Messiah comes. . . .

The passage in Gikatilla's writings is technical in nature, and contains the term "light of countenance" which is not explicit in the Zohar: the matter of the shining of Moses' face and the horn of the Messiah in Gikatilla's composition are a part of the description of the attribute. The Zohar contains no theoretical description of this attribute, but only its visionary revelation. Without the parallel in Gikatilla's writings we would have been completely ignorant of the integral link between the shining of Moses' face and this Tikkun, since the shining of the face appears in the Zohar only when R. Simeon b. Yohai expresses his excitement, in his reaction to the description of the revelation of the Tikkun, comparing himself to Moses. Likewise the messianic significance of the revelation of the Idra, presented here as an intermediary stage between the revelation of Sinai and the messianic epoch, is logical in accordance with Gikatilla's version, which links this Tikkun with the "horn of the Messiah."[107] The Zohar circle would seem to have had a "dry" technical description like Gikatilla's in its possession, and the author of the Zohar introduced into it the experiences of the circle, including the mystical and the messianic element. In my opinion, the opposite view, namely the claim that Gikatilla drew his technical description from the Zohar, is philologically quite impossible.

Rabbi Joseph of Hamadan

In order to determine which is the earlier version of this *Tikkun*, and even to answer the general question of whether Gikatilla's description of the thirteen attributes is prior to the thirteen attributes in *Idra Rabba*, we will have to turn to another Kabbalist, Rabbi Joseph of Hamadan.[108] Research into this perplexing Kabbalist, whose origins remain undetermined,[109] was commenced by Gershom Scholem[110] and continued by such important scholars as Alexander Altmann,[111] Ephraim Gottlieb[112] and, until this day, by Moshe Idel;[113] and some of Joseph of Hamadan's writings have appeared in recent scientific publications.[114] Sufficient use of this research literature has not yet been made with respect to the Zohar, since scholars generally believed that R. Joseph was merely imitating the Zohar with which he was already familiar. Certainly his style is similar to that of the Zohar— at times he also writes in Aramaic and uses terms with which we are acquainted through the Zohar. We also find parallels between the contents of his writings and the Zohar, and above all with the *Idrot*. Some of his very bold anthropomorphic descriptions have parallels in the *Idrot*, and some go beyond those of the *Idrot*; the *Idrot* only describe the divine faces, and R. Joseph describes every single limb, including the breasts and the pubic hair.

The relationship between R. Joseph and the Zohar certainly merits further research. R. Joseph was a contemporary of R. Moses de Leon,[115] and the Zohar is never mentioned by name or quoted in his writings (he refers only to "the aid that will come to me from above"[116]). Hence, detailed comparison between R. Joseph's works and between the Zohar and the other members of the circle is required. Such a comparison can be of assistance in the question of the relationship between the description of the thirteen attributes in the *Idra*, which are parallel to the "locks of the beard," and Gikatilla's aforementioned description. The general assumption is that Gikatilla "stripped" the beard away from the attributes since the bold anthropomorphism was not in keeping with the nature of his Kabbala. Certainly the anthropomorphic element, like the sexual element, is more moderate in Gikatilla's writings than in the Zohar. This is not the correct explanation, however. Firstly, Gikatilla also knows about the "supernal *tikkunim* which are called the beard," not however in the *sefira* of *Keter* (crown) but in the *sefira* of *Tif'eret* (splendor).[117] And secondly and most importantly, R. Joseph of Hamadan, who had absolutely no prejudices against anthropomorphism, does not follow the *Idra* either: the thirteen attributes of *rahamim* (compassion) are described on several occasions in his writings, but never once are they linked to the beard,[118] although a description of the beard does exist in his writings.[119]

There is one description of the thirteen attributes in R. Joseph of Hamadan's works that lends itself to comparison with the *Idra* and with Gikatilla's aforementioned composition and that has certain affinities with both of them.[120] On the one hand it is of a completely anthropomorphic nature as in the Zohar, but on the other hand it does not link the thirteen attributes to God's beard, but to other limbs, such as the eyes, ears, and the nose; it also contains various details not mentioned in the Zohar, but which are mentioned in R. Gikatilla's composition. I shall illustrate this through a parallel in R. Joseph of Hamadan's composition to the second article cited above, in Gikatilla's work and in the Zohar (in fact in R. Joseph of Hamadan's work the passage describes the twelfth article). It will be seen that R. Joseph also finds within the article the source of the shining of Moses' face, and the lighting of the face, like Gikatilla, and unlike the Zohar:

> The twelfth light parallels *ve-nakeh* [and exonerates]. . . and parallels the Supernal Face of the Supernal Form Blessed be He.[121] And of this it is written "the Lord make his face to shine upon you, and be gracious unto you" and from there two hundred and fifty worlds give light, and thence the face of Moses our teacher shone, as it is written: "for the skin of Moses's face shone."[122]

Hence, it would seem that the members of the Zohar circle were familiar with a common text describing the thirteen attributes of compassion as lights or springs, like the known texts of *Hug ha-'Iyyun*, and the different members of the circle elaborated it and completed it, each giving it an anthropomorphic nuance according to his inclination and combining it with other texts known to them. This method is certainly employed frequently in the writings of R. Joseph Ashkenazi and R. Joseph of Hamadan. Both, for instance, developed a *Hug ha-'Iyyun* treatise that describes the thirty-two paths of wisdom;[123] such a method is not foreign to the Zohar either.[124] A clear example of this, which also deals with the subjects under discussion, is to be found in a commentary on the thirteen attributes by R. Moses of Burgos[125] of the Gnostic Kabbalists' circle, which interprets the attributes in accordance with God's stature (the beard is also mentioned there, p. 309), elaborating on "what was revealed to our lord R. Ishmael." Such a description of the creation of the *Idra* could also apply to the composition of the main body of the Zohar, since the identification of the thirteen lights with the "locks of the beard" at times seems in the Zohar a rather artificial compounding of two descriptions.

(We have found a passage in *Livnat ha-Sappir* that represents a kind of intermediary stage between Gikatilla and the *Idra*. It is written in a language like that of the Zohar and uses the term "the Ancient One," but it calls the thirteen attributes "springs of salvation" as Gikatilla does, without identifying them with the beard:

> "Good Oil" [Ps. cxxxiii, 2] these are the thirteen streams of pure balsam which flow from the thirteen springs of salvation, the thirteen attributes of the Ancient One, firstly "on the Head" [ibid.] this is *Hokhma* [Wisdom]. . . and secondly "on the Beard" [ibid.] this is *Hesed* [Lovingkindness]. What is *pi middotav* [the skirts of his garment]—all of them [*middotav* means also: His attributes].[126]

The use of this verse from Psalms for the description of the supernal abundance going down onto the beard of the Small Countenance and onto his *middotav* also exists in the Zohar (Zohar, III, 7b; 88b; 295b—*Idra Zuta*). The passage from *Livnat ha-Sappir* apparently recognizes only the existence of the lower beard, because this passage also shares in the monotheistic conception described below.)

In order to determine whether R. Joseph of Hamadan based his conception on the *Idrot*, a comparison of the method employed in each of the sources is also necessary. The *Idrot* are based, as it is known, on the dualism of two Countenances which in general are opposed to each other: the "Large Countenance" namely "the long-suffering God" which is parallel principally to the *sefira* of *Keter* (Crown);[127] and "the Small Countenance," "the Impatient One," which is parallel to the lower *sefirot* apart from *Malkhut* (Kingship), namely the male *sefirot*, with *Tif'eret* (Beauty) in the center. This is not so in R. Joseph of Hamadan's conception. He sees *Keter*, which is the "Large Countenance," only as the brain of the single male divine form, or encircling his head.[128] The "Small Countenance" in R. Joseph's writings is a name for the *Shekhina* (divine presence) and is female. With such a difference, the entire nature of the method is of course modified, and its dualism is greatly mitigated,[129] since the dual sexuality of the divinity is the very foundation of all the doctrine of the Kabbala, and also contains within it the element of harmony, love, and erotic union, and more simply than in the doctrine of the *Idra* (indeed the *Idra* also establishes the harmony between the Countenances "at a propitious hour"). How is this difference to be interpreted? If we say that R. Joseph is influenced by the Zohar and is imitating it, we will have to conclude that he strayed from the words of the *Idra* here. We might then ask how he could have made such an error in a subject that is so general and basic in the *Idrot*. We will particularize our question in the study of the following statement by R. Joseph: "And there is no hair in the beard of the Small Countenance. And therefore there is hair in the beard of the male, and there is no hair in the beard of the female which is the Small Countenance, which is the *sefira* of *Malkhut* who adorns herself in front of the Holy King Blessed be He."[130] How could anyone imitating and continuing the *Idra*, a large part of which is devoted to the description of the beard of the Small Countenance and its locks, claim that the Small Countenance has no beard, like the woman formed in his image? Gershom Scholem's explanation that this is not an error but an intentional change that R. Joseph made in the Kabbala of the *Idra*,[131] is also problematical: anyone attempting to imitate the *Idra* may be presumed to respect the Zohar, and how would he not accept its opinion in such a fundamental matter? Moreover, if he disagrees with the whole doctrine of the Zohar, why would he imitate it?

However, on closer study, the interpretation, "Small Countenance" = *Malkhut* is not so strange. This would seem to have been the original interpretation of the Zohar circle, and of the first version of *Sifra di-Tsni'uta*, and only subsequently was it changed in the *Idrot*. In this case, R. Joseph had a source to draw from, and did not depend on the Zohar in our possession. Certainly the homiletic logic behind the dualism of the Small Countenance opposite the Large Countenance is more suited to male and female than to two males. Let us now study the opening sentence of *Sifra di-Tsni'uta* (Zohar, II, 176a): "For formerly when there was no balance, they did not look each other in the face, and the kings of ancient time died." If we were not familiar with the *Idra*, we would have said that the two looking each other in the face are the male and the female, *Tiferet* and *Malkhut*, and not the two males, the Large Countenance and the Small Countenance. Indeed another section of the Zohar, which from several points of view might well be called *Idra*[132] too, opens with a parallel text, which deals explicitly with male and female: "When their faces were turned to one another, it was well with the world:

'How good and how pleasant' (Ps. cxxxxiii, 1), but when the male turned his face from the female, it was ill with the world." It should also be noted that this sentence is based on the talmudic description of the cherubs in the Temple (according to the rabbis of the talmudic era too they were male and female),[133] and elsewhere the Talmud calls the two cherubs "Large Countenance and Small Countenance";[134] it may be supposed that this epithet is one of the sources for the Zoharic phraseology, "Large Countenance" and "Small Countenance,"[135] and for the two faces referred to at the beginning of *Sifra di-Tsni'uta*. Another factor contributing to the interpretation of the first sentence of *Sifra di-Tsni'uta* as referring to male and female is the use of the word "balance" (*matkela*), which means harmony of erotic union.[136]

Moreover, without the *Idrot*, I think it unlikely that we would have interpreted "Small Countenance" in *Sifra di-Tsni'uta* as the male and not the female, since nowhere in *Sifra di-Tsni'uta* does the use of the term imply this. (It even seems that the meaning of the descriptions of the locks of the beard of the Small Countenance in the third chapter of *Sifra di-Tsni'uta* [Zohar, II: 177b] which commences: "Nine are said to be the locks of the Beard," does not deal at all with the divine countenance, but with the beard of mortal man, and in accordance with the Zoharic physiognomy which links the divine countenance to the human countenance. This is the simple explanation of the sentence: "Whoever is found among them [i.e. the nine locks of the beard] is found strong and robust," and the two beards, the human and the divine, are explicitly mentioned again subsequently: "When any one[137] dreams that he takes the upper beard of a man in his hand. . .and all the more so when the supernal beard irradiates the inferior."[138]) Further, I have found one passage where R. Joseph cites his own version of the doctrine of the *Idra*, relating the Small Countenance to the *Shekhina*, in the name of "a few Kabbalists said,"[139] showing that this is not an independent elaboration of the *Idra*, but that he heard it in the discussions of the circle. Indeed we will study below an exceptional passage from *Idra Rabba*, which is interpreted in accordance with this doctrine. R. David ben Judah he-Hasid also supports R. Joseph's interpretation of the "Small Countenance" as a name of the *Shekhina*,[140] and he is a very important witness since, as I shall demonstrate subsequently, he was also connected with the Zohar circle, and while a few stylistic influences of R. Joseph of Hamadan are to be found in his writings, his Kabbalistic doctrine was quite different, and his interpretation of the Small Countenance cannot be attributed to the direct influence of R. Joseph.

The second aspect of R. Joseph's doctrine is, as said, the unity of the male image of the deity.[141] This unity seems to contradict the doctrine of the *Idra*, which R. Joseph's doctrine resembles in its anthropomorphic nature. It could be asserted that R. Joseph modified the *Idra* for theological reasons, and changed it from dualistic to monistic. In response, however, it should be noted that from this point of view R. Joseph's doctrine resembles that of the early Kabbalists and the Kabbalot of the other members of the circle, such as the passages from *Livnat ha-Sappir* and R. Joseph Gikatilla[142] cited above, and even the Kabbala of the main body of the Zohar, which contains no trace of dualism or of antagonism between *Keter* and *Tiferet* (parallel to the Small Countenance and the Large Countenance in the *Idrot*). A meticulous study of the main body of the Zohar will reveal that many of the descriptions existing in the *Idrot* also exist in the Zohar itself, but in a monistic framework. Thus we see that the change occurred precisely in the *Idra*, and the dualistic element was introduced here. To cite but one example, in the *Idra* (Zohar, III, 129b, etc.) the eyes of the Large Countenance were described as two that are one (the right only), as against the two eyes of the Small Countenance, which indicate the dualism of *Din* (Judgment) and *Rahamim* (Compassion), characterizing the latter Countenance.[143] We will also study a section of the main body of the Zohar that contains a similar homiletic logic, namely the Zohar homily (Part I, 123a) on the verse (Gen. xxiii, 1): "And the lives of Sarah were one hundred years and twenty years and seven years" (literally, one hundred year, twenty year, and seven years):

What is the difference that the word "year" [*shana*] is used each time in the singular, whereas with the number seven it is in the plural [*shanim*], as it is written: "one hundred year and twenty year," and then "seven years"? But there is no contradiction. The one hundred years contains all this, the Holy One Blessed be He is crowned with one hundred from a most secret place, by the secret of the one hundred benedictions pronounced each day.[144] Similarly, "twenty year," because it is written *shana* in the singular, is the secret of the unification, and Thought and Jubilee are never separated from each other. But the "seven years" are separate and go out separately from the secret world above, and although everything is still a unity, there is however a difference, they diverge into Judgement and Compassion in several respects, as is not the case in the supernal region. And hence of those seven years we have *shanim* [in the plural] and not *shana* [in the singular]. And they are all called "life". Thus "the life [in Heb. lives] of Sarah was" means "really was," having been created and established in the supernal regions.

This passage does not speak about the Countenances but about the ten *sefirot*. It is not dualistic and lays particular stress on the fact that the ten *sefirot* are "all a unity." Nonetheless, there is a difference between the three supernal *sefirot* and the seven lower ones. The three supernal ones are in a greater unity, because *Keter*, the supernal *sefira* called here "The Holy One Blessed be He" is included with the Supernal Originator, and its unity also continues with *Hokhma* and *Bina*, called here "Thought" and "Jubilee" (these names are very prevalent for these two *sefirot*), two *sefirot* that are always coupled and never separated, and that are described thus many times in the Zohar.[145] Thus it is appropriate to refer to these three in the singular, "one hundred year [*shana*] and twenty year [*shana*]",[146] but the seven inferior *sefirot* do not belong to the "secret world above" because they differ from each other in aspects of judgment (*din*) and compassion (*rahamim*).Therefore, the plural is ascribed to them, as is said of the Small Countenance in the *Idra*. Another affinity to the literature of the *Idrot* can be found in the expression "the most secret of all places," which is a name of the Large Countenance,[147] but here it is a name for the Originator, Ein Sof.[148] In view of this affinity to the doctrine of the *Idra*, another writer elaborated the passage in our possession in the spirit of the Kabbala of the *Idrot*. Thus, instead of the sentence "the Holy One Blessed be He is crowned from a most secret place," the version "twenty year [*shana*] which is crowned from a most secret place"[149] is conserved in Rabbi Joseph Angelet's *Livnat ha-Sappir*, composed only a generation after the Zohar; and the author of *Livnat ha-Sappir* also expressed his doubt about this: "perhaps it is a writer's error as in some versions." R. Joseph Angelet then cites another adaptation, not contained in the Zohar, which refers to the Ancient One and the Small Countenance:

On a parallel to the name of God, *Ehyeh*[150] and its signs [Gen. xxii, 16] "By Myself I have sworn the name of the Ancient of Days as the Small Countenance swore unto Abraham[151]—by the character *Yod* [*bi*=by myself, can also be interpreted as "by *yod*"] have I sworn." And whoever meditates [or enters] twenty years is taken into account: "From twenty year [*shana*] old and upward" [Deut. i, 3, etc.], precisely "and upward."[152] It may also be said one hundred years is parallel to the *Ayin* [nothingness][153] that includes everything. And from it one hundred benedictions extended. Twenty years include *Hokhma* and *Bina*, each

includes ten. These seven years diverge and go out separately
from the world above as Judgment and Compassion, by the secret
"Yours, oh Lord is the Greatness."[154] And they are all called "life"
and the soul of whoever has this knowledge is bound up in the
bond of eternal life.[155]

'Primordial Man'

The same is even more emphatically the case with regard to a section
that has been conserved in the *Idra Rabba* itself which sharply opposes
the position of the rest of the *Idra*. This passage adopts the monistic
position of R. Joseph of Hamadan, which sees in the Small
Countenance the female element, indispensable for the completeness
of the male divinity, that is, the Large Countenance.

> *Tana.* Rabbi Simeon said: All those attributes and all those words
> I wish to reveal only to those who were weighed in the balance,
> and not to those who neither entered[156] nor went out, for he who
> enters and does not go out, would that he had never been created.
> The sum of all is this: The most Ancient One and the Small
> Countenance are all one. He was all, He is all, He will be all;[157]
> He will not be changed, neither is He changed, neither has He
> been changed. He was adorned with these adornments, and has
> perfected Himself in that form which comprehends all forms,[158]
> in that form which comprehends all names. A form which
> appears as this form is not that form, but is only like that form.
> When the crowns are joined together, then all becomes one
> perfection, because the form of *Adam* [primordial man] is the
> form of the supernals and inferiors which are included therein.
> And because that form comprehends the supernals and the
> inferiors, the Holy Ancient One shaped his adornments and
> shaped the adornments of the Small Countenance in this form.
> And if you say: What is the difference between the two, all is
> in the one balance. The ways are separated by us, however: from
> this side, compassion emanated and from the other side,
> judgment comes into being.[159] It is from our side that they are
> different from each other and these secrets were not revealed
> except to the reapers of the holy field,[160] as it is written, Ps. xxv,
> 14: "The secret of the Lord is with those who fear Him".[161] Also
> it is written, Gen. ii, 7: "And the Lord God created [*va-yyitser*]
> Man [*Adam*]," with two "*yods.*" He completed the adornments
> within adornments like a seal. This is *yyitser*. Why are there two

"*yods*"? This is a secret of the Holy Ancient One and a secret of the Small Countenance. What is *va-yyitser* [shaped]? Tsar is a shape [*tsura*] within a shape.[162] And what is a shape within a shape? The two names which are called the full name of the Lord God.[163] And this is the secret of the two "*yods*" of "He created a shape within a shape." He shaped the complete name—the Lord God. And in what are they included? In this supernal form which is called *Adam* which includes male and female,[164] and thus it is written, *et ha-Adam* [the Man], which comprehends male and female. . . . And what is all this for? In order to bring into them the most secret of all things, which is the soul, which all life above and below depends on and is established in. (Zohar, III, 145a–b).

The section opens with a caution and even a curse against those who are not worthy of the revelation of its secret. They are termed here as those "who did not enter or go out," the same expression used in the preface to *Sifra di-Tsni'uta* to denote those who do not interpret the book in the correct manner.[165] As opposed to these wicked people, for whom it would have been better if they had not been created, there are those who "were weighed in the balance." R. David b. Judah he-Hasid, in his version in *Sefer ha-Gevul* (which will be discussed below in greater detail), rather than this phrase, quotes "who entered and came out of *bei Idra Kaddisha* [the Holy Assembly Hall]."[166] This is far more suited to the contrast in the following sentence and was probably the initial version. The version printed in the Zohar is most interesting. Those who "were weighed in the balance" are those who are married, as I showed in detail in the previous chapter.[167] The indication that those who are unmarried are unworthy is not by chance here. The serious transgression of celibacy is closely connected with the substance of the section: it must not be revealed to the single, because it deals with the completeness of male and female. In the essential part of the section too we find the word "balance": "all is in the one balance." This last phrase comes in answer to the question: "What is the difference between the two; or what is the difference between the "Holy Ancient One" (i.e., the Large Countenance) and the Small Countenance?" And there are two meanings here: a) in fact, there is no difference between the two,[168] and b) the two are together in a marriage.

What was the theological error of the unmarried who "did not come in and go out" and are not "God fearing"? Logically, this was the doctrine of the *Idra* itself developed in the previous pages of the Zohar, since the passage under discussion proposes an alternative to it. The main doctrine of the *Idra* is, as already noted, the dualism of the two male forms, the Large Countenance and the Small Countenance, one of which is entirely compassion and the other principally judgment, and only at "the propitious moment" are they in harmony, when the supernal face looks upon the inferior face and mitigates its judgment. As opposed to this doctrine, which contains a dualism and even a kind of homosexuality, the author of the section under discussion preaches a pure faith in the unity of God and his unchanging eternity, all the changes and distinctions being on the side of the recipients only ("from our side"). This concept, which seems to resemble the position of the philosophers, also exists among the Kabbalists of the Zohar generation.[169] Indeed, the Kabbalistic nature of the passage, which contains an extreme anthropomorphic ideology, is clarified subsequently: the unity and completeness of the divinity is expressed in that it assumes the most complete form possible: the form of Man. The completeness of this form is in the unity of male and female, and these are the Large Countenance and the Small Countenance. A soul penetrates into this androgenous form, the soul being the essence of the supreme divinity, called here, rather than *Ein Sof* (the term normally used in the Kabbala), "the most secret of all things" (this is also the meaning of the term "most secret" in the Zohar proper and in the writings of R. David b. Judah he-Hasid, although in the rest of the *Idra* it denotes the Large Countenance[170]). In the seventeenth century this doctrine captivated the Sabbatian theologian Abraham Miguel Cardozo who attributed it to his Messiah, Sabbatai Zevi, perhaps precisely because it contradicts the spirit and the doctrine of the rest of the *Idra*, developed subsequently in the Lurianic Kabbala.[171] Going back to our subject and the late thirteenth century, the contradiction between the rest of the *Idra* and this passage is exactly the same as the fundamental differences we saw between the doctrine of the *Idrot* and R. Joseph of Hamadan.

The most prominent difference between the doctrines was, as noted, in the gender of the Small Countenance. Hence we will offer additional proofs that in the passage quoted "the Holy Ancient One" and "the Small Countenance" are male and female. These two faces are indicated in the passage by the two "*yods*" of the word *va-yyitser* (created), in the verse "and the Lord God created Man," and on account of these two "*yods*" Man achieved his completeness, namely he was comprised from male and female. This can also be learned from parallels in the Zohar,[172] and in particular by a study of the midrashic source developed by the Zohar, that is, *Midrash Otiyot de-R. Akiva*:[173] " 'And the Lord God created the Man'. *Va-yyitser*—why are there two '*yods*'? One for *yetser ha-tov* [the good inclination] and one for *yetser ha-ra* [the evil inclination]. Another explanation: two yods, one for the creation of Adam and one for the creation of Eve. Another explanation: *va-yyitser*, why two 'yods'? One for the face before him and one for the face behind him." In this midrash, which explains the same verse in the same way, the two "yods" are male and female, whether they are "Adam and Eve" or whether they indicate the "two faces" which were included in Man when he was first created, according to the midrash.[174] The use of the term "face" fits the Large Countenance and the Small Countenance. The homily on the two *yetsarim* (inclinations) also parallels the description of compassion and judgment going out separately from these faces according to the Zoharic passage under discussion.

The two faces of primordial man were interpreted from the outset in the Kabbala as alluding to the divine male and female (as could have been predicted a priori), and sometimes they were also compared to the two cherubs[175] who, as indicated above, were also seen as male and female, and also contributed to the creation of the Zoharic doctrine of the faces.[176] The midrashic and Kabbalistic parallels to the passage quoted have already been noted by Moshe Idel,[177] who determined by virtue of them (and also by virtue of other Gnostic and midrashic sources[178]) that R. Joseph of Hamadan's interpretation of "Small Countenance" is more suited to the midrashic sources than the doctrine of the *Idra*, in which the "Small Countenance" is male. Here I merely continue and develop the logic of these arguments, and draw the required conclusions as regards the writing of the Zohar. I also reinforce the argument by showing that the passage before us is not a source adapted in accordance with a different doctrine, but that it actually and explicitly expresses a view contrary to the one prevalent in the *Idra*. (Perhaps in the aforesaid *Sefer ha-Gevul* an allusion was also conserved to the fact that this section of the *Idra* derives from a specific source; the homily on the two *"yods"* is cited there from *Mekhilta de-R. Simeon*,[179] and most of *Idra Rabba* is not indicated in such a way, such indications being infrequent in *Sefer ha-Gevul*).

Yet another difference in terminology sets this passage apart from the rest of the *Idra*. The term *Adam* in the *Idrot* indicates precisely the Small Countenance and not the Large Countenance (perhaps according to "son of man" [*bar enash*] as opposed to 'Ancient of days" in Dan. vii, 13) which is explicitly denied this name in certain contexts;[180] this is also true in the parallels in the writings of Gikatilla.[181] We have already seen this specified in *Sifra di-Tsni'uta* (Zohar, II, 177a): "Concerning that "honored of honor" it is written (Jer. ii, 6) "No man (*ish*) passed through it and no man (*Adam*) lived there." *Adam* is without, *Adam* is not included within, all the more so *Ish*. In the above passage, on the other hand, the "supernal form" called *Adam* comprises, as noted, the Large Countenance and the Small Countenance, and also, as the soul within him, *Ein Sof*. Indeed, in another part of *Idra Rabba* (Zohar, II: 139b) there is a parallel passage, but it differs symbolically. There, *Adam* is the Small Countenance, and the soul within him is his inner part, which is the Tetragrammaton (in total contrast to the "secret..." of the passage above).[182] We have found, however, a parallel in terminology for the passage quoted above in another part of the Zohar:

> Man has four names: *Adam, Gever, Enosh, Ish*—and the highest of them is *Adam*, as it is written [Gen. i, 27]: And God created man [*Adam*] in his image. Said R. Judah to R. Isaac: Why then is it written [Exod. xvi, 3], "The Lord is a man [*ish*] of war;" why is it not written *Adam*? He replied: The secret of the Lord is to those who fear Him. Said R. Judah: I too am one of them,[183] yet I have not been privileged to hear this.[184] Said the other: Go to R. Abba, for I learn from him only on condition that I should not tell. So he went to R. Abba, and found him discoursing and saying: When is there said to be completeness above? When the Holy One Blessed be He sits on His throne, and until he sits on His throne there will not be completeness. (Zohar, III, 48a)

While this passage is not taken from the *Idra*, but from the main body of the Zohar in the portion *Tazria*, it belongs to the *Idra* not only by virtue of the subject, but also because in R. David b. Judah he-Hasid's *Sefer ha-Gevul* it appears, in a Hebrew translation and with slight changes, exactly after the passage from *Idra Rabba* cited above![185] (Another hint that the portion belongs to the *Idrot* is to be found in a quotation from *Sifra di-Tsni'uta* cited in the portion *Tazria* several lines after this passage.[186]) Several more sentences were added there (in *Sefer ha-Gevul*) explaining Man's sitting on the throne in a sexual fashion, as the completeness of the pairing of the male with the female, and this would seem to be the correct interpretation (and not as in *Tikkunei Zohar* where this sitting is explained concerning the entry of the soul, i.e., the divinity, into the *sefirot*[187]). It follows then that this portion was once part of the *Idra* and was removed from it during another editing, apparently because of the terminology that contradicts most of the doctrine of the *Idra*, even more conspicuously here than in the portion previously cited above. The narrative framework of this passage, in which the revealer of the secret is not R. Simeon b. Yohai but R. Abba, does not fit the narrative of the *Idra*. Here too the editor interfered: in R. David b. Judah he-Hasid's *Sefer*

ha-Gevul the expounding scholar is R. Simeon b. Yohai and the
questioner is R. Abba, and not R. Judah (but further on in the passage,
as we will see below, the roles are reversed, both in the Zohar version
and in R. David's version). We have found another case in the Zohar
where the editor apparently separated an inconsistent passage from
the *Idra*, and attributed it to R. Abba, who had a special status in
R. Simeon b. Yohai's Zoharic circle.[188] This is the *Idra* known in print
as *Idra de-Vei Mashkena*,[189] Zohar, II, 123b, in which R. Abba teaches
the doctrines of the *Idra* that R. Simeon b. Yohai failed to teach prior
to his death, and these doctrines likewise are not exactly identical
to the rest of the *Idrot*. Even if we change the names of the scholars
in accordance with the *Sefer ha-Gevul* version, the narrative
framework will not correspond exactly to that of *Idra Rabba*, because
in the *Idra* R. Simeon b. Yohai is discoursing to the scholars, whereas
here he has to be sought out. If this is the case, the passage under
discussion might have been cited in *Idra Rabba* (when it was still
there) as a quotation from a previous edition of the *Idra*. This might
also be concluded from the marked parallel between the passage's
narrative framework and the preface to *Idra Rabba*,[190] and from the
doctrine expounded in the passage, which comprises, as we saw, a prior
stage in the creation of the doctrine of the faces.

Later in the section of the portion *Tazria*, after the passage cited,
the debate between R. Judah and R. Isaac continues, but this time
according to the Zohar version (this passage is not quoted in *Sefer
ha-Gevul*) they submit their difficulties to R. Simeon b. Yohai and not
to R. Abba. I shall cite this passage here, because it contains another
version of the *Idra*'s doctrine of the faces, and another usage of the
term *Adam*:

> *Tana.* From the Lamp of Darkness [*botsina di-Kardinuta*] issued
> 325 sparks traced out and linked together from the side of *Gevura*
> and when these entered the Body, it was called *Ish* [Man]. And
> not *Ish* as it is taught [Job, i, 1]: "a perfect and upright man,"
> "a just man" [Gen. vi, 9] but *Ish* here is a man of war as it is
> written: "because of all the end is judgment and all is one." Said
> R. Judah: Why? He could not answer.[191] So they went and asked
> R. Simeon, who replied: . . . But thus it is taught, all is in one
> balance[192] and all is one. And because the lower judgments are
> attached to the hair of this one, he is called stern Judgment; but
> when the hair is removed, he becomes mitigated and the lower
> judgments are not present. Therefore he is called clean, for
> somebody is called "clean" only if he came out of the side of
> uncleanness, and when he comes out of the side of uncleanness

he is called "clean," as it is written [Job xiv, 4] "Who can bring
a clean thing out of an unclean thing?", out of an unclean thing
to be sure. And there it is written [Lev. xiii, 40] "And the man
whose hair is fallen off his head is bald; yet he is clean." Come,
I will show you: on the head of this man, *butsina di-Kardinuta*,
and because of this the skull of the head of this man is completely
red like a rose and the hair is red within red, and suspended
from it below are the inferior crowns which bring judgment in
the world, and when the hair is removed and shaved by supernal
mercy, he is all mitigated and is called clean by his name. Said
R. Judah: If he is called by his name, he is called "holy" and
not "clean." He answered: This is not so. Something is called
"holy" only when the hair hangs, since holiness lies in the hair,
as it is written [on the Nazirite, Numbers, vi, 5]: "He shall be
holy, and shall let the locks of the hair of his head grow." And
that man is called clean, because he belongs to what hangs from
it below, and therefore the hair is removed and he is purified.
Come and see: Anybody who is on the side of judgment and the
judgment is joined in him, is not purified until the hair is
removed and he is purified. And if you say this of *Adam*? This
is not so. Because he is the completeness of all, and all
compassion is found within him. Therefore, it is not so, because
all holiness[193] and holy things are joined[194] within him. But this
one is from the side of judgment and judgment is joined within
him, he is not mitigated until his hair is removed. Similarly, the
Levites who came from this side of judgment were not purified
until their hair was removed, as it is written [Numbers, viii, 7]:
"And thus you shall do to them to cleanse them: Sprinkle
purifying water upon them, and let them shave all their flesh."
And so that they would be more mitigated, the Priest who is on
the side of supernal mercy, should wave them, as it is written
[Numbers viii, 11]: "And Aaron shall wave the Levites before the
Lord as a wave offering." Just as for the supernal Man [*Ish*] when
he desires to be more mitigated, the supernal mercy is displayed
in him and he mitigates the world below, and this *Ish* is included
in *Adam*. And when God wants to wage war, he wages war
throught that *Ish*, as it is written: "The Lord is a man (*Ish*) of
war." Through this very *Ish*. And he does not wage war through
him until he removes the hair of his head, so that all the inferior
crowns which are held in the hair will be released and broken.
(Zohar, III, 48b—49a)

This passage is unlike the one preceding it; in the first passage only one image is referred to, which is called *Adam* when complete, and *Ish* when incomplete, whereas in the second passage there are two images. While it is said at the end of the latter passage that "this *Ish* is included in *Adam*," this does not negate the existence of the two different images. The aforesaid expression is explained subsequently: when *Adam* mitigates Ish and amends him by shaving, then he can use him to fight against the enemy (perhaps the author had seen as examples soldiers with shaven heads), and then it is possible to talk about harmony, and the merging of *Ish* in *Adam*. The contradictory wording of this sentence is certainly intended to mitigate and conceal some of the dualism, and is perhaps a later addition. In any case the doctrine of the passage is very similar to that of the *Idra*: there too the lower face is mainly judgment, because it emanated from the sparks of the Lamp of Darkness,[195] and there too it requires amendment and cleansing, and the amendment is effected with the aid of the supernal face, called here, as in the *Idra*, "Supernal Mercy,"[196] and depicted in the figure of the High Priest.[197] The adjective "holy," attributed to this face because of its hair, is also echoed in *Idra Rabba*, where it is noted that every single lock of the hair of the Large Countenance are four hundred and ten locks of hair according to the number of the word *kadosh* (holy in gematria) (Zohar, III, 128b).[198]

Alongside the profound parallels between this passage and the *Idra*, important differences also exist. The main difference is the name *Adam*, attributed here most emphatically to the supernal face, the Large Countenance of the *Idra* (and *Ish* which is attributed to the Small Countenance); this clearly opposes what is specified above in *Sifra di-Tsni'uta* and the consistent usage in the *Idrot*. We have seen three different versions of the *Idra* doctrine, and in each one this basic term serves in a different way. This demonstrates the existence of different directions and different lines of thought in drafting of the doctrine, which must have had their source in different Kabbalists who developed them together and discussed a text together (the recurring use of *tanya* [it has been taught] in this passage, as in all the *Idra* literature, would seem to point to such a text). We shall bring proof of this from a fourth use of the term *Adam* in the same context, and this time not in the Zohar, but in the writings of a member of the Zohar circle: in the writings of R. Joseph Gikatilla[199] we have found a parallel to one section of *Idra Rabba* (Zohar, III, 139b), where verses from the Psalms (cxviii, 6–9) are expounded in a similar way: "The Lord is on my side, I will not fear. What can man (*Adam*) do to me? . . . It is better to trust in the Lord than to put confidence in man

(*Adam*). It is better to trust in the Lord than to put confidence in Princes." But while in the Zohar *Adam* is the Small Countenance, in Gikatilla's writings *Adam* is the world of the angels.

Moshe Idel in his detailed article on the idea of "The World of the Angels in the Image of Man" (Heb.) also dealt with this parallel, considering that Gikatilla uses the *Idra* "while secretly contending its anthropomorphic elements."[200] I am inclined to contest this supposition, because elsewhere Gikatilla uses the term *Adam* for his parallel to the *Idra*'s Small Countenance.[201] It seems rather that Gikatilla does not depend here on the Zohar version, but is associated with the conflict we saw in the *Idra* regarding *Adam*, and while working on the Zohar he elaborates the same motif and adds another interpretation. Such an explanation falls into line with what we have already seen in other cases as regards the relationship between the Zohar and R. Joseph Gikatilla. Additional proofs will reinforce this argument.

Firstly, Gikatilla's homily, according to which *Adam* are the angels, better fits the literal meaning of the verses of the Psalms interpreted, which contain an opposition between *Adam* and the Divinity, than the Zohar interpretation by which Adam is the Small Countenance. Further, Gikatilla's interpretation is related to the idea of the world of angels in the image of man (*Adam*), which has deep roots in the literature of the rabbinic scholars of the talmudic era (which also uses the term "princes" to refer to the angels[202]) and in the Gnostic and Kabbalistic literature (principally that of the "*Iyyun* Circle") and in the other writings of Gikatilla and even in the Zohar; these were collected by Idel in his article. Idel also demonstrated the importance of this idea in the Kabbala of R. Joseph of Hamadan, and if this is so, then these two Kabbalists, who are members of the Zohar circle, have a similar position in this too, since R. Joseph of Hamadan, despite his anthropomorphism, does not call his image of the divinity *Adam* in any of his writings, but the "supernal form." He reserves the name *Adam* for the world of the angels, as seen in the examples cited by Idel, who also showed there the interesting development of this idea in *Tikkunei Zohar*. Before reviewing other differences between this passage from Tazria and the *Idra*, we should note the existance of another passage, printed as one of the Toseftot at the end of the Zohar in later editions, which appears to be another edition of the passage cited from *Tazria*. It adds to the impression of difficulties within the Zohar circle regarding formulation of the "faces". Rather than the doctrine of the faces, this edition deals with the *sefirot* of *Hesed* and *Gevura*. The interlocutors are also different, being this time R. Judah and R. Abba, who conversed at the beginning of the section in the portion *Tazria* and on coming to a more profound subject, gave way to R. Simeon b. Yohai. Apparently R. Abba, who was not considered sufficiently authoritative by the author of the section dealing with the faces, was adequate for this edition. This parallel was printed as "Tosefta 9," in Zohar, III, 303a, in a Hebrew translation (and perhaps also an adaptation) which seems to be the work of R. David b. Judah he-Hasid.[203]

"And Aaron shall offer the Levites before the Lord for an offering" [Num. viii, 11]. R. Judah asked R. Abba: Why did the Priest wave the Levites? He answered: To what can this be compared? What is done to a baby who is crying and angry? Said R. Judah: they rock him and shake him in order to quiet him.[204] Said R. Abba: Judah, Judah, this word[205] comes to you and you did not enquire into it? Will your ears not hear what your mouth speaks. This is the attribute of angry and agitated *Gevura*. As it is written [Gen. xlix, 5]: "Simeon and Levy are brothers, instruments of cruelty are in their habitations," and (Gen. xlix: 7]: "Cursed be their anger, for it was fierce, and their wrath, for it was cruel . . ., because they are strong and obdurate in their anger and wrath to go out and do judgment, to destroy and annihilate human beings. Then the Priest, who is the supernal mercy [*Hesed*], waves this side of the Levites[206] which is the attribute of strength [*Gevura*], in order to quiet and to pacify its anger and wrath so that the hairs would be broken from all their edges[207] and would not grow strong. R. Judah came and kissed his hands. And when judgement is awakened in the world, the Patriarch Abraham sets aside all the judgments which are found daily and they do not stand before him. Thus it is written [Ps. vii, 12] "And God is angry every day."[208]

Shaving of the Hair

Going back to the "official" version of the portion *Tazria*, we saw that the section quoted differs from the *Idra* in the use of the term *Adam*. The difference between the Zoharic sources, however, does not end there. There is another motif which shows that the *Idra* we have in our possession was not known to the author of the section in the portion *Tazria*. Another passage in the portion *Tazria*, a few lines below the aforementioned section, demonstrates the author's apparent ignorance of the special virtue of the beard, to which a great part of the *Idra* literature is devoted.

"And if his hair be fallen off from the front part of his head" [Lev. xiii, 41]. We learn that there are two kinds of faces. And what are these faces? This front part is called the face of wrath. And all those who derive from that face are bold, stern and cruel. But when the hair is removed from that side of the face, all these are removed and rendered powerless. For, as we have learnt:[209] All those who derive from the hair of the head are superior to the others and not bold-faced like them. And all those who derive from the side of the hair of that face are bold and stern. (Zohar, III, 49a)

The description of the beard here is completely negative; the face adorned with the beard is the "face of wrath" and only when shaven is it mitigated. This description contrasts very sharply with the climate of fervor and mystery surrounding the subject of the beard in the *Idrot* (it is "the most honored of all things"; explicit mention of it in the Scriptures is below its dignity, and woe to anyone who holds it in his hand). In truth, in the *Idrot* too, on a parallel to the beard of the Large Countenance, there is also a description of the beard of the Small Countenance, which is essentially judgment. Notwithstanding, the attitude toward the beard in each of the sources cannot be compared. The passage from the portion *Tazria* seems unaware of the existence of the holy beard at all (the "two kinds of faces" are both elucidated with respect to the Small Countenance, before and after he is shaved). Indeed, the judgment in the Small Countenance's beard in the *Idra* is not mitigated by shaving (heaven forbid), but by mingling its hairs with those of the Large Countenance which descend upon it from above.[210] The hairs of the head of the Small Countenance are mitigated in the *Idra* in a like manner, but in the passage from the section *Tazria* they also require shaving by the supernal face, namely the high priest, according to the passage cited above, and to another passage cited below (regarding Korah).

This difference also indicates an element common to the two sources, and this is the very need for improvement and adornment (*tikkun*) of the divine hair, and in both cases the supernal face adorns the inferior face. In the *Idra*, however, this adornment is also transmitted to flesh and blood Kabbalists, who expound homilies on the locks (*tikkunim*) of the beard, and extol its curls,[211] and no parallel usage is mentioned in the section in *Tazria*. The myth of shaving, however, also seems to have had a ritual side. An allusion to this in conserved in another place in the Zohar, portion *va-Yehi*, Part I, 217a, in which a reprimand is delivered to one of the members of Rabbi Simeon b. Yohai's circle, who saw a vision and did not understand the Kabbalistic allusion concealed in it, and did not act accordingly: "This man has not yet plucked the hairs from the head of his Master, nor shorn the Matron." This shows that the *tikkun* of shaving was also effected through dealing with the secrets of the Kabbala, like the extolling of the beard of those assembled in the *Idra*; and there may even have been people who shaved themselves symbolically, like the Levites and Korah in the portion *Tazria*. The narrative in the portion *va-Yehi* also shows that the subject of shaving was once connected with the *Idra*, because it refers to the "holy *Idra* of Rabbi Simeon and the other comrades" and to the death of the three comrades in the course of the *Idra*.[212] On the other hand the section in *va-Yehi* makes no mention whatsoever of *Idra Zuta*, and uses an alternative description of the day of R. Simeon b. Yohai's death.

Moreover, even though the *Idra* makes no mention of the shaving of the inferior face, symbolized by the shaving of the Levite who is called "clean," nor of the holy Nazirite who symbolizes the supernal face which does not require shaving, it can be proven that they existed there in some stage of the drafting of *Idra Rabba*. The section quoted in the Zohar just before *Idra Rabba*, and which serves as a kind of introduction describing the anticipated content, states that the *Idra* will deal precisely with the aforesaid elements. The fact that this promise is not fulfilled is very suspicious, especially since the subject of the Nazirite is the only reason alluded to in the Zohar for the inclusion of *Idra Rabba* precisely in this place in the book, in the portion *Nasso*, which deals with the Nazirite (there is in fact one other possible reason),[213] and in several places *Idra Rabba* is referred to as *Idra de-Nazir* (this is so in *Sefer Livnat ha-Sappir*). The section before the *Idra* states:

Now with regard to the Levites it says: "And thus shall you do unto them to cleanse them: sprinkle the water of purification upon them, and let them cause a razor to pass over all their flesh" [Num. viii, 7]. After the hair has been removed and all the details performed, the Levite is designated "clean," but not "holy." But the Nazirite, having abstained from the side of rigor, is designated "holy" and not simply "clean." Because it is written thus: "All the days of his Nazirite vow. . . .in which he consecrates himself to the Lord, he shall be holy, he shall let the locks of the hair of his head grow long." This is explained by the passage, "and the hair of his head was like pure wool" [Dan. vii, 9] inasmuch as the Nazirite in this regard resembles the celestial pattern. R. Judah said: It is indeed by his hair that the Nazirite is distinguished as holy. This is an allusion to "his locks are

curled" [Song of Songs, v, 11]. A teaching of R. Simeon says: "Did
men but understand the inner significance of the Scriptural
passages regarding the hair as in the secret of secrets,[214] they
would acquire a knowledge of their Master by means of the
superior wisdom. Until here the secrets of the Torah, from here
onwards [namely *Idra Rabba*] the crowns (or secrets) of the Torah.
And her merchandise and her hire shall be holiness to the Lord
[Is. xxiii: 18).[215]
(Zohar, III, 127b).

Apart from the elements in this section that do not exist in the
Idra,[216] the section also contradicts the doctrine of the *Idra*. The verse,
Song of Songs, v, 11: "his locks are bushy and black as a raven," serves
in the *Idra* to describe the black hair of the Small Countenance, as
opposed to the white hair of the Large Countenance, in accordance
with the verse [Dan. vii, 9] "And the Ancient of days did sit, whose
garment was white as snow, and the hair of his head like the pure
wool." However, the section above expounded on these two verses with
regard to the supernal face, which is parallel to the holy Nazirite.[217]
The section may have been based on the sayings of the rabbis who
saw in the two figures one revelation,[218] and perhaps the passage in
our possession does not see a contradiction in this, since it does not
relate at all to the color expressed in the verses (the words "black as
a raven" are not cited, and "pure wool" could also express other traits).
In this too, a relation can be found to the section above from the portion
Tazria, where the head of *Ish* (Man), was red and not black, in contrast
to the description of the Small Countenance in the *Idra*,[219] which
attributes the color red to the hair of the *Shekhina* (Zohar, III, 141b),
in accordance with Song of Songs vii, 5: "the hair of your head is like
purple."

The section in the portion *Tazria* is not then a true *Idra*, but
it does reflect a parallel attempt to draft the doctrine of the divine
faces. This section has a parallel, in fact, which does not yet contain
this doctrine, in the Zoharic section on the portion *Korah*:

"In the morning the Lord will show who are his and who are
holy" [Num. xvi, 5]. Why "morning" and why "holy' rather than
"clean"? But these [namely Korah and his congregation who
were Levites and not priests like Aaron] are on the side of "clean,"
and the priest is "holy." Moses meant this: In the morning the
crown of the Priest is active, and if you are priests, then in the
morning perform the service of the morning and the Lord will
make known who is just His—that is to say the Levite—and who

is "holy" that is to say the Priest—"and He shall bring near Himself." The test will only be made by "morning." If it is meet for you to remain on the side of judgment, then morning will not endure you, for it is not the time of judgment. But if it is meet for you to remain on the side of grace, then as it is the time thereof, you will remain with it, and it will accept you. (Zohar, III, 176b)

This section explains that "morning" and the "crown of the priest" are the *sefira* of *Hesed*, and the degree of the Levite is judgment. This is the usual meaning of these symbols that are prevalent in the main body of the Zohar.[220] They correspond to what we saw in the alternative version to the above section from the portion *Tazria*, where the *sefirot* of *Hesed* and *Din* also replaced the faces (that of R. David b. Judah he-Hasid). In contrast to that section, however, the idea of the purification of the supernal beings is not included here, and "Korah's" name is not used here to allude to the supernal haircut [Korah is of the same root as *kereah* = bald]. This is not the case in the parallel to this passage in the aforementioned section in portion *Tazria*, appearing between the two passages already cited from there. Here, the subject is expounded in accordance with the doctrine of the faces, although using the terminology of the portion *Tazria* which calls the lower face *Ish*:

> The greatest of all the Levites is Korah, whom God made below in the image of what is above, and called him Korah. When? When he shaved because of him that "*Ish,*" as it is written [Lev. xiii, 40]: "He is bald" (*kereah*). And when Korah saw that he had no hair on his head and he saw Aaron adorned with the adornments of kings, he felt that he was belittled and envied Aaron. God said to him: I made you in the image of what is above; if you do not wish to go up to the heights, go down to the lower regions. (Zohar, III, 49a)

Although the subject of the Nazir and shaving of the hair of the divinity was taken out of the *Idra*, it was not rejected in the Kabbala of other members of the Zohar circle, and first and foremost in that of R. Joseph of Hamadan. This Kabbalist accords supreme importance to these themes, which he deals with in most of his *Idra*-like writings, describing the "supernal form." The way in which he employs these ideas not only testifies to their presence in the *Idra* circle, but can also explain the reason for their removal: the narrative of the hair was connected with the idea of the destruction of the worlds and the

doctrine of the *shemittot* (which deals with the destruction of the world
and its resetting in fixed cycles of time), and it was therefore omitted
by the final editor of the *Idra*. We will see below that at a later stage
another myth expressing the idea of the destruction of the worlds was
introduced into the text of the *Idra*,[221] the myth of the "death of the
Edomite kings," and the new myth replaced the old one. It may easily
be surmised that the final editor was opposed to the doctrine of the
shemittot; indeed, we find in the writings of the most likely final editor,
R. Moses de Leon, a vigorous disputation against the adherents to
this doctrine in its customary form.[222] Not all the members of the circle
agreed with Moses de Leon in this respect, and he may have directed
the disputation against certain of them. Proof of this exists not only
in the writings of R. Joseph of Hamadan and the writings of others
(such as R. Bahya b. Asher),[223] whose membership in the circle may
be doubted by some, but also in the *Sifra di-Tsni'uta* itself, which I
will quote presently, and which alludes to the doctrine of the *shemittot*
and relates it to the idea of the destruction of the worlds. In the *Idrot*
which were meant to interpret this book, only the idea of the
destruction remains.[224]

> Thirteen derive from the thirteen of the most honourable one
> [namely "the locks of the beard"]. Six thousand years derive from
> the first six, the seventh above them alone becomes powerful.
> And the whole becomes desolate for twelve hours, as it is written:
> "It was formless and void" etc. . . . In the thirteenth He will raise
> up these through mercy, and all these six will be as before, as
> it is written [Gen. i, 1]: "created,", and then it is written [Gen.
> i, 2] "it was", since it already was,[225] and at the end of the
> "Formless and the Void and Darkness," "the Lord alone shall
> be exalted on that day" [Isa. ii, 11].[226] (*Sifra di-Tsni'uta*, Zohar,
> II, 176b)

The ideas in this passage relate to the sayings of the rabbis that
always served as a basis for the doctrine of the *shemittot* (perhaps this
is indeed their meaning[227])—*Rosh ha-Shana*, 31a: "Six thousand years
the world exists, and during one (thousand years) it is destroyed, as
it is said 'the Lord alone shall be exalted on that day.' " This midrash
and this verse from Isaiah are also used by the proponents of this
doctrine in the above mentioned disputation that R. Moses de Leon
wrote against them.

The subject of the Nazirite and his hair appears frequently in
R. Joseph of Hamadan's writings,[228] as for instance in his commentary
on *Eser Sefirot*:[229]

And the holy hair, which are known channels, draws from this source. And those channels which shine on several worlds which God created and encircle the Supernal Form are a secret of the Nazirite, as it is written: "he let his hair grow long." Because this is the holy hair[230] growing one thousand years until it reaches a certain limit. When it reaches that certain limit it immediately cuts[231] those channels and they return to their former position. Accordingly the rabbis said: "A king cuts his hair daily."[232] And God's day is one thousand years as it is written [Ps. xc, 4] "For a thousand years in your eyes are but as yesterday when it is past."[233] And the honored fire which cuts that holy hair which really emanated from Him is called the primordial light. When God first wished to create the world, he created His world like this world, and brought light out from the attribute of the *Keter* to illuminate it, and it could not tolerate that supernal light and he destroyed it. Accordingly the talmudic sages said in this respect: It teaches that "God created and destroyed worlds" until he concealed that hidden light for the righteous. . . .[234] And this is the attribute (the *sefira* of *Keter*) even in the seventh millenium of which it is written "And the Lord alone is exalted on that day" when those ten *sefirot* are not revealed, this *sefira* stands firm and does not ever change.

In contrast to the Zohar, the growing of the hair here is not related to judgment and uncleanness, but to the Emanation which must be limited. In any event this passage deals with the destruction of the worlds, which are related to millennia and to the shaving of the Nazirite's hair; the bringing together of these two themes is the same as the result of the joining of the doctrine of the section in the portion *Tazria* with the allusion to the doctrine of the *shemittot* in *Sifra di-Tsni'uta*. Interestingly, the destruction of the worlds is presented here as a consequence of an abundance of light, which could not be tolerated. Such a version of the idea of the destruction of the worlds precedes the famous "breaking of the vessels" in the Lurianic Kabbala, the reason for which was the large amount of lights.[235] I have not found this among the early Kabbalists. *Sefer ha-Bahir* does talk about the "flaw" of too much light, but in a mystical and epistemological rather than ontological context.[236] The Zohar ascribes the destruction of the worlds to the flaw of the lack of "balance" or sexual harmony,[237] and not to an abundance of light. We have indeed found in the Zohar a related section, according to which the worlds could not tolerate the abundance of light; here, however, this did not lead to the destruction of the light, but rather to the covering and attenuation of it.[238] R. Joseph's writings incorporate and develop the motifs circulating within the Zohar circle, and they are appropriate for an independent member of this group.

Others besides R. Joseph testify to these ideas, which were current in the Zohar circle. We have also found such ideas in R. Bahya b. Asher's Commentary of the Torah, portion *Nasso*, Num. vi, 3.

> I have already explained to you in the portion *Emor* who the High Priest resembles, and here the Nazirite is above him, because he is above the attributes, he cleaves to the actual supernal mercy, and because he is crowned with the attribute of the Naziriteship he is called Nazir after the word *nezer* [Naziriteship or crown].

The Nazir's standing here resembles his standing in the portion *Tazria* in the Zohar and in the section preceding the *Idra*. In this case too, a description of the Nazir's hair follows, with the use of the terms "his locks are curled" and the "hair of his head was like pure wool," and in contrast to the doctrine of the *Idra*. On the other hand, in several details which are not in the Zohar at all, R. Bahya's words resemble those of R. Joseph of Hamadan. Thus it seems to me that the interpretation of the word "Nazir" as deriving from the word *nezer,* crown (an allusion to the *sefira* of *Keter*) is also alluded to in the words of R. Joseph cited above, and according to them the secret of the Nazir is in the channels that surround the supernal form. R. Bahya goes on to explain the growing of the Nazirite's hair as symbolizing the spreading of the Emanation, and this also corresponds to R. Joseph's conception. There is an exact parallel to R. Bahya's words in *Sefer Ta'amei ha-Mitsvot*, second version.[239]

Rabbi David Ben Judah He-Hasid

We will continue our study with the aid of another Kabbalist, R. David b. Judah he-Hasid.[240] Gershom Scholem also pioneered the research into this Kabbalist, and since then considerable progress has been made by Scholem's pupils, the late Ephraim Gottleib,[241] and Amos Goldreich and Moshe Idel. One of R. David's major works appeared in a critical edition with an important introduction by Daniel Matt, and other writings have been published by Idel. In this case, too, as in the case of R. Joseph of Hamadan, the research literature has not been exploited for the study of the Zohar. This is surprising, since it is well known that R. David was the first to use the Zohar and to translate and adapt large sections of it; he even wrote a complete book entirely based on *Idra Rabba*, *Sefer ha-Gevul*, which still exists only in manuscript form. At the beginning of his research into R. David, Gershom Scholem wrote of *Sefer ha-Gevul* the following very true statement: "Any true study of the *Idrot* must be based on this book."[242] And it is with this book that I will begin my investigation.

Sefer ha-Gevul is in fact basically an expanded and elucidated Hebrew translation of *Idra Rabba*. The translation differs from the source, however, in more than language. Large sections of the *Idra* are not contained in the book, and the book contains passages that are not in the *Idra*; some are from other places in the Zohar with which we are familiar, and for some there is no extant source. Even the passages of the *Idra* quoted are often not in the same order as in the Zohar and their wording differs. I was able to study one of these changes with facility, thanks to Amos Goldreich's work, which furnishes a precise description and detailed comparison with the *Idra*.[243] Goldreich showed that the structure of the Zohar *Idra* is more compact and pleasing than that of *Sefer ha-Gevul*. Goldreich studied the problem in depth and rejected the possibility that the page order of *Sefer ha-Gevul* or of the *Idra* in his possession might have been confused, or that R. David changed the order for reasons of method. His conclusion (on page 34 of his work on *Sefer ha-Gevul* was: "The omissions [in the order of the *Idra*] are in the main absolutely arbitrary, and there is no justification for them, other perhaps than the wish to distort and efface the original structure of the *Idra*, in an effort to create from *Idra Rabba* a new work called *Sefer ha-Gevul*, to be attributed to R. David."

I shall suggest here another solution: the source of many of the differences between *Idra Rabba* and *Sefer ha-Gevul* is the *Idra* that was in R. David's possession. I am not referring to a changed order of the pages, rather R. David was familiar with the work before it assumed its final form, while it was still in the raw stage. This was indeed a "Zoharic" text and not a "proto-Zohar" text such as those with which R. Joseph Gikatilla or Joseph of Hamadan were familiar. However, since originally it was a kind of report of the discussions of the circle, it still awaited an editor to give it the final polish, to add to and take away from it and arrange its parts suitably. R. David found it in this state and attempted to improve it to the best of his ability: by translation and commentary and with additions of his own. There is no attempt at plagiarism by R. David. The way he uses the *Idra* must be understood in light of his status in the Zohar circle, a status that will be described below through other of his extant writings, some of which were published only recently. Even without such a study, I do not see how a different order could help R. David to claim authorship of the *Idra*. In accordance with the philological rule of *lectio difficilior*, if the order in *Sefer ha-Gevul* is more difficult, this indicates that it is more original and was elaborated in later versions.

In our study of "Primordial Man"[244] we examined one passage incorporated in the *Idra* in *Sefer ha-Gevul* that does not figure in the Zohar *Idra*. We perceived that this is not an addition, but that the passage belonged to the *Idra* originally and was removed by an editor, because it reflects a view not consistent with the *Idra*. I cannot develop this further in the present framework, but I will add an opposite example, an apparent "omission": the impressive myth of the death of the kings of Edom appears in *Idra Rabba* three times, and far apart from each other.[245] Hence, the complete absence of this subject in *Sefer ha-Gevul* is blatant. Goldreich (p. 63) attributed R. David's omission to theological difficulties. This assumption is contradicted by a text, which includes this myth, published by *Idel* (after Goldreich's work) and identified by him as reflecting R. David b. Judah he-Hasid's thought.[246] The only remaining explanation for the "omission" is that the subject of the "Kings of Edom" was not in the version of the *Idra* with which R. David was familiar. This corresponds to the conjecture that I proposed some years ago, that the mention of the death of the Kings of Edom in *Idra Rabba* alludes to the fall of the last remnant of the Crusader kingdom in Eretz Israel in 1291.[247] At the time I expressed this opinion "rather hesitantly" because of chronological difficulties associated with the writings of Gikatilla, R. Bahya, and Joseph of Hamadan, whom I assumed had already used the *Idra* in a prior period; I attempted to resolve this by "conjecturing" that these Kabbalists were familiar with an earlier edition of the *Idra*. This conjecture is confirmed now through the comparison with *Sefer ha-Gevul*, which in turn confirms the reason we proposed for the "omission" in *Sefer ha-Gevul*. Indeed, it seems that this passage was not in the *Idra* of the other contemporary Kabbalists either. In R. Joseph Gikatilla's writings this secret was not taken from the *Idra* and is closer to its form in the writings of the "Gnostic Kabbalists."[248] R. Joseph of Hamadan was completely unaware of the relation between the Kings of Edom and the idea of the worlds that were destroyed at the beginning of the Emanation, as is shown precisely in his extensive homilies on the portion of the "Kings of Edom," in which these kings are reckoned as demonic forces in the sphere of *Sitra Ahra*, and nothing more.[249]

Another "omission," which is very important for an understanding of R. David's relation to the Zohar, is the absence in

Sefer ha-Gevul of the "narrative framework" of the *Idra* and the names of its rabbis. This might be explained by the fact that the "narrative framework" was not complete in the *Idra* which R. David had in his possession. Such an explanation is certainly valid for some of these "omissions," and corresponds to the thesis we presented above, that the "narrative framework" was perfected in the final editing of the *Idra*. This is not, however, the entire explanation. If we add the fact that nowhere in his writings does R. David mention the Zohar[250] or the *Idra* as a literary composition (his use of the term *Idra* will be discussed below), and nor does he note that he is translating or elucidating any book whatsoever (apart from *Sifra di-Tsni'uta*, which he refers to in the same way as the *Idra* in its quotations from *Sifra di-Tsni'uta*[251]), it is natural that an impression of plagiarism emerges. This is further strengthened by the fact that he precedes the adaptation of the *Idra* with his own preface, in which he explains to the reader his Kabbalistic and practical objective and method, as if it were entirely his work. The same is true of the conclusion of the book: "I have arranged this book and called it *Sefer ha-Gevul* and I began it from the Most Ancient One until the natural world so that you will be free of all doubt and thought and will not require profound conceptions since this is the limit [in Hebrew: *ha-gevul*]."[252] The conclusion that this is an attempted plagiarism also presents difficulties. Firstly, can a book such as the *Idra* be plagiarized? Would anyone believe that R. David was the author? Could R. David think that he was the only one to possess this book? Further, in certain places, the rabbis of the *Idra* are nonetheless mentioned in *Sefer ha-Gevul*,[253] and such negligence is hardly suited to the method of a plagiarist. Amos Goldreich, who most meticulously described the relevant findings in *Sefer ha-Gevul*, was compelled therefore, out of great intellectual honesty, to assume that this was a "hesitant, inconsistent plagiaristic tendency, which was apparently unaware of itself right up to the end."[254]

Apart from the intrinsic difficulty in it, this solution does not relate to the other strange aspects of R. David's attitude to the Zohar. In *Sefer Mar'ot ha-Tsove'ot*, for instance, instead of omitting the "narrative framework" from the Zohar passages, R. David even adds to them; alongside translations of authentic Zohar sections (and some that were not conserved in the Zohar in our possession, and which are to be found in all his writings[255]) he attributes Kabbalistic words of other Kabbalists to the Zohar rabbis. He even adds his own words, which are at times attributed to R. Hiyya, and sometimes they are accompanied by Zoharic blessings for their author, uttered by R. Simeon b. Yohai.[256] (Thus some of his sayings even appeared in the printed Zohar, and other sayings of his are quoted by Kabbalists as if they were Zohar dicta.[257]) In my opinion, all this is explained by the fact that R. David himself belonged to the Zohar circle (and not that he is "eager to have his alter ego accepted into the circle of *havrayya*," as maintained by one important scholar, who furnished an excellent description of R. David's writings, but failed to depart from the conventional conclusions drawn by the research literature[258]). He joined it at a relatively late stage when most of the Zohar had already been written and was almost at the final editing stage. The circle remained in existence, however. Since he was close to its leaders and familiar with its method of action, R. David allowed himself on the one hand to translate, elucidate, and disseminate Zohar writings within his own writings, and on the other hand to continue to write in the Zohar style. If his old friend, R. Moses de Leon, ascribed the words of the shared circle to rabbis such as R. Hiyya, why should R. David not do so too? It is not surprising that R. David also ascribed to the rabbis of the Zohar sayings of other Kabbalists, since they also belonged to the same circle, and their names have already been mentioned above: R. Moses de Leon, R. Joseph Gikatilla, R. Joseph ben Shalom Ashkenazi ha-Arokh, and R. Todros Abulafia.[259] In this he followed the usage of the Zohar itself, which ascribed the words of its circle to the *Tannaim*. In contrast, the words of R. Azriel of Gerona were introduced by: "And I have seen in the commentary of some Kabbalists."[260]

Solid proof exists of R. David's intimate relations with the authors of the Zohar. Firstly, R. David knew one of the sources cited in the Zohar, which is not known from anywhere else and was suspected of being from the fictive "celestial library." In *Sefer ha-Gevul* and *Mar'ot ha-Tsove'ot* he cites from it more than was cited in the Zohar.[261] Secondly, according to *Or Zaru'a*, Rabbi David's later book[262] (not yet in print), R. David personally knew the members of the *Idra*. This can perhaps already be deduced from the preface to the book:[263] "Because all the words (of the rabbis) are an allusion to him[264] who entered and departed from *bei Idra*." This is Zohar rhetoric and we have already discussed its meaning.[265] It is doubtful whether it was known and in use, other than in reference to the defined *Idra* circle, and perhaps also to the place where they met. Scholem indeed maintained that the reference was to a "mysterious conception also called by other Kabbalists in this period "entrance to *bei Idra*",[266] but I have found no reference to this in other contemporary Kabbalists, other than the following example that Scholem cited from *Livnat ha-Sappir*:[267] "And I understood in *Midrash ha-Ne'elam* [the term used for the entire Zohar in this book] from the *Idra de-Vei Mashkena*,[268] that wherever it is written in the midrash 'come you to *bei Idra*,' it means: come in to see the light of God. And the proof is that it says there. . . ." As proof, a section from the Zohar (II, 128b) is cited here, in which *Idra* appears as a symbol for God. So it is clear that *bei Idra* is not a usual expression for the author of *Livnat ha-Sappir*, but the language of the source that he is attempting to explain through proofs and parallels. Indeed the expression "come you to *bei Idra*" does not appear in the Zohar in our possession, but the author of *Livnat ha-Sappir* explicitly affirms on several occasions that this is the version he had before him. This rhetoric at the beginning of *Or Zaru'a* also posed difficulties for one of the copyists of the book, who replaced the above expression in one manuscript by "he who entered and departed in this commentary (in Hebrew: *be'ur da* instead of *bei Idra*)."[269]

Even without the proof from *Livnat ha-Sappir*, it can still be maintained that *bei Idra* in *Or Zaru'a* is general rhetoric, and we have already raised the possibility that R. David employed a similar usage in this book with the combination "*tsni'ut ha-sefer*."[270] There is one example that precludes any such assumption. In one place in *Or Zaru'a*[271] we read: "A question asked by the members of the *Idra*:[272] why do all the nations say 'Amen'. You will find 'Amen' in all seventy tongues. And the rabbis replied. . . ." This interesting question and its answer (which I will not quote at length here) do not appear in the *Idra* or anywhere else in the Zohar. This is direct evidence of the active relation between the author and the actual *Idra* Circle, and not the composition of the *Idra*, which he never mentions by name. The narration appears extremely authentic because it does not idealize this Circle in any way; the "members of the *Idra*" are described here as people who do not know an answer to their question, and they ask other rabbis. Perhaps this lowered status of the members of the *Idra* added to the difficulty of the copyist who had been troubled by the word *Idra* in the previous case. Here he determined: "A question asked by the rabbis of that generation [in Hebrew: *hai dora* instead of *bnei ha-Idra*] and the sages replied to them."[273] Perhaps the use of the singular form of the verb "replied" in Hebrew alludes to the fact that the source referred to one sage, and then the picture becomes simpler: the members of the *Idra* ask the question of the scholar at their head, as the rabbis of the *Idra* in the Zohar used to ask their rabbi, R. Simeon b. Yohai.

The proofs that follow will be taken from such questions. Not from questions addressed to R. Simeon b. Yohai, but from questions addressed to R. David b. Judah by his disciples, in which they asked him to explain the doctrine of the *Idra*. The text of the questions and answers makes it quite clear that R. David is considered as one of

the remaining members of the *Idra* Circle, and his authority stems
from this. Here too the *Idra* is not referred to as a composition, but
as a "group," and its leader is not called R. Simeon b. Yohai, but "the
head of the group," even though it refers to the person who expressed
R. Simeon b. Yohai's views in the composition of the *Idra*. Indeed, the
impression is given that the asker and the respondent knew the
identity of the rabbi of the previous generation, concealed behind the
Zohar's R. Simeon b. Yohai. The responsum appears in a single
manuscript[274] and was published by Moshe Idel,[275] who studied its
Kabbalistic significance[276] and dealt with the identity of its author.
With respect to our study, I will quote here the beginning of this
answer (with corrections from the manuscript):

> The answer that my venerable teacher R. David gave to my
> question on the secret of the two heavenly Countenances that
> were never separated and will never be separated.[277] Wisdom
> cries without[278] and the locks of the hair of the head of the group
> are curls,[279] mounds of curls.[280] Even though you are a reaper of
> the field[281] and supreme secrets are not concealed from you, but
> hidden in the treasures of your room,[282] notwithstanding[283] here
> is the answer to what you asked. The head of the group knew,
> said the members of the group, the secrets of *Genesis Rabba*:[284]
> "We saw supernals below and inferiors above."[285],[286]

The second question and responsum was also published by Idel,
together with a detailed study.[287] I will quote part of it:

> And this is the answer given by my venerable teacher R. David
> to my question to examine in detail to what degree in the actual
> *sefira* the "eyes" and the "nose" and the "mouth"and the "beard"
> and *Orekh Anpin* [the Large Countenance or the Long-Suffering
> One] and the Small Countenance allude. Said my venerable
> teacher R. David: It seems to me according to what I learnt from
> my teachers that all these names allude to a most high place
> which is *Ein Sof* which is ten *tsahtsahot* [brightnesses]. . . .and
> *Orekh Anpin* alludes to the supreme *Keter* of the ten which is
> the Large Countenance, and Small Countenance alludes to the
> crown ['*atara* = *Shekhina*] within it[288]. . . . . All these things are
> transmitted from one man to another and could not be written,
> and if I did not love you I would not have written them. But since
> I know that they are hidden with you, I have written them to you.

I believe that the expression "hidden with you" alludes to the existence of the *Idra*,[289] and in particular if we compare this expression to "hidden in the treasures of your room" which we saw in the previous reply, where the expression "your room' [Hebrew: *hadarkha*] would seem to allude to the word "*Idra*" (Assembly). Such an allusion also exists perhaps in the rhetoric concluding the passage quoted by Idel from *Sefer ha-Gevul*,[290] and which mentions "his holy law which he gave us from his treasure-house." Whether or not this is the case, the anthropomorphic secrets expounded by R. David here are secrets of the *Idra*. It should be noted that he does not refer to his intellect and understanding or to celestial aid,[291] but to what "I learnt from my teachers," "because these are things transmitted from one man to another." These are not merely words! Thanks to Moshe Idel's research work, scholars will no longer disregard R. David and his Kabbala, or apologize in their work for discussing such an unimportant Kabbalist. Idel found that R. David in his writings expressed and faithfully developed very ancient traditions which prevailed in Israel for centuries (at the same time he was also open to receive mystical doctrines from elsewhere,[292]) and also considerably influenced the future history of the Kabbala and in particular the Lurianic Kabbala.[293] As a receiver of tradition, R. David is likely to be a member of a group, and the contents of this tradition indicate the Zohar as his group. First and foremost of these contents is his famous doctrine of the "ten *tsahtsahot*" and their anthropomorphic image, mentioned in his responsum above.[294] This doctrine is close to the *Idra* and refers to it. Since R. David wrote these words shortly after the Zohar was written, it might easily be assumed that the teachers to whom he alludes there are the authors of the Zohar. Idel certainly noted that R. David's Kabbala is not identical to the Zoharic Kabbala.[295] To my mind, however, this difference results from the nature of this group, each of the various members of which dealt with the ancient traditions in his own independent manner (we already saw that in the actual Zohar, and in the actual *Idra*, various orientations were preserved). While the doctrine of the ten *tsahtsahot* is not an essential part of the Zoharic Kabbala, and does not appear in the writings of R. Moses de Leon,[296] it can be proved that it is also known in the Zohar. It appears there in several sections (the word *tsahtsahot* is sometimes translated in Zoharic language as *tehirin* and sometimes it appears in other places in other guises), and these are connected to the doctrine of the *Idra*, as we heard from R. David.[297]

This study of R. David b. Judah he-Hasid shows us that inquiry into the Zohar must also encompass the fourteenth-century continuers, imitators, and commentators. A comprehensive discussion of the question of the Zohar will also include, *mutatis mutandis*, R. Joseph Angelet, who belongs to this circle and has many ties with it. Even though his relation to the Zohar would seem to be different from R. David's—he quotes from it explicitly and in Aramaic, and even writes his own compositions in Aramaic—he obviously saw himself as an authorized continuer of the Zohar circle.[298] The discussion will also encompass the book *Berit Menuha*, which includes Aramaic passages introduced by the expression "R. Simeon b. Yohai said";[299] and above all such a discussion will comprehend the author of *Ra'aya Meheimna* and *Tikkunei Zohar*.

I see this chapter as a contribution to the comprehensive research that still remains to be undertaken.

APPENDIX 1: (Appendix to Note 248) Catharsis of Thought, The Doctrine of *Gilgul* and the Death of the Kings

The idea alluded to in *Sha'arei Ora* in the place indicated in the note, according to Gikatilla and to most of the early Kabbalists, requires "numerous orally transmitted kabbalot, things that are the mysteries of the world." I will summarize very briefly the conclusions that I drew from their allusions, and I hope to expand on this subject in another context. Gikatilla is apparently alluding to the dualism of good and evil existing in the *sefira* of *Hokhma* (which is also called Thought—Mahshava) and in the *sefira* of *Keter*, even if it is *Rahamim* (mercy) which is not mixed.[300] This dualism is apparently connected to the arbitrariness prevailing in Thought ("Be silent! Thus it occurred in thought"), from which "the righteous suffer, the wicked thrive," and the capriciousness and arbitrariness of the complete pardon of the *Keter* ("and I shall be gracious to whom I shall be gracious" [Ex. xxxiii, 19]); it is also presented here as stemming precisely from the height of the *Keter*, which is above any causation. This dualism has profound roots in early Judaism, as noted by Moshe Idel.[301] In the circle of the "Gnostic Kabbalists" this idea gave birth to a secret doctrine, according to which the world, which is merely the Thought of the creative God, is cleansed in the course of the emanation, of the supernal evil. This process is called the *sod ha-ibbur*, and it includes the idea of the destruction of the worlds, as well as the idea of the catharsis of the impaired souls through transmigration (the *sod ha-ibbur* was confined to the subject of souls only at a relatively late period). This catharsis was used to interpret the subject of Cain, Abel, and Seth, who transmigrated in Moses, and the Ten Martyrs headed by R. Akiva (of his martyr's death as the "reward" for preserving his Torah it is said: "be silent! Thus it occurred in thought," BT, Menahot, 29b), who were elevated to a cosmic level, and whose death became the means for world redemption, as we found also in other cases in Jewish martyrology.[302] Apparently the death of the Ten Martyrs by the "Kingdom of Edom" was the *Tikkun* [restitution] of the blemish of the "Kings of Edom" in their Zoharic sense, even though the Kings of Edom were not specifically mentioned in this context in the Gnostic circle.[303] The relationship between the Kings of Edom and the Ten Martyrs is explicit in the Zohar and in the writings of the Zohar circle,[304] and the Kings of Edom are also linked there with the sphere of the Divine Thought: the term *malkhei* (kings of) is understood also as an invalid thought, in the expression *nimlakh be-da'ato* [changed his mind], as is apparent for instance in the expression *Shi'er malkhin* [gave due proportion to certain kings], attributed to *Sifra di-Tsni'uta.*[305]

The myth of the Kings must also be related to those supernal lights, which were pursued by the "light of Thought" thus causing the continued Emanation, and which, when reintegrated, become the ten palaces called *Ein Sof.*[306] (These lights, and the idea of the catharsis of Thought gave birth to the final stage of the development of the myth under discussion in Jewish thought—the idea of "light which contains thought" and 'light which does not contain thought" in the Kabbala of Nathan of Gaza.[307]) Such an interpretation does not, however, invalidate the actual existence of the Kings. Both R. Moses Cordovero's "abstract" interpretation of their nature and R. Isaac Luria's "mythical" explanation are based on the plain meaning of the Zohar.[308] The secret tradition concerning the cleansing of Thought is the basis for the Lurianic doctrine of Catharsis.[309] In R. Isaac Luria's doctrine, too, there is a close connection betwen the myth of the transmigration of the souls and the emanation and cleansing of the worlds, as well as between the death of the Kings of Edom and the Ten Martyrs.[310] The dead Kings of Edom were alluded to in the Zohar not only in the *Idrot*, but also in Zohar, I, 223b, where they are identified with "the children of the east country" (in Hebrew: *benei kedem*, which also means "primieval men") (Kings 1, v, 10). On the idea and its sources see also above.[311]

──────── APPENDIX 2: Rabbi Todros Ben Joseph Abulafia ────────
And Rabbi Simeon Bar Yohai

This chapter proposes the theory that the writer of the Zohar, seemingly R. Moses de Leon, reflected in his composition the life of

an actual group and added to it literary elements of his own. While
we indicated several possible members of this group, we did not
determine which personality is represented, albeit partially, by the
figure of R. Simeon b. Yohai. There is no special reason to identify
this figure with the author. On the contrary, R. Simeon b. Yohai is
not represented in the book as an author (*Idra Zuta* was written by
R. Abba—Zohar, III, 287b), and not all the book takes place in his
lifetime (below, paragraph 6). I cannot be definitive in the matter, but
I do suggest that one possibility be considered, and that is that the
personage of R. Simeon b. Yohai in the Zohar is in fact the Kabbalist
R. Todros ha-Levi Abulafia. This assertion is based on the following
considerations:

1. Many of the most esoteric doctrines of the Zohar are alluded to
   in the writings of R. Todros (see above, Appendix 1), and he was
   in possession of pseudo-midrashic sources that are also elaborated
   in the Zohar and are not known from elsewhere (above, n. 39).
2. R. Todros' firm ethical position as regards sexual promiscuity, and
   in particular as regards the permissiveness that was allowed with
   the Moslem female servants is reflected in the Zohar and in the
   Hebrew writings of R. Moses de Leon.[312]
3. R. Moses de Leon, who drafted the Zohar in its written form, was
   well acquainted with R. Todros and his son R. Joseph, and
   dedicated several of his books to R. Joseph.
4. R. Todros's son was also a Kabbalist, and in the Zohar we find R.
   Eleazar the son of R. Simeon.
5. The Zohar was written when R. Todros was already an old man;
   in fact he died in 1283[313] during the course of the Zohar's
   composition and the activity of the Zohar group. Likewise the story
   of R. Simeon b. Yohai's death is recounted in the Zohar (in *Idra
   Zuta* and in *Midrash ha-Ne'elam*), and in several sections he is
   referred to as though he were dead (see for instance Zohar, II, 123b).
   Of course, we do not have to attribute all the sections in which
   R. Simeon b. Yohai is portrayed as alive to the period prior to 1283.
   The author of the Zohar here followed the method of Plato, who
   wrote the Socratic Dialogues many years after the death of his
   teacher Socrates, who was merely his spiritual mentor in his way
   of writing.[314]
6. R. Todros was the head and the rabbi of the Castile community
   (at times he is referred to simply as "the Rabbi"), bringing together
   Torah and greatness.[315] At the same time he was considered the
   head of the Castile Kabbalists. The Zohar itself also considers itself
   a part of this group of Kabbalists.[316]

7. R. Todros b. Joseph married into a family renowned both for its wealth and its Torah learning (he himself was also descended from great Torah scholars). Thus the poet Todros b. Judah Abulafia wrote in his eulogy: "And he married into Torah and greatness... and he is rich and wise..."[317] R. Pinhas b. Yair, who in the Zohar is referred to as R. Simeon b. Yohai's father-in-law and not his son-in-law as he is in the Talmud, is described as he who by virtue of his piety also received honor and blessings of this world, Zohar, III, 72a (he is always called "pious" = *hasid* in the Zohar, and several people were called by such an epithet in the Middle Ages).

8. If we meticulously compare the series of poems dedicated to R. Todros b. Joseph by the poet Todros b. Judah Abulafia,[318] we find that the descriptions of R. Todros are similar to those of R. Simeon b. Yohai in the Zohar. We certainly receive the impression that both sources are describing one man and from a common viewpoint, although the frivolous poet was certainly not a member of the actual Zohar group, and did not discern in his rabbi all that they discerned. It should be noted that these poems are the principal source for a knowledge of R. Todros apart from general words of admiration uttered by R. Isaac Ibn Latif, R. Yeda'yah ha-Badrashi, and R. Isaac Albalag, and apart from what can be deduced from R. Todros's actual writings.

Here are a few of the parallels: in the eulogy on R. Todros's death (poem 431), he is described as sustaining the ten *sefirot* and the entire cosmos (the beginning of the poem); and his degree is superior to that of the angels (line 45), and compare Zohar, I, 4a; and as abolishing the decrees (line 52), and see Zohar, III, 15a. R. Todros is also called here "the tree of knowledge and of life" (line 45), and compare Zohar, I, 218a: "A great tree, mighty in both worlds, which is R. Simeon, son of Yohai," and also in *Ra'aya Meheimana*—Zohar, III, 223b and *Tikkunei Zohar, Tikkun* 6, 23b; and he is also called *tanoui* (= *Tana*, line 57). R. Todros desires here to see "the dead who own fortified stages" (line 49), and this can perhaps be paralleled with R. Simeon b. Yohai's attempt to find out with whom he will dwell in Paradise (*Zohar Hadash*, 19a, *Midrash ha-Ne'elam*).[319] His death is considered a unification with God ("Entered into the rock, and hid in the dust" Isaiah ii, 10) and as true life (lines 49–50), and compare the end of *Idra Zuta*. R. Todros is considered a "sea of goodness" and the source from which rivers flow (lines 51, 56), and compare Zohar, III, 23a: "Alas for the world when R. Simeon shall depart, and the fountains of wisdom shall be closed." After R. Todros's death no one remains who can understand "Bible and mishnas, gemaras and toseftas and baraithas and haggadas and midrashes" (lines 59–63), and in

Zohar, I, 217a, "And R. Simeon ascending on them with a scroll of
the law, and also with all manner of books containing the hidden
expositions and Agadahs. They all ascended to heaven and were lost
to view. When R. Judah woke he said: In truth, since the death of
R. Simeon wisdom has departed from the earth." Perhaps the word
Agadata is mentioned here precisely because R. Todros is known as
the exponent of the *Aggada* in his book *Otsar ha-Kavod*. On R. Todros's
death, the words of the rabbis remained sealed without keys (lines
62–63), and compare Zohar, II, 174a: "When R. Simeon reflected on
this subject....he said: All the treasures of the supernal King are
disclosed by means of one key." And on his death the light was
concealed and no longer diffuses his light (line 34, and see also poem
428), and compare Zohar, II, 86b: "R. Simeon is such a light; he
illuminates everyone," and compare also Zohar, I, 156a, and the
expression *butsina kadisha* (holy lamp) which is also the standard
epithet of R. Simeon b. Yohai in the Zohar. We can also find an
interesting parallel for the following image: "The fields of the stages
[*ma'alot*] he made reaped and the vineyards of grace he made
harvested" (line 47), and compare R. Simeon b. Yohai's complaint at
the beginning of *Idra Rabba*, Zohar, III, 127b: "And the reapers of
the field are few, and those who are at the end of the vineyard do not
attend."[320] *Ma'alot* means stages, and is equivalent to *dargin* which
is one of the usual names for the *sefirot* in the Zohar. It is also said
in the eulogy: "And the cares bloomed in the flower beds and he
watered them by bloody tears in place of rivers" (line 38). This might
perhaps be compared with what is said after the death of R. Simeon
b. Yohai at the end of *Idra Zuta*, Zohar, II, 296b: "and all the comrades
are drinking [*shateyan*] blood." It is possible to interpret this as
shotetim dam ["are dripping blood"],[321] but the expression *shateyan*
is easier to explain from the word *shtiya* [drinking].[322]

　　　Certainly R. Todros b. Joseph's style in his Kabbalistic writings
does not resemble R. Simeon B. Yohai's style in the Zohar. In contrast
to the Zoharic abundance, R. Todros is very wary of revealing
Kabbalistic secrets and confines himself to allusions. However, R.
Simeon b. Yohai might also have acted in this way if he had written
his own words in a book that would reach a broad public; certainly
his attitude in the Zohar to the revealing of Kabbalistic secrets is
characterized by a marked ambivalence.[323]

3

Christian Influences on the Zohar

One of the outstanding features of the Zohar is its receptiveness to ideas from other sources and its ability to adapt them to its own particular style and way of thought. A far from negligible factor that facilitated this receptivity was the book's pseudo-epigraphic format, which freed its author from the cares and criticisms of his contemporaries. It should not surprise us therefore that a leading source of such influences on the Zohar was Christianity since, as we know, its author lived in a Christian milieu. Further, the nature of Christianity as a daughter-religion (or, rather, a sister-religion) of Judaism, an alternative interpretation of a common scriptural tradition, made it all the easier for the two religions to influence one another and for the Zohar to become an expression of this mutual influence.

Needless to say, the Zohar is emphatically a Jewish, not a Christian work. It adopted basic concepts from a variety of sources and combined them together, creating an amalgam that presents a complete, albeit diversified, picture of the Jewish religion. In spite of the originality of this picture, there is no mistaking the Jewish spirit that permeates it—that spirit which made it possible for the Zohar to strike such deep roots among the Jewish people, making it a decisive factor in shaping the temper and outlook of Jewish life, particularly during the sixteenth to eighteenth centuries. (In passing, it should be noted that, although the author of the Zohar allowed himself to be influenced by Christianity, this does not mean that he felt any affinity for the "Gentile Nations," and particularly for those who converted to their faith. Quite the opposite is true—see note 90).

Thus, there is no basis to the claims of Christian Kabbalists that the Zohar contains Christian beliefs. On the other hand, those Kabbalists did have some grounds for their claims, since the Zohar does contain many texts of Christian origins (of which the Zohar's author was quite conscious); however, in the Zohar these formulations were transformed into an integral part of the Jewish-Kabbalistic worldview. In this article I shall present a number of examples of Christian influence found in the Zohar, although the esoteric nature

of the material calls for intensive research in order to uncover this
influence. I shall begin my examples with a discussion of the doctrine
of trinity in the Zohar.

The Doctrine of Trinity

It is a well-known fact that the Zohar frequently describes the
Godhead as a threefold unity, doing so in different ways.[1] The tenfold
structure of the Kabbalistic *sefirot* can actually be fitted into a
threefold division, particularly in accordance with a certain passage
from *Pirkei de-Rabbi Eliezer*—a passage on which the Zohar often
bases itself (see note 15)—thus remaining within the realm of
traditional Judaism.

Notwithstanding, it is my contention that the Christian doctrine
of the trinity also influenced the threefold formulations in the Zohar
(it should be noted that the very interest demonstrated by the Zohar
in tripartite formulations is itself due to Christian influence).[2] I shall
illustrate this[3] through a study of triparte formulations that the Zohar
brings concerning the divine names, *Adonai Eloheinu Adonai,* in the
verse "Hear O Israel the Lord our God, the Lord is One" (Deut. vi,
4), the verse par excellence proclaiming the unity of God. In the Zohar
(II, 53b) we read the following:[4]

Hear, O Israel, *Adonai Eloheinu Adonai* is one. These three are
one. How can the three Names be one?[5] Only through the
perception of faith: in the vision of the Holy Spirit, in the
beholding of the hidden eye alone.[6] The mystery of the audible
voice is similar to this, for though it is one yet it consists of three
elements—fire, air and water, which have, however, become one
in the mystery of the voice. Even so it is with the mystery of the
threefold Divine manifestations designated by *Adonai Eloheinu
Adonai*—three modes which yet form one unity. This is the
significance of the voice which man produces in the act of
unification, when his intent is to unify all, from the Infinite (*Ein-
Sof*) to the end of creation. This is the daily unification, the secret
of which has been revealed in the holy spirit.

Tishby, in relation to this passage and others,[7] wrote: "The
Zohar's presentation of the mystery of the Trinity, however, is quite
different from the Christian one....There is no denying the possibility,
nonetheless, that despite his firm anti-Christian attitude, the author
of the Zohar might have been influenced in his formulation

of the mystery of the Godhead by the theology of the rival faith." It is this possibility that I have set out to substantiate here.

First, I should like to point out that there are passages which attempt to prove the validity of the Christan Trinity on the basis of the verse "Hear O Israel" in the book *Pugio Fidei* by Raymond Martini,[8] a Christian contemporary and fellow countryman of the author of the Zohar, who had never heard of the Zohar, as well as in a work quoted by Maimonides in his *Ma'amar Tehiyat ha-Metim* (Essay on the Resurrection of the Dead).

It should also be noted that the author of the Zohar himself, R. Moses de Leon, was aware of the paradox of the threefold unity found in the *Shema'* ("Hear O Israel") and its similarity to the Christian principle of trinity. Evidence of this is found in his book *Shekel ha-Kodesh,*[9] which concludes with a discussion of the mystery of unity found in *Shema'*. This discussion is presented in the context of a fictitious questioner inquiring about the inherent contradiction within the belief in a threefold unity, alluding to the Christian nature of such a belief. Such allusions are to be found, in my opinion, in the following remarks of the questioner: "This matter causes much confusion," and "the one who understands this, trembles with fright lest he commit a transgression by speaking of it." The beginning of the response to the questioner also contains such allusions:

> For though it is true that no one in the Land of Israel has ever asked this question. . . .For it is just as you said, that a person should guard his words and thoughts from consideration of this lest the foundation [of his faith] collapse and his thoughts bewilder him. Therefore the master of mysteries may he rest in peace, [i.e., King Solomon, in Eccles. v, 5] taught: "Take care lest your mouth cause you to sin."

It seems to me that in the last words of this passage R. Moses de Leon expressed his apprehension concerning incidences of apostasy grounded in Kabbalistic studies which occurred in his own day, such as the case of R. Abner of Burgos. In *Shekel ha-Kodesh*, he writes:

> Question: You have already discussed[10] the mystery of unity and the mystery of *Adonai Eloheinu Adonai*,[11] speaking of the mystery of unity as regards these three names. And you have also spoken of the mystery of holiness found in the holy triad, "Holy, holy, holy (Isaiah vi, 3)." Even though all this is fine and good, would it not have been proper to demonstrate God's unity, in the mystery of its quality and knowledge, through negation[12]

alone, saying only "God is one," as is found in the mystery "God will be one" (Zechariah xiv, 9). Likewise, in the verse ". . . Holy is the Lord of Hosts," why is "holy" found three times" Is this not a very confusing matter? Although there is truth to be found[13] in the matters you have raised, it is still difficult to come to terms with them. The person who understands them, fears and trembles lest he commit a transgression by speaking of them; and, therefore, he places a harness on his mouth. And then again if, as you suggest, you will find out that these things are as you thought, why are not the ten *sefirot* three, just as the mystery of unity is threefold . . .

It is interesting to note that R. Moses de Leon also grapples in the above passage with the problematics of the ten *sefirot*—why they are not threefold as is the Unity of God (and not only why they are not considered one—a philosophical question)—apparently because the tripartitite formulations were of such obvious importance to him. Indeed, in writing his response to the questioner in his work after he confirmed the unity of three,[14] de Leon also responds to this latter question:

> And as to what you have said concerning the *sefirot* [divine emanations], that they are ten and not three or more, you have made your point very clear. Nevertheless, all the *sefirot* are contained within the mystery of the triune singularity, as our sages teach us [*Pirkei de-Rabbi Eliezer*, 3]: "The world was created through ten sayings, and of three are they comprised— wisdom, understanding[15] and knowledge—forming a single secret of reality". (*ibid.*, p. 134)

Indeed, Abner of Burgos also relied on this triad of wisdom, understanding, and knowledge in order to show the authenticity of the Christian trinity. Y. Baer, citing Abner of Burgos,[16] drew a parallel between his words and the words of the Zohar in the *Midrash ha-Ne'elam* in *Zohar Hadash*, Section Genesis (Mosad ha-Rav Kook ed., 4a) and in III 290a—b (*Idra Zuta*), and in the commentary of R. Azriel of Gerona in his *Commentary to the Aggadot* (see note 13), claiming that not only could such (trinitarian) quotes be used for Christological interpretations, "but that the aforementioned Kabbalist writers had made use of the idea of the Christian Trinity in their works." Further study of these matters leads us to a reevaluation of the work of Christian Kabbalists. Clearly, they frequently falsified quotes from Jewish Kabbalistic sources, but our appraisal of how much truth or fiction is to be found in these passages must change once we acknowledge that some of the passages from the Zohar on which they based themselves really do show signs of Christian influence. In passing, one should note that the most persuasive argument of Christian Kabbala was the fact that here were Jews who claimed Jesus came to the mystery of of the trinity by way of the Kabbala (see G. Scholem's article on the beginning of Christian Kabbala [also note 16] p. 178f.). In addition, it is quite possible that in those few places where the Zohar text of the Christian Kabbalists is more Christological that that found in Jewish hands, the original formulations were preserved by the Christians, while the Jewish copyists either expurged or softened them, for obvious reasons.

This was the case, in my opinion, in the passage on the mystery of unity found in the *Shema'*, quoted by Gershom Scholem[7] from the writings of the apostate Paul of Heredia. I. Tishby, in alluding to the threefold formulations in the Zohar[18] which we mentioned above, has already noted: "The views in the Zohar that I have discussed make it easier to understand how the apostate Paulus de Heredia could fabricate a Christian 'Zoharic' extract dealing with the mystery of unification through the recital of the *Shema*." However, in my opinion one can even go one step further. Careful scrutiny of de Heredia's quote shows that it is really an expunged passage from the Zohar, nowhere preserved by Jewish hands. G. Scholem, in the article mentioned above, noted that this passage was very cleverly forged, far more so than any other Christian texts, such as *Iggeret ha-Sodot* and *Galei Rezaya* (and I certainly do not doubt that these works were forged). Scholem also noted that, from the conspicuous linguistic usages in the Latin text, one can discern that this is a translation of a passage originally written in the language and style of the Zohar. I am in perfect agreement with this assertion and I will cite several examples below. Scholem did not go into details. However, my conclusions concerning this "forgery" are much more far-reaching than those of Scholem, and I shall now elucidate the reasons for this claim.

Firstly, I find it difficult to believe that in the Middle Ages there was a forger so expert that the linguistic style of the Zohar would be apparent even in a Latin translation of his work (I am familiar with the works of several forgers of the Zohar, from the earliest, such as the author of *Tikkunei Zohar* and R. Joseph of Hamadan, to the more recent, such as R. M. H. Luzzatto—all of whose forgeries are readily detected, because they did not succeed in accurately imitating the language of the Zohar). Secondly, this passage contains a certain detail (itself somewhat unclear) that adds nothing to the passage or its Christian intent, but is evidently connected to other passages in the Zohar discussing the same topic. I refer to the phrase *mensura vocis,* the Latin term by which our passage denotes the third member of the trinity—the Holy Spirit.[19] While I could not trace the exact source of this term to the Zohar (its Aramaic equivalent *shi'ura de-kola* appears nowhere in the Zohar),[20] the idea that the three divine qualities are contained in the voice (i.e., the voice of one reciting the *Shema'*) exists in the Zohar. This concept was noted earlier in this chapter (note 7) and is also found in several places in the writings of Moses de Leon[21] in connection with the symbolism of voice and speech that is developed so elaborately in both the Zohar and in his writings.[22] The connection between this voice and the Holy Spirit is also found in the Zohar passage alluded to previously—one can comprehend the unity within the three by means of voice and the Holy Spirit. Similarly, one finds in the writings of Moses de Leon:[23] "The Holy Spirit is speech activated by the voice."[24]

In the passage cited by Heredia, we find strong emphasis placed upon the mystery surrounding the second element of the Trinity—the Son. While the origin of this element is assuredly Christian, in my opinion its use in no way implies a forgery. It is quite possible that these words came from the author of the Zohar himself, for allusions to such concepts are to be found in other passages of the book, as we shall see further on in this study. But first let me remark that this even constitutes a kind of proof of the authenticity of this passage: the very beginning of Heredia's passage does appear in extant editions of the Zohar (as Gershom Scholem correctly noted), in III, 263a.[25] This Zohar passage, concerning the first of the three divine names in the verse *Shema' Yisrael,* contains the following statement: "And this is called the father." While it is true that the term "father" is regularly applied in the Zohar to the *sefira* of *Hokhma* (Wisdom), as it is clearly alluded to here, it is nevertheless unusual for the Zohar to simply enumerate the different names of the divine spheres unless they fit within a specific framework of discourse. Hence, only if we assume that Heredia's addition referring to "son" is authentic will the use of the term "father" seem appropriate within this discourse.

Moreover, it seems to me that if someone wishes to falsify a document, he will forge an entire passage, so as not to be caught in the act of falsifying material, rather than attach a forged section to an authentic passage. This is so especially after we have noted that there are other passages in the Zohar discussing the triune qualities of the *Shema',* which the forger certainly would have known (it is hard to imagine that his forgery just happened to chance on the same idea that appears in the Zohar in these places). One might ask why Heredia did not hinge his forgery on one of these passages, which would have suited his purposes better than the one in question—a passage discussing five elements and not the three found in the *Shema'*.

All of these considerations have convinced me that the passage Heredia brings is an authentic Zohar passage, which was apparently later abridged because of its Christian connotation and then woven into another discourse on the *Shema'*. This change was very likely made by the author of the Zohar himself, who was frightened by his own daring after the first version of his work had been disseminated, reaching Heredia inter alia. Other such instances of this phenomenon—different recensions of the same passage, all written by the author of the Zohar—have been well attested.[26]

Let us now focus on the subject of the "Son" found in Heredia's passage commenting on the second name of God (Elohenu) in the *Shema'*. Heredia writes:

> Elohenu id est deus noster[27] profunditas fluminum et fons scientiarum[28] quae procedunt ab illo patre et filius vocatur[29] Ait aut rabbi Symeon: hoc arcanum filii no revelabitur unicuique quosquam venerit messias ut ait Isaias cap. XI.[30] Quia repleta erit terra scientia dei sicut aquae maris operientes.

Is it possible that these words, shrouding the concept of the Son within a mystery not to be revealed until the advent of the Messiah, could have been written by the author of the Zohar? I would think so. First of all, the style permeating the Latin "translation" is definitely that of the Zohar. We find similar expressions in the Zohar in different contexts (not about the "Son"), but worded differently enough to suggest that the Heredia passage is authentic, not something copied from another place in the Zohar, but rather a passage sharing authentic stylistic traits with the Zohar, even to the extent of employing the verse from Isaiah in the same manner. Thus, for example, we find in Zohar II, 68a: "But the words of the Master will light up the world until the Messianic king comes, as it is written: 'And the Earth shall be filled with the knowledge of God. . .' [Isa. xi:9]." Similar passages are found in Zohar III, 23a and III, 236b, the latter referring specifically to the *Shema'*: "A secret which was given only to the sages and must not be revealed. R. Simeon fell silent. He laughed and cried, and said: I will say that this is certainly the hour of grace and there is none like this generation until the Messianic king comes."[31]

The Son

In certain sections of the Zohar the subject of the Son is presented as a matter that is obscure and indecipherable. In Zohar I, 3b we find the following passage:

> "In the beginning" *[bereshit]*: this is the key which encloses the whole and which shuts and opens. Six gates are controlled by this key which opens and shuts. At first it kept the gates closed and inpenetrable; this is indicated by the word *bereshit*, which is composed of a revealing word with a concealing word. *Bara* is always a word of mystery, closing and not opening. Said R. Jose: Assuredly it is so, and I have heard the *Botsina Kadisha* [Sacred Lamp][32] say the same, to wit, that *bara* is a term of mystery, a lock without a key, and as long as the world was locked within the term *bara* it was not in a state of being or existence. Over the whole there hovered *tohu* [chaos], and as long as *tohu* dominated, the world was not in being or existence. When did that key open the gates and make the world fruitful?[33] It was when Abraham appeared, as it is written,[34] "These are the generations of the heavens and of the earth *Behibaream*" [When they were created]. Now,[35] *Be-hibaream* is an anagram of *Be-Abraham* [through Abraham], implying that what was hitherto sealed up and unproductive in the word *BARA* has by a transposition of letters become serviceable, there has emerged a pillar[36] of fruitfulness: for *BARA* has been transformed into *EIVER* [organ], which is the sacred foundation on which the world rests.

What we have here is another version of the myth regarding "the Holy One who creates worlds and destroys them,"[37] or how the Holy One desired at first to create his world using only the quality of strict judgment as its foundation, but after deliberation added to it the quality of mercy.[38] This idea is developed in the *Idrot*, as in Zohar, III, 128a, referring to Genesis xxxvi, 31: "And these are the kings that ruled in the land of Edom before a king reigned over the children of Israel." Here, however, the idea is developed quite differently. The word *bereshit* is the *sefira* of *Hokhma*[39] containing within it the letters of the word *bara* and *shit*[40] (Aramaic for six). The *sefira* of *Hokhma* (which at times can be referred to as the father) can be conceived as a key that can open the womb of the *sefira* of *Bina* (intuition—the "mother"), causing her to give birth and replenish the emanations sustaining the existence of the world expressed by the word *shit*. These emanations are the six *sefirot* from *Hesed* to *Yesod*, indicated by the Hebrew letter *vav* of the divine name (it goes without saying that the key here is clearly a phallic symbol). However, the key in the passage is not only capable of opening, but also shutting, a condition somehow signified by the word *bara*. Why the word *bara* is closed rather than open is a mystery left unexplained by the Zohar. Instead it prefers to rely on the statement of *Botsina Kadisha*—R. Simeon b. Yohai (the same R. Simeon mentioned in Heredia's passage, on whose authority the son is also declared an indecipherable mystery). At the start of creation, the "key" chose to use the second option—*bara* (*bara* appears twice in Genesis i, 1—once internally within the word *bereshit*, sharing the same first letters in the Hebrew, and secondly as a separate word following the word *bereshit* within the verse)—and thereafter followed a period of *tohu* (chaos), characterized by barrenness.[41] This period also coincides with the generations preceding the patriarch Abraham, for upon his birth the six (*shit*) emanations mentioned above, and which he symbolizes,[42] emerged, causing the letters of the word *bara* to rearrange themselves into the word *eiver*: organ—the male reproductive organ and also the first Hebrew letters forming Abraham's name.

What is the meaning of the word *bara* and why is it considered a "term of mystery?" It seems possible that the reason why the Zohar surrounds this topic with such a veil of secretiveness, identical to that which surrounds the mystery of the son in Heredia's passage, is because both passages may hint at the same subject: the Hebrew word *bara* is also the Aramaic word for son (*bera*). The correctness of such an interpretation of *bera* in the above passage from the Zohar can be shown by a parallel passage in the *Sifra di-Tsni'uta*. This book is, as its name suggests, an "arcane text" of hidden lore which consists entirely of anonymous laconic and indecipherable statements. A major portion of these statements are explained in the *Idrot*. However, the quote referred to above, which we are about to examine in depth, is not discussed in that work. Nonetheless, this passage is clearly parallel to the one found in the Zohar. The two passages complement and clarify one another and, as the word *bara* is interpreted as son in the *Sifra di-Tsni'uta*, we can readily apply this interpretation to our cryptic Zohar passage as well.

We read the following in the beginning of the fifth chapter of the *Sifra di-Tsni'uta* (Zohar, II, 178b): " '*Bereshit bara*,' *bereshit*—a separate statement, *bara*—half a statement; father and son; concealed and revealed." This cryptic passage can readily be deciphered on the basis of the talmudic passage (*Rosh ha-Shana* 32a)—" '*bereshit*' is also a statement (one of the ten by which God created the universe)" for if *bereshit* is considered a complete statement, then *bara*, which is half of that word, must be half of one statement used to create the world. The rest of this cryptic statement may then be readily understood, based on the parallel Zohar passage from I, 3b: "Concealed and revealed" refers to the two halves of the word *bereshit—bera*—concealed; *shit*—revealed. Father and son are therefore *bereshit* and *bera*, for *bereshit* is the *sefira* of *Hokhma* known as the father, while *bera*, according to its Aramaic reading, is the son[43]—confirming and complementing my interpretation of the parallel Zohar passage, *bera* which is prior to Abraham is the "son."

Further examination of this sentence from the *Sifra di-Tsni'uta* calls to mind other associations. The relationship found here between the two "statements" (a whole and a half) and "concealed and revealed" reminds one of the talmudic discussion on the two forms of the letter *mem* found within the Hebrew alphabet. We are told in *Shabbat* 104a that: "An open *mem* and a closed *mem* represent an open (revealed) statement and a closed (concealed statement)." On these words, Rashi comments: " 'An open statement and closed statement'—this refers to matters which one may discuss, and matters which one is commanded to leave closed, such as the mystic speculations on the Divine Chariot." Since the son referred to in the *Sifra di-Tsni'uta* is linked with a closed/concealed statement, we have here yet another source shedding light on the aura of mystery surrounding the son in Heredia's passage—it is a clear parallel to the mystic speculations on the Divine Chariot.

Still another association comes to mind regarding the "son" and the closed *mem*, which is explained in the Talmud as a closed statement (*ma'amar sagur*). If this association or allusion is really present in the text, then its origin is most assuredly Christian: for Christians interpreted the closed, final letter form of the Hebrew letter *mem* in the middle of a word, found in Isaiah ix, 6, as signifying the closed womb of the virgin from which Jesus had issued. This interpretation is to be found in the Christian work *Pugio Fidei* (see note 8),[44] a work from the same general area and period in which the Zohar was written, but whose author had no knowledge of it whatsoever. Within this Christian work, the subject of the son of the virgin is connected to the talmudic passage referring to the "closed statement." This, then, may represent yet another source for why the son is referred to as "half-a-statement" and as closed.

The Zohar's view on this matter becomes clearer if we recall that the closed form of the *mem* is the symbol of the barren male (according to *Sefer ha-Bahir*[45]) representing the *sefira* of *Bina* (called the masculine world in Zohar passages such as II, 101b) when its womb is closed and barren (see Zohar, III, 156b). The picture becomes even clearer if we recall that *bara* in Zohar I, 3b, when described as closed and barren, also relates back to *Bina*, as does the son in Heredia's passage (see note 29). This *sefira* (referred to as freedom and the world to come) has many eschatological associations throughout Kabbalistic literature and its relationship to the son may in part explain why the mystery of the son will not be revealed until the advent of the Messiah (as stated in Heredia's passage).

Moreover, the closed *mem* found in Isaiah ix, 6 is not only interpreted in messianic terms by the Christians, but in the Talmud as well (Sanhedrin 94a), where its closed character is seen to signify the hidden date of the end of days. In the Zohar (III, 156b) we find a similar statement that the *mem* of Isaiah ix, 6 was closed at the time of the destruction of the Temple and will only be reopened at the time of Redemption. This condition of destruction and exile, as it relates back to the closed *mem*, is parallel, I feel, to the period of *tohu* (chaos) signified by *bera* in the Zohar passage examined previously. If we accept this, *tohu* (chaos) then not only refers back to the generations prior to Abraham, but signifies Israel's condition of exile up to the Messianic era.[46] It is even possible that the time of exile is marked as the time of the son (*bera*), since the exile signifies Christian domination under a regime whose god is the son. The theme of barrenness connected with the "son" (the closed *bera* that is barren as opposed to the *eiver*-male reproductive organ) may possibly allude to the Christian monastic ideal, to which the Zohar is absolutely opposed.[47] From this, we can more readily understand how the idea of the Messiah who splits open the closed womb of the *Shekhina*, signified by the closed letter *mem*, developed in later Kabbalistic thinking—an idea which had its beginnings in the Zohar,[48] in which midrashic, Kabbalistic, and Christological speculations were combined. These Christological speculations were used, however, by the Zohar to convey something quite the opposite of their original intent: in the Zohar the time of the "son" is definitely not the Messianic era; on the contrary, it refers to the period of exile. The "son" is seen as defective and marred by barrenness, while the Messiah is a transformed version of this "son" (*eiver* [organ] instead of *bera*[49]), who will in the future rectify this defect. We can perhaps trace here ideas influenced by Joachim of Fiore, who awaited a messianic period of the Holy Spirit that was to come only at the conclusion of his own times, the period of the son. The splitting open of the closed letter *mem* in the messianic era is comparable to the transformation of the "closed/concealed" to the "open/revealed" described in the terminology employed in *Sifra di-Tsni'uta*. Here too we find an allusion to the idea that all of the Torah's secrets will be revealed in messianic times.[50] Another expression of this theme is the transformation of *bera* to *eiver* in Zohar I, 3b. A similar theme is also found in the mending and subsequent revealing of the letter *tsadi*, in I, 2b, which shall be examined later in this study; all of this can also be seen as parallel to the idea found in Heredia's passage that the mysteries of the "son" will be revealed in messianic days (i.e., the "repair" of the son and his emergence from concealment to revelation).

However, there is still more to this melange of motifs and associations. An additional association forces itself upon us when we examine the aforementioned quote from the *Sifra di-Tsni'uta*. On studying this sentence, which connects the "son" with the words or statements God used to create the world and the word *bereshit* (in the beginning), the reader cannot ignore the echoes in this passage of the opening words of the Gospel of John. "In the beginning there was the word [Greek, *logos*] and the word was of God and God was the word." Later in the same chapter (i, 14) the word is even identified as the "son." The opening phrase of John's Gospel bears an obvious parallel to the first words of the Torah—"In the beginning God created"—and it would have been astonishing if Christians had not tried to draw some correspondence in content between the verses. This connection could easily have been made by interpreting the word *bara* in Genesis i, 1 according to its Aramaic rendering—son—especially if they utilized the statement of the rabbis discussed previously: " 'In the beginning' (i.e., the word *bereshit*) is also a statement (by which God created the world)."[51] This interpretation would have carried even more weight had Christians added to it the talmudic passage that designated the closed final *mem* as a "closed statement" along with their own understanding of this letter as representing the womb of the virgin, as mentioned above.

It was only a short time after these associations occurred to me upon reading the statement in *Sifra di-Tsni'uta* that I came across a passage written by a Christian thinker some one hundred years before the time of the Zohar which includes all the abovementioned elements: the comparison drawn between Genesis i, 1 and the Johannine Gospel, the Aramaic connotation of *bar(a)* in Genesis i, 1, and the idea of the "son" as a closed or even an "abridged statement"—parallel to the *Sifra di-Tsni'uta*'s "half a statement"— born of a closed womb, albeit the Christological connection between the closed *mem* as the womb and the closed statement is not explicitly stated in this text. I refer to a passage in Alexander Neckam's book *De Naturis Rerum*.[52] There is no need to assume that the author of the Zohar knew of this book or drew material from it, for Neckam was far from the originator of these exegeses. Even if Neckam did know some Hebrew,[53] he certainly could not have known enough to compose such complex literary connections that require a clear command of the Jewish sources and the ability to deal with them adequately. I personally am convinced that these interpretations reached Neckam through written sources, sources which, as such or in variant terms, were also known to the author of the Zohar. The distance between Neckam's England and Spain makes it hard to assume that there was any direct influence, although it is possible that Neckam may have come across sources for his writings while in France where, we are told in the editor's introduction to his book, he spent some time before writing this book.

The first chapter of *De Naturis Rerum* discusses the correlations between the opening verses of Genesis and those of John's Gospel[54] in the same manner as was suggested above. The openings of both books are not seen as contradictory but as complementary to one another: according to one, the "son" is from the "father" while, according to the other, the father is found in the son. These two claims both represent scriptural truth in accordance with Christian faith.[55] Neckam even cites the "Holy Spirit" as secretly alluded to in both these passages.

After a lengthy discourse of these ideas, Neckam substantiates them by interpreting the various combinations of the Hebrew letters found in the word *bereshit* (in the beginning): *ab* (father), *bar* (son), *esh* (fire = Holy Spirit), and *yesh* (existence). He even interprets the final letter *tav* as signifying the cross,[56] among other things.[57] We are, however, concerned here primarily with the following passage concerning the son:

> ...et habebis *bar*, quod apud nos idem est filius. Ecce quonammodo in principio Geneseos est *verbum inclusum*. Verbum igitur quod omnia continet duabus litteris inclusum est, ad disignandum quia *in utero beatissimae Virginis erat abbreviandum verbum* quod pro nobis abreviatum est. (pp. 7–8)

Here are all the elements found in the sentence from *Sifra di-Tsni'uta*. *Bar* (son) is found within *bereshit* and is designated as a closed statement. This "statement" is interpreted by Neckam as the virgin's womb and is certainly connected with the closed *mem* identified in the Talmud as a "closed statement." All these elements are seen as interrelated in much the same fashion as Raymond Martini viewed them. There is even a a Christological parallel to the expression "half a statement" found in *Sifra di-Tsni'uta*: the statement (the son—Jesus) had to be limited (*erat abbreviandum*) within the virgin womb. [This expression has a long history in Christian theology, beginning in Romans ix, 28 where Paul quotes Isaiah x, 23—"for a decree of annihilation has the Lord of Hosts carried out in the Land." The Hebrew words *kala ve-neheratsa*, translated by the English "decree of annihilation," were rendered in New Testament Greek *logon. . . syntemnon*, coming down to us in their Latin form in the Vulgate as *verbum. . . breviatum* (in some textual versions the participle is active and in others passive). What results from all this is the following understanding of the verse from Isaiah: "An abridged statement will God bring to earth." Certainly, Paul himself never suggested such a reading, but some of the later Church fathers interpreted the "abridged statement" as an allusion to Jesus as the *logos*.[58]] Also of interest is another explanation given by Neckam in his grammatical treatment of the term "a closed statement" (*verbum inclusum*). This phrase may also be translated as "a closed word" (*verbum*, as does the Greek word *logos*, has both these connotations), and according to Neckam "every word consisting of two letters (such as *bar*—son) is a closed matter." One would surmise that the source of Neckam's statement was some work on Hebrew grammar from Neckam's period, but I have yet to trace its source and its precise contextual meaning. (Perhaps he is referring to a two-letter closed syllable?)

The Exegesis of Genesis 1:1

Within this context, it should be noted that Christian discussions of Genesis i, 1 may have exerted a general influence on the way the Zohar interpreted this verse. In Zohar I, 15b we read: " 'The Lord, our God, the Lord.' These are the three stages corresponding to the divine mystery found in 'In the beginning God created.' " As was demonstrated earlier in this work, the triune of "the Lord, our God, the Lord" (*Adonai Eloheinu, Adonai* found in the *Shema'*) is originally a Christian formulation, which is here given as a parallel to the first three words of the Torah.[59]

Furthermore, it seems that the very reading of Genesis i, 1 in such a way that the word "God" is considered the object of the verb "created" rather than its subject (as in the aforementioned passage of the Zohar), is of Christian inception. In Christian-Jewish polemic literature, Jewish writers are extremely critical of such a reading, viewing it as a wholly Christian distortion. R. Yom-Tov Lipmann of Muelhausen (fourteenth–fifteenth centuries) in his *Sefer he-Nitsahon* (*Parashat Bereshit*, para. 4) wrote:

"In the beginning God created." Here the heretics have erred in saying that *bereshit* is the Holy One, who is called the First One, and that he created Elohim [God]—which they interpret to mean as Jesus. This is a malicious fabrication. And even if they erred, have they not the eyes to see the continuation of the verse—"the heavens and the earth"? If another creation which had occurred prior to the world's were cited in this verse, as they claim, would not the text have added a conjunctive *vav*, reading the text as follows—"*and* the heaven and the earth." In addition, the meaning of *bereshit* is "in the beginning/at first" and not, as they mistakenly interpret it, "the First One."

It is interesting that R. Yom Tov, who was a Kabbalist, did not perceive the existence of such an interpretation also in the Zohar (at the beginning of the aforesaid passage, I, 15a: "Thus, by means of this 'beginning' the Mysterious Unknown created this palace. This palace is called Elohim"). There may have been some measure of feigned innocence in his affirmation.

This Christian interpretation of Genesis i, 1 (in which "God" is considered the object of the sentence) seems to be very old, for the rabbis of the Talmud (in Megilla 9a) already attack it: "It is told that Ptolemy the King assembled seventy-two elders...and he said to them...'Write down for me [in Greek] the Torah of Moses your teacher." God caused them all to be of one mind so that each of them translated the first verse: 'God created in the beginning [*bereshit*]." On this passage Rashi comments: "So that no one could say that *bereshit* was a noun and that there are two sovereign realms, one having created the other." Rashi's understanding of this rabbinic passage seems to be substantiated by the reading of the verse in the extant text of the Septuagint: there the word order is the same as in the original Hebrew—"In the beginning God created (*En arxei epoiesen ho Theos*) and not "God created in the beginning." Following Rashi's suggestion, there is then no reason to assume that the rabbis in this passage are referring to a Greek translation—where the word order was changed—different from the one found in the Septuagint; but we can rather conclude that they are referring to the same Greek rendering, in which the word God appears in the nominative form, as the subject and not the object of the sentence (*ho Theos* and not *ton Theon*), but since Hebrew is a language without case endings, the rabbis described the sense of this translation in terms of word order. Be that as it may, the Zohar nevertheless interpreted the word God in Genesis i, 1 as the object of the verb "created," following a Christian tradition attacked by Jewish polemicists throughout the ages. One should note though that the Zohar is not unique among the Kabbalistic writings of its generation in using this interpretation of Genesis i, 1; it is also found in other Jewish writings preceding the Zohar.[60]

The Letter Tsadi—Allusion to Jesus?

We shall now turn to another parallel text in the Zohar that will, in my opinion, also contribute to our understanding of the subject of the "son" who is concealed until the coming of the Messiah, according to the passage by Heredia and the above-mentioned parallels. The passage below is a section of a lengthy passage on the creation of the world, during which each letter of the alphabet approaches the Creator and asks that he use it to create the world and to begin the Torah. (This motif in general and many of its particulars are taken from the *Midrash Otiot de-R. Akiva, op.cit.*, n. 2) This is what the Zohar (I, 2b) writes about the letter *Tsadi*:

> Enters the *Tsadi* and says: "O Lord of the Universe, may it please You to create with me the world, inasmuch as I am the sign of the righteous (*tsaddikim*) and of Yourself who are called righteous (*tsaddik*), as it is written, 'For the Lord is righteous, He loves righteous deeds' (Ps. xi, 7), and hence it is meet to create the world with me.
>
> The Lord answered: "O *Tsadi*, you are *Tsadi*, and you signify righteousness, but you must be concealed, you may not come out in the open so much lest you give the world cause for offense. For you consist of the letter *nun* surmounted by the letter *yod* which is the holy covenant."[61] And this is the mystery of how God created the first man: with two faces.[62] In the same way the *nun* and the *yod* in the *Tsadi* are turned back to back like this— צ —, and not face to face like this— צ . The Holy One, blessed be He, said to her further: "I will in time divide you in two[63] so as to appear face to face,[64] but you will go up in another place."

I have dealt with this passage at length in another part of this book,[65] proving that it contains the idea of the concealed righteous man (*tsaddik*) who, although he is the foundation of the entire world, must conceal himself and the secrets of his doctrine. In this he is similar to the *sefira* of *Yesod*, called *Tsaddik*, symbolized by the masculine organ which is concealed despite being the source of corporeal splendor.[66] I posited that the passage was referring to

R. Simeon b. Yohai, the literary hero of the Zohar, and I showed that this passage (the part about the letters *nun* and *yod*) also indicates a certain flaw in the mystical-sexual existence of R. Simeon b. Yohai, which will be repaired through coupling between him and the *Shekhina*. While I do not renounce this interpretation, I wish to add another level of understanding to it. In my opinion, this description was also influenced in a decisive manner by the image of Jesus, as it was understood by the Zohar. The literary persona of R. Simeon b. Yohai in the Zohar is syncretistic, combining the figure of Jesus, as well as others, with the qualities of the historic R. Simeon b. Yohai.[67] The fact that R. Simeon b. Yohai is described in the Zohar as the son of God also supports this hypothesis.[68]

I base my argument that this passage refers to Jesus on several points. First, there is a striking parallelism between the ideas contained in this passage and those contained in the other passages that I interpreted above, and which I tried to show were alluding to Jesus. Thus, God's statement that *tsadi* will have to be concealed until its repair is clearly parallel to *bera* (son), which is to remain sterile until its repair by *eiver* (organ);[69] the subject of *bera* and *eiver* is parallel, in turn, to the impotent "son" in *Sifra di-Tsni'uta* and the statement of R. Simeon b. Yohai, according to the passage by Heredia, that the subject of the son will be revealed only with the coming of the Messiah. It seems to me, as well, that the very rationalization of the need for concealment—"so as not to give the world cause for offense"—hints at the idea's association with Christianity; in the social reality of the Middle Ages, there was clearly good reason for concealment and esotericism regarding such an idea. Additional study of the text (concerning the letter *tsadi*) raises further parallels between it and the above text dealing with *bera* and *eiver*. God refused to create the world with the letter *tsadi*, claiming that it was flawed and needed to remain concealed until its repair. *Bera* is likewise flawed (impotent and unable to procreate) until later, when it will be reformed and will become *eiver* (an organ). Even the method of repair is similar: in one instance the switching of the letters *yod* and *nun* which comprise the letter *tsadi*, and in the other instance the switching of the order of the letters in the word *bara* (created). The type of flaw is also similar: *bara*'s defect is one of impotence and *tsadi*'s flaw is the absence of sexual harmony, as reflected in the male and female being turned back to back and thus not in a proper position for mating, a problem similar to that of impotence. First and foremost, both passages deal with a first opportunity to create the world (potentially or actually) which is unsuccessful. In my discussion above about *bara* and *eiver*, I pointed out that this is, in fact, another version of the myth concerning the

"Death of the Kings of Edom." The text here concerning *tsadi* parallels the subject of the Kings of Edom even more closely. The flaw in these kings' existence responsible for their death was celibacy, remedied only by the last of them, who married.[70] Elsewhere, this defect is described in the following words (Zohar, II, 176b, at the beginning of *Sifra di'Tsni'uta*): "Until there was a balance[71] they were not looking *face to face* and the ancient kings died." The phrase "face to face" is the very expression used regarding the repair of the letter *tsadi* in our text. Above, I speculated that perhaps the subject of *bera* and the "Kings of Edom" was connected to Christian hegemony ("Edom" is a well-known appellation for Christianity) and that impotence or celibacy is connected to the monastic ideal in Christianity.[72] I now further suggest that this letter *tsadi* perhaps refers to Jesus and to his successors, that is, the celibate popes.

Another argument strengthens the connection between the letter *tsadi* and Jesus. In my opinion, the above text concerning *tsadi* is actually a reworking of a text from the *Midrash Otiot de-R. Akiva* that deals with the same letter; there the letter *tsadi* is explicitly connected with Jesus. While the text in its extant form is clearly anti-Christian, I maintain (and shall attempt to prove) that the text in its original, uncensored version bore a completely different character. Apparently the author of the Zohar was familiar with this first version, which he reworked in the above text. This assumption about such a first version is consistent with my view of *Otiot de-R. Akiva* generally—that is, that it originated in Jewish circles which shared many Christian views.[73] This midrash's influence on our text from the Zohar is not surprising for, as stated, the text is taken from a work which is itself a reworking of a particular section of this midrash.[74]

The following is the text from *Otiot de-R. Akiva* which, in my opinion, influenced this section in the Zohar:[75]

> Why does *tsadi* have two heads? Because it is Jesus of Nazareth who seized two heads—one of Israel and one of Edom—and stood and led people astray. And because Israel saw him thus, they found him and crucified him on the cross. On what did they base themselves: "If your brother, your own mother's son entices you in secret" (Deut. xiii, 7)—[your mother's son, but] not the son of your father.[76]

There are numerous variant readings in the manuscripts of this text, and it is not easy to determine the original version that may have influenced the author of the Zohar, for it is precisely texts such as these that are most liable to distortion by censorship—both internal

and external.[77] Notwithstanding, I am of the opinion that the text was
originally more sympathetic to Jesus than it is in its present form.
Firstly, the very linkage of Jesus with the letter *tsadi*, which evokes
first and foremost the association of *tsaddik* (righteous person),
supports this contention.[78] Further, after the above anti-Christian
homily, one of the manuscripts[79] cites (with some textual differences),[80]
another homily that interprets the *tsadi* as the Messiah-king. It may
be assumed that in the original version these two homilies were one.
The second homily (following the anti-Christian text) reads as follows:

> Another interpretation: Why does *tsadi* have two forms (i.e., one
> when it appears in the middle of the word and one when it is
> the final letter of a word)? This is the true branch (*tsemah
> tsedaka*) (as in Jeremiah xxxiii, 15, "In those days and at that
> time, I will raise up a *Branch of Righteousness* of David's
> line. . ."). And why does it have two heads? This is the Messiah
> son of David, as it is written: "A shoot shall grow out of the stump
> of Jesse" [Isaiah xi, 1].[81] Why is he called Messiah? Because he
> is the head of all.[82] And why is the bottom part (of the *tsadi*) bent?
> Because it is burdened and sick from Israel's sins (an explanation
> very suitable also for Christians!). And why is the other *tsadi*
> (the one that concludes a word) straight? Because God testifies
> to Israel through his prophets that he is a true branch, as it is
> written: "See a time is coming—declares the Lord—when I will
> raise up. . .[The verse continues: ". . . . a true branch of David's
> line."] [Jer. xxiii, 5) And why does *tsadi* have two heads? One is
> for "branch" (*tsemah*) and one is for "righteous" (*tsaddik*).

Probably in the original version of *Otiot de-R. Akiva*, the two
heads of the letter *tsadi* did not expound the negative two-faced quality
of Jesus (as it appears in the printed version), who made himself the
head both of Edom (the gentiles) and also of Israel. Perhaps it
originally alluded to the two facets of Jesus's personality: one human
and one divine (speculation about these facets and their interrelations
caused many controversies in the Christian church). Indeed, I found
an allusion to this problem in another manuscript,[83] which says the
following about the letter *tsadi*: "And it is Jesus of Nazareth who
siezed two heads—one was the head of Israel and the other an image
without any substance." "An image wihout any substance" is a clearly
derogatory expression referring to the Christian belief in Jesus's
divine nature.

As already stated, I believe this text was reworked by the author
of the Zohar: the result is the above passage about the letter *tsadi*.

The author of the Zohar added some Kabbalistic[84] and other aspects
to the figure of Jesus; he even incorporated, as already stated, the
idea of the "concealed *tsaddik*." The two heads of the letter *tsadi*, which
are interpreted at length in *Otiot de-R. Akiva*, become, in the Zohar,
the letters *yod* and *nun* which comprise the letter *tsadi*. Who knows—
perhaps this was the case also in one of the versions of *Otiot de-R.
Akiva*, and perhaps *yod* and *nun* even stand for *Yeshu ha-Notsri* (Jesus
of Nazareth).

(The description of the *tsadi* as comprised of the letters *yod* and
nun exists also in *Sefer ha-Bahir*, para. 61. However, it may easily be
assumed that it was taken from *Otiot de-R. Akiva*. The Zohar may
well have used this intermediary version, with the symbolic meaning
attributed to the letters which it contains. From *Sefer ha-Bahir*, the
idea also passed to *Sefer ha-Temuna* [Lemberg 1892, 59b–60a].)

Perhaps the *yod* and *nun* in the Zohar here symbolize not only
the masculine and feminine principles whose union is defective—both
in the realm of the earthly *tsaddik* and in the cosmic, divine
sphere[85]—but also the duality of the divine and human principle (or
the analogous duality of the body and soul) which the author perceived
in his persona of the *tsaddik*;[86] and it is this dualism that will be
harmonized in the days of the Messiah. It is interesting that the Zohar
illustrates this dualism through Adam, who was created with two
faces; perhaps this comparison supports the hypothesis that the letter
tsadi is a reference to Jesus who, according to the Christians, came
to the world only in order to rectify the sin of Adam.

If the letter *tsadi* does indeed refer to Jesus (and it seems to me
that the evidence presented has been quite convincing), then this text
clearly expresses the Zohar's ambivalence toward Jesus. On the one
hand, the letter *tsadi* is defective, symbolizing the exile and the
dominion of the gentiles; on the other hand, God says to it, "O *Tsadi*,
you are *Tsadi* and you signify righteousness!"

(Incidentally, I have found a profound eschatological exposition
on the letter *tsadi* being comprised of *yod* and *nun*, in Rabbi Yom Tob
Muelhausen's Commentary on the Alphabet.[87] There, the *yod*
connected to the neck of the *nun* refers to the reign of Jesus during
the exile, while the simple *tsadi* symbolizes the coming of the
Messiah.)

I should like now to refer briefly to further aspects of Christian
influence on the Zohar.

The Zohar has known views on the *tsaddik* who descends
to hell to raise up and save the souls of the wicked (see, e.g., Zohar,
III, 220b). This idea, it is well known, occupied an important place
in later Jewish mysticism—in Lurianic Kabbala, Sabbateanism, and

Hasidism. M. Piekarz discussed the subject at great length in "The Beginning of Hasidism" (*Bi-Ymei Tsmihat ha-Hasidut*),[88] describing the development of the idea from the Zohar and later Kabbala, until the beginning of Hasidism; his book both summarizes the work of the scholars who preceded him and introduces new information. I wish to note that one stage must perhaps be added to this development, a stage prior to the Zohar and which served as a source of inspiration; I am referring, of course, to the Christian stage. The Zoharic image of the *tsaddik* descending to hell to bring up the wicked may be based on the oft expressed Christian view of the activity of Jesus of Nazareth. This Christian view was known to medieval Jewry, and we have found that it served as an important basis for the anti-Christian polemic in *Sefer Nitsahon Yashan* (*op.cit.*, n. 16), pages 92, 100, 102. The editor (M. Brauer), in his notes there, refers the reader to the source of the idea in the writings of the Church Fathers. (In the Talmud [Hagiga, 14b] we find that R. Yohanan descended to hell after his death to bring up R. Elisha b. Avuya, but this is presented as a unique case.)

Another idea that the author of the Zohar took from Christianity is the relationship of love between the Messiah's disciples (in Christianity, and in the Zohar: R. Simeon b. Yohai's followers), and the unification (of the disciples in particular and of all Israel in general) into one body whose foundation is the Messiah (or the *tsaddik*), and where each of them is a part of his fellow. This idea exists in several places in the New Testament (e.g., Romans xii, 5), and in a formulation very similar to that of the Zohar (and even more so to that of Lurianic Kabbala). The idea was also of great importance in Lurianic Kabbala, in Sabbateanism, and in Hasidism. For a more detailed discussion of this idea, its development and its New Testament sources, see the relevant section in this work (note 15).

Another related theme is the epithet, "limbs of the lady," which is used to refer to Israel in the Zohar (III, 231b. And in *Ra'aya Meheimana* we also found "limbs of the Shekhina"—Zohar II, 118a, III, 17a). Such an epithet has to be related to the Christian conception of the church (parallel to *Knesset Israel* which in the Kabbala is identified with the *Shekhina*) as the body of God (Corpus christi or Corpus domini), and the church members as its limbs.

Moving on to a completely different subject, it is sometimes possible to find a Christian nuance in one place in the Zohar, when it discusses an idea developed fully in other places in the same work without any such nuance. For instance, a basic idea in the Zohar (and in the Kabbala in general) is that of the apparent flaw caused to the divinity through Israel's sins. Several layers can be discerned in this idea: firstly, we have the talmudic stratum, which is of a midrashic and ethical nature, and deals with God's love for Israel. In consequence, in every place of Israel's exile the *Shekhina* is with them (Megilla 29a), and by their sins Israel weaken the strength of the Creator (Leviticus Rabba 23, 12, etc.) The Kabbalists (including the author of the Zohar) added a more precise technical (almost magical) nuance to this—every action of man on earth induces a consequence in the supernal realm, and hence transgressions flaw the divinity.[89] Various aspects of this idea are developed in several places in the Zohar, and in one of them (II, 32b) we found this idea: " the Holy One accepts willingly the consequences of Israel's transgressions (from which demons were created which must pour out their wrath on someone) in place of Israel, and atones for their iniquity, since they are His sons and He loves them." The theme of God suffering in place of mankind is an important element in Christianity, and since I have found no such theme in the works of the rabbis of the Talmud,[90] this would seem to me to be a Christian touch.[91] The description of the king's mother (the *sefira* of *Bina*) interceding for the king's prisoners and liberating them (I, 220b) is strongly reminiscent of the role of Jesus's mother in medieval Christian writings and art.

Another important expression in the Zohar which bears the imprint of Christian influence is that of "reapers of the field," the Zoharic name for the Kabbalists. As can be demonstrated from the context in one place (Zohar, III, 127b, at the beginning of *Idra Rabba*), this is a translation from the New Testament (Luke x, 1–2, and its parallels). Once this epithet was coined, very different Kabbalist explanations were added to it in the Zohar (in many places, and in the Hebrew writings of R. Moses de Leon). I discussed at very great length the development of the expression and its explanations elsewhere (cf. note 15).

The author of the Zohar quite consciously used great quantities of Christian material in his splendid work. I suspect that such material is incorporated in the Zohar also in many other themes. I discussed at length, for instance, the *Tikkun Leil Shavu'ot*, in the chapter on "The Messiah . . ." (p. 00), and proved that the central event described in the Zohar, the assembly of *Idra Rabba*, is in fact the *Tikkun Leil Shavu'ot*. I showed there that a mystical nature was attributed to *Shavu'ot* already by the Tana'im, and this originated in the identication of this holiday with the giving of the Torah. I now further conjecture that the Christian Pentecost may have influenced this theme in the Zohar; this holiday was already of an indubitable mystical character in the New Testament (Acts 2), since the Holy Spirit came down to Jesus's disciples on this occasion (although it is certain that it was the mystical nature of the Jewish holiday that was continued in the New Testament interpretation). In this context, it should be noted that the Dominican friars (who were contemporaries and fellow countrymen of the author of the Zohar), held their gatherings at Pentecost! For all we know, these gatherings may have influenced the description of the gathering of R. Simeon b. Yohai and his followers in the *Idra Rabba*. If this is indeed the case, it constitutes a brilliant illustration of the process of borrowing and influence in the development of the same religious holiday in Judaism and Christianity, even though there was no love lost between these two sister faiths. Just as the Jewish component in Christianity did not increase the Christian's love for the Jews, so it is impossible to deduce from the Christian influences on the Zohar any affection on the part of the Zohar's author towards Christians. In fact, the Zohar is extreme in its antipathy towards the nations of the world.[92] Indeed, it seems to me that the spiritual affinity between the two religions was among the causes for the animosity between them.

Finally, no study of Christian influences on the Zohar would be complete without mention of Y. Baer's study, "The Historical Background of the *Ra'aya Meheimana*" (Hebrew) *Zion* 5 (1939–40), pages 1–44, in which he discusses the decisive influence of Franciscan thought upon the latter sections of the Zohar, the *Ra'aya Meheimana* and the *Tikkunei Zohar*.

Notes

Preface

1. Y. Liebes, "New Trends in the Research of Kabbala" (Hebrew). *Pe'amim* (forthcoming).

2. "Ha-Mashiah shel ha-Zohar—li-Dmuto ha-Meshihit shel Rabbi Shim'on Bar Yohai," in *The Messianic Idea in Jewish Thought. A Study Conference in Honour of the Eightieth Birthday of Gershom Scholem Held 4-5 December 1977*, ed. S. Re'em (Jerusalem: The Israel Academy of Sciences and Humanities, 1982), 87–236.

3. "Keitsad Nithabber Sefer ha-Zohar," in *The Age of the Zohar, Proceedings of the Third International Conference on the History of Jewish Mysticism*, ed. J. Dan (Jerusalem 1989) (= Jerusalem Studies in Jewish Thought 8), 1–71.

4. "Hashpa'ot Notsriyyot al Sefer ha-Zohar," *Jerusalem Studies in Jewish Thought* 2 (1983), 43–74.

5. *Immanuel 17* (1983–84), 43–67.

Chapter 1

1. Gershom Scholem, "The Idea of Redemption in the Kabbala" in *Explications and Implications, Writings on Jewish Heritage and Renaissance* (Hebrew) = *Devarim be-Go*, Tel Aviv 1975, pp. 191–216.

2. Ibid., p. 195.

3. Ibid., pp. 209f.

4. Ibid., p. 199.

5. Ibid., p. 213.

6. The latter includes *Sifra di-tsni'uta* ("The Book of Concealment"), an anonymous mishna, as it were, which is explained in the other *Idrot* (II, 176b–179a); *Idra Rabba* (III, 127b–145a), the largest of the works in this category (hence its name "*Rabba*," which means "large"); *Idra Zuta* (III, 287b–296b), which tells of the death of R. Simeon bar Yohai and is called "*zuta*" (small) in comparison to *Idra Rabba*; and *Raza de-Razin* (II, 122b–123b), which is not to be confused with another work of the same name that deals with physiognomy (II, 70a–75a). On *Idra de-vei-Mashkena* see below, note 109. There are allusions to the unique Kabbalistic ideas of the *Idrot* in other parts of the *Zohar*, especially in the section called *Sitrei Torah*. Several other isolated passages also contain Kabbalistic teachings characteristic of the *Idrot*; noteworthy among them is the passage at III, 48a–49a.

The word *idra* in the *Zohar* means "room" and refers derivatively to a Kabbalistic "gathering" or "event" of the sort described in *Idra Rabba* and *Idra Zuta*. The word can also be used in the sense of "session" or even *Sanhedrin*. *Idra* also denotes the proceedings at the gathering, and the word in this sense is already used in the *Zohar* itself to refer to the work that records what was said at the gathering.

Idra in the sense of "room" also has symbolic meanings and is sometimes used to refer to the *Shekhina* (II, 128b) or to other divine entities. On these and other usages of the term, see Yehuda Liebes, "Sections of the Zohar Lexicon" ([Hebrew] = "Perakim") (Ph.D. diss., Hebrew University, Jerusalem, 1977), pp. 93–106.

7. For example, I, 119a; I, 139a–140a; III, 212b.

8. For example, II, 9a–b; on that passage, see below. Elsewhere (II, 258a), the *Zohar* describes the unfolding of the generations as a descent through the body of the Holy One; at the End of Days the process will reach his feet and the Messiah will arrive. One who knows the mystery of his stature (*shi'ur komah*) thus also knows the time of redemption, apart from the other advantages ascribed to him in *Sefer Shi'ur Koma*, a work of *Merkava* mysticism. We shall see below that such a person also facilitates the advent of the Messiah.

9. On the development of messianic symbolism in the later Kabbala see Yehuda Liebes, "The Author of the Book Tsaddik Yesod Olam—the Sabbataian Prophet, Rabbi Leib Prossnitz," *Da'at I* (1978), pp. 73–120, 77f., n. 29.

10. Version Wertheimer S. A., (A. I. Wertheimer—new edition), *Battei Midrashot*, I–II, Jerusalem 1950–1953, Vol. II, p. 368; see also *Eccles. Rabba* to Eccles. xi:8; and see also below, p. 50.

11. This is Maimonides' position.

12. Along with the association of the *Idra* with the occasion of the giving of the Law at Mt. Sinai, there are also parallels between Moses and R. Simeon bar Yohai. Moreover, we find in the *Zohar* (III, 163a) that Moses in Paradise conducts something very similar to *Idra Rabba* for the generation of the desert. It is called "the day of the marriage celebration" (*yoma de-hillula*); the same term is applied to the *Idrot*. The text tells there of the radiance of Moses' face, which is so great that he cannot be seen; that is so in *Idra Rabba* as well (III, 144b). The bridal canopy that is present in the *Idra* also appears in the account of the gathering conducted by Moses, where it is identified with the veil covering Moses' face (Exod. 34:33) and with the "clouds of glory" that went before the Israelites and guided them in the desert. The theme of love, which is extremely important in *Idra Rabba*, is also of prime importance here, so much so that the gathering in Paradise is called the "academy (*metivta*) of love."

13. See Z. Bacher, *Aggadot ha-Tanna'im* III, Berlin 1932, pp. 48, 63–67.

14. See, for example, *Nistarot shel Rabbi Shim'on Bar Yohai* and *Tefillat Rashbi*, published in Y. Even Shemuel (ed.), *Midreshei Ge'ula*, Jerusalem and Tel Aviv 1954.

15. *Sukka* 45b. Other figures from rabbinic literature could also have served in that role. It seems to me, however, that the author of the *Zohar* decided on R. Simeon because of the messianic element in his characterization, which sets him apart from the others.

16. *Sukka* 45b; see also PT *Berakhot* vi:2, 13d.

17. *Gen. Rabba* xxxv:2, where R. Simeon's partners are Abraham and Ahiyah the Shilonite.

18. That is, a sage, following the *Tanhuma* to the portion of Noah (3), commenting on II Kings xxiv:14 and Isaiah xxii:22.

19. It is interesting to note that in the Talmud, too, R. Simeon is optimistic in his forecast.

20. It has that meaning in Dan. ii:35 and in the *Targumim*, and in two places in the *Zohar* (I, 116a and Zohar Hadash to Song of Songs 61a). The circular shape of the *Idra* may have had associations with the circles once formed by the ancient mystics (see Appendix II).

21. *Targum* to Cant. vii:3; *Cant. Rabba*, ad. loc.; *Targum* to Cant. iii:4.

22. Cf. *Ketubot* 111a.

23. While the continuation of this passage is concerned with the secret of redemption as explicated on the basis of the letters of the Ineffable Name, the allusion here is to another, simpler mystery, upon which the author had already expounded in the past; it is not clear, however, what he had in mind.

It may have been the seventy-two–letter name of God etched onto Moses' staff, to which he was probably referring earlier (8b) in speaking of the crown with which God was adorned at the time of the Exodus and with which the Messiah will be adorned. On the seventy-two–letter name, see II, 52a. The reference might also be to what was said earlier: "When the Holy One will awaken to restore the worlds and the letters of His name will shine, having reached perfect completion, *Yod* with *He*, *Vav* with *He*, so that all is one perfect whole. . ."(8a). If that is so, the phrase "letters of the Holy Name" refers simply to the Tetragrammaton.

24. Cf. II, 47b.

25. I have been unable to establish definately what is meant here, as I have not found a discussion of the verse anywhere else in the *Zohar* (except in its later imitation, *Ra'aya Meheimana*). In the rabbinic literature I found a discussion of it only in *Yalkut Shim'oni* to Psalms, 708.

26. The word *razin*, "mysteries," also has an ontological significance.

27. Cf. *Hagiga* 5b: "The Holy One, blessed be He, has a place and its name is Secret."

28. At that time marvelous and miraculous events would begin to occur. The stage after that would arrive in 1400, when the *tikkun* of the Holy One blessed be He would be completed. In the next stage, in 1532, the dead in the Land of Israel would be resurrected, and in 1676 those outside the Land of Israel. The next stage is the seventh millenium, when the *sefira* of *Malkhut* would gather new souls in order to maintain the world at a higher level. This stage is explained in detail, at times with the help of parallel Zoharic expressions, in Moses de Leon's Hebrew work "Seder Tehiyyat ha-Metim" (printed at the end of his book *Ha-Nefesh ha-Hakhama*, Basel, 1608), where it is formulated as a polemic against the doctrine of the cosmic cycles as understood among the followers of Solomon b. Aderet. According to another passage (I, 119a), based on similar calculations relating to the mystery of the letter *vav* in the Tetragrammaton, the first stage is to begin in 1300, and the subsequent stages will follow more closely: the second stage is the coming of the Messiah in 1306, and the redemption of the *Shekhina* culminates in 1312. The description of the seventh millenium resembles and complements that in the first passage.

29. See G. G. Scholem, *Major Trends in Jewish Mysticism*, New York 1961, p. 186.

30. I, 65a; II, 226a, 268b.

31. See E. Gottlieb, *Studies in the Kabbala Literature* (Hebrew), Tel Aviv 1976, p. 459, n. 176; on the passage and its meaning, see Liebes, above n. 9, p. 85, n. 74.

32. The author of the *Zohar* makes the point that a person may raise his hands heavenward only in prayer and entreaty; to do otherwise is arrogance (III, 195b). We find the same expression also in III, 287a.

33. The name Abba may call to mind the patriarch Abraham or even Jotham ben Uzziah, who is commended there by R. Simeon for the respect he paid his father (based on Rashi's commentary to *Sukka* 45b). His name may also be associated with R. Abbahu, an important figure in *Merkava* mysticism; see Urbach E. E., "The Traditions about Merkabah Mysticism in the Tannaitic Period" (Hebrew) in *Studies in Mysticism and Religion presented to Gershom Scholem*, Jerusalem 1967, p. 21.

34. Another early "version" of *Idra Rabba* appears at II, 14a–15a, as part of *Midrash ha-Ne'e'lam*, which according to Scholem is the oldest portion of the *Zohar*; see Scholem, *op. cit.* (above n. 29), p. 182. This passage too deals with the mystery of redemption, but here the third personage joining R. Simeon and his son is R. Hiyya, not R. Abba.

35. On this see inter alia, the well-known testimony of R. Isaac of Acre printed in Abraham Zacuto, *Sefer Yuhasin*, Frankfurt 1925, pp. 88f.

36. On this see my doctoral dissertation, Liebes, above n. 6.

37. See G. G. Scholem, *Elements of the Kabbalah and its Symbolism (Pirqei Yesod be-Havanat ha-Kabbala u-Smaleha)*, Jerusalem 1976. pp. 213–58; and see also Scholem, *The Messianic Idea in Judaism*, New York 1971, pp. 251–56. I would like to note in this connection that the verse "When the storm passes the wicked man is gone, but the righteous is an everlasting foundation" (Prov. x:25) in its literal meaning does not contain the idea that the righteous man is the foundation of the cosmos, as Scholem suggests in the second article (p. 251). In the Bible, the world *olam* does not mean "universe" or "cosmos" (the biblical term for which is *tevel*), but is an adverb meaning "forever."

38. The first was Abraham, the lone believer in a world of godless men. Of him it is said: "For he was only one when I called him" (Isa. vi:2), and his attempt to rescue the inhabitants of Sodom is in keeping with that description. He is called "pillar of the world" (*Ex. Rabba* ii; Maimonides, *Hilkhot Avodat Cokhavim* i:2), a title which calls to mind Prov. x:25 as expounded in Hagiga. Another figure to whom the title "righteous, foundation of the world" can aptly be applied is Hanina ben Dosa, of whom a heavenly voice said, "The whole world is for the sake of My son Hanina" (*Berakhot* 17b; *Ta'anit* 24b). For something of the popular character and views of R. Hanina, which might make the title "*hasid*" more appropriate for him than the title "*tsaddik*," see for example *Avot* iii:9–10; *Ta'anit* 25a; *Berakhot* 34b. On the distinction between *hasid* and *tsaddik*, see Scholem, above n. 37, pp. 213–58.

39. On "righteous" in *Sefer ha-Bahir*, see Scholem, above n. 37, pp. 216–24, and also Scholem, *Ursprung und Anfange der Kabbala*, Berlin 1962, pp. 134–43.

40. Cf. Ketubot 62b.

41. See, for example, I, 66b; the parallel between the two situations is clearly described in I, 153b.

42. See Liebes, above n. 6, pp. 144f.

43. See Gottleib, above n. 31, pp. 59–87.

44. This is the view argued by Scholem in his *Leket Margaliot*, Tel Aviv 1941, p. 14, and it is further strengthened by the parallels I bring below from the "Gnostic Kabbalist" circles; see also Liebes, above n. 9, p. 106, n. 170. On the idea that the *sitra ahra* is made of the sparks of destroyed worlds and its connection with the "Gnostic Kabbalist" circles see G. G. Scholem, "Kabbalot R. Ya'akov ve-R. Yitshak, Benei R. Ya'akov ha-Kohen," (Hebrew) in *Mada'ei ha-Yahadut*, II (1927), pp. 165–293, 33.

45. Cf. Zohar Hadash, Parashat Va-Yera, 26b–c.

46. On this circle, see Scholem, above n. 44, and G. G. Scholem, "An Inquiry in the Kabbala of R. Issac ben Jacob ha-Cohen" (Hebrew) *Tarbiz II–V*, (1931–34). Scholem also noted the connection between them and the author of the *Zohar*, but called attention to the difference between their respective creative powers; if the imagination of the *Zohar*'s author, as he put it, was productive, that of the members of his circle was merely reproductive (G. G. Scholem, "R. Moshe of Burgos, the Disciple of R. Issac" (Hebrew) in *Tarbiz*, III, pp. 258–86; IV, pp. 54–57, 207–25; V, pp. 50–60, 180–98, 305–23; *idem Tarbiz*, III, p. 280). On the close personal ties maintained by the author of the *Zohar* with R. Todros Abulafia and with his son Yosef, of which we know from letters written by Moses de Leon, see G. G. Scholem, "Shenei Kuntresim le-R. Moshe de Leon" (fragment from *Shoshan Edut; Sod Eser Sefirot Belima*) in *Kovets al Yad*, VIII (XVIII), Jerusalem 1976, pp. 325–84. 327.

47. Published by Scholem, "R. Moshe," above n. 46, *Tarbiz*, IV, p. 208.

48. See Scholem, "R. Moshe," above n. 46, *Tarbiz*, III, pp. 266, 280; see also Scholem, *Kabbalot*, above n. 44, p. 28; and Farber Assi (ed.), *A Commentary on Ezekiel I, By R. Ya'acov ha-Kohen* (Hebrew), Jerusalem 1978 (photocopied), Introduction, p. 1.

49. Isaac of Acre, *Otsrot Hayyim*, cited in Gottleib, above n. 31. pp. 341–42, n. 32.

50. An echo of the polemic of the Catalonian scholars and their followers, the Kabbalists of the circle of Solomon b. Adret, against the *Zohar*, which continues the line of the Kabbalists of Castile, is perhaps to be heard in a passage at the end of *Or-ha-Ganuz*, a commentary on *Sefer ha-Bahir* written by Meir ibn Sahula (see also G. G. Scholem, *Catalogus Codicum Hebraicorum. . . Bibliotheca Hierosolymlitana (= Kitvei Yad be-Kabbala)* (Hebrew), Jerusalem 1930, p. 147):

I explain this book not because my wisdom is greater than all those who preceded me, for it is from their waters that I drink. I am jealous for the Lord, the God of Israel, and for those who expound books and books of the Gentiles, copying out their alien beliefs and calling them secrets of the *Torah*. Therefore I resolved to reveal the glory of God as I received and understood it from my teachers, R. Joshua ibn Shu'eyb and R. Solomon of Barcelona, who received it from Nahmanides, who received it from R. Isaac the Blind, the son of R. Abraham ben David, who received it from the prophet Elijah.

This is the expression of a pupil of R. Joshua ibn Shu'eyb and of Solomon b. Adret, who continued the way of the Gerona Kabbalists and accepted only Kabbalistic techniques handed down by their teachers. Ibn Sahula sharply attacks those who adopt unauthorized Kabbalistic doctrines and call by the name "secrets of the *Torah*" explications of gentile books, from which they copy alien beliefs. It is very likely that the target of this attack is the author of the *Zohar*. Ibn Sahula was a contemporary of Moses de Leon, hailed from the same city and undoubtedly knew him well. The position he espouses here explains his absolute refraint from citing the *Zohar* in any of his writings. The *Zohar*, after all, is unmatched (to those who know that it is pseudepigraphic) in its daring and innovation, and so ran against the spirit of the followers of Solomon b. Adret. It was also suspected of using alien sources and "copying their beliefs." Moreover, a part of the *Zohar* is actually called "secrets of the Torah" (*Sitrei Tora*). It is also possible, however, that Ibn Sahula's attack is directed against the philosophers, who used foreign sources and called their writings "secrets of the *Torah*."

51. See II, 48b; see also Isaac ha-Kohen's *Ma'amar 'al ha-atsilut ha-semalit* (Scholem, above n. 44, p. 100), where the word Leviathan is interpreted as a cognate of the words *livvuy*, accompaniment, and *zivvug*, coupling. A similar symbolism appears in *Sefer Ma'arekhet ha-Elohit*, especially in chapter 8.

52. Scholem, above n. 44, p. 111. The idea of the force of evil having a name equivalent to that of the force of good that battles against it appears quite frequently in later Kabbalistic writings, and was developed in particular by Samson Ostropoler.

53. See G. G. Scholem, *Shabbatai Sevi, The Mystical Messiah*, Princeton, New Jersey 1973, p. 308, n. 291. However, there is no clear evidence to indicate that Isaac ha-Kohen intended to identify the serpent with the Messiah by *gimatria* as well. Moses of Burgos noted how advantageous it was that King David was descended from "worshippers of other gods" (i.e., Ruth, a Moabite), "for when the seed becomes good again, there is nothing better; it lacks nothing, for it knows all the ways of good and all the ways of evil, and in all it goes to do the will of its Creator" (*Sefer Ammud ha-Semali*; Scholem, above n. 46, p. 222). This kind of thinking was not far removed from that of the

Shabbatians. On the sources in the *Zohar* of several Shabbatian ideas in this vein see Liebes, above n. 9, n. 88. Other points of contact between the messianism of the "Gnostic" circle and the Shabbatians are the Messiah's identification with the *sefira* of *Yesod* and his being called by the name "tsaddik." Moreover, the verse "the righteous shall live by his faith" (Hab. ii:4), frequently cited by the Shabbatians as referring to Shabbetai Sevi, was interpreted in the "Gnostic" circle as an allusion to the Messiah.

54. Scholem, above n. 44, p. 82.

55. Scholem, "R. Moshe" above n. 46, p. 190.

56. See J. Dan, *The Esoteric Theology of Ashkenazi Hasidism* (Hebrew) (= *Torat ha-Sod shel Hasidut Ashkenaz*), Jerusalem 1968, pp. 193–94.

57. Scholem, "R. Moshe," above n. 46, p. 225.

58. For the dates, see Scholem, above n. 46, p. 265.

59. See, for example, the passage based on Ruth iii:13 published by Scholem in ibid., above n. 46, p. 323.

60. *Otsar ha-Kavod*, Warsaw 1879, 14a; *Pesahim* 54a.

61. *Pesikta Rabbati* xxxiv, which is also based on Zech. ix:9.

62. See Liebes, "Perakim," above n. 6, pp. 371–75.

63. See Liebes, "Perakim," above n. 6, p. 361.

64. See Liebes, "Perakim," above n. 6, p. 359, n. 48; pp. 362–66.

65. In many places in the *Zohar* the ten *sefirot* are reduced to three, and we should not discount the possibility that the author was influenced by the Christian trinity. The Kabbala of the *Idra*, too, involves the three *partsufim*—divine configurations—of *Arikh 'Anpin, Ze'er Anpin,* and the *Shekhina*. The same triad occurs in the discussion of the three Sabbath meals (II, 88a). It is possible, indeed, that R. Simeon and his son allude respectively to *Arikh 'Anpin* and *Ze'er Anpin*, for they are called " *'anpe ravreve ve-'anpe zutare"*—a notion derived from the description in *Sukka* 5b, commenting on Ezek. ix:14, of the faces of the Cherubs—and the author of the *Zohar* may have related this to the two supreme *partsufim*. However, it seems that the *Zohar*'s intention here is primarily to denote these three personages as embodying the three "lines" according to which the system of the *sefirot* is arrayed: right, left, and center. The reference here, however is not to the *sefirot* of *Hesed, Gevura,* and *Tif'eret,* which are usually the principal points of these lines in the *Zohar,* but to the inner essences of the lines, which are the *sefirot* of *Hokhma, Tevuna* (or *Bina*), and *Da'at* (*Hokhma* being the inner essence of *Hesed, Tevuna* of *Gevura,* and *Da'at* of *Tif'eret*; in *Idra Rabba*, III, 136a, the inner essences are called *mohin*—marrow; this notion is greatly elaborated in the Lurianic Kabbala). That this is the intention of the author of the *Zohar*

is established by his allusion to the statement from *Pirkei de-Rabbi Eliezer*, iii, "The world was created by ten sayings, and they are included in three: in wisdom (*hokhma*), understanding (*tevuna*) and knowledge (*da'at*)." (Luria, too interprets the role of the three personages in this way, in *Nitsotsei Orot* to this place in the opening passage of *Idra Rabba*.)

It is further established, moreover, upon examination of an exactly parallel passage in *Midrash ha-Ne'e'lam* where the use of the statement from *Pirkei de-Rabbi Eliezer* is even more obvious (II, 14b). The author goes on there to say that Abraham is *Hokhma*, Isaac is *Tevuna*, and Jacob is *Da'at*, that is, a division parallel to the division into the three lines of *Hesed, Gevura,* and *Tif'eret* (II, 14–15). A similar statement appears in the writings of Isaac ha-Kohen (Farber, above n. 48, p. 51) and the very same triad occurs in de Leon's Hebrew works, such as *Sefer Sheqel ha-Kodesh*, London 1912, pp. 104, 134. The three personages at the opening of *Idra Rabba* may thus be seen to parallel *Hokhma, Tevuna,* and *Da'at*, and R. Simeon, who is in the middle, is *Da'at*. If that is so, R. Simeon in this context does not symbolize the *sefira* of *Yesod*. This is not necessarily a contradiction, for *Da'at* may be regarded as the inner essence of *Yesod*. Both *Da'at* and *Yesod* are on the "middle line" (*Da'at* above and *Yesod* below), and both have to do with the matter of coupling. *Da'at*, as we have said, is one of the *mohin*; it is that which spreads to the lower organs of the body and as such is the source of the drop of semen. Elsewhere in the *Idrot*, *Da'at* is regarded as a symbol of the tongue, which is considered analogous to the male organ (see *Sefer Yetsira* i:3). The male organ apparently is involved in the baser, physical coupling (i.e., the kiss; see III, 165a, and Zohar Hadash to the Song of Songs, 63a). *Da'at* brings about coupling between the upper *sefirot* (*Hokhma* and *Bina*), while *Yesod* is involved in the coupling of the lower *sefirot* (*Tif'eret* and *Malkhut*). (See II, 176b; II, 123a, where *Da'at* is the spiritual content of *Tif'eret*; the sexual aspect of *Da'at* is further developed in *Tikkunei Zohar*, tikkun 69, 99a). *Da'at* thus can very aptly be symbolized by R. Simeon, for he unites within himself its sexual and intellectual aspects.

R. Simeon's status among his fellows is nonetheless often described in the *Idrot* as that of the *sefira* of *Yesod*. He is compared to the Sabbath, his six fellows (those who remained after the death of the three) being likened to the weekdays (III, 144b–145a); and the Sabbath is a symbol of *Yesod* (see Tishby I., *The Wisdom of the Zohar*, An Anthology of Texts, I–III, Oxford University Press, Oxford G.B. 1989, pp. 1215–1325; Gottlieb, above n. 31, pp. 259–61). This passage in the opening of *Idra Rabba* was one that influenced the Shabbatean movement (see the prophetic statement addressed by Nathan of Gaza to three sages: "You are three. . .and if you can become ten, you will have the merit of being of assistance to my friend Shabbatai" (cited in Scholem G., *Studies and Texts Concerning the History of Sabbetianism and its Metamorphosis* (Hebrew), Jerusalem 1974, p. 230). The ten subsequently became twelve, the number of the Israelite tribes (ibid.), which also brings to mind the twelve apostles of Jesus; this parallel gives further support to a messianic interpretation of the *Idra*.

66. See Liebes, above n. 6, pp. 355–58.

67. Cf. the wording of the oath taken by God in *Pirkei Hekhalot Rabbati* (Wertheimer, above n. 10, Vol. I, p. 85), which brings together heaven, earth, and *yoredei merkava*. The author of the *Zohar* surely regarded his heroes as *yoredei merkava*, the true mystics.

68. Cf. *Targum Onkelos* to Ex. xiii:18, *Mishna Shabbat* vi:4; *Onkelos* to Deut. xxii:5.

69. That the word *tikkun* can mean both "jewel" and "world" calls to mind the similar dual meaning of the Greek word "cosmos."

70. See *Shabbat* 59b; 63a; *Mo'ed Katan* 16b; *Ta'anit* 23a; PT *Ta'anit* iii:12, 67a.

71. I, 218a; II, 16a (*Midrash ha-Ne'e'lam*).

72. See also II, 14b (*Midrash ha-Ne'e'lam*).

73. See the description of the wedding canopy spread over the heads of the sages in *Idra Rabba* III, 135a.

74. Maimonides uses the word with this significance in *Mishne Tora, Hilkhot Yesodei ha-Tora* viii:1; his usage in this instance is influenced by the Arabic. Cf. Saadya Gaon's commentary to *Sefer Yetsira* (ed. J. Kafeh, Jerusalem 1972, p. 31b). It did not yet have this meaning of "a solemn occasion" in rabbinic Hebrew, where it means simply "in the presence of" (e.g., PT *Sanhedrin* i:3).

75. It was customary to preface Kabbalistic works with a philosophical apology; see, for example, *Sefer Ma'arekhet ha-Elohut*.

76. For example, III, 106b (based on *Nidda* 13b), which also cites the verse from Ecclesiastes.

77. Thus at III, 84a, R. Simeon expounds the verse "Turn ye not unto the idols, nor make to yourselves molten gods" (Lev. xix:4) as a prohibition against looking at women.

78. See I, 8a.

79. See Scholem, above n. 37, pp. 41–47.

80. In associating the secrets of the Kabbala with engagement in proscribed sexual relations, the *Zohar* may have been influenced by the association in Hagiga ii:1 of the restrictions on expounding the laws of incest with the restrictions on expounding the account of Creation (*Ma'ase Bereshit*) and the account of the Chariot (*Ma'ase Merkava*).

81. See the version of this document published in W. Rabinowitsch, *Zion*, V, 1940, pp. 125–26; and Scholem's study of it, ibid., pp. 133–60. The pledge

taken by Luria's students and the opening of the *Idra* are both concerned primarily with the guarding of secrecy.

82. The expression *ne'eman ruah* in the sense of "guardian of a secret" also occurs in *Tsavva'at R. Eliezer ha-Gadol*, 39, which was written by the author of the *Zohar*; see *Sefer Orhot Hayyim*, Jerusalem 1966, 48a.

83. See also I, 202a.

84. See III, 159a.

85. The two aspects of the Torah are also called the Tree of Knowledge and the Tree of Life, the latter derived from Prov. iii:18: "She is a tree of life to them that lay hold upon her." These two trees symbolize the *sefirot* of *Malkhut* and *Yesod*. The Tree of Life is primarily the Kabbala, and the Kabbalist who studies it is also called thus. R. Simeon is himself called a "mighty tree" (I, 218a). This symbol is further elaborated in *Ra'aya Meheimana*, where R. Simeon is likened to the trunk of a tree and his disciples to branches growing out from him (II, 223b). For the use of a similar symbolism in rabbinic literature, see *Ta'anit* 7a; *Pesahim* 112a; *Avoda Zara* 7b; and see also Liebes, above n. 6, pp. 118-24.

86. Hence the relationship between *Yesod* and circumcision—only to a circumcised person can the secrets of the Torah be disclosed. This idea is already to be found in *Aggadat Bereshit* (ed. Buber, ch. xvi), which relates that only when Abraham had been circumcised did God reveal His "mystery" to him. The *Zohar* contains a similar notion in its statement that God revealed himself fully to Abraham only by virtue of his circumcision (I, 91a). The idea in *Aggadat Bereshit* is not precisely the same, for there God does not reveal himself or his secrets to Abraham because of the circumcision, but rather the circumcision itself is God's "mystery," and by virtue of it Abraham's seed will be beneficient. The *Zohar* might thus appear to take the idea a step further, but even that step, it seems, was known in ancient times. *Aggadat Bereshit* makes the connection between the mystery and circumcision by means of the verse: "The secret of the Lord is for those who fear Him; to them He makes known His covenant" (Ps. xxv:14)—the very same verse that is cited at the beginning of *Idra Rabba*. While the verse is cited in *Idra Rabba* in order to link the secret to fear, the relationship to circumcision is suggested, and it is made explicit with reference to the same verse elsewhere in the *Zohar*.

87. The association between "Righteous" (*Yesod*), "seed," and 'light" is supported by the verse "Light is sown for the righteous" (Ps. xcvii:11); cf. Maimonides, *Mishne Tora, Hilkhot De'ot* iv:19: "Semen constitutes the strength of the body, its life and the light of the eyes." In the writings of Plato, Socrates' teachings are likened to a spark of light and to seed that is sown in souls; on this see J. G. Liebes, *The Trial and Death of Socrates by Plato*, (Hebrew) Jerusalem-Tel Aviv 1972, p. 152.

88. See III, 139b.

89. See also Liebes, above n. 6, p. 244.

90. The reason given for this further on, is that the letter *tsadde* is formed of the letters *yod* and *nun*, which are male and female joined back-to-back. This back-to-back form represents a defect, and the *tsadde* is thus not to be revealed until that defect is corrected. The flaw is on the one hand ontological and epistemological, but on the other, as I shall argue later, it is also a defect in the private life of R. Simeon. Hence, just as the letter *tsadde* must be concealed because of this defect, so too must R. Simeon; and that is the idea of the hidden righteous one. These two defects are remedied by the messianic *tikkun* of the *Idra*, and after the *tikkun* it is no longer necessary to keep the secrets hidden. This passage on the letter *tsadde* seems originally to have been concerned with Jesus, another figure that influenced the portrayal of R. Simeon in the *Zohar*. On this see my article, "Christian Influences in the *Zohar*" (below). Cf. *Mo'ed Katan* 16a–b: "As the thigh is concealed, so are the words of the *Torah* concealed."

91. Compare: As *hip* must be concealed so must be the words of the Torah; *Mo'ed Katan*, fl 15.

92. Another reason for the pseudepigraphic mode is the freedom it allows the author. A comparison between the *Zohar* and the Hebrew writings of de Leon reveals the extent to which he gave free rein to his imagination in the *Zohar*, and how far superior this work is to his arid Hebrew writings, most of which were never even printed.

93. On this notion see G. G. Scholem, *The Messianic Idea in Judaism*, above n. 37, pp. 251–56. Scholem did not trace the origin of the idea to the *Zohar*, but placed it later, in the eighteenth century. Moreover, while the *Zohar* does not, as far as I can tell, contain the tradition of the thirty-six just men, it does present R. Simeon as the quintessence of the thirty just men who sustain the world. Furthermore, the relationship between the notion of 'righteous, foundation of the world" and the number of thirty-six is already explicitly drawn in *Sefer ha-Bahir* (ed. Margaliot, 101). I believe that R. Simeon of the *Zohar* and the ideas associated with him are the source from which the idea of the thirty-six just men was developed in the eighteenth century. The question of who picked up the idea from the *Zohar*, developed it and spread it among his contemporaries in the eighteenth century remains to be investigated. There was a significant difference between R. Simeon of the *Zohar* and the later traditions about the hidden just men: the *Zohar*'s R. Simeon may be hidden from others, but he is himself very aware of his special status. This sets him apart even from Moses, who was unaware of the radiance of his face (Ex. xxxiv:24); R. Simeon, by contrast, was aware (III, 135b). The Hasidic tales are not uniform on this point, only some of them describe the just man as being unaware of his own status. The idea of the hidden just men is of tremendous importance for an understanding of Hasidism. It helps make sense of the discrepancy between two motifs in Hasidic thought, the "dualistic" aristocratic conception that divides people into "men of matter" and "men

WORD OF THE WEEK
The Subject: God ordains certain men to hell on purpose

Isaiah 64:8 - 0 Lord, thou art our Father; we are the clay; and thou our potter; and we all are the work of thy hand.

work - Hebrew: Maaseh · an action (good or bad); product; transaction; business

Romans 9:20-23 - Who art thou that repliest against God? Shall the thing formed say to him that formed it, why hast thou made me thus? Hath not the potter the power over the clay of the same lump, to make one vessel unto honour and another unto dishonour - What if God willing to show his wrath, and to make his power known, endured with much long suffering the vessels of wrath fitted to destruction: And that he might make known the riches of his glory on the vessels of mercy, which he hath afore prepared unto glory.

fitted - Greek: katartizo · to complete thoroughly; fit; frame; arrange; prepare. Thayer says this word speaks of men whose souls God has so constituted that they cannot escape destruction; their mind is fixed that they frame themselves.

Men get angry to think that we serve a God that can do as it pleases him. They actually think that an almighty God thinks the way they think and that he could not possibly form-fit a vessel to hell merely to show his wrath and power. Paul said he does. Men have difficulty perceiving a God that predestinates men (Rom. 8:29) on whom he desires to show his grace (unmerited favor) and mercy, that he may shower them throughout eternity with the riches of his glory. We like to believe that we must give him permission if he is to operate in our hearts and minds. The Lord said, "My thoughts are not your thoughts, neither are your ways my ways. As the heavens are higher than the earth, so are my ways higher than your ways and my thoughts than your thoughts (Isaiah 55:8,9)". Our God is in the heavens: he hath done whatsoever he hath pleased (Psalms 115:3). He doeth whatsoever pleaseth him (Eccl 8:3). Thou, 0 Lord, hast done as it pleased thee (Jonah 1:14). Whatsoever the Lord pleased, that did he in heaven, and earth, and in the seas, and in all deep places (Psalms 135:6). He does all his pleasure (Isa. 46:10; Isa. 44:24-28; Eph. 1:5,9; Philippians 2:13). It is Jesus that holds the keys to death and hell (Rev. 1:18), not Satan. God will intentionally cast these evil vessels of wrath into hell and lock them up for eternity because it is not his pleasure to draw them to him (John 6:44). This doctrine angers men, though it is taught throughout the pages of God's Holy Book. Men do not have a Biblical view of the living God when they think he is not in control of all things including the minds and hearts of all men. God is not only love to the vessels of mercy, but he is a consuming fire (Deut. 4:24) upon the vessels of wrath fitted to destruction. We do not serve a God who is Superman that can only shake mountains, implode blackholes, and explode quasars. The God of the universe can harden and soften the hearts of men at will (Rom. 9:18; Ezek. 36:26). He giveth not account of any of his matters (Job 33:13).

GRACE AND TRUTH MINISTRIES
P.O. Box 1109, Hendersonville, TN 37077
Jim Brown - Bible Teacher · Local: (615) 824-8502 | Toll Free: (800) 625-5409
https://www.graceandtruth.net/

of form" and holds that one can cleave to God only via an intermediary, who is the *tsaddik*, and the conception reflected in such "democratic" tales as those relating the virtue of cowherds able to move the upper worlds by their whistling. The opposition between the two tendencies becomes reconcilable when these boors are viewed as hidden just men or *tsaddikim*. The idea of the hidden just man who sustains the world has a parallel in the faith of certain Shi'ite Muslim sects which believe in a hidden *imam* who sustains the world until the final redemption; on this see H. Lemans, *Ha-Islam*, Jerusalem 1955, pp. 111–15.

94. Weeping occurs regularly in the *Zohar* before profound discourses, and is an expression of the intensity of feeling stirred up by the dilemma of whether to reveal or to conceal.

95. This has a parallel in *Bava Batra* 89b: "Woe to me if I speak, and woe to me if I do not speak." See also *Zohar*, I, 11b. In the Talmud, however, the expression does not refer to the problem of revealing esoteric knowledge but to matters of judgment.

96. This letter was published and analyzed by Scholem in *Sefer Bialik*, Tel Aviv 1934, pp. 141–55.

97. II, 133b–134b.

98. The motif of the "herald" is taken from Dan. iii:4; in the *Zohar* it becomes part of the description of the heavenly "royal court."

99. The expression "reapers of the field" as a designation for Kabbalists appears frequently in the *Zohar*; see also II, 240b and *Zohar Hadash*, Midrash ha-Ne'e'lam to Ruth, 85d, where the field symbolizes the *sefira* of *Malkhut*. The idea of the "Field" as a designation for the *Shekhina* is derived from the expression "a field of holy apples," which is taken in turn from rabbinic exegeses of the verse "See, the smell of my son is as the smell of a field which the Lord hath blessed" (Genesis xxvii:27); *Ta'anit* 29b comments "as the smell of a field of apples." Another homily on the same verse relates that "When Jacob went in to his father, Paradise entered with him" (*Gen. Rabba* lxv:22). In the *Zohar*, the heavenly Garden of Eden is one of the designations of the *Shekhina*, and thus the set of associations and identifications: field = field of apples = Garden of Eden = *Shekhina*. This is explained at length at III, 84a. A Kabbalistic interpretation of "apples" is presented at I, 142b, according to which the apples are the three Patriarchs, or the three *sefirot* of *Hesed, Gevura,* and *Tif'eret*. See also I, 85a–b; III, 74a; III, 287a; III, 133b. The idea of the "field of apples" in this Kabbalistic sense also occurs in Moses de Leon's Hebrew writings: see Scholem, "Shenei Kuntresim" above n. 46, p. 365. For the source of the idea in the legends of R. Azriel see Tishby I., *Commentarius in Aggadot Auctore R. Azriel Geronensi* (Hebrew), Jerusalem 1945, pp. 36f.; and see also Scholem, above n. 50, pp. 194f.

If the field is the *Shekhina*, it still remains to be seen why the Kabbalists are called its reapers. One possibility is that the Kabbalists clear the *sefira* of *Malkhut* of thorns and weeds, which is how the Kabbalists themselves sometimes understood it; see Hayyim Vital's second introduction to *Sefer Etz Hayyim*. This, however, is not the principal meaning here; the word "reaping" is not really appropriate to the act of clearing thorns and briars, and the *Zohar*, moreover, elsewhere relates explicitly (I, 156a) that the "reapers of the field" are those who distribute the divine plenitude that comes from the *sefira* of *Malkhut* to the lower worlds, including themselves; and this is how the role of the Kabbalists is defined.

The expression "reapers of the field" may well have been taken by the author of the *Zohar* from the New Testament: "After these things the Lord appointed another seventy. . .and said he unto them: The harvest truly is great, but the labourers are few" (Luke x:1–2; see also Matt. ix:37). De Leon's use of ideas and phrases from the New Testament should not surprise us. He was very receptive to outside sources and enjoyed the protection of pseudepigraphic writing.

100. *Cant. Rabba* viii:11; PT *Berakhot* iv:1, 7d.

101. The story of the "four [who] entered the *pardes*" (*Hagiga* 14b) is about mysticism; Rashi's interpretation of the phrase is that "they went up to the firmament near there." Maimonides in *Hilkhot Yesodei ha-Tora* (iv:13) interprets the word *pardes* as a reference to theosophy, while the Kabbalists regarded it as an acronym for the four levels of meaning in the Torah (*peshat*, the plain meaning; *remez*, the symbolic meaning; *derash*, the homiletic meaning; and *sod*, the esoteric meaning). This acronym does not appear in the *Zohar* (except in *Ra'aya Meheimana* and *Tikkunei Zohar*), though it seems to have been Moses de Leon who first introduced it in his Hebrew works, which, according to Scholem, were written after the *Zohar*; see Scholem, *Pirkei Yesod*, above n. 37, pp. 58–60. Like many other thirteenth-century works, the *Zohar* did, however, conceive of the Torah as consisting of several superimposed layers, usually four in number; see P. Sandler, "The Problem of 'pardes' and the Quadrilateral Method." ([Hebrew] Li–v'ayat "pardes" ve-ha-Shita ha-Meruba'at), *Sefer Urbach*, Jerusalem 1955, pp. 222–35. The parallel between *pardes*, grove, and *kerem*, vineyard, also appears in *Seder Eliyahu Rabba* (ed. Ish Shalom), ch. vii, which contains the statement: "Israel is the vineyard of the Holy Blessed One; do not look into it."

102. Cf. *Seder Gan Eden* (Jellinek A., *Bet ha-Midrasch*, I–IV [Hebrew] Jerusalem 1967, Vol. III, pp. 131–33), which was written by the author of the *Zohar* (see G. G. Scholem, above n. 1, pp. 274–75).

103. See *Zohar*, II, 4a, where it is said that "Knesset Israel" is called a vineyard; and III, 45b, where the people of Israel are likened to a vineyard.

104. PT *Berakhot* vi, 9a; and see also *Midrash Shoher Tov* to Ps. xvi:1.

105. The source of this idea is *Gen. Rabba* xlix:2, but it is not developed there and the disclosure of the secrets is not limited to God-fearing. It appears in several places in the *Zohar*; e.g., III, 234a—where, however, a distinction

is made between the secrets of the upper *sefirot* and the secrets of the lower "world of separation" which may be disclosed; see also I, 236b, where the notion is related to circumcision. Maimonides cites the verse "The secret of the Lord is for those who fear Him" in his introduction to the *Guide of the Perplexed* with reference to the need to conceal the secrets of the Torah from the masses, and it is cited in this sense at the beginning of many works originating in the *iyyun* and Gnostic Kabbalist circles; see G. G. Scholem, "The Commentary of R. Issac to Ezekiel's Chariot" (Hebrew) in *Tarbiz, II*, pp. 188–217. p. 194, and *idem, Kitvei Yad*, above n. 50, pp. 17, 204. In the wicked generation of *Idra Rabba*, the time of Moses de Leon, only the participants in the *Idra* were found fit for the disclosure of the secrets and therefore, as is stated at the end of the *Idra*: "From that day the companions did not stir from R. Simeon's house, and when he disclosed secrets only they were there present" (III, 144b).

106. This idea is much elaborated in the *Zohar*; see, e.g.: I, 7b.

107. *Sefer ha-Bahir* (ed. Margoliot), 68–69.

108. This view of the prophet Habakkuk stems from the theophanous description in chapter iii, which is the *haftara* for the second day of Shavuot, and also from his interest in eschatology and the end of the exile, as related in chapter ii. This combination of elements is characteristic of the principal trend in Jewish mysticism. It is interesting to note that the rabbis ascribed to Habakkuk an intimacy with God resembling that of Honi Ha-Me'aggel, since Habakkuk, too, drew a circle, stood within it and said he would not budge—until he heard what God would say through him. This story is based on Hab. ii:1: "I will . . . set me upon the tower (*matsor*), and will look out to see what He will speak by me"; the word *matsor* is interpreted by the midrash as meaning "circle." There is an allusion to it in Ta'anit 23a, where Honi's deed is described as resembling that of Habakkuk. The full story appears in a number of midrashim—the midrash to Ps. vii:17 is an example—and is related by Rashi in his commentary to Hab. ii:1 and by Kimhi in his commentary to Is. xxi:8. Incidentally, this verse from Isaiah is cited in *Sefer ha-Bahir* (88), where the lion in the verse is apparently taken as an allusion to Habakkuk, the numerical value of whose name by *gematria* is equivalent to that of the word *arye*, lion, as noted in the commentaries of Rashi and Kimhi. This understanding of the *Sefer ha-bahir* accords with its own earlier precedent of viewing Habakkuk as the paradigmatic mystic. Habakkuk's importance to Jewish eschatology was recognized in *Pesher Habakkuk*, a work originating in the Dead Sea Sect. Habakkuk was said to have come by his mystical powers by virtue of his experience as the child restored to life by the prophet Elisha (II Kings iv:8–38); his soul left him and then returned to his body, enabling him to see things never seen by man during his lifetime.

109. Based on what we know about *Idra de-vei-Mashkena*, any candidate for identification with it must meet the following conditions: a) it must be a work in the style of the *Idrot* and contain a special Kabbala; b) it must deal

with the mysteries of the Tabernacle; c) it must describe an assembly held before *Idra Rabba*; d) in the course of it, something similar to death must occur to several of the participants, probably R. Yose, R. Hezkiah, and R. Jesse; e) it must deal with that aspect of the worlds whose essence is primarily *Din*; f) it most probably begins with the verse: "O Lord I have heard the report of Thee and am afraid." According to *Sefer Livnat ha-Sapir*, a commentary on the *Zohar* written a generation after it by Joseph Angelet (as was recently proven by I. Felix, this is his correct name, rather than Angelino) and mistakenly attributed to David b. Yehuda he-Hasid, *Idra de-vei-Mashkena* is the portion of the *Zohar* at II, 127a–146b. While this section deals with the mysteries of the Tabernacle, it does not meet any of the other conditions listed above and thus cannot be *Idra de-vei-Mashkena*. In the printed versions and in several manuscripts of the *Zohar*, the section that begins with the words "Secret of secrets" (II, 122b–123b) is entitled *Idra de-vei-Mashkena*. While this section is in the style of the *Idrot* and deals with *Ze'er Anpin* and with *Din*, it deals not at all with the mysteries of the Tabernacle, nor does it describe anything like a death. Furthermore, this *Idra* takes place after R. Simeon's death and thus cannot be the event referred to by R. Simeon at the beginning of *Idra Rabba*. In speaking of earlier and later *Idrot* I am referring not to the time of their composition but to the time at which the events related in the *Zohar* "occurred."

110. *Hagiga* 14b: "Four *entered* the Garden (*pardes*)...and R. Akiva emerged unharmed"; the Talmud (ibid., 15b) relates this entering and emerging from the *pardes* to the verse: "The king has brought me to his chambers" (Cant. i:4). There may be another associative link here between *pardes* and *idra*, for *idra* means "chamber." The author of the *Zohar* explicitly links the *idra* to the "*Idra* of the World to Come" (i.e., the Garden of Eden = *pardes*), to which the three companions ascended after the departure of their souls (III, 144a); cf. also the frequently used expression "chambers of the chariot" (e.g., *Cant. Rabba* to that verse).

Paralleling the expression, "entered and emerged," it is also said of R. Akiva that he "went up unharmed and came down unharmed" (*Hagiga* 15b); the latter expression is used in reference to his ascent to and descent from heaven, which Rashi identifies as the Garden.

111. They die because, in revealing the secrets, they "fail to mind the honor of their Creator," and the rabbis said of such a one that "he who fails to mind the honor of his Creator would better never have come into the world" (*Hagiga* 16a). See also Moses de Leon's Hebrew work *Shoshan Edut*, in Scholem, "*Shnei Quntresim*," above n. 46, p. 345, where "entering without emerging" refers to apostasy, as also in the writings of Gikatila cited in Gottlieb, above n. 31. p. 277.

112. Cf. the use of this verse at the beginning of *Tsava'at R. Eliezer ha-Gadol*.

113. That is, the death from which he returned, for the *Zohar* holds Habakkuk to be the child restored to life by the prophet Elisha. In reaching

this conclusion the author of the *Zohar* draws upon the wording of Elisha's prophecy to the child's mother: "You will embrace a son" (II Kings iv:16), deriving the name Habakkuk from the word *hoveket*, embrace.

114. Commenting on the verse, "For man shall not see Me and live" (Ex. xxxiii:20), the rabbis stated that "In their lifetimes they do not see, but in their deaths they do see" (*Num. Rabba* xiv:36). This notion is developed in many places in the *Zohar*; e.g., I, 7a (with reference to Habakkuk).

115. Cf. the pledges sworn by the disciples of R. Shalom Shar'abi in the Beth El Yeshiva in Jerusalem in the eighteenth century. These pledges concern the obligation of the signatories to love one another and are among the most moving texts to be found in a legal document. See the bibliography on them by S. H. Kook, *Kiryat Sefer*, 24, 1959, pp. 16–18; cf. also the pledge undertaken by the students of R. David ben Zimra (including Isaac Luria), published by B. D. Kahane in *Birkat ha-Arets*, (Hebrew) Jerusalem 1904, p. 61.

116. See for example III, 187a: "*le-Ya'akov lo it'hazei hakhi ela be-dugma*" —"Jacob could do this only in a symbolic way." Jacob is contrasted here with Moses, whose coupling with the *Shekhina* was not symbolic but mythic. As the *Zohar* puts it, Moses' coupling was "physical" (*be-gufa*), meaning that it actually took place during his lifetime, while Jacob's was "spiritual" (*be-ruha*), that is, it was carried out symbolically through his coupling with his wife Rachel, and only after his death did he cohabit directly with the *Shekhina*.

117. On the ordination controversy in Safed, see H. Z. Dimitrovsky, "Rabbi Yaakov Berab's Academy" in *Sefunot*, VII, 1963, pp. 41–102.

118. In *Sanhedrin* the ordination is performed not by R. Akiva but by R. Yehuda ben Babba; it is clear, however, from the names of those receiving ordination that the story refers to the same event as that mentioned in *Yevamot*; apparently there were a number of different traditions as to who performed the ordination.

119. For example, N. Krochmal, I. Nissenbaum, Y. Levinsky; see Encyclopedia Judaica, s.v. *Lag ba-Omer*.

120. Benayahu Meir, *The Toledoth Ha-Ari* (Hebrew), Jerusalem 1967, p. 319; see also pp. 165f.

121. See Liebes, above n. 9, pp. 87–88, nn. 88–89.

122. See *Bet ha-Behira* on the above passage from *Yevamot*; the tradition is also mentioned in the Tur, *Orah Hayyim* 493; see also Encyclopedia Judaica, loc. cit.

123. See also R. Nahman of Bratslav, *Sefer Liqqutei Moharan*, I, p. 61.

124. On the spread of this practice see M. Halamish, *Kiryat Sefer*, LIII (1978), pp. 534–56.

125. Based on *Berakhot* 6b: "When the Blessed Holy One enters a synagogue and does not find ten (worshippers) there, he immediately becomes incensed, as it is written, 'wherefore, when I came, was there no man?' (Isa. 1:2)"; the *Zohar* (III, 126a and elsewhere) interprets the word "man" to refer to both the full *minyan* and to the supernal "body" that is completed through it.

126. Cf. the expression "organs of the Shekhina" in *Ra'aya Meheimana* and *Tikkunei Zohar* (e.g., III, 17a). The idea bears comparison with Christian notions according to which all believers are organs of the Church, which is the body of God, *Corpus Domini*. The source of this idea is Rom. xii:5. On the development of this idea by Nathan of Gaza see H. Wirshovski, "On the Spiritual Love" ([Hebrew] "Al ha-Ahava ha-Ruhanit") in *Qovetz Hotsa'at Schocken le-Divrei Sifrut*, Tel Aviv 1941, pp. 180–92; on its development by Moses Hayyim Luzatto, see Y. Tishby, *Kiryat Sefer*, LIII (1978), pp. 181–82.

127. Cf. *Avot* v:17. Another messianic group whose members were commanded to love one another was that of Jesus' disciples; cf. John xiii:34–35: "A new commandment I give unto you, that ye love one another; as I have loved you, that ye also love one another. By this shall all men know that you are my disciples, if ye love one another."

128. Each of these "versions" develops a particular aspect that is also found in the *Idra*, and *Idra Rabba* is apparently the final development that comprehends them all. Thus, these "versions" can be used to elucidate various aspects of the *Idra*. The version discussed here (III, 59b–64b) is primarily concerned with love. While it does not share the usual concern of the *Idrot* with the Kabbala of the *partsufim*, it does share their characteristic narrative framework: a solemn opening that deals with the question of love and with R. Simeon's authority to disclose secrets, followed by each of the companions speaking in turn. Moreover, the word *tanna*, which is used frequently in the *Idrot*, opens a number of clauses in this section, heightening its dramatic impact by creating the impression that its statements are fragments of an ancient mishna. This section, *Idra Rabba*, and *Sifra di-tsniu'ta* all begin with this word, and it also occurs in *Yevamot* 62b, a passage that influenced *Idra Rabba*.

This section is related to the discourse that precedes it, which discusses the flaw inherent in the separation between male and female, taking the description of the cherubs in the temple as its basis. According to the Talmud (*Yoma* 54a), the cherubs were male and female and were interlocked; when they faced each other, it was a sign that Israel was doing God's will (according to *Bava Batra* 99a). The first "version" of the *Idra*, which follows this discourse, develops the idea as follows: It happened once that the world was in need of rain, and R. Simeon was approached to beseech God for mercy. The need for rain is not, of course, a messianic matter, but its fulfilment is of such terrestrial and historical importance as to make it parallel redemption (see *Ta'anit* 7b). R. Simeon deals with the problem by bringing about a coupling of male and female, which is precisely what he does in the matter of Israel's redemption. In so doing he bases himself on the many statements by the rabbis likening rainfall to marriage and copulation (e.g., *Ta'anit* 10b). R. Simeon here identifies the remedy for the defect in the relations between male and female with love among his disciples.

129. The inference is to *Yesod* and not *Tif'eret*, as is established by the citation of the verse "and be thou wholehearted (*tamim*). . ." (Gen. xvii:1), which was spoken to Abraham before his circumcision. The *Zohar* frequently relates the notion of wholeheartedness (*temimut*) to circumcision and to *Yesod* (e.g., III, 163b), for Abraham was able to perfect his virtue, which was love, only through circumcision.

130. It is especially appropriate that the *tikkun* of the Torah should take place on the night of Shavuot, the festival marking the giving of the Torah, and accordingly *Idra Rabba* is the *tikkun* performed on that night; see Appendix A.

131. The verse from Habakkuk is also expounded with reference to the Messiah by the "Gnostic" Kabbalists.

132. This is derived from the verse "All the paths of the Lord are mercy and truth unto such as keep His covenant and His testimonies" (Ps. xxv:10). The author apparently relates mercy (*hesed*) to *Arikh Anpin* and truth (*emet*) to *Ze'er Anpin*. These paths, from which the commandments of the Torah pour forth, are also the organs and sinews of *Ze'er Anpin*, who is the supernal man in whose image God created man. This is the *Zohar*'s explanation for the relationship noted by the rabbis between the number of the commandments and the traditional number of the organs of the human body.

133. The rabbis use this term for the practical *mitsvot*, intending by it to refer to the main body of the Torah, the principal part (*Berakhot* 63a). The *Zohar*, however, takes the word in its concrete meaning, and thus locates this "body" precisely between the outer garments and the soul. The term still refers to the *mitsvot*, but the new meaning attached to it by the *Zohar* lowers their status. Aware of the plain meaning of the term, the *Zohar* uses it to contrast those who concern themselves with the practical *mitsvot* and those who engage in Kabbala. Cf. the use of the term by R. Azriel: see Scholem, above n. 37, pp. 47–49.

134. Solomon Ibn Gabirol uses the expression "soul of the soul" in his poem "Keter Malkhut." In the *Zohar* the expression is sometimes used to refer to the highest part of man's soul (e.g., II, 56b).

135. The description of the ontological sources of the Torah in relation to one another is similar to the description of the Torah as consisting of outer garment, body, soul, etc.

136. The expression derives from the verse: "And there hath not risen a prophet since in Israel like unto Moses, whom the Lord knew *face to face*" (Deut. xxxiv:10).

137. This conception of the *mitsvot* of the Torah as stern judgment that is ameliorated only for select individuals appears already in *Sefer ha-Bahir*, 66, 192, and elsewhere.

138. *Otsar ha-Kavod*, Warsaw 1879, 22b,c. R. Todros Abulafia belonged to Moses de Leon's circle.

139. See also *Eruvin* 13a: "And when I came to R. Ishmael, he said to me: My son, what is your work? I said to him: I am a scribe. He said to me: My son, be careful in your work, for your work is the work of heaven. Should you leave out a letter or add one, the whole world will be destroyed."

140. Cf. Scholem, *Kitvei Yad*, above n. 50, p. 205.

141. A parallel to this passage in *Idra Rabba* appears in the writings of R. Azriel of Gerona (see G. Scholem, *New Remnants from the Writings of Azriel of Girona* [(Hebrew) *Seridim Hadashim mi-Kitvei R. Azriel mi-Gerona*], in *Sefer Zikkaron le-A. Gulak ve-S. Klein*, Jerusalem 1942, pp. 211–12), who makes use of the same verse from Isaiah. The connection between the Messianic era and the number seven, with the number six related to the pre-Messianic era, is also found elsewhere. On this notion in the writings of Abulafia, see M. Idel, *Studies in Ecstatic Kabbalah*, State University of New York Press, Albany, New York 1988, p. 51.

142. *Mishne Torah, Hilkhot Melakhim* xii:4–5 (English translation: Yale University Press).

143. Ibid., *Hilkhot Teshuva* ix:9–10.

144. See M. Idel, *"The Writings of R. Abraham Abulafia and His Doctrine"* ([Hebrew] *Kitvei R. Avraham Abulafia u-Mishnato*) (Ph.D. diss., Hebrew University, Jerusalem, 1976), pp. 395–418.

145. See, for example, the *Sod ha-Levana* of Jacob Hakohen, published by Scholem, in "Kabbalot," above n. 44, pp. 78–79.

146. See Maimonides, *Guide of the Perplexed*, III:51. Maimonides ascribes such a mystical meaning to the rabbinic legends about the six righteous men who died by a kiss, the foremost among them being Moses. See also H. Wirszubski, *Three Studies in Christian Kabbala* (Hebrew), Jerusalem 1975, pp. 13–22. Despite R. Simeon's denunciation of those who "enter the Garden and do not emerge," his suspicion that they died because of the sin of disclosing secrets, and the fact that R. Jesse's death is elsewhere described as a punishment, he nonetheless extols the manner of their departure and regards it as a great and meritorious attainment. Cf. the attitude expressed by R. Todros Abulafia in *Sefer Otsar ha-Kavod*, Tractate

Hagiga, where he extols Ben Azzai, one of the four who entered the Garden, who "looked and died."

147. At the end of *Idra Zuta*, R. Simeon's soul, too, departs at the word "Life."

148. In his *Nitsotsei Zohar*, Margaliot wonders how it is that R. Hezekiah and R. Jesse are alive in the *Zohar* at III, 71a, since according to this passage the event described there took place after the death of R. Simeon and of his son R. Eleazar. Rather than leading us to suppose, as Margaliot suggests, that the sages in the passage are a different R. Hezekiah and a different R. Jesse, this seems to reflect the method of *Zohar*'s composition, presenting the same stories in successively more developed versions.

149. The Sages, too, may have seen this as praiseworthy: see PT *Sanhedrin* x:2, 28b, where Hiel the Bethelite, who refounded Jericho in the days of Ahab at the cost of his sons (I Kings xvi:34), is called a "great man."

150. Jericho is an appropriate term for the *Shekhina* for several reasons. First, it can be derived from *yerah* (moon), a symbol of the *Shekhina*. Second, the circling of Jericho seven times by Joshua's men recalls the seven upper *sefirot* that influence the Shekhina. R. Eleazar of Worms compared the circling of Jericho to the circling of the altar on Hosha-'ana Rabba (*Sefer ha-Rokeah*, 221). The parallel is striking: on each of the first six days of Sukkot the altar is circled once, while on the seventh day (Hosha-'ana Rabba) it is circled seven times; and so too at the conquest of Jericho: for six days it was circled once a day, and on the seventh day it was circled seven times. In the *Zohar* the circling of the altar is interpreted as symbolically representing the circling of the *Shekhina* (e.g., III, 24a). This idea is also developed by R. Bahya b. Asher, a contemporary of the author of the *Zohar*, in his book *Kad ha-Kemah*, s.v. "*Arava*"; see also Y. D. Wilhelm, Sidrei "Tikkunim," *Alei Ayin—Minhat Devarim*, The S. Schoken Jubilee Volume (Hebrew), Jerusalem 1948–52, pp. 125–46, especially p. 133. Third, it is said of Jericho that it "was shut up tight" (Josh. vi:1), which is appropriate to the description of the *Shekhina* as a virgin, as explained in *Tikkunei Zohar* (58, 92a). See on this also R. Meir Poppers, *Sefer Me'orei Or*, s.v. "Jericho." Fourth, Jericho was the first of Israel's conquests and therefore was dedicated, like first fruits and other first things, to God. This may parallel the identification of the *Shekhina* with the priestly tithe (as, e.g., in II, 138b). Fifth, Jericho was conquered on the Sabbath (according to *Midrash Tanhuma*, Naso, xxxi), and in the *Zohar* the *sefira* of *Malkhut* stands for the Sabbath (or an aspect of the Sabbath).

151. This identification appears several times in the *Zohar* (see, e.g., III, 84a) and in Moses de Leon's Hebrew works as well (*ha-Nefesh ha-Hakhama*, II, Basel 1608). There the *Shekhina* is the Heavenly Garden of Eden, while the lower Garden of Eden exists in the material world. This is also the view of Nahmanides in *Sh'ar ha-Gemul* (*Kitvei Ramban*, II, Jerusalem 1964, pp. 295–97).

152. In contrast to the Tree of Life, which is the *sefira* of *Tif'eret*. The Tree of Death is identical with the Tree of Knowledge, on account of which death came into the world; see also Liebes, above n. 6, pp. 122f, n. 7.

153. This follows clearly from the above passage (III, 120b–121a), and from the passage cited below from *Zohar Hadash*, where "falling to one's face" is later described as surrender of the soul to the God. Luria drew a connection between the *Shekhina* and the *Sitra Ahra* in this context, because "her feet descend to death." The conception of the *Shekhina* as a creature interested in death is not in and of itself surprising, for it is known from other parts of the *Zohar*; see Scholem, above n. 37, pp. 300–302; and see also Tishby I., above n. 65, Vol.III, pp. 970–71, who mistakenly related this creature to the *Sitra Ahra*.

154. The *Zohar* (III, 121a) emphasizes this extensively and in the sharpest terms. For example, "A man must make his soul (or himself) and his will (or his devotional intention) cling to his Maker, and shall not come before Him with a false intention." The author excoriates anyone who entices the Blessed Holy One without true *kavvana*: "Woe unto him who would beguile his Maker with a distant heart and without true intention, as it is written, 'But they beguiled Him with their mouth, and lied unto Him with their tongue; for their heart was not steadfast with Him' (Ps. lxxvi:36–37)." "Beguiling" with the proper intention, on the other hand, is deemed positive, as the passage in the *Zohar* states: "Happy is the man who knows how to beguile and worship his Maker with the will and intention of his heart."

These lines clearly embody a polemic against those who "beguile" by falling on the face without being wholehearted in their intention. It is not clear from this passage why anyone would do this, or how, or what in fact is meant by "beguiling." This becomes clearer from a parallel passage in *Zohar Hadash* (Teruma 42a). There the author of the *Zohar* likens the worshiper to a monkey in the mountains in the presence of another animal that wants to kill it; the monkey adopts a strategem of playing dead, and the other animal is satisfied by this and does not kill it. De Leon buttresses this discourse by noting that Psalms xxv, an alphabetically structured psalm recited in an attitude of falling on the face, lacks a verse beginning with the letter *kuf*, which stands for *kof* (monkey). The preying animal is the *Shekhina*. A worshiper who falls on his face in the manner of this myth obviously has no intention of actually giving himself up to death; he only pretends to do so in order to "beguile" the beast. The tone of the author's comments conveys the impression that such "beguiling" was indeed practiced by contemporaries of his, against whom his polemic is addressed. In the view of the *Zohar*, the "beguiling" will not succeed unless the worshiper truly intends to deliver up his soul (the *Shekhina*, it seems, is not so naive). Temptations offered the *Sitra Ahra*, on the other hand, are in fact only semblances (see, e.g., III, 102a), and that, too, is evidence that the reference here is to the *Shekhina*. On surrender of the soul to death while falling on the face see also Moses de Leon's Hebrew work, *Sefer ha-Rimmon* (Ms. Bodlein 1607), p. 33.

155. See for example I, 59b. Luria used the expression with clearly sexual implications in his song for the first Sabbath meal; see Y. Liebes, "Sabbath Meal Songs Established by the Holy Ari" (Hebrew), *Molad*, IV (1972), pp. 540–55, 543.

156. According to II, 129a, the motion of falling on the face at the end of the Amida prayer is to be understood as concealment of one's face, for it is at this point (during the benediction of "Sim Shalom," which is the last in the prayer) that the coupling between *Yesod* and *Malkhut* is completed. Coupling ought to be performed in circumstances of modesty, and one has therefore to conceal his face and refrain from looking.

157. The notion of "feminine waters" has two sources, the one cosmological-mythical and the other physiological. The first is related to the ancient notion that "supernal waters are masculine and lower waters are feminine" (e.g., PT *Berakhot* ix:3, 14a; *Gen. Rabba* xiii:13; *Zohar* I, 29b); as for the second, "waters" is the term used for the sperm of the male and the discharges of the female released during copulation. Since the *Zohar* describes the couplings of a male and female (*Tif'eret* and *Malkhut*) which are cosmic, these two realms readily merge in its descriptions (see also, I, 60b, 244b).

158. See *Sha'ar ha-Kavvanot*, "Inyan Nefilat Apayim," Jerusalem 1902, 46d–47c.

159. This notion does not appear in the *Zohar*, for there the coupling between *Abba* and *Imma* (*Hokhma* and *Bina*) is permanent and unceasing and therefore has no need for assistance from below.

160. This is true in general of the Kabbala; see Scholem, above n. 1, pp. 325–50. In this regard Isaac of Acre is an exception; his mysticism is of the "pure" sort and resembles the Sufi method (see Gottlieb, above n. 31, pp. 231–47).

161. See, for example, III, 41b; just as there are ten *sefirot* of faith, so there are ten *sefirot* below of unclean magic. There are those who cling to the former and those who cling to the latter. The *Zohar* often relates this notion to a rabbinic saying: "If one comes to defile himself, he is given an opening; if one comes to cleanse himself, he is helped" (Shabbat 104a; *Zohar* I, 54a, 62a; III, 53b).

This kind of mystical magic is ascribed mainly to the wizard Bilaam (e.g., III, 207a; II, 21b–22b). In these passages Bilaam is likened not to just any Kabbalist, but to the greatest of mystics, Moses himself. This too is based on a rabbinic statement: " 'there hath not arisen in Israel a prophet since like unto Moses' (Deut. xxxiv:10)—but there did among the nations of the world. Who was this? Bilaam." (Sifre, Deut. 357). This gave the author of the *Zohar* a good opportunity to liken the greatest of mystics to the greatest of wizards, the only difference between them being that the former clung to the forces of holiness, the latter to the forces of defilement.

162. This is marked in all the writings of Merkava mysticism. For one example, see the midrash, *"Ele Ezkera"* (op. cit. [above, n. 101], IV, pp. 64–73), in A. Jellinek, *Bet ha-Midrash*, I–IV (Hebrew), Jerusalem 1967.

163. On the relationship between study, *devekut*, and *tikkun*, see the especially forthright passage at II, 213b.

164. Tishby, above n. 98, p. 40.

165. On the question of *devekut* and theurgy, see also Gottleib, above n. 31, pp. 38–55.

166. Cf. his statement on the originality of his description of the beard of *Attika Kaddisha* (see n. 176 below).

167. This is a mythic-midrashic motif; see Appendix I. It also appears in *Idra Rabba*, III, 135a.

168. Cf. that passage, I, 8a: " 'His handiwork'—those are the bearers of the sign of the covenant by the side of the bride. These bearers of the sign of the covenant are called 'his handiwork', as it is written: 'The work of our hands, establish Thou it' (Ps. xc:17). That is the sign of the covenant sealed in the flesh of man." It appears that the author of the *Zohar* understood the verb k-n-n (establish) as meaning "to seal," though it is hard to see on what basis. He may have been influenced associatively by the midrash on Eccles. v:5 (which verse he cites immediately before the present passage): "The work of your hands—what is to the work of man's hands? his sons and daughters" (Shabbat 32b).

169. This is the motif of love among the companions and between them and the *sefirot*, which was discussed above in our analysis of the opening of *Idra Rabba*.

170. Cf. the passage from the "Gnostic Kabbalists" in Appendix I (p. 77), according to which the verses recited before prayer are the *tikkun* of the bride and her adornment.

171. This may be the source of the designation *Tsaddik ha-Emet* by which R. Nahman of Bratslav frequently referred to himself.

172. For example, in the writings of Moses Cordovero; see J. Ben-Shlomo, *The Mystical Theology of Moses Cordovero* (Hebrew), Jerusalem 1965, pp. 95–100. The idea is explained at length in the *Zohar*, III, 204b.

173. For example, at II, 135a–b, which is the passage recited by Hasidim in welcoming the Sabbath. It also appears in II, 134a–b. In many places in his writings Luria develops the idea found here into a notion of *tikkun* which involves the enlargement of the female to the size of *Ze'er Anpin* before their perfect coupling.

174. The drawing of ethical or political conclusions from the behavior of the supernal configurations is characteristic of *Idra Rabba*. Here we see a kind of 'reverse symbolism"; not only do we extrapolate from the lower to the supernal world, but also the converse. Some of the precepts for human conduct derived in this way appear quite bizarre in their earthly political context. For example, "From this we learn that whoever wants the king to hear him should run his hand through the king's hair, lifting the hairs from the king's ear; then the king will listen to all that he wants to say" (III, 295a–*Idra Zuta*). It should be noted here that the descriptions of the supernal configurations in the *Idra* are often based on theories of physiognomy, which is the art of judging character on the basis of a person's facial features. The reverse is also sometimes the case; for example, the description of the art of physiognomy in the *Zohar* (the section "Raza de-razin" in the chapter on the Torah portion of Jethro) takes the descriptions of the supernal configurations in the *Idra* as the source of its ideas.

175. On the connection between the *tikkun* of *Attika* and the night of the *Idra*, which is the night of Shavuot, see below, Appendix I.

176. The act of taking hold of the beard—in addition to the discourses on it—itself harbors holy secrets, and R. Simeon in *Idra Rabba* thus expressed his trepidation before expounding on the beard: "Woe unto him who stretches out his hand to the precious supernal beard of the Holy Old One, the hidden, sealed from all . . .the beard that no man, prophet or holy person came near to see" (III, 130b). The end of his statement alludes to the fact that the beard of the Blessed Holy One is not mentioned in the Bible or in the legends of the rabbis, not even in the Song of Songs, which is interpreted as an allegory on the Blessed Holy One. R. Simeon explains this omission as follows: "You may say: The beard is not mentioned, and all Solomon said was 'His cheeks' (Cant. v:13), forebearing explicitly to say 'beard'. But in *Sifra di-Tsni'uta* we learned that whatever is hidden and concealed and is not mentioned or disclosed—that thing is supreme and precious above all, and for that reason it is kept sealed and hidden. The author of the *Zohar* goes on from this to develop the association between the beard, the sexual organ, and *Yesod*. In *Idra Rabba* grasping the beard is related to oath–taking: "He who stretches out his hand (i.e., and takes hold of his beard) to swear an oath is as one who swears by the thirteen *tikkunim* of the beard (of *Attika Kaddisha*)" (III, 131a). Immediately after this warning, R. Simeon turns to R. Isaac and tells him to twirl the supernal beard, an indication that while expounding on this subject the companions held their beards.

177. The term "sweetening" in the sense of mitigating stern judgment comes from the Spanish; see G. G. Scholem, above n. 29, p. 388, n. 44. This "sweetening" is generally effected by the coupling of male and female, for the female by herself has judgment as her primary characteristic, and she is "sweetened" by being linked to the male.

178. This theory, known to many peoples, reached the *Zohar* via *Sefer ha-Bahir*; see G. Scholem, *Das Buch Bahir*, Darmstadt 1970, p. 112. It also appears in *Midrash Temura*; see Wertheimer, above n. 10, Vol. II, p. 195.

179. This understanding appears often in the *Zohar*, especially in relation to Abraham, whose virtue, *hesed*, was fully realized only with his circumcision (III, 142a). A saying that recurs frequently in the *Idrot* is *"Hesed* depends on mother's *mouth"* (ibid.). The *Zohar* calls the female's restored private parts, which the passage goes on to describe, "the covering of the entire body"; the meaning of "covering" apparently being opposite to that of "private parts." On this see also Liebes, above n. 6, p. 243.

180. See Scholem, above n. 44, pp. 82, 112. The verse is also used in a messianic context in Moses de Leon's Hebrew work, *Shekel ha-Kodesh*, London 1911, p. 90.

181. See *Sanhedrin* 68a.

182. The impression of this contrast is intensified when we consider that the deaths of R. Akiva and his associates (the ten who were martyred by the Roman regime) are explained in the *Zohar* (II, 254b–255a) as symbolic of the separation of good from evil in the Divine Thought at the beginning of the emanations. This separation on the one hand signified a purgation (catharsis) of the Godhead, and on the other the creation of the forces of evil. The notion of the purgation of the Divine Thought thus parallels the idea of the "death of the kings." According to *Zohar Hadash* (*Tsav*, 46c), the second *sefira* of *Sitra Ahra*, which parallels "pure thought"—the *sefira* of *Hokhma*—on the side of holiness, is called "evil thought." See M. Idel, "The Evil Thought of the Deity," *Tarbiz*, XLIX (1980), pp. 356–64. If so, then the death of R. Akiva, which created the "kings" that died, is the reverse counterpart of the death of R. Simeon, which effected their *tikkun*. Furthermore, the bodies of the ten martyrs were handed over to the "kingdom of wickedness" whereas R. Simeon's death in the *Zohar* is meant to bring about the end of that kingdom (the "kings of Edom," i.e., Rome and its successors, the Christian kingdoms) and to lead to the building of Jerusalem.

183. Cf. perhaps the statement by Meir Aldabi that "the womb has three chambers"; *The Paths of Faith* (*[Hebrew] Shevilei ha-Emuna*), Vilna 1818, 95b.

184. See Appendix II. It should also be borne in mind that the *Zohar* views the high priest's entry into the Holy of Holies as involving the soul more than the body; see *Midrash ha-Ne'e'lam*, *Zohar Hadash* 19a, where it is also stated that the Holy of Holies is a symbol of Paradise. The *Shekhina*, moreover, is often called "Paradise" in the *Zohar*.

185. See Idel, above n. 144, pp. 416–17. Idel there cites another instance of this as well. R. Simeon was not a *kohen*, a descendant of the priestly line, nor is there any evidence that Moses de Leon was. But that in itself does not obstruct the spiritual self-identification of the *Zohar*'s author with the figure

of the priest. As Idel shows, Abulafia by his own testimony was neither priest nor Levite, but that did not prevent him from describing himself in the image of the high priest.

186. This view of the natural condition of the Gentile nations was widespread in the Middle Ages. Cf. *Kuzari*, iv:23.

187. For example, *Ex. Rabba* xxi:5; *Mekhilta Beshallah* xv:2; and in the *Zohar*, e.g., II, 54b; cf. also the designation "kingdom of wickedness" used by the author of the *Zohar* to refer to the *Sitra Ahra* (II, 134b).

188. The source of this idea is the *Kuzari*, iv:23. The description of the *Sitra Ahra* as a husk occurs in the writings of Azriel of Gerona and may have its origins in the writings of the *Hasidei Ashkenaz*, who envisioned the chariot as a nut. They did not, however, identify the shell with the forces of evil; for them it represented Judgment. The symbol of the nut and its shell appears frequently in the *Zohar*; see Liebes, above n. 6, pp. 20–27. On the idea among the Hasidei Ashkenaz and its possible sources, see J. Dan, "Hokhmath ha-Egoz, Its Origin and Development," *Journal of Jewish Studies*, XVII (1966), pp. 73–82; J. Dan, *'Alei Sefer*, V (1978), pp. 49–53; J. Dan, *The Esoteric Theology of Ashkenazi Hasidim*, Jerusalem 1968, pp. 208–10. Dan believes that the idea should be traced back in time to the talmudic mystics. See also Abraham b. Azriel, *Sefer Arugat ha-Bosem* (ed. E.E. Urbach), Jerusalem 1947, p. 168; A. Altmann, "Eleazar of Worms" Hokhmath ha-Egoz," *JJS*, XI (1960), pp. 101–13.

189. On the stages in the life of Moses de Leon see Scholem, above n. 29, pp. 186–87, who however maintains that the *Zohar* was written between 1280 and 1286. Tishby, however, maintains that the writing of the main body of the *Zohar* began in 1293 (Tishby, above n. 65, Vol. I. pp. 95–96).

190. The expression used there—*di-shkil be-matkela*—may also mean that the book is written in poetic meter, which is in fact true of *Sifra di-Tsni'uta*, especially in its early chapters. My rendering of *matkela* as "balance" follows Isaac the Blind, from whom I believe the author of the *Zohar* took the idea of the balance with two pans, though it may also have earlier sources. See the commentary of Isaac the Blind to *Sefer Yetsira*, printed as an appendix to a mimeographed collection of lectures by Scholem, *Ha-Kabbala in Provence*, Jerusalem 1963, pp. 8f.

191. *Qav ha-Midda*; see Liebes, above n. 6, pp. 146–51, 161–64, 327–31. On the notion of the "line of measure" in the writings of Azriel of Gerona, who calls it *kav ha-yosher*, see Y. Tishby (ed.), above n. 98, (above, n. 164), pp. 89f.

192. See for example *Merkava Shelema*, Jerusalem 1972, 38b.

193. This balance resembles another, which also weighs the souls before they enter the world and determines whether they shall belong to the Holy

Side—the *sitra di-kedusha*, or to the *sitra ahra* (II, 95b–96b); on this balance see Liebes, above n. 6, pp. 327–35.

194. *Berakhot* 61a. This midrash is based on the myth recounted by Aristophanes at Plato's *Symposium*; see also L. Ginzberg, *The Legends of the Jews*, Philadelphia 1956, V, pp. 88–89, n. 42.

195. See Tishby, above n. 98, p. 86; see also *Sefer Ma'arekhet ha-Elohut* (Mantua, 1558), especially chapter 8.

196. See for example *Zohar*, I, 91b; for a discussion of the idea, see Tishby, above n. 65, Vol. III, pp. 1355–56.

197. This is derived from Gen. v:2, and from the rabbinic teaching in *Yevamot* 63a.

198. This notion appears in scores of places in the *Zohar*; see, e.g., III, 141b; see also: Liebes, above n. 6, p. 33. The idea is also found in *Sefer ha-Bahir* (ed. Margaliot), 172.

199. The rabbis said this of one who does not fulfil the command to "be fruitful and multiply" (*Yevamot* 63b).

200. For example, at III, 7b; see also Liebes, above n. 6, pp. 277f.

201. According to the midrash (*Gen. Rabba* vii:5), the demons are spirits for whom God did not create bodies before the day was sanctified. The author of the *Zohar* explains this bodilessness as of the demons in that they are not connected to the Godhead, which is called *guf* (body; e.g., III, 143a,b). In the *Zohar* the demons are sometimes identified with the general notion of the *Sitra Ahra*, and therefore bodilessness is ascribed exclusively to the *Sitra Ahra*. The author of the *Zohar* affirms the rabbinic statement that an unmarried person is not called "man" but also explains it in that he is remote from the Godhead, which is called Man (III, 5b). From this it derives another reason for denying the name "man" to the *Sitra Ahra*: the celibacy of the kings of Edom (III, 292a), who were removed from reality in that they were neither "man" nor "body." This view of the *Sitra Ahra* is related to other statements elsewhere in the *Zohar* (II, 112a) about its barrenness. Accordingly, a person who does not engage in reproduction becomes part of the *Sitra Ahra*. On the whole issue of bodiless demons who are not called man see Liebes, above n. 6, pp. 54–55, 190.

202. This comes about through levirate marriage. The dead brother returns to life as the child of his wife and his brother. The Kabbala thus transforms the "name" of the brother, which is preserved by the levirate marriage, into his soul. This is also based on the verse "He will renew your life (*nefesh*)" (Ruth iv:15). Levirate marriage was interpreted in this way by the Gerona circle as well. (See Liebes, above n. 6, pp. 110, 294–96.) Reincarnation in this way is punishment, for one who returns to the world in this manner descends from his former rung, in which he was connected

with the male world (*Bina*), and comes to be associated with the female world (*Malkhut*), as expressed in this world in that his former wife becomes his mother (see II, 100b). Most of the *Zohar*'s chapter on the Torah portion of Mishpatim is devoted to the subject of levirate marriage; see also Moses de Leon, *Sod Yibbum* (printed with his book, *Ha-Nefesh ha-Hakhama*, Basel 1608).

203. Thirteen years, according to PT *Shevi'it* ix:1, 38d.

204. Published in *Sefer Yuhasin*; reprinted in Tishby, above n. 65, Vol. I, pp. 13–15.

205. Not only does the male below dwell between two females; *Yesod* (or *Tif'eret*) is located between *Bina* above it and *Malkhut* below it. Jacob's two wives, Leah and Rachel, allude to these two.

206. *Sefer ha-Rimmon*, p. 57.

207. For example, III, 132b.

208. In those passages where it is explained that the Messiah is of the *sefira* of *Yesod*.

209. See II, 57b; III, 69a. The idea already appears in *Ex. Rabba*, xxx and in *Tanhuma*, Aharei Mot, xii. These statements belong to a larger group of assertions stating that Israel's exile is the exile of God (e.g., Megilla 29a). This led the Sages to conclude that Israel's redemption is above all the redemption of God—a view that appears diametrically opposed to the Christian view of the Saviour, for here the Saviour is not sacrificed for the world, but rather the salvation of the world is his own salvation. The author of the *Zohar*, who retained this view, nonetheless introduced a resemblance to the figure of Jesus into the messianic figure of R. Simeon in that R. Simeon, too, brings about salvation through his death, though Jesus' death was one of suffering while R. Simeon's is one of bliss. Nor was it beyond the conceptualization of the *Zohar* to describe the Messiah as suffering the pains of Israel. In II, 212a, de Leon depicts him sitting and suffering with the sick. The image is taken from *Sanhedrin* 98a, but the *Zohar* shifts its location from the gates of Rome to one of the chambers of Paradise. It states, moreover, that the Messiah's sufferings take the place of sufferings that would otherwise have come upon Israel. The *Zohar* applies this line of thought to chapter liii of Isaiah, an interpretation known to us primarily from Christianity, and one against which Nahmanides had argued most forcefully.

210. The sources for this is *Lam. Rabba* iv:19.

Notes to Appendix I

1. For this purpose the *mitsvot* were formulated into liturgical poems called *azharot*; some notable examples of these were composed by Saadya Gaon and Solomon Ibn Gabirol.

2. By engaging in study of the Torah and above all its secrets, the companions deck the *Shekhina* with twenty-four adornments, which parallel the twenty-four books of the Bible (following the Jewish reckoning), and with the help of their study of these holy books the bride is adorned. This parallel has its origin in *Cant. Rabba* iv:11, and *Ex. Rabba* xli. According to Wilhelm (p. 127), the bride's twenty-four ornaments have their source in the twenty-four ornaments mentioned in Is. iii:18–24, though by my count twenty-five types of jewelry are mentioned there. For a similar image, cf. Revelation xxi:2: "And I saw the holy city, new Jerusalem, coming down from God out of heaven, prepared as a bride adorned for her husband."

3. He also appears as such in *Tikkunei Zohar*; e.g., *Zohar*, I, 22a, where he is called *Sava De-Savin*. This figure combines the figure of the Old Man in the *Zohar* with the philosophical notion *sibat ha-sibot*, the cause of causes or First Cause. In the same way, the concept *'illat ha-'illot* became *'illat 'al kol 'illa'in*, the Most Supreme. A figure of this sort appears in the writings of the rabbis. The Talmud reports that on Yom Kippur the high priest, Simon the Just, saw an old man wrapped in white in the Holy of Holies (*Menahot* 109b), and the Jerusalem Talmud adds, "it was the Shekhina." It should be noted that in the period of the writing of the *Zohar*, Simon the Just was considered a mystic.

4. It is possible that the description of *Tikkun Leil Shavu'ot* begins only at I, 8a; if so, this parallel should not be taken into account.

5. For example, *Shabbat* 88b: "Wretched is the bride who whores under her bridal canopy"—an allegory on the sin of the Golden Calf.

6. See Wilhelm Y.D., above n. 150, pp. 125–130.

7. *Tikkun*, ibid., p. 127.

8. Cited in ibid., p. 126.

9. See Farber, above n. 48, p. 78, n. 12, and pp. xvi, xvii; Scholem, "The Commentary of R. Issac" above n. 104. p. 202; the beginning of *Sefer Ammud ha-Semali* by Moses of Burgos (above, n. 47); Todros Abulafia, *Sefer Sha'ar ha-Razim* (Munich Ms. 209; National and University Library, Jerusalem, microfilm no. 1625), pp. 46, 52; and the statements of R. Isaac in Scholem, "Kabbalot," above n. 44, p. 82.

10. I:34.

11. See Scholem, "Rabbi Moshe," above n. 46, *Tarbiz*, III, p. 286.

12. Ibid., p. 194.

13. Ibid., pp. 266–67.

14. In his commentary to Ex. xxxi:19, which is based on Hullin 133a: "The word 'remnant' refers to a learned sage, as in the verse which concludes 'and among the remnants whom the Lord calls.'"

15. See Scholem, "R. Moshe," above n. 46, *Tarbiz*, V, p. 322.

16. Cf. *Zohar*, II, 138b.

17. See S. Lieberman, "Mishnat Shir ha-Shirim," in G. G. Scholem, *Jewish Gnosticism, Merkabah Mysticism and Talmudic Tradition*, New York 1960, pp. 118ff. Lieberman proves that *Midrash Shir ha-Shirim* is the same as the *ma'ase merkava* and the *shi'ur koma*, and that according to the mystics it was revealed at Mt. Sinai, or at least, that the day when it was given was as great as the day on which the Torah was given. See also the talmudic and midrashic sources in which the mystical visions of the Tannaim are compared to the revelation at Sinai, in Urbach, op. cit. (above, n. 33), pp. 6–11.

18. See I. Weinstock, Studies in Jewish Philosophy and Mysticism (*Bema'agelei ha-Nigle ve-ha-Nistar*), Jerusalem 1970, p. 198.

19. See Lieberman, op. cit. (above, n. 17), pp. 118f.

20. *Mekhilta*, Beshallah, Shirat ha-Yam, IV, and parallels. The rabbis associate this description with the same verse as that used by the *Zohar*: "I beheld till thrones were placed, and one that was ancient of days did sit: his raiment was as white snow, and the hair of his head like pure wool" (Dan. vii:9).

21. *Sha'ar ha-Kavvanot*, Concerning Shavu'ot.

22. Venice 1763, p. 49a.

23. See also: Natan Shapira, *Sefer Tuv ha-Arets*, Venice 1655, 75b.

24. See G. G. Scholem, *Shabbetai Sevi*, above n. 53, pp. 214–15.

Notes to Appendix II

1. *Tanhuma*, Ki Tissa, xxxi; *Pirkei de-Rabbi Eliezer, xlvi*.

2. *Pirkei de-Rabbi Eliezer*, loc. cit.

3. See the text called *Sidrei Shimusha Rabba*, published and analyzed by Scholem in *Tarbiz*, XVI, 1945, pp. 196–209.

4. Ibid., p. 205.

5. Ibid., p. 200.

6. Shavuot is also associated with *Bina*.

7. According to *Midrash Mishlei*, ix (ed. Buber).

8. Cf. *Pirkei de-Rabbi Eliezer, xlvi*.

Chapter 2

The subject dealt with in this essay requires systematic study in a wide range of literature, and this framework is not the place for it. This chapter concentrates on points raised in my lecture at a study day. Its aim basically is to serve as a methodical guide and to provide examples for the way in which I anticipate future research.

1. The reader will find a detailed survey of the history of Zoharic research in I. Tishby: *The Wisdom of the Zohar*, Oxford 1989, pp. 30–55.

2. G. G. Scholem summed up these studies in his book: *Major Trends in Jewish Mysticism*, York 1961, pp. 156–243 (the book was first published in 1941). He summarized the contents of this book also in the entry on the Zohar in the *Encyclopedia Judaica*.

3. The letter was translated and examined by Tishby (cf. n. 1), pp. 13–17.

4. Alexander Altmann, *Sefer Or Zarua le-R. Moshe de Leon: Mavo Text Criti ve-He'arot*, *Kovetz al Yad*, 9 (19), 1980, pp. 243–44. Altmann's view that *Sefer Or Zaru'a* is the first of Moses de Leon's writings also presents difficulties. However, the subject cannot be developed in the present context.

5. Tishby (above n. 1).

6. Eliyahu Peretz, *Ma'alot ha-Zohar—Mafte'ah Shemot ha-Sefirot*, Jerusalem 1987, pp. 8–9, 129–67.

7. See for instance: Moses de Leon, *Ha-Nefesh ha-Hakhama*, Basel, 1608 (photocopy: Jerusalem 1969), fol. 6, p. 1b (in *Seder Tehiyat ha-Metim*): "Tilkot nefashot ha-ta'anugim." The difficult language "nefashot ha-ta'anugim" occurs twice on the same page, and is also found in the manuscripts (according to Yonah Weinhoven's critical ed.). The original expression in Zohar, II, 10a, however, is: "le'alkata nafshin be-ta'anugei kedusha." Thus it is understood that "be-ta'anugim" is a description of the method of gathering (*lekita*), and not as in Moses de Leon's version.

8. See below, n. 298.

9. See Altmann (above n. 4), pp. 240–43.

10. See Alexander Altmann, *Midrash Alegori al Pi Derekh "Ha-Kabbala ha-Penimit" al Bereshit 24*, in his book: *Panim shel Yahadut*, Tel Aviv 1983, pp. 68–75.

11. Zohar, I, 170a contains a section that is basically only an Aramaic translation of a passage from R. Joseph's *Ta'amei ha-Mitzvot*; cf. A. Altmann, *Li-She'elat Ba'aluto shel Sefer Ta'amei ha-Mitzvot ha-Meyuhas le-R. Yizhak ibn Farhi*, KS 40 (1965), p. 265. On this section and its deviation from the

doctrines of R. Joseph, cf. Moshe Idel: "The World of Angels in the Image of Man" ([Hebrew], *Mehkarim be-Kabbala, be-Filosofia Yehudit uve-Sifrut ha-Musar vehe-Hagut*), presented to I. Tishby, Jerusalem 1986 (Jerusalem Studies in Jewish Thought, Vol. 3, 1984), pp. 51–52. Cf. also n. 12.

12. There are many such passages dispersed through the Zohar and the *Zohar Hadash*, all of which cannot be mentioned here. One was already recognized by the printers—Zohar, I, 211b–216a. Some of these passages were identified as part of *Tikkunei Zohar*, and others are still to be identified: see for instance below, n. 88, or the radical passage incorporated in *Sifra di-Tsni'uta*—Zohar, II, 177b–178b; or the passage dealing with the problem of choice and knowledge printed at the end of *Zohar Hadash* and at the end of R. Shem Tov b. Shem Tov's *Sefer ha-Emunot*; or the passage printed in the Zohar, II, 38a–39b. Other passages belong to R. Joseph Angelet (cf. below n. 298), and others bear the imprint of the school of R. Joseph of Hamadan or R. David b. Judah he-Hasid (see below nn. 140, 203). In this respect, I would call the reader's attention also to the passages on the *Pikkudin* (see Efraim Gottlieb, *Mehkarim be-Sifrut ha-Kabala*, Tel Aviv 1976, pp. 215–30), which in contrast to the *Pikkudin* in the preface to the Zohar, parallel in order and style to those in Moses de Leon's *Sefer ha-Rimmon*, are in the same order as those of Maimonides and those in R. Joseph of Hamadan's *Ta'amei ha-Mitzvot*, for instance; even their style at times seems different from that of most of the Zohar—this is particularly prominent in the mitsvot discussed also in the preface to the Zohar.

13. See: Gershom Scholem, *Kabbalat R. Yitzhak ben Shlomo ben Avi Sahula ve-Sefer Ha-Zohar*, KS 6 (1927–1930), pp. 109–18; Gershom Scholem, *ha-Tsitat ha-Rishon min ha-Midrash ha-Ne'elam*, Tarbiz 3, 1932, pp. 181–83; Avraham Yitzhak Green, *Perush Shir ha-Shirim le-R. Yitzhak Ibn Sahula*, from *The Beginning of Jewish Mysticism in Medieval Europe—Proceedings of the Second International Conference on the History of Jewish Mysticism*, Jerusalem 1987 (*Jerusalem Studies in Jewish Thought*, 5, 3–4), pp. 400–401.

14. Such as "tashlum" in the sense of "shlemut" (wholeness)—Part 1, 126a (*Midrash ha-Ne'elam*).

15. See, for instance, how the *Midrash ha-Ne'elam* (I, 98a–99a) adapts the talmudic story (Sanhedrin, 68a, and parallels) of the death of R. Eliezer the Great (and for instance: *min'al she'al ha-imum*—"the shoe on the shoe tree" which seemingly he did not find sufficiently spiritual, he changed, without explanation, to *sandal shel yibum*—"the sandal of the levirate marriage"; R. Akiva's request to study a chapter on *netiat kishuim*—"the planting of cucumbers" becomes in the *Midrash ha-Ne'elam* a lesson on *Ma'aseh ha-Merkava*—Ezekiel's vision). Compare as against this the delicate, splendid use that the author of *Idra Zuta* makes of the same story. On ideological contradiction between the *Midrash ha-Ne'elam* and the main body of the Zohar, cf. n. 222 below.

16. Zohar, I, 181b–182a. This is a symbolical midrash on Zohar, I, 126a–129a, *Midrash ha-Ne'elam*. In the main body of the Zohar, too, Abraham's servant is the angel Metatron sent in order to return the souls for the resurrection of the dead. However, as is not the case in *Midrash ha-Ne'elam*, he is identified here with the *Shekhina*, and the whole interpretation of the episode changes in the spirit of the Kabbalistic symbolism.

17. Cf. Gershom Scholem, *Kabbalot R. Ya'akov ve-R. Yitzhak benei R. Yaakov Ha-Kohen, Madda'ei ha-Yahadut* 1 (1927), pp. 33–34.

18. Cf. below, nn. 39, 125, and appendix. This circle was also responsible it would seem for the writings of the *"Sefer ha-'Iyyun* circle," cf. M. W. Verman, "Sifrei ha-Iyyun" (thesis presented to Harvard University, 1984), pp. 173–78. The Zohar contains many passages that are parallel in style and contents to the writings of the *ha-'Iyyun* circle, and which are based on the same sources; cf. Gershom Scholem, *Ikvotav shel Gabirol ba-Kabbalah* in: A. A. Kabak and A. Steinman (eds.), *Ma-asaf Sofrei Eretz Israel le-Sifrut ule-Divrei Mahshava*, Tel Aviv 1940, pp. 167–70. See also my article: "Sefer Yetzira Etzel R. Shlomo Ibn Gabirol ve-Perush ha-Shir Ahavtikha" in *The Beginning of Jewish Mysticism. . .*, above n. 13, pp. 73–98.

19. I am referring to *Tikkun Leil Shavuot*. Cf. above, pp. 56. *Tikkun Hatsot* in the Kabbalistic group is also spoken of in the section attributed to the rabbis in R. Isaac Ibn Sahula's exegesis of the Song of Songs, Green ed. (above n. 13), p. 433: "and our rabbis interpreted this allegorically: 'the flowers appear on the earth' [Song of Songs, ii, 12]—those engaged in the study of the Torah for its own sake; 'the time of the singing of the birds is arrived' (ibid.)—to sing to their Creator together. 'And the voice of the turtle is heard in our land' (ibid.)—this is the Angel of Countenance come to gather the souls of the righteous to sing to their Creator in the night." The source of these words of "the rabbis" has not been preserved, but they would seem to me to belong to the *Midrash ha-Ne'elam*.

20. Ibid., pp. 123–28.

21. Cf. ibid., pp. 182–84.

22. Recently, Moshe Idel also raised the possibility of the Zohar having been composed by a group, referring to the freedom of exegesis common to this circle. See: M. Idel, *Kabbalah—New Perspectives*, New-Haven and London 1988, p. 380, no. 66.

23. Different sections are to be distinguished likewise within the *Midrash ha-Ne'elam*. The *Midrash ha-Ne'elam* already employs the words of the Zoharic *Matnitin* and *Tosefta*, and from various points of view is close to *"Sitrei Torah"* (see Gottlieb, above n. 12, pp. 203–4). Further, there are motifs common to the *Midrash ha-Ne'elam* and to the *Idra*, that do not appear in the rest of the Zohar: for instance—the 400 worlds anticipated for every righteous man (*Midrash ha-Ne'elam*—Zohar, I, 124b; *Idra Rabba*—Zohar, III,

128b; *Idra Zuta*—Zohar, I, 288a), or the account of R. Simeon b. Yohai's death (*Midrash ha-Ne'elam—Zohar Hadash, Bereshit*, ed. Mosad ha-Rav Kook, 18d–19a; and in contrast *Idra Zuta*. At the beginning of *Idra Zuta* R. Simeon b. Yohai alludes to the account of his death in the *Midrash ha-Ne'elam* and reconciles the contradiction in this since several more years were then added to his life). Perhaps the author of the *Midrash ha-Ne'elam* (Zohar, I, 121b) had a version of his own on the myth of the death of the Kings of Edom (see appendix, below), and according to it God created six men, each of whom inherited from Adam a certain trait, and all impaired the divine trait (according to *Pirkei de-R. Eliezer*, chap. 53, and to Sota, 10a—the Talmud indeed speaks of five, and not six as in the *Pirkei de-R. Eliezer*, but in the Talmud they are a "kind of heavenly prototype" and not only "resembled Adam"; the Zohar was apparently influenced by both versions). These six together are "Seth," the son of Adam, according to the meaning of his name in Aramaic. Cf. below n. 239.

24. Gershom Scholem, *Ha-Im Hiber R. Moshe de Leon et Sefer-ha-Zohar* in: *Madda'ei ha-Yahadut* 1 (1926), p. 12.

25. *Sefer ha-Rimmon*, ed. Elliot Wolfson, Atlanta 1988, p. 392. Cited also by Scholem (above n. 2), p. 398.

26. See above, p. 56.

27. See: A. Jellinek, *Moses Ben Schem-Tov de Leon und sein Verhaeltniss zum Sohar*, Leipzig 1951. Jellinek did not talk about a group explicitly and its existence is implied only in his assertion that Moses de Leon is the principal author (*Haupturheber*) of the Zohar (p. 23). Cf. also chapter 1, pp. 4–6.

28. Ashkenazi traditions were at the foundation of the Sephardi Kabbala even before the Zohar. There are many examples of this in scholarly studies, including Prof. Moshe Idel's as yet unpublished, special comprehensive work on this subject. Concerning the Ashkenazi customs in the Zohar, cf. Yaakov Katz, *Hakhra'ot ha-Zohar bi-Dvar Halakha* in his book, *Halakha ve-Kabbala*, Jerusalem 1984, pp. 34–51. Also Israel Ta-Shma, *Be'era shel Miriam* in *Jerusalem Studies in Jewish Thought*, 4 (1985), pp. 269–70.

29. Cf. Gershom Scholem, *R. David b. Judah he-Hasid Nekhed ha-Ramban*, KS 4 (1927–1928), pp. 303–6; and in the preface of D. C. Matt (ed.), *The Book of Mirrors: Sefer Mar'ot ha-Tzove'ot by R. David ben Yehudah he-Hasid*, Brown University 1982, p. 1. In this respect, the testimony of R. Joseph Angelet, one of the leaders of the Zoharic circle in Saragossa, is interesting (cf. below n. 298). At the end of his book, *Kuppat ha-Rokhelin*, which bears throughout the stamp of the Zohar, he writes: "and we will conclude the year 5071 (= 1311 C.E.). . .and the sixth year to the exile of our brothers in France and the second year to the exile of Avignon. And I wrote this composition from the stones of the sanctuary at the top of every street (according to

Lamentations iv, 1), that is from the sages of France, and from what I received from the other sages and from what the gracious Giver of knowledge gave me...."

30. For an example of this method, see Israel Ta-Shma's article: *Ha-Pores Sukat Shalom—Berakha ve-Gilguleha* in *Asufot* 2, 1988, pp. 177–89. According to this article, Moses de Leon attributed a certain passage to *Yerushalmi* and used it with this label in many places, both in his own books and in addenda that he added secretly to other books. However, as Ta-Shma also attests, a passage of this kind is quoted as words of the *Yerushalmi* by other authors too and without connection with the activities of Moses de Leon. Why then should we not suppose that just as they were familiar with it he was also familiar with it? Incidentally, an important source should be added to the subject discussed there: R. Joseph Angelet's *Sefer Kuppat ha-Rokhelin*, Ms. Bodeley, OPP. 228, p. 29.

31. Jerusalem 1970, pp. 167–93.

32. Cf. below, concerning n. 239.

33. Zohar, II, 114a; *Zohar Hadash, Ki Tavo*, ed. Mosad ha-Rav Kook, 60a. Gottlieb, ibid., p. 172.

34. In addition to the parallel below, there is another parallel in Zohar, III, 26b; but, as Gottlieb noted there, this is certainly not R. Bahya's source, for it contains only part of what he quoted as *Midrash de-R. Simeon b. Yohai.*

35. Scholem, *Ha-Tsitat* (above n. 13), p. 183: "From here it is proved that the author of the *Midrash Ha-Ne'elam* originally intended to be more precise in alluding to his sources."

36. In his Torah exegesis, Genesis i, 20, and quoted by Gottlieb (above n. 31), p. 171. Recently I found that this sentence is quoted here under the same title (*be-Midrasho shel Rabbi Shim'on bar Yohai*), but there another sentence is added to the citation, which proves that it is not taken from Bahya. This is a conclusive proof to my point, that this is a different *midrash* and is not taken from the Zohar. See: Yosef Alashqar, *Sefer Tsafenat Pa'aneah*, Jerusalem 1991, p. 122a.

37. See Gershom Scholem (ed.), *Sod Ilan ha-Atzilut le-R. Yizhak; Kuntras mi-Masoret ha-Kabbalah shel Sefer ha-Temunah* in *Kovetz Al-Yad*, new series E (1951), p. 91 and n. 103. The relationship of the *Sefer ha-Temunah* circle to the Zohar is complicated and cannot be dealt with here.

38. The manuscript of the tract (in the previous note) ends with the following words: "This is a lofty and awesome book, in the wisdom of the Kabbala, of R. Akiva and his pupil R. Simeon b. Yohai of blessed memory." See Scholem, ibid., p. 67. The mention of R. Akiva together with R. Simeon b. Yohai shows that the attribution is not influenced by the Zohar.

39. See Scholem (above n. 24), p. 12. Scholem's assertions are still true, even if he himself retracted them (in his later writings, Scholem does not deal with his earlier question, how the elderly and honorable R. Todros would relate to the doctrine of the young, lowly R. Moses de Leon as if they were hidden secrets that he heard from his rabbis). I have already proved, moreover, that the Zohar is not the source of the midrash cited by R. Todros, but that it was known by the author of *Sefer ha-Emunot* in a more complete version containing details not present in the Zohar. See chapter I (above n. 19), pp. 219–21. See also: Asi Farber Ginat, "Tefisat Ha-Mercava be-Torat ha-Sod be Me'ah ha-Shalosh Esreh—Sod ha-Egoz ve-Toldotav" (doctoral thesis submitted to the Hebrew University Senate, Jerusalem 1987), pp. 145–59. In the context of such midrashim, the problem of *Midrash Yehi Or* should again be alluded to; this is a kind of Zohar in Hebrew that is frequently cited in R. Israel al-Nakawa's *Menorat ha-Ma'or.* I rather think that much remains to be learned on the subject of this work.

40. In several versions of the Zohar the copyist changed R. Yohanan's name to R. Simeon b. Yohai in order to adapt it to the general usage in the Zohar; see my article, ibid. The determining of R. Simeon b. Yohai as the protagonist of the Zohar is inherent of course to the content of the Zohar, as shown in chapter I, pp. 00.

41. See below n. 88. The midrash quoted there was transposed to the main body of the Zohar too. See also below n. 239.

42. Moshe Halamish (ed.), *Perush Kabbali le-Bereshit Rabba le-R. Josef b. Shalom (He-Arokh) Ashkenazi*, Jerusalem 1985, p. 259. See also the editor's preface, p. 13. The editor conjectured that the quotation from R. Simeon b. Yohai was an interpolation of one of the copyists, but offered no basis for his hypothesis.

43. Zohar, III, 70a. See also Zohar, III, 25a, where the wording is even further removed, as noted by Halamish (see previous note).

44. *Zohar Hadash, Bereshit Midrash ha-Ne'elam* (Mosad ha-Rav Kook edition), 11a. The wording is amended here: "and R. Aha said: they did not teach thus, but the souls of the wicked that come out of the body are the demons in the world."

45. Such as several lines before: "we learn: he who comes to be purified is aided." The source is BT, Shabbat, 104a.

46. Zohar, II, 118a, *Ra'aya Meheimana*, and so forth. Likewise (in a mixture of Hebrew and Aramaic) in part of the *Tikkunim* in *Zohar Hadash*, Mosad ha-Rav Kook edition, 118c: "as was said by the sages of Matnitin: the souls of the wicked are the demons in the world." Also Zohar, III, 16b, *Ra'aya Meheimana*: "and it was said: the souls of the wicked are the demons in the world." Compare too Zohar, I, 28a—29b, which belongs to *Tikkunei Zohar*: "the souls of the wicked are really the demons of the world."

47. See my article, *Ketavim Hadashim be-Kabbala Shabta'it mi-Hugo shel R. Jonathan Eybeschuetz*, Jerusalem Studies in Jewish Thought, 5 (1986, printed in 1988), pp. 240–41.

48. *Perush Bereshit Rabba* (above n. 42), p. 79. See also p. 243.

49. Cf. Tishby, The Wisdom of the Zohar, III, Jerusalem 1989, p. 1453, n. 94.

50. See: Levi Ginsberg, *Agadot ha-Yehudim*, I, Ramat Gan 1966, p. 194, n. 98.

51. Para. 1170 (Jerusalem 1973, p. 578): "the souls of the wicked on their death are demons." See R. Margaliouth's note in *Nitsotsei Zohar*, Zohar, III, 70a, para. 5.

52. See above n. 23.

53. See Commentary on *Sefer Yetsira*, Jerusalem 1965, 13a (commentary of R. Joseph attributed to R. Abraham b. David).

54. See below n. 123.

55. It should be noted that in order to explain the component "genos" in "androgenos" in the midrash, R. Joseph uses the modern Greek form "yenika" (woman), *Perush Bereshit Rabba* (above n. 42), p. 133, proving that both he and those who heard him were conversant with this language. His Ashekenazi origin and his German traditions have already been discussed by other scholars.

56. On ancient mythical sources see my article *The Kabbalist Myth of Orpheus* (Hebrew), in Moshe Idel and Warren Zev Harvey (eds.), *Shlomo Pines Jubilee Volume on the Occasion of his Eightieth Birthday*, Part I (Jerusalem Studies in Jewish Thought, vol. VII), Jerusalem 1989, pp. 425–59; see also below in the Appendix.

57. This is stated in the introduction to *Idra Rabba*. See chapter 1 (above n. 19), pp. 00.

58. The name of the composition is generally translated as "The Book of Concealment" (Gershom Scholem), or "The Book of Concealed Mystery." According to Zohar, III, 146b (the passage is in the portion of *Nasso* after *Idra Rabba* [on this section, see n. 88 below], but it is included in the translation of the *Idra* at the end of *Sefer ha-Gevul* which will be dealt with below, Ms. Jerusalem, 80 3921, 59a), its name comes from the word "tsni'ut" (modesty), as in *Kiddushin* 71a: "When the lawless became rife, the name of the Holy One was transmitted to the modest in the priesthood" (on the relationship between mysticism and modesty, see below n. 116). The composition is also perhaps called: "The Great Secrets"—see below n. 214. Another possibility is raised by Zohar, I, 217a, which recounts that after the death of

R. Simeon b. Yohai the words of the Kabbala, which had been abundant during his lifetime, decreased, and only what had been lain by to be kept remained of them, like the manna in the desert, which was placed in a pot. The expression "to be kept" (*mishmeret*), is translated here by *leatsna'uta* (see Targum Jonathan for Exodus, xvi, 23, and Targum Onkelos for Exodus, xvi, 24). Perhaps the Zohar refers to the few and secret matters contained in *Sifra di-Tsni'uta* in this way (compare the preface of *Sifra di-Tsni'uta*, which will be cited and elucidated below). If this is the case, the writings of *Sifra di-Tsni'uta* are the remains of the writings of R. Simeon b. Yohai, and not their source, even though this thesis contradicts R. Simeon b. Yohai's many quotations from *Sifra di-Tsni'uta* in the *Idra*; possibly in one edition *Sifra di-Tsni'uta* was considered the source, and in another the summary. The name *Sifra di-Tsni'uta* might also be the translation of *Sefer Yetsira*, from the Arab word, *Zana'a*, which means *yatsar* (created). Certainly, *Sifra di-Tsni'uta* also deals with the mysteries of the Creation (in the Cremona edition *Sifra di-Tsni'uta* was included in the portion *Bereshit*) and according to the secrets of the Hebrew characters, as in *Sefer Yetsira*. Cf. also the last sentence of the book (Zohar, II, 179a): "And the Tseniuta of the King was crowned"; this mystery is perhaps the Creation. On the Sabbatean interpretation of the book, see my article (above n. 47), pp. 264–76.

59. On the meaning of the name, and the number, scope and contents of the Assemblies, see my doctoral thesis, *Perakim be-Milon Sefer ha-Zohar*, Jerusalem 1977 (new edition, 1983), pp. 93–107, and chapter 1 (above n. 19).

60. One example out of many—the serpent with its tail in its mouth (Zohar, II, 176b). On this subject and its interpretation by the Sabbateians, see my article (above n. 47), pp. 304–20. Cf. also, for instance: "*Bereshit* is the speech, but *bera* is the speech halved" (Zohar, II, 178b), which is explained at length in the chapter, "Christian Influences on the Zohar," pp. 146–152. I have found a parallel in the Zohar, I, 3b, for one element in this chapter (but not in the *Idrot*); most of the chapter, however, is interpreted only in accordance with external parallels.

61. See below, on the subject of the "Small Countenance," nn. 132, 137.

62. See below n. 67, and above n. 81 (but see n. 83), and n. 198. (On the other hand what I wrote in my article (above n. 47), p. 287, n. 74, should be amended, because the quotation referred to there exists in a different form at the beginning of *Sifra di-Tsni'uta*.

63. For instance, we find in *Sifra di-Tsni'uta*, II, 176a: "And the kings of ancient times died. . . . Until that head of all desires prepared and inherited vestments of honor." Whereas the *Idra Rabba*, III, 135a, develops the theme: "This is the tradition described in the *Tseni'uta di-Sifra*: Before the Ancient of the Ancient Ones prepared His conformations, He formed certain kings, collected certain kings, engraved certain kings, and gave due proportion to certain kings; but they did not subsist until He expelled them, and concealed

them for the time being. . . . But all these did not subsist until the White Head of the Ancient of the Ancient Ones was disposed. . ." Cf. also below n. 94.

64. III, 133a (*Idra Rabba*): "We have learned in *the Sifra di-Tsni'uta*: What is this which is written *pesha'* (transgression)? If they win, it passes over; it they do not win, the word 'transgression' stands." II, 141a (*Idra Zuta*): "And in the *Sifra di-Tsni'uta* is the same called Glory (*Hod*), and Honor (*Hadar*), and Beauty (*Tif'eret*). And it is beauty that Passes over Transgression, as it is written (Prov. xix, 11): 'and His Beauty passes over transgression.' " *Sifra di-Tseniu'ta*, II, 177a, however, merely states: "There exists a path to forgive [literally to pass over transgression], as it is written, Prov. xix, 11: "And it is His Beauty to pass over a transgression.' "

65. In *Sifra di-Tsni'uta*, II, 178a: "He made it in man, in two: in the general and the particular. Then were contained in the particular and the general, legs and arms right and left." In *Idra Rabba*, III, 143a: "We have learned in the *Sifra di-Tsni'uta*: that in man are comprehended the Supernal Crowns in particular and in general." We will see that the correct version is in *Sifra di-Tsni'uta*, *bi-tren* (= in two) and not *kitrin* (crowns).

66. *Sifra di-Tsni'uta*, 178a: "The Ancient One requested it and the serpent came upon the female"; *Idra Rabba*, II, 143a: "And we have learned in the *Sifra di-Tsni'uta* that when the Most Holy Ancient One desired to see whether the judgments could be mitigated, and whether these two could adhere together (the supernal Adam and Eve). . .which the world could not bear because she had not been mitigated and because the strong serpent polluted her."

67. II, 291a (*Idra Zuta*): "In the 'Book of the Aggada' it is said: Since *El De'ot* is the Tetragrammaton (Samuel I, ii, 3) do not read *De'ot* (of knowledges), but *Edut* (of testimony). Moreover, also, although we have placed that matter in the *Sifra di-Tsni'uta*, in another form, all that is mentioned of it is correct." This matter is not mentioned at all in the *Sifra di-Tsni'uta* in our possession.

68. Sweet cakes. Perhaps, changing the meaning, from "*tiriaka*," which is also written "*triaka*" (see Rashi and Nachmanides on Exodus, 34), a Greek word which means a drug against snake venom, which is also depicted at times as mixed with honey (inter alia its ingredients were also snake flesh, see Maimonides, ibid.).

69. See quotation in n. 183, and the background in the articles mentioned; see also nn. 264–69. The *Sifra di-Tsni'uta* concludes with the words (II, 179a): "Blessed is he who enters into and comes out from it, and knows its paths and ways."

70. See below n. 165.

71. See Scholem (above n. 24), and see in my book (above n. 59), p. 3.

72. It is attributed in several manuscripts to R. Shem Tov of Faro. Cf. Moshe Idel, *Perush Esser Sefirot u-Sridim mi-Ketavim shel R. Yosef ha-Ba mi-Shushan ha-Bira*, in *Alei-Sefer*, 6–7, 1979, pp. 82–84. My thanks go to my friend Prof. Moshe Idel for the typed critical edition that he prepared and placed at my disposal.

73. Ms. Munich, 305, 59b–62b. See: G. Scholem, "Colours and their Symbolism in Jewish Tradition and Mysticism" in *Diogenes* 109, 1980, p. 71 and no. 93. I do not agree with Scholem's assumption there, that the author of the text is R. Joseph Gikatilla. The vehement anthropomorphic description contradicts the nature of Gikatilla's Kabbala, as does the definition of evil as absence and annihilation and a return to the *Ein Sof.* Such characteristics are far closer to the Kabbala of *Sefer ha-Yihud*, and the Kabbala of R. Joseph of Hamadan, in whose writings there is a parallel composition on the secret of colors, included in his book *Toledot Adam* (in *Sefer ha-Malkhut*, Dar el Beida, Casablanca 1930, 102a–103a. On the identification of the composition see Gottlieb (above n. 12), pp. 251–55). However, the author of *Sod ha-Gevanim le-Mineihem* is not to be identified with Joseph of Hamadan, the author of the most independent homilies, but is yet another author belonging to the same circle. The stylistic influence of Gikatilla is habitual in the writings of this circle.

74. I devoted my lengthy article to an elucidation of these (above n. 19).

75. See below nn. 245–49.

76. On different editions of the *Idra* (and on authors whose relation to the *Idrot* had not been known previously) see chapter 1 (above n. 19), pp. 00. We shall see below that R. David ben Judah he-Hasid was familiar with a version of *Idra Rabba* previous to the printed one. See also above n. 23.

77. In his book in English (above n. 2), pp. 194–96.

78. See Altmann (above n. 4), pp. 235–40; Asi Farber, *Keta Hadash mi-Hakdamat R. Yosef Gikatilla le-Sefer Ginnat Egoz*, Jerusalem Studies in Jewish Thought, I, 1981, pp. 158–76. These studies show that R. Moses de Leon used intensively, and even copied textually, long passages from R. Joseph Gikatilla's *Ginnat Egoz*, which he incorporated in his book, *Or Zaru'a*.

79. Asi Farber, *Ikvotav shel Sefer ha-Zohar be-Kitvei R. Yosef Gikatilla* in *Alei Sefer* 9, 1981, pp. 70–83. I do not agree with this author's view that R. Joseph translated these passages from the Zohar since they are not written in his usual style (p. 72). Farber also makes the further claim that the Zohar is not accustomed to translate an entire passage textually. In reply, I would say: firstly, this also applies to Gikatilla, who is likewise an independent and individual Kabbalist; secondly, Farber, in making this claim, is quoting from Ephraim Gottlieb, who was referring to the relationship between the Zohar and R. Bahya ben Asher. However, the frequent use of such an argument can lead one to think that in fact the reverse might be true. Thus, Farber's

assertion is based on a false foundation, as we already saw when we dealt with R. Bahya and the Zohar. Indeed Peretz in his study (above n. 6) demonstrates precisely that it is the Zohar which uses Gikatilla's writings. On Gikatilla and the Zohar, cf. also, Gottlieb (above n. 12), pp. 97–98.

80. In the books *Sha'arei Ora* and *Sha'arei Tsedek* this influence is evident above all in the last chapter, which deals with the *sefira* of *Keter* (Crown). Most of the last chapter of *Sha'arei Tsedek* is not included in the printed book, Krakow 1881 (photocopy Jerusalem 1967), and was published by Gottlieb (above n. 12), pp. 132–62.

81. Joseph Gikatilla, *Sha'arei Ora*, Warsaw 1883 (photocopy Jerusalem 1960), Chap. 3–4, 37a, Chap. 6, 74a; Joseph Gikatilla, *Sha'arei Tsedek* (ibid.), 17a. Noted already by Scholem (above n. 24).

82. The Aramaic translation of Ecclesiastes, ix, 2: "all things depend on fortune."

83. Zohar, II, 177a: "all things in this Fortune exist and are concealed." More precisely in *Idra Zuta*, Zohar, III, 289b: "all things depend on fortune".

84. As I heard from my teacher, the late Prof. Ephraim Gottlieb.

85. In *Sefer ha-Rimmon* (above n. 25), pp. 193–94: "And truly all things depend on fortune. . .and truly this matter is also the great fortune upon which the Book of the Law depends."

86. *Sha'arei Ora* (above n. 81), Chap. 1, 12a: "And this is the fortune that even the Book of the Law in the Temple depends on." (In the previous sentence it is called "the fortune of all fortunes" and there are other superlatives there in this syntactical structure which is customary in the Zohar). The same sentence exactly is also to be found in *The Secret of the Thirteen Attributes emanating from the Supreme Crown and are called the Springs of Salvation* (Hebrew) in Gershom Scholem, Catalogus Codicum Hebraicorum, National Library, Jerusalem (Hebrew), Jerusalem 1930, p. 223. Scholem asserted that the composition belonged to Gikatilla after the book was printed.

87. See Wolfson's comments in his preface to the edition of *Sefer ha-Rimmon* (above n. 25), pp. 51–53. On pp. 53–55, Wolfson indicates another case (the symbolism of the Sabbath meals) where Gikatilla is closer to the path of the Zohar than R. Moses de Leon.

88. *Sha'arei Ora* (above n. 81), Chap. I, 13a: "And this is the saying of the sages of blessed memory, do not read (Deut. xxv, 3) *macca rabba* (a mighty blow), but *mikoh rabba*" (from the greed "thus" [= *koh*]). Also in Zohar, II, 145b: "And as R. Eleazar said: what is *macca rabba*, namely a blow (*macca*) from thus (*koh*)." Indeed the entire passage differs from the usual style of the Zohar as formulated by R. Moses de Leon. (Two passages of this "Zohar section," immediately after the *Idra Rabba* and part of which deals with the

same subject, are cited in the book named in the research literature, *Ta'amei ha-Mitsvot*, Second Version, which in other places does not use the Zohar—see: Gottlieb [above n. 31], p. 195. Both these passages are in Hebrew, and differ greatly from the usual style of the Zohar. The first passage is attributed in *Ta'amei ha-Mitsvot* to "our rabbis," and in the Zohar it is introduced by the word, *Tana*, used to introduce a talmudic source in the Talmud: "*Tana*, whoever emerges from the stage of fear and robes himself in humility attains thereby a higher degree" [Zohar III, 145a]. The second passage is quoted in *Ta'amei ha-Mitsvot* in the name of a "sage," with whom the author of *Ta'amei ha-Mitsvot* disagrees.) On another passage from this section of the Zohar (Zohar, III, 146b) see above concerning n. 58. See also below n. 198.

89. Cited in Scholem's article (above n. 24), p. 12, n. 40. In his later book (above n. 2), p. 195, Scholem offers the explanation that R. Moses de Leon quoted from the Zohar and referred to it as *Sha'arei Ora* (Gates of Light) alongside quotations from Gikatilla's book, *Sha'arei Ora*. If this thesis is correct, Rabbi Moses de Leon himself finds a special relationship between the Zohar and Gikatilla.

90. Such a possibility was also raised by Joseph b. Shlomo, in his edition of *Sha'arei Ora*, Jerusalem 1971, vol. 1, p. 162.

91. Above n. 86.

92. Scholem (above n. 86), p. 19. Compare also his assertions above, relative to n. 25.

93. Ibid. (above n. 86), p. 224, and n. 8: "Hence it is proved that the author drew from more complete sources than our version of the Zohar." Compare also his other assertion, relative to n. 92.

94. It should be noted that in the enumeration of the *tikkunim* it also does not correspond to the *Sifra di-Tsni'uta* we have before us. In the *Sifra di-Tsni'uta* (Zohar, II, 147a) this *tikkun* ("those hairs that hang down, neither is one preeminent above another"), is in fact the ninth *tikkun*.

95. In Micah vii, 18–20, according to the Kabbala of the *Idrot*, thirteen attributes of compassion of the "Large Countenance" are mentioned, or of the "Crown" in Gikatilla's terminology. The thirteen attributes enumerated by Moses (Exod. xxxiv, 6–7), which are contained in nine (Numbers xiv, 18), are the attributes of the "Small Countenance."

96. In another version, noted by Scholem, 425. The number 325 also reoccurs in a parallel that we will cite from the Zohar (in R. Joseph of Hamadan's parallel, however, the number is 250). We will again find this in another place, below n. 195.

97. Compare *Sha'arei Ora* (above n. 81), 101a.

98. Micah, vii, 18. See above n. 95. "Pardons iniquity" is indeed mentioned in Moses's thirteen attributes, but not as the second attribute.

99. In Scholem's edition, according to the manuscripts he had before him, "and the secret: the skin of my face shone" is also added, and I omitted it in accordance with Ms. Parma 966 (in the Institute for Manuscript Photocopies in Jerusalem: S 13053).

100. "Secret of the Thirteen Attributes" (above n. 86), p. 222.

101. Compare *Sifra di-Tsni'uta*, Zohar, II, 177a.

102. See explanation in chapter 1 p. 20.

103. Compare R. Simeon b. Yohai's words at the beginning of *Idra Zuta*, Zohar, III, 288a; and Zohar, I, 88b. The homily before us, however, means the opposite.

104. In visionary style of Daniel, chap. vii.

105. Equals "iniquity."

106. See chapter 1 p. 23.

107. This parallel from Gikatilla's writings should be added to the proofs of the messianic nature of the *Idra* which I presented in chapter 1 (above n. 19).

108. Cf. also, above nn. 10, 11, 73.

109. Most scholars attached little importance to his name which infers a Persian origin, since we have no knowledge of the existence of Kabbala in Persia in this period, and they considered him an exclusively Spanish Kabbalist. An exception is Shelomo Pines, who in a conference compared R. Joseph's Kabbalistic doctrines to a Persian doctrine; and certainly these Kabbalot contain elements that differ radically from all that is known. In refutation of the Persian origin, I shall refer to a homily of R. Joseph that gives a Kabbalistic meaning to the fact that "we pray towards the east." It is difficult to imagine that anyone familiar with the communities to the east of Eretz Israel, such as in Persia, which pray to the west, should write thus. See J. Zwelling, *Joseph of Hamadan's Sefer Tashak . . .*, A Dissertation Presented to. . . Brandeis University, 1975 (Xerox University Microfilms, Ann Arbor), p. 117.

110. G. Scholem (above n. 86), p. 81; G. Scholem, *Einige kabbalistische Handschriften im britischen Museum*, Jerusalem 1932, pp. 11–33.

111. Above nn. 10, 11.

112. In his book (above n. 12), pp. 251–55.

113. Above, n. 72; Moshe Idel, *Seridim Nosafim mi-kitvei R. Joseph ha-Ba mi-Shushan ha-Bira, Da'at* 21, 1988, pp. 47–55; etc.

114. *Sefer Tashak* (above n. 109); M. Meir, "A Critical Edition of the 'Sefer Ta'amei ha-Mitsvot' attributed to Isaac Ibn Farhi," presented to Brandeis

University, 1974) (University Microfilms, Ann Arbor); Midrash on Genesis xxiv (above n. 10). My friend Prof. Moshe Idel placed at my disposal other editions that he prepared and photocopies of manuscripts of R. Joseph.

115. This was proved by Altmann who showed that R. Menahem Recanati used many of R. Joseph's writings in the early fourteenth century; cf. Altmann (above n. 11).

116. *Sefer Tashak* (above n. 109), p. 2. This aid he attributes subsequently precisely to his baseness and smallness ("Since I am not worthy to say even something as small as an ant's egg, since my knowledge is as of the most insignificant of the Jews, I am completely and utterly worthless") which aroused divine compassion. Likewise, p. 103. The relationship between the attribute of humility and revelation is customary in Jewish mysticism, and this was the basis for my book, *The Sin of Elisha, the Four who Entered Paradise and the Nature of Talmudic Mysticism* (Hebrew), Jerusalem 1986. For an interesting parallel, cf. my article: "Mysticism and Reality: Towards a Portrait of the Martyr and Kabbalist R. Samson Ostropoler" in I. Twersky (ed.), *Jewish Thought in the Seventeenth Century*, Harvard University Press 1987, p. 240.

117. *Sha'arei Ora* (above n. 81), 62b.

118. The attributes of compassion are called by him as in the Zohar, *mekhilan de-rahamei* (I have found no such reference in early Aramaic), and are described sometimes as parts of God's garments (in accordance with the meaning of the word *middotav* [= garments, but also attributes] in Ps. cxxxiii, 2). Cf. for instance in *Sefer Tashak* (above n. 109), pp. 129–30.

119. *Sefer Tashak* (ibid.), pp. 109–12, etc.

120. *Toledot Adam* (above n. 73), 56b–58b.

121. The addition of "Blessed be He" to an abstract description is habitual in R. Joseph's writings. Cf. for instance *Sefer Tashak* (above n. 109), p. 129: "One thing (*pitgam had*) Blessed be He."

122. *Toledot Adam* (above n. 73), 58b.

123. R. Joseph Ashkenazi's adaptation was printed in the preface to his commentary on *Sefer Yetsira* (above n. 53), 10a–11a. R. Joseph of Hamadan's adaptation is to be found in his *Toledot Adam* (above n. 73), pp. 54–55.

124. Cf. above n. 18.

125. Published by Gershom Scholem, *Tarbiz* 5 (1934), pp. 305–16.

126. *Livnat ha-Sappir*, Jerusalem 1913 (Photocopy print: Jerusalem 1971), 66c. The printing house attributed the book to R. David b. Judah he-Hasid, but the true author is R. Joseph Angelet; cf. G. Margoliouth, *Hebrew*

and Samaritan Manuscripts in the British Museum, part 3, London 1915, p. 72. On *middotav*, garments or attributes, cf. above n. 118.

127. Whatever is said in the Zohar vis-à-vis the "Large Countenance" is expounded vis-à-vis the *Keter* in the writings of Gikatilla and of R. Joseph of Hamadan. Even in the Zohar itself the parallels are not unequivocal. In one place in *Idra Zuta* (Zohar, III, 288a–b) this face is made up of three "heads," which are *Ein Sof, Keter* (these names are not explicit here), and the supernal aspect of *Hokhma*.

128. *Sefer Tashak* (above n. 109), p. 104. The *Keter* is sometimes called *Or makkif* (*Or* with the letter "Ayin" = "encircling skin") and in several parallels in R. Joseph's writings it becomes *Or makkif* (*Or* with "Aleph" = "encircling light"); this would seem to be the origin of this conception in R. Isaac Luria's Kabbala, as pointed out to me by my friend Moshe Idel. For other sources of R. Isaac Luria's Kabbala, see below concerning n. 235, and in n. 293.

129. This dualism can also be of a strong nature. In one place I have found that R. Joseph calls the "Small Countenance," who is the *Shekhina*, "another God." Cf. *Toledot Adam* (above n. 73), 109a.

130. *Sefer Tashak* (above n. 109), p. 112.

131. In his article in German (above n. 110), p. 20.

132. Zohar, III, 59b. In chapter 1 (above p. 19), pp. 00, n. 00. I discussed this section and its traits, and compared it with the beginning of *Sifra di-Tsni'uta*. I was already of this opinion, even without the proof from R. Joseph.

133. *Yoma* 54a. See also *Baba Batra* 99a.

134. *Sukkah* 5b. To be precise, it does not use this term for the two cherubs in the Temple, but for the "face of the cherub" and the "face of the man" in the Chariot (Ezekiel x, 14).

135. This was the supposition of Moshe Idel, cf. below n. 177. There another source for this name will be mentioned.

136. Cf. below n. 167.

137. The two versions existing in print give this formula.

138. The continuation, "the supernal is 'abounding in mercy,' but the inferior is just 'mercy'" seems to me to be an addition that was introduced here from *Idra Rabba*, Zohar, III, 140b, since it does not fit the context. The nine *tikkunim* are not related in any other place in *Sifra di-Tsni'uta* to the attributes of compassion; their meaning is power and strength.

139. See below n. 143.

140. Cf. below concerning n. 288. The term *Ze'ira* (small) for the *Shekhina* also exists in *Zohar Hadash, Ki Tissa*, Mosad ha-Rav Kook edition, 45b, but the passage does not belong to the author of most of the Zohar. Cf. Moshe Idel, *Demut ha-Adam she-me'al ha-Sefirot, Da'at* 4 (1980), p. 46, n. 37.

141. See the expressions cited above, concerning and in n. 121.

142. Gikatilla adopts an intermediate position. Alongside the unity and the continuity of the two *Sefirot*, we have found in his writings that *Keter* and *Tif'eret* look each other in the face. Cf. *Sha'arei Ora* (above n. 81), 101a. The Aramaic terms "Small Countenance" and "Large Countenance" do not appear in the writings of Gikatilla. In one section, *Sha'arei Ora*, Chap. 7, 77a, he expounds the term "The Long-Suffering One" (*Erekh Apayim*) vis-à-vis the *sefirot* of *Hesed* (mercy) and *Bina* (intelligence) (the homily on *Bina* resembles the subject of 'Large Countenance' [*Arikh Anpin*] in the Zohar); he also mentions "the Impatient One" [*Ketsar Apayim*] (cf. Prov. xiv, 17), but does not expound on this subject, noting only "that it is profound and with God's help you will still grasp the matter." For a clear instance of this intermediary position, cf. below n. 181.

143. Compare in R. Joseph of Hamadan's *Toledot Adam* (above n. 73), 104a: "And a few Kabbalists said that in the attribute *Malkhut* there are two eyes and in the bridegroom, who is the King, the Lord of Hosts, there is only one eye."

144. Cf. *Menahot*, 43b.

145. Cf. for instance Zohar, III, 4a, 120a, 290b (*Idra Zuta*). Cf. below concerning n. 277.

146. Compare in *Sifra di-Tsni'uta*, Zohar, II, 178b: " 'Yod' is either perfect or imperfect. When alone, it is a hundred, but if two letters are put (= 'vav' and 'dalet,' which form the name of the character 'yod') it is twice reckoned— the hundred and twenty years [Gen. vi; 3)."

147. Cf. for instance Zohar, II, 165b: "The most Ancient and most Secret One." The passage belongs to the Kabbala of the *Idrot*, and like them it describes the veil that this Ancient One spreads below him.

148. This is also the meaning of the similar combination in the exceptional passage in *Idra Rabba* cited below—cf. regarding n. 170. Accordingly, R. David b. Judah he-Hasid determined in *Sefer ha-Gevul* (above n. 30), 53b: "Every mention of the most Ancient One is an allusion to the supernal *Keter*. . . . and of the most Secret One to the Cause of Causes (= God), who is even more secret than the thoughts."

149. *Livnat ha-Sappir* (above n. 126), 28d. This version was printed in copies of the Zohar in brackets as an alternative version.

150. That is, "twenty year" and another "hundred" together are twenty-one, in gematria *Ehyeh*, and this name in the Kabbala signifies the *sefira* of the *Keter*. The name *Ehyeh* (= "I shall be") is drived from Exod. iii, 14.

151. Zohar, III, 130a (*Idra Rabba*): "the name of the Ancient One is concealed from all, and is not mentioned in the Law, save in one place, where the Small Countenance swore to Abraham, as it is written 'By myself have I sworn said the Lord—said the Small Countenance.' " Namely, the name of the Ancient One is "Yod" and the Small Countenance swore by it to Abraham.

152. This apparently means: Anyone who studies (or "who enters" if we read *de'ayil* instead of *de-ayen*) the secret of "twenty year" is considered the son of the Large Countenance, and he is "upward" of the merit of he who is twenty years old, since he who reaches this age is considered to be the son of the Holy One Blessed be He according to Zohar, II, 98a.

153. *Ayin* is the *sefira* of *Keter*, and equals a hundred.

154. I Chronicles xxix; 11. From this verse the customary names of the seven inferior *sefirot* in the Kabbala were determined. Its use here is far from the habitual style of the Zohar.

155. According to 1 Samuel xxv; 29. Whoever added this benediction here was following the regular usage of the Zohar, which often opens or concludes its homilies with blessings connected with the homily, for instance the matter of "life" here. Compare all this passage also with *Livnat ha-Sappir* (above n. 126), 44c.

156. In another version: who neither entered nor went out. Cf. also below.

157. Compare in the New Testament, John's Revelation, i, 8. See also my article (above n. 56).

158. Cf. my book (above n. 59), pp. 50–51.

159. This seems to me the correct version; it is a combination of the two versions printed on this page of the Zohar.

160. On this term for those who hold the secret, see chapter 1 (above n. 19), pp. 00. See below with regard to n. 281.

161. On the use of this verse, Ps. xxv; 14, cf. below n. 183.

162. According to *Berakhot*, 10a.

163. Genesis Rabba, xiii, 3.

164. See *Yebamot*, 63a: Any man (*adam*) who does not have a wife is not a man, as it is said (Gen. v; 2): "Male and female He created them, and called their name Adam."

165. See above, concerning n. 69.

166. *Sefer ha-Gevul* (above n. 54), 53b. This phrase in the writings of R. David will be discussed further below, with regard to nn. 264–69. See also below n. 183.

167. In chapter 1 p. 68.

168. There are several such occurrences in Zoharic phraseology. See for instance on the preceding page (Zohar, III, 141a): "they are weighed in one balance," and see also below n. 192.

169. Cf. *Ma'arekhet ha-Elohut*, Mantua 1558 (Xerox, Jerusalem 1963), 5a–7b.

170. See above nn. 147–48.

171. See Gershom Scholem, *Sabbatai Sevi, The Mystical Messiah*, translated by R. J. Zwi Werblowsky, Princeton 1973, p. 908. Scholem notes there that the doctrine of *Sefer Raza de-Mehemanuta*, which is based on this passage from *Idra Rabba*, "contains almost no trace of really Lurianic views." In my opinion it is also related to the passage that was chosen to serve as a foundation for the doctrine. On the true author of *Raza de-Mehemanuta*, see my article: *Abraham Miguel Cardozo—the author of "Sefer Raza di-Mheimanuta" which is attributed to Sabbatai Tsvi* (Hebrew), KS 55 (1980), pp. 603–16; KS 56 (1981), pp. 373–74.

172. See Zohar, III, 46b. The passage does not employ the specific *Idra* expressions: "Large Countenance" or "Holy Ancient One" or "Small Countenance." It explains that the two "yods" are male and female, *Tif'eret* and *Malkhut*, and this is the meaning of the names "Lord God" included in the "full name."

173. In Avraham Wertheimer (ed.), *Batei Midrashot*, 2, Jerusalem 1956, p. 412.

174. Leviticus Rabba xiv, 1.

175. See the quotation from R. Abraham b. David in Gershom Scholem's, *Reshit ha-Kabbala*, Jerusalem and Tel Aviv 1948, p. 79.

176. See above, with regard to nn. 132–35.

177. In his book (above n. 22), p. 135.

178. Cf. the talmudic passage, Sanhedrin 111a: "What did Moses see? R. Hanina b. Gamla said: he saw the 'Long-Suffering One'; and our Rabbis said: he saw 'Truth.'" This section hints at the antiquity of the *Idra*'s doctrine of the divine faces, in which *Erekh Appayim* (the Long-Suffering One) (in Aramaic *Arikh Anpin* = the Large Countenance) is the name of the supernal face, while "Truth" (*Emet*) is one of the indubitable names of the lower face, the face of the Small Countenance. My affirmation concerning the Large Countenance is further reinforced by this talmudic section, which goes on

to identify *Erekh Appayim* with *Orekh Yamim* (the Length of Days) (Sanhedrin 111b, likewise in Rashi), and the other indubitable name of the Large Countenance is "Ancient of Days" (perhaps, as Moshe Idel noted, we should relate to this also the habitual usage of *Orekh Anpin* instead of *Arikh Anpin* in the writings of R. Joseph of Hamadan and R. David b. Judah he-Hasid). As regards "Truth," Prof. Moshe Idel drew my attention to the fact that the Gnostic Markos, in a passage that many scholars consider to indicate a Jewish background, maintained that the revealed divine face is called "aletheia," which means "truth" in Greek, and this face has a clearly female nature (and not only because "aletheia" in Greek and *emet* in Hebrew are feminine as regards the grammatical gender), in contrast to the supernal concealed divinity which is of the masculine gender.

This affirmation reinforces our theory that the face of the Small Countenance was originally of the female sex. Markos' doctrine was presented by the Church Father Irenaeus, *Adversus Haereses*, XIV, 1. See also translation and research in Idel (above n. 11), pp. 2–15, and the references there to other research literature. Idel noted in his article, that the figure of "Aletheia" in Irenaeus, apart from its famous parallel to the figure of *Shi'ur Komah* and the other parallels, is also parallel to the angel called *emet* (= Truth) which according to *Midrash Genesis Rabba* viii, 5 (Theodor Elbeck, ed., p. 60), was cast from heaven and returned and grew from the ground. "Aletheia," likewise according to Markos, "was brought down from her supernal place of dwelling." The midrash is indeed based on verses of the Psalms, but the name "Aletheia" is also quoted there (the Greek word, although miscopied in the manuscripts, was recognized by the editors, even though they did not indicate the Gnostic parallel). The name of the concealed male face is not given in Markos' writings and there is no basis for supposing that this is also the Long Suffering One in his doctrine. The name "the Long Suffering One" in its Greek form does however exist in this period, and served in Orphism as a name for the supernal face of the Divinity, as I noted in chapter 1 (n. 19) and discussed at length in my article referred to above in n. 55. Another possible midrashic source for the Small Countenance as the name of the *sefira* of *Malkhut* is the myth of the waning of the moon (*Hullin* 50b), which is interpreted in the Kabbala as the "diminution" of the *Shekhina*. This "diminution" is expressed in Zoharic language through the verb *ze'ar* which appears also in *Ze'er Anpin*; see for instance Zohar, I, 20a.

179. *Sefer ha-Gevul* (above n. 50), 53b.

180. See Zohar III, 136b (*Idra Rabba*): "And also the Victory of Israel will not lie nor repent: for He is not a man (*Adam*), that he should repent" [I Sam. xv, 29]. For what reason? Because it was not of that place which is called *Adam*, for the face and the nose were not uncovered, but the forehead alone, and wherever the face is not found, it is not called *Adam*." A precise interpretation is that only the forehead of the Large Countenance is not called "*Adam*," but the entire face is so called, as we see in Mishna *Yebamot* xvi, 3.

Such an interpretation is not confirmed by the usage of the *Idra*, however, which does not attribute the name *Adam* to the Large Countenance. See also n. 181.

181. See *Sha'arei Ora* (above n. 81), 39b: "But if the attribute of *Netsah* (Victory) went up through the channels and cleaved to the *Netsah* of *Ratson* (Willpower) [in *Sha'arei Tsedek* (above n. 75), 18a: to the forehead (*metsah*) of *Ratson*; and this is the correct form according to the Zohar, see previous footnote, and at the beginning of the section there] in the head of the *Keter*, it does not repent. The reason is that the attribute of *Netsah* has already gone up to a place that it is not called *Adam*, and this is the place that is called *Keter*; but if the attribute of *Netsah* stands below in the attribute of *Tif'eret*, repentance is possible, because in the place called "figure as the appearance of a man above upon it" (Ezek. i, 26], it stays." Here the problem indicated in the previous note does not exist, because Gikatilla recognized only one figure, and the *Keter* (crown) is its forehead. Compare his words in "The Secret of the 13 Attributes" (above n. 86), p. 221, on the verse, Numbers xxiii; 19: "God is not a man (*ish*) that he should lie." "God" is the *Keter*, and *ish* apparently replaces *adam*.

182. These two together gave birth in the Kabbala of *Tikkunei Zohar* to the idea of *Adam be-orah atsilut* (a man in the way of Emanation), which is the Supernal God filling the vessels of the *sefirot*, and is indicated by the Tetragrammaton, the letters of which, written out in full, equal ADM (*Adam*) in gematria. On the idea, its sources and references, see my book (above n. 59), pp. 34–35, 56. See also R. Joseph Gikatilla's conception in his commentary of "The Guide for the Perplexed," in the passage that was also introduced at the beginning of *Kuppat ha-Rokhelin* (see Gottlieb, above n. 12, pp. 116–17). This conception, and in particular the form it assumed in *Kuppat ha-Rokhelin*, is in my opinion one of the sources of the Lurianic doctrine of "Primordial Man." See also below n. 186.

183. Compare the beginning of *Idra Rabba*, Zohar, III, 127b: "Rabbi Abba arose and said to him (to R. Simeon b. Yohai): If it pleases the Master to reveal, because it is written: 'The secret of the Lord is with those who fear Him.' And well do these companions fear the Lord; and now they have entered into the *Idra de-Vei Mashkena* (assembly of the house of the tabernacle). Some of them have only entered, and some of them have also departed." See above, concerning n. 161. See also chapter 1 (above n. 19) pp. 00.

184. Compare with the contradictory language in Zohar, III, 55b (*Tosefta*): "The manners of the Master of the world are thus? It would be better if we had not heard them! We heard and we did not know!"

185. *Sefer ha-Gevul* (above n. 55), 51a–53b.

186. Zohar III, 48b: "As taught in the most high secret in *Sifra di-Tsni'uta*..." (compare the term "most secret of all things" [*Raza de-Razin*] below n. 215), and its source (with modifications) in Zohar, II, 178a–b (*Sifra*

di-Tsni'uta). The contents of the quotation do not fit exactly into the discussion expounded by the section. The existence of the quotation in this section complicates the question of its relationship to *Sifra di-Tsni'uta,* since most of the section contradicts the determination in *Sifra di-Tsni'uta,* cited above, that *'adam* is without. . ., all the more so *ish'.*

187. See my book (above n. 59), p. 49. See above n. 182.

188. On this, see chapter 1 p. 21. See also below, n. 191.

189. See chapter 1, p. 36.

190. The parallel passage from *Idra Rabba* is cited above, in n. 183.

191. In several versions, we also find: "R. Isaac could not answer." I think, however, that the reference is to R. Abba, who is the exponent of the preceding passage. If this is true, this passage is considered more profound than the preceding one.

192. See above n. 168.

193. In Moses Cordovero's version, *Or Yakar,* 12, Jerusalem 1983, p. 202: "a holy thing." Perhaps it should be: "a completely holy thing."

194. In *Or Yakar,* "were seen."

195. Zohar, III, 135b (*Idra Rabba*). The *Idra* expounds on 370 sides on which the spark extends (and compare ibid., 133b and commentary on *Nitsotsei Zohar*). The number 325 is also mentioned, however, in the *Idra* and in its parallels—see above n. 96. On *butsina de-cardinota,* see in my book (above n. 59), pp. 145–55, 160–67.

196. In *Idra Rabba* two kinds of mercy (*hesed*) are described, one of the Large Countenance and the other of the Small Countenance—Zohar, III, 133b; but the phraseology "supernal mercy" exists only in *Idra Zuta*—Zohar, III, 289b. This same term also exists in *The Secret of the Thirteen Attributes* (above n. 86), p. 223.

197. Zohar III, 132b (*Idra Rabba*)—first lock. Compare *The Secret of the Thirteen Attributes* (above n. 86), p. 222.

198. In one place, Zohar, III, 146b, we found that the Levite is also called "holy" and not only "clean." This refers to a quotation from *Tseni'uta di-Sifra,* which is not in the *Sifra di-Tsni'uta* in our possession. However, this place belongs to a later stratum, as noted above n. 88.

199. *Sha'arei Ora* (above n. 81), 50a.

200. Idel (above n. 11), p. 49.

201. See above n. 181.

202. Idel (ibid.), p. 43, n. 161. I have not found his source.

203. According to Amos Goldreich: "R. David b. Judah he-Hasid's *Sefer ha-Gevul*—Methods of Adaptation of a Zoharic Text after the appearance of the Zohar" (Hebrew), M.A. thesis, Tel Aviv University, under the guidance of Ephraim Gottlieb, 1972 (mimeograph), p. 46, with author's handwritten appendix. A copy of the thesis, including the handwritten appendices, exists in the Scholem Collection at the National University Library in Jerusalem. The identification is based on the style and parallels. The passage seems like a translation from the Aramaic (see the following notes). I found another version of this passage in: *Tsafenat Pa'aneah* (above n. 36), p. 20a. It is quoted there in the name of 'The Zohar sages' (*Hakhmei ha-Zohar*). Other passages by R. David he-Hasid are quoted there, as by other Kabbalists, as 'Midrash ha-Ne'elam.' See the preface by Moshe Idel, p. 30.

204. This was cited as a correct view in *Sefer ha-Gevul* (above n. 47), 53b: "And so the Priest would wave the Levites as a wave offering before the Lord in order to quiet his anger as someone rocking and shaking a crying child." This subject is also mentioned in *The Book of Mirrors. . .* (above n. 29), p. 82: "Therefore the Priest was obliged to show a joyful face in order to throw off and vanquish the side of stern judgment, which is the left, so that it will not rule over the world. Therefore the Priest would wave the Levites in order to quiet and pacify their anger and their wrath." Here, however, it is not clear whether the waving is as R. Judah or as R. Abba. Goldreich alluded to these parallels in his work.

205. *Milah* instead of *davar*. This is an Aramaism.

206. The phrase "which is the attribute of *Gevura*" is an explanation given by the translator into Hebrew.

207. This is a misreading of the original Zohar: *mi-shilshuleihon*. See Goldreich, ibid. In *Tsafenat Pa'aneah* (above n. 203) it reads correctly.

208. "Abraham" and "El" (God) are common symbols of the *sefira* of *Hesed*. *El* is the characteristic name for the *sefira* of *Hesed* in the writings of Joseph Gikatilla, but in the Zohar it also denotes the attribute of judgment. See the discussion of the double sense of this name, based on this verse in Psalms, in Zohar, III, 30a–31b. It gives the impression of a true discussion reflecting the divergences of opinion in the Zohar circle.

209. From here, this is a Kabbalistic elaboration of a source dealing with physiognomy. The *Idrot* literature also establishes that the hairs of the beard are sterner than the hairs of the head. For example, Zohar, III, 131b (*Idra Rabba*).

210. See for instance Zohar, III, 140a–b.

211. See Zohar, III, 139a (*Idra Rabba*): "Said R. Simeon to R. Eleazar his son: Rise my son and expound [literally: curl] on the lock of the holy beard (or king)."

212. This event is related in *Idra Rabba*, Zohar, Part III, 144a.

213. In chapter 1, pp. 74–82, I showed that the convening of the *Idra Rabba* must be seen as *Tikkun Leil Shavu'ot*, and the portion *Nasso* is always read on the Sabbath closest to Shavu'ot.

214. *Raza de-Razin* (secret of secrets) is the name of the Zohar section that deals with physiognomy—Zohar, II, 70a–75a (other parts related to it were printed in *Zohar Hadash*, portion *Yitro*, in which other sections printed there and dealing with the same subject belong to *Tikkunei Zohar*). The *Idra* which deals with the supernal faces is closely related to this section (for examples, see above, concerning n. 34, and in n. 209), and may have also been called by this name in its first edition. We have also found that *Sifra di-Tsni'uta* is called "Supreme Secret"—see above n. 195.

215. Isa. xxiii; 18. The verse continues: "for her merchandise shall be for them that dwell before the Lord, to eat sufficiently, and for ancient covering." The talmudic sages said in *Pesahim* 119a: "What is 'for ancient covering'?—That which covers the things that the Ancient of days covered; and what are they? The secrets of the Torah. And some say: That which reveals things that the Ancient of days concealed; what are they?—Meanings of the Torah." According to R. Moses de Leon's version, *Nefesh ha-Hokhama*, Basle 1608 (Xerox copy, Jerusalem 1969), fol. 3, 3b: "And to the covering of ancient things that the Ancient of days revealed." For some other versions of this sentence, see J. H. A. Wijnhoven's critical edition, *Sefer ha-Mishkal*—Text and Study, (diss. presented to Brandeis University, 1965 (University Microfilms, Ann Arbor), p. 49.

216. For instance in Zohar, III, 132a (*Idra Rabba*).

217. Perhaps in accordance with *Nedarim* 9a, which describes the Nazirite whose "locks are arranged in curls."

218. *Hagiga*, 14a.

219. When the dew descending from the Large Countenance reaches the head of the Small Countenance, a red coloring also appears there—Zohar, III, 135b (*Idra Rabba*).

220. See examples in the corresponding entries in Kabbalistic Lexicon *Erkhei ha-Kinuyyim* (in Moses Cordovero, *Pardes Rimmonim*, chap. 23).

221. See below, concerning nn. 245–49.

222. *Nefesh ha-Hakhama*, Basle (above n. 215), fol. 6, 1b, Wijnhoven (above, ibid.), p. 92–93. Compare Zohar, II, 10a; ibid., 253a. The doctrine of the *shemittot* is indeed mentioned (albeit without the Kabbalistic connection) in *Midrash ha-Ne'elam*. *Zohar Hadash*, Mosad ha-Rav Kook (ed.), 16d.

223. See Gottlieb (above n. 31), pp. 233–37. R. David b. Judah he-Hasid also possessed the doctrine of the *shemittot*. See Matt (above n. 29), pp. 102–7,

in the English part, pp. 31–33. At the beginning of *Livnat ha-Sappir* (above n. 126), the author attempts to bring many proofs of the relationship between our *shemitta* and the *sefira* of *Malkhut*, apparently as a disputation against others of his comrades in the Zohar circle, such as R. David b. Judah he-Hasid, who maintained that we are in the *shemitta* of *Gevura* (this is also the view adopted by *Sefer ha-Temuna*). R. Moses Cordovero, who also contended that our *shemitta* is the *shemitta* of *Malkhut* is influenced, I think, by *Sefer Livnat ha-Sappir* and continues its controversy. On Cordovero's view, see Berakha Zak, "Three Times of Salvation in R. Moses Cordovero's *Or Yakar*" (Hebrew) in Zvi Baras (ed.), *Messianism and Eschatology*, Jerusalem 1984, pp. 281–84. See below n. 227.

224. This explains R. Isaac Luria's opposition to the doctrine of the *shemittot* in his commentary on *Sifra di-Tsni'uta, Sha'ar Ma'amarei R. Simeon b. Yohai*, Jerusalem 1959, 46b. He considers that the aforesaid doctrine derived from a misunderstanding of the idea of the destruction of the worlds.

225. See *Genesis Rabba* i, 16: " 'And the earth was'—because it already was." See also *Sefer ha-Bahir*, Margaliouth edition, para. 2.

226. See also at the end of *Sifra di-Tsni'uta*, Zohar, II, 179a. Compare the *Midrash ha-Ne'elam* to the Song of Songs, *Zohar Hadash*, Mosad ha-Rav Kook edition, 62d–63a.

227. The talmudic passage continues: "Just as the Sabbatical year drops one year every seven years, so the world drops a thousand years every seven thousand years." Such an idea already existed in the Slavonic Book of Enoch, xi, 81: "So that the week will become like the seven millenia and the eighth day like the beginning of the eighth millenium, and like the first day of the week it will always recur." In my opinion, this should be linked with the doctrine of Time expressed in chapter 17 of this book. According to this doctrine, the time divided into periods originates in the great eternity, which is also called "the world of creation," and it is to this that it will return. On this concept and its sources see: Shlomo Pines, "Eschatology and the Concept of Time in the Slavonic Book of Enoch," in R. J. Zwi Werblowsky (ed.), *Types of Redemption*, Leiden 1970, pp. 72–87. The combination of these two doctrines resembles the Kabbalistic view of the *sefirot* which return in the *shemitta* and jubilee to the *sefira* of *Bina*, which is called World or Eternity (*Olam*). A doctrine similar to that of the Book of Enoch, but with the addition of an astrological nuance, exists in R. Abraham bar Hiyya's *Megilat ha-Megalleh*, Berlin 1924, pp. 8–11. For a review of the doctrine of the *Shemittot* and its development see: Israel Weinstok, *Be-Ma'agalei ha-Nigle ve-ha-Nistar*, Jerusalem 1970, pp. 153–241.

228. See for instance in *Sefer Tashak* (above n. 110), p. 105.

229. Paris Mss. 853, 80b–81a (typescript by Moshe Idel). See Idel (above n. 72), p. 75.

230. I added this word in accordance with the parallel section in the Sassoon Ms. 290, p. 666 (typescript by Moshe Idel).

231. This is the correct version, as it appears in the Sassoon Ms. In the Paris Ms. the word "cuts" is replaced by 'conceals.'

232. *Ta'anit* 17a, where a proof from the Nazir is cited. This saying of the talmudic sages is cited in several places in R. Joseph's writings (as in the Sassoon Ms., ibid.) as follows: "The rabbis said: God cuts his hair every day," and it is characteristic of R. Joseph to introduce his views into the words of the talmudic sages. See example below, n. 234. In the Sassoon Ms. (p. 667) he also presents a proof of this from the angels who are created and abolished daily, and created anew in the morning, according to *Hagiga* 14a.

233. *Genesis Rabba*, viii, 2.

234. This is a combination of two sayings of the talmudic sages: *Genesis Rabba* iii, 7, *Hagiga*, 12a. On the idea of the concealed light in talmudic literature, see my book (above n. 116), pp. 159–61.

235. See Isaiah Tishby, *The Doctrine of Evil and the "Kelippah" in Lurianic Kabbalism* (Hebrew), Jerusalem 1963, pp. 21–61.

236. *Sefer ha-Bahir*, Margaliouth edition, 190: "It teaches that that light was very great and no creature could look at it, so God concealed it for the future *tsaddikim*."

237. See above, n. 167, and the references there. See also below in the Appendix.

238. Zohar, III, 204b: "The first light that God created was so bright that the worlds could not endure it. God therefore made another light as a vestment to this one, and so with all the other lights, until all the worlds could endure the light without being dissolved." The phrase "until all the worlds could endure" may allude to the period of breaking, but such an interpretation is not essential. Perhaps the Zohar passage is merely the Neoplatonic doctrine of the Emanation in a Kabbalistic guise.

239. R. Bahya's words were cited on a parallel to *Ta'amei ha-Mitsvot*, 2nd version by Gottlieb (above n. 31), pp. 202–3.

240. See also above, concerning n. 140.

241. In his book (above n. 12), pp. 249–50.

242. Scholem (above n. 29), p. 308. In various parts of this article Scholem also introduces various conflicting views about R. David as a source for knowledge of the Zohar. See below n. 261.

243. Goldreich (above n. 203). My friend Dr. Goldreich also placed at my disposal his own handwritten copy of *Sefer ha-Gevul*, with important notes.

244. Above n. 185 and regarding it.

245. Zohar, III, 128a; 135a–b; 142, namely before the *tikkun* of the Large Countenance, before the *tikkun* of the Small Countenance, and before the *tikkun* of the female.

246. Moshe Idel, "The Evil Thought of the Deity" (Hebrew), *Tarbiz* 49 1980, p. 364.

247. Chapter 1, p. 66.

248. *Sha'arei Ora* (above n. 81), chap. 9, 98b. See Appendix at the end of this chapter.

249. For instance, in *Toledot Adam* (above n. 73), 97b–102a. This is also true of the other Gnostic Kabbalists—see Scholem (above n. 17), p. 34. We have also found this in Zohar, I, 177b.

250. Scholem (above n. 29), p. 302, determined that R. David never calls the Zohar by name. Goldreich, in his work (above n. 203), pp. 96–101, examined the places that would seem on the face of it to contradict this assertion. He concluded, however, that they are insubstantial, and that the initials S. H. in R. David's writings indicate *Seni'ut* (= *Tseni'ut*) *ha-Sefer*, namely *Sifra di-Tsni'uta*, and not *Sefer ha-Zohar*.

251. All the quotations from *Sifra di-Tsni'uta* cited in *Sefer ha-Gevul*, are also cited in *Idra Rabba*. In R. David's *Or Zaru'a* (Bodely Ms. 1624, at the Institute for Manuscript Photocopies in Jerusalem: S 17202, p. 8b), however, I also found the following occurrence: "And HE, being full of mercy [the Hebrew, *rahum*, may be interpreted as 'mercied upon'], forgave their iniquity" (Psalms lxxviii; 38), "And HE," He is called "and He." That is what is written [Job xxiii; 13] "And He is in one." "Full of mercy" because he is merciful [*rahaman* = giver of mercy]. "Full of mercy"—merciful it should have been! What is "And He being full of mercy"? But to intimate to you here in the secret of faith (as in Zoharic language: "*be-Raza de-Meheimenuta*"), a wonderful secret in *Tsni'ut ha-Sefer*: that even "supernal *Keter* [these two words are missing in this manuscript, and I completed them from the other manuscripts where sometimes the letters were written reversed, as a token of secret], which is called 'And He' is itself full of mercy of the Cause of Causes, because the Cause of Causes has mercy on those below him, since the way of the father is to be merciful to those who come out of his loins. And understand, and be silent to the Lord." I also found this homily in a section by R. David. In both the versions that have been conserved, the indication *Tsni'ut ha-Sefer* is missing. These versions, one of which is in *Sefer ha-Gevul*, and the other in the book *Ma'or va-Shemesh*, were quoted and compared by Moshe Idel in his article "Kabbalistic Materials from the School of Rabbi David ben Judah he-Hasid" (Hebrew), Jerusalem Studies in Jewish Thought, Vol. II, 1983, p. 172. This homily does not appear in the *Sifra di-Tsni'uta* with which we are familiar, and its terminology, e.g., "the Cause of Causes,"

does not fit in this work. It may however have been an interpretation of another version with which R. David was familiar, in which he might have changed the terminology. He may possibly have interpreted the expression "most Secret One" as the "Cause of Causes," as was his wont (see above n. 148). A similar homily also exists in the same circle, in R. Joseph b. Shalom Ashkenazi's commentary to *Sefer Yetsira* (above n. 53), 30b. "Supernal *Keter* is 'blessed' by the Cause of Causes and *Hokhma* is 'blessed' by Supernal *Keter*." This comparison was cited by Goldreich (above n. 203), p. 87. *Tsni'ut ha-Sefer* here may just be rhetoric, however, like "the secret of faith" and "wonderful secret." Compare the subject of *bei Idra* (below, concerning nn. 266–69).

252. See Scholem (ibid.), p. 308. Ibid., pp. 308–9, the preface is also printed.

253. See above, concerning n. 188.

254. Goldreich (above n. 203), p. 58.

255. This subject requires extensive study and does not come within the scope of this chapter. I will merely indicate comments made concerning him by other scholars. Gershom Scholem commented on several passages from *Sefer Mar'ot ha-Tsove'ot*—Scholem (above n. 24), p. 314, and on another passage from *Or Zaru'a* (a passage belonging to *Midrash ha-Ne'elam* which is designated as "*Yerushalmi*" just as this midrash is designated in the writings of R. Moses de Leon and Ibn Sahula)—Scholem (ibid.), p. 322. Scholem (ibid.), p. 324–25, commented on many Zohar sections that are not in our possession and that were in the possession of the author of the "Lexicon of the Zohar." See also Scholem (above n. 86), p. 48. Notwithstanding, the important question of the above-mentioned lexicon and its relation to R. David has not yet been exhausted. For other such passages from *Mar'ot ha-Tsove'ot*, see Matt (above n. 29), p. 15. Another Zoharic passage was published by Moshe Idel in his article "Rabbi David b. Judah he-Hasid's Translation of the Zohar and his Lexicon" (continued) (Hebrew), *Alei Sefer* 9 (1981), pp. 88–91. On Zoharic versions by R. David which are superior to those in print, see Moshe Idel, "Rabbi David b. Judah he-Hasid's Translation of the Zohar and his Lexicon" (Hebrew), *Alei Sefer* 8 (1980), pp. 68–70. I. Tishby disagreed with one of the points raised here by Idel—the originality in the Zohar of "Adam" as the abbreviation of "*Adam—David—Messiah*," a question that cannot be unequivocally settled. See I. Tishby, "Messianism in the Time of the Expulsion from Spain and Portugal" (Hebrew), Jerusalem 1985, p. 141.

256. See Scholem (above n. 29), p. 313. Matt (ibid.), pp. 17–18.

257. See above n. 203 and regarding it.

258. See Matt (above n. 29), p. 17.

259. See Scholem (ibid.), pp. 313–17. Matt (ibid.), pp. 11–13. There are many other pertinent examples.

260. See Matt (ibid.), p. 11. R. David ascribes one passage of R. Azriel to *Tannaim* of the Zohar, and twice in two different elaborations, in the first to R. Hiyya and in the second to R. Simeon (Matt, ibid.). We can perhaps resolve the question by supposing that R. David had a special feeling for this passage, and so repeated it. R. Azriel sent this passage from Gerona to Burgos; in many manuscripts it is included in the writings of the "Gnostic Kabbalists" who were connected, as already mentioned, with the Zohar circle, and it is ascribed to R. Jacob ha-Cohen—see Scholem (above n. 17), pp. xii–xiii. It may already have been attributed to this scholar in R. David's lifetime.

261. Scholem (ibid.), pp. 310, 318–20. Scholem's position on this book is not clear-cut. On p. 310, after noting that R. David described this book in two of his works and added information on what is said in the Zohar, he concludes his discussion thus: "And if this is so—then it is significant!" On p. 319, however, he writes "If we scrutinize R. David's words, we must understand that that book of Sar Shalom Gaon is not a visible revealed book in the earthly world, but a mysterious inner book which is revealed to the vision of the Kabbalists who scrutinize their inner thoughts and 'profess the unity of God in their hearts'—in other words, all this is a spiritual matter and not something of the material world." It is unclear to me whether by making the book an "internal mystery" Scholem contradicts his previous words, or whether he still maintains the allusion to the inner knowledge that R. David had concerning the aforesaid book of the Zohar. Scholem's view that a scrutiny of R. David's words shows that he is not referring to an earthly book is essentially incorrect and is based on a faulty version which he had in his possession. The correct version (*Mar'ot ha-Tsove'ot*, Matt ed., p. 197) reads thus: 'He who wishes to know those characters written within each and every *keter*, will profess the unity of God and thus he will succeed in all. And I once inscribed those written and known letters in every single *keter* [= *sefira*] from the 'Supreme Book of the Chief of Fifty [= *Sar ha-Hamishim*]' written by Sar Shalom Gaon in the city of Mittburg, and I carried this name with me." In the version Scholem had, the words from "and I once inscribed" up to "every single *keter*" are missing, and thus it appeared that the book is revealed in the profession of the unity of God. According to the complete version, however, this book is earthly, and contains indications for this profession (the same indication for the word *yihud* [=profession, or meditation of unity] as in the writings of R. Isaac Luria already exists here in my opinion). In Scholem's version the name of the city Mittburg is replaced by meaningless words, an error that also contributed to his view of the unearthly character of the book. Mittburg is probably the town of Magdeburg, as Goldreich surmised (above n. 203), pp. 3–4.

262. See Matt (ibid.), p. 6.

263. Two of the manuscripts are indicated in the notes below.

264. In the Bodely ms. (above n. 251) it is written *li* (= to me) and the correction *le-mi* (= to he who) is written over it. Possibly the error is intentional or Freudian. In the other manuscripts: *le-mi*.

265. Above, notes 69, 183. The expression *bei Idra* (= hall of assembly) exists in the Zohar, e.g., Zohar, III, 127b (*Idra Rabba*): "The companions entered the *bei Idra*." See also my book (above n. 59), p. 49. The expression (Zohar, III, 134b; *Idra Rabba*) "Happy are those who are in that Supreme Holy Assembly" is translated by R. David in *Sefer ha-Gevul* (above n. 58), 39a, "Happy is he who is in the supreme holy *bei Idra*." See also, *Mar'ot ha-Tsove'ot* (above n. 29), p. 116: "And the secret in this. . . is for all who enter *bei Idra*."

266. Scholem (above n. 29), p. 321.

267. *Livnat ha-Sappir* (above n. 126), p. 28a.

268. See above n. 183 and its references.

269. Sassoon ms. (1064) 1006. In the Institute for Manuscript Photocopies in Jerusalem, S 9576.

270. See above n. 251.

271. Bodely (above n. 25), 246b. This matter is also mentioned by Scholem (above n. 29), p. 321–22.

272. For instance in the London ms. 771.1 (in the Institute for Manuscript Photocopies in Jerusalem, S 5454), 22a. In the Bodely ms. "from the *Idra*."

273. Sassoon (above n. 269), p. 106.

274. Milan-Ambrosiana ms. 62 (in the Institute for Manuscript Photocopies in Jerusalem, S 14614), 3b.

275. Idel (above n. 251), pp. 194–96.

276. The subject discussed in the answer, the union of *Hokhma* and *Bina* as opposed to the union of *Tif'eret* and *Malkhut*, is very important for the history of the Kabbala, as Idel explained. I will add that this problem also greatly preoccupied R. Isaac Luria in his early writings. He himself wrote an answer that somewhat parallels R. David's answer, and which was printed in his book *Ets Hayyim*, Jerusalem 1910, 10c–d; and in *Sha'ar Ma'amarei Rashbi*, Jerusalem 1959, 63b.

277. See above n. 145.

278. Proverbs, i, 20.

279. Song of Songs, v, 11.

280. *Erubin*, 21b.

281. See above n. 160. The "reapers of the field" are also mentioned in Zohar, III, 143a, several lines before the words of R. Simeon b. Yohai that are quoted subsequently.

282. See below, after n. 289.

283. According to the manuscript. According to Idel: "all of it."

284. This is a reference to the subject of the two Countenances which appears in *Genesis Rabba* viii, 1 (Idel's note).

285. *Pesakhim* 50a; *Baba Batra* 10b. In *Idra Rabba*, Zohar, III, 143a, the section is ascribed to R. Simeon, who is alluded to prior to this as the "head of the group" (Idel's note).

286. Some corrections to the printed version of this responsum can be found in the Hebrew version of this article.

287. Idel (above n. 140), pp. 41–42.

288. See above, concerning n. 140.

289. Idel (ibid.), pp. 43–44, considered that this was a reference to other of R. David's writings. I think that the expression "What I intimated to you in the verse 'my loved one is pure and red' " cited at the end of the responsum, relates to the explanation of this verse at the beginning of the same responsum and not in another place.

290. Idel (ibid.), p. 43.

291. Only at the end of the responsum did he note "and notwithstanding, the answer of the tongue is from the Lord" (Proverbs xvi; 1).

292. Idel considers that R. David drew his doctrine of the *kavanot* (intentions), according to which man when praying sees in his mind the colors that represent the objects of his *kavana*, from the countries of the Orient. See: M. Idel, "La Prière Kabbalistique et les Couleurs" in: *Prière, Mystique et Judaïsme, Coll.*, Strasburg 1984, pp. 107–19.

293. In his article (above n. 140), Idel indicated R. David's influence on the Lurianic conception of "Primordial Man" (and see also above n. 182). In another article—Moshe Idel, "Once More about R. David b. Judah he-Hasid" (Hebrew), *Da'at* 7 (1981), pp. 69–71—he showed R. David's influence on the Lurianic doctrine of the Divine Countenances. In this respect I will note that in a drawing at the end of *Sefer ha-Gevul* (above n. 71), 53a, the following explanation appears, and it contains terminology considered extremely Lurianic: "From the nose upwards the face is called Leah female of Israel and from the nose down it is called Rachel. All are in the female *malkhut* of the Small Countenance which is called *tif'eret*." These words are included in most manuscripts of *Sefer ha-Gevul* (e.g. in New York ms. in JTS, mic. 2193, Scholem Coll., photostat 36, 81a). The drawing and its explanations are absent in the only manuscript in which a date prior to the Lurianic Kabbala is specified—16 Kislev, 1559, namely the Jerusalem ms. 4080. On this subject, see Scholem !above n. 86), pp. 48–49. This does not, however, constitute proof

that the words are a later Lurianic addition, since large sections of *Sefer ha-Gevul* are missing in this manuscript, and the drawings in general differ greatly from one manuscript to the next. Even if this is a Lurianic addition, it is interesting that anyone wished to elaborate R. David's writings in this way. We have found such an elaboration in the writings of R. Joseph of Hamadan (Dr. Amos Goldreich showed me one such example).

294. Idel (above n. 140), pp. 41–55. See also: Idel, "The Sefirot above the Sefirot" (Hebrew), *Tarbiz*, 51, 1982, pp. 239–80.

295. Idel (above n. 140), p. 54.

296. Here I must amend what I wrote in my essay, "Tsadik Yesod Olam—Mitos Shabbeta'i," *Da'at* 1 (1978), p. 93, n. 107, where I attributed to R. Moses de Leon a section by R. David which had been transposed in his book.

297. *Tehirin* - see Zohar, II, 259a. Another translation of this word in the language of the Zohar is *hivrin*—Zohar, III, 129b (*Idra Rabba*). Another guise of this idea is the subject of the nine "lights of thought" which will be discussed in the Appendix. All this is dealt with in my essay (ibid.), pp. 93–94.

298. Iris Felix recently demonstrated that Angelet is the correct name of the scholar who was known in research literature as R. Joseph Angelino. R. Joseph Angelet's consciousness of ensuring the continuity of the Zohar is attested to, for instance, by the following sentence from *Kuppat ha-Rokhelin* (above n. 30), p. 41b: "And his wife's name was Mehetabel and we explained it in the Holy Assembly (see Zohar, III, 142a, *Idra Rabba*), and nothing more should be revealed here." We have already seen some of his Zoharic writings above (concerning nn. 126, 155). All his books are filled with Zoharic expressions (in addition to quotations from all the known and unknown members of the Zohar circle), and it is sometimes extremely difficult to draw the line between those Zoharic sections that he himself wrote and "original Zohar" passages. At times evidence of proto-Zoharic layers also appears in his writings. We found in *Kuppat ha-Rokhelin*, 167b, for instance, a dialogue between R. Simeon b. Yohai and R. Hiyya, written in Hebrew, and R. Hiyya appears in the dialogue as greater than his companion. Only some of the Zohar passages are indicated in his books as quotations from *Midrash ha-Ne'elam* (which is how he refers to the entire Zohar generally in *Livnat ha-Sappir* and in his commentary to *Sha'arei Ora*, but in his earlier book, *Kuppat ha-Rokhelin*, he uses mainly the name "Zohar").

R. Joseph Angelet also wrote several passages printed in the Zohar, for example the messianic passage which constitutes the portion *va-Yeshev* in *Zohar Hadash*, Mosad ha-Rav Kook ed. 29a–d. (His messianic concept in my opinion reveals the influence of Christianity, particularly as regards Joseph and his tribulations, which are the reason for the exiles.) This passage is parallel to *Livnat ha-Sappir* (above n. 126), 55c–56d. The entire passage is written in the style and spirit of R. Joseph. The *Livnat ha-Sappir* version, and its parallel in *Kuppat ha-Rokhelin*, p. 154, contains the hope for the redemption in the year 88 [= 1328 C.E.]. This year was extremely important in the life of R. Joseph Angelet, and he anticipates it in various ways (see also *Livnat ha-Sappir* 9c, 25b, 26b, 39a, 65d). In the passage in *Zohar Hadash*, due to the absence of a certain sentence which exists in *Livnat ha-Sappir*, the end of the Zohar is actually reckoned 280 years later. However, the aforesaid sentence appears in R. Moses Cordovero's version in *Or Yakar* after the portion *be-Hukotai*, vol. 13, Jerusalem 1985, p. 218 (Cordovero's version is closer to *Kuppat ha-Rokhelin* than to *Livnat ha-Sappir* or *Zohar Hadash*). This year was also predicted in *Ra'aya Meheimana*, Zohar, III, 252a, but in a completely different homily. The same year is mentioned in *Livnat ha-Sappir* 98b, in a passage written by the author of *Ra'aya Meheimana and Tikkunei Zohar*, although it does not exist in the same form in the Zohar in our possession (the passage of the *Tikkunim* printed in *Zohar Hadash* 102c resembles it). This topic is one of the points of contact between the author of *Tikkunei Zohar* and the author of *Livnat ha-Sappir*; although there is a great difference between them we have found many parallels of content and style (e.g., *Kuppat ha-Rokhelin* began, although it did not finish, explaining the word "bereshit" [= in the beginning] with seventy Aramaic commentaries, like *Tikkunei Zohar*, as emerges from its language on p. 11a onwards). *Livnat ha-Sappir* is also the first to quote *Tikkunei Zohar* (*Livnat ha-Sappir*, 95b–100b. The source of the passage is not indicated and only short sections appear in the same form as in *Tikkunei Zohar*, but the style proves that they belong there. This passage is missing in most of the *Livnat ha-Sappir* manuscripts). The section which constitutes the portion *Ki Tissa* in *Zohar Hadash* also appears to belong to R. Joseph Angelet, resembling both in style and content the aforementioned section from the portion *va-Yeshev* (part of it was printed in *Livnat ha-Sappir*, 86d–88a, and this part was also printed as an addendum to Zohar, II, 276a–277a). Several stages can be discerned in R. Joseph Angelet's relation to the Zohar. His first book is apparently "Twenty-Four Secrets" (very many manuscripts of which exist, including for instance at the end of Jerusalem ms. 10 1959). In the manuscripts the book is anonymous, but there are substantive proofs that it is the work of R. Joseph Angelet. The first to identify the author of this work was Moshe Idel in his essay, "Patterns of Redemptive Activity in the Middle Ages" in Zvi Baras: Messianism and Eschatology—A Collection of Essays (Hebrew), Jerusalem 1984, p. 264 and n. 46). This book contains no explicit quotation from the Zohar, but only from *Sifra di-Tsni'uta*, from which there are, as known, explicit quotations in the actual Zohar too. It is interesting to note that when R. Joseph Angelet quotes from "Twenty-Four Secrets" in his later book *Livnat ha-Sappir*, he tends to incorporate in his quotations sections from the Zohar with are not in "Twenty-Four Secrets." See *Livnat ha-Sappir*, 4b, where part of the "secret of the souls" from "Twenty-Four Secrets" is cited, and in which a passage from Zohar, III, 58a is incorporated.

299. Avraham of Granada, *Berit Menuha*, Jerusalem 1959, 4b, etc.

300. See *Sha'arei Ora*, chap. 10 (above n. 81), 105a–b, the subject of "Laban (in Hebrew, *lavan* = white) the Syrian" who is as against "the White Head" and who can "completely root out the whole" (according to the Passover Haggada).

301. See Idel (above n. 246), pp. 356–59. See also my article (above n. 18). p. 91.

302. In addition to the well-known case of Jesus, I wish to point out the quasi-mythical status achieved by the "Woman and her Seven Sons" in the Book of Maccabees IV. They were exalted to the level of a "holy and harmonious symphony," and were likened to the seven days of Creation which surrounded the "God-fearingness," obviously a symbol of the Sabbath day (Maccabees IV, xiv, 3–7. According to the manuscripts, it was the days that surrounded the God-fearingness [*eusebian*] while the brothers surrounded the number seven [*hebdomada*], and the editors for their own reasons tried to change this). Their mother symbolizes the Sabbath day and the fear (the fear is normally called "the fearing understanding" [*ho eusebes logismos*] and the entire book is dedicated to its praise—see ibid. i, 1; this degree is also attributed to the mother of the sons—ibid. xvi, 1). The Woman and her Sons are also likened to the moon and the seven stars (ibid., xvii, 5). There may also be an allusion here to the possibility that they will become fixed in the heavens, like the seven Pleiades in the Greek myth. The Woman is also called "mother of the nation" (*meter ethnous*)—ibid., xvi, 29, and the victory of the people over their oppressors is attributed to her and to her sons—ibid. xvii, 9–10. In the talmudic midrashim on the Woman and her seven Sons there is no echo of this Jewish-Hellenistic myth. It may, nonetheless, have influenced in a hidden way the emergence of the Kabbalistic myth of *Bina* with the seven *sefirot*, which are the days of Creation, and their destruction and *tikkun*. Even if this is not the case, it still constitutes an example of the similitude in the patterns of Jewish myth in its various periods and its many forms.

303. See "Isaac ben Jacob ha-Cohen, an essay on the left-sided Emanation" (Hebrew) in Scholem (above n. 17), pp. 86–89; Todros Abulafia, *Sha'ar ha-Razim*, Bnei Brak 1986, pp. 35–37, 64–65, 119–20, 227–28; Todros Abulafia, *Otsar ha-Kavod*, Warsaw 1879 (photocopy bound with *Sha'ar ha-Razim*), 14b, 22c, 27b; Amos Goldreich (ed.) "*Sefer Mei'rat Einayim* by R. Isaac of Acre," A Critical Edition, Jerusalem 1984, pp. 29–37. See also *Sefer ha-Bahir*, Margaliouth ed., para. 194–95; Idel (above n. 246), pp. 358–59; Farber (above n. 39), pp. 169–89).

304. See the sources cited by Idel (ibid.), pp. 360–64.

305. Cited above in n. 63.

306. Zohar, III, 65a. The passage is sometimes called *Idra*. See above n. 297.

307. See in my article (above n. 296), p. 85, n. 74 and p. 92; also in my article (above n. 47), pp. 268–71.

NOTES 227

308. On these two interpretations, see I. Tishby, "Towards an Understanding of the Methods of Abstraction and Mythologization in the Kabbala" (Hebrew) in his book: *Netivei Emuna u-Minut*, Ramat Gan 1964, pp. 23–29.

309. On this doctrine see Tishby, ibid., and Tishby (above n. 235). On its sources, see Idel (above n. 246), p. 643.

310. See *Sha'ar Ma'amarei Rashbi* (= Lurianic Commentaries on the Zohar), Jerusalem 1959, 65b–67b. The article was copied from the handwriting of R. Isaac Luria himself, and was written when he initially began to study Kabbala. This is the first place that deals with this subject, which is not yet called here the "breaking of the vessels." The first half of the article is devoted to the Ten Martyrs, and the second half to the death of the Kings.

311. Above nn. 25, 56.

312. See F.J. Baer, "Todros ben Judah ha-Levi and his Time" (Hebrew), *Zion* 2, 1937, pp. 36–44.

313. See Scholem (above n. 24), p. 11. The mention of the year 58 [= 1298] which appears in the title of Todros ben Judah's eulogy below must be an error.

314. See J. G. Liebes, "Illumination of the Soul and Vision of the Idea in Plato" in *Studies in Mysticism and Religion* (Hebrew) presented to Gershom G. Scholem, Jerusalem 1968, pp. 149–61.

315. See Baer (above n. 312), and the poems of Todros ben Judah (below n. 318).

316. See chapter 1 p. 16.

317. *Gan ha-Meshalim ve-ha-Hidot* [The Garden of Parables and Enigmas], David Yellin (ed.), Part I, Jerusalem 1932, poem 431, p. 183, lines 77–78.

318. Idem, pp. 164–84, poems 419–31.

319. "Fortified [= *betsurot*] stages" are perhaps stages in Paradise, in accordance with "a place was fortified [= *nitbatser*] for him in hell" (*Sanhedrin*, 110a).

320. On this line see chapter 1 p. 32.

321. Compare: Zohar, I, 99a, *Midrash ha-Ne'elam*: "He found R. Akiva dead, then he rent his clothing and tore his flesh, and the blood flowed down his body (in another version on his beard)." See in the place indicated in n. 322.

322. See Daniel Chanan Matt, *Zohar*, New York-Ramsey-Toronto 1983, p. 298.

323. See chapter 1, pp. 26–30.

Chapter 3

1. Some examples of this may be found in the article by I. Tishby, *Kudsha-berikh-hu Orayta ve-Yisrael kola had* (Hebrew), KS 50 (1975), pp. 668–74.

2. Nevertheless threefold formulations are also found in early Hebrew literature and these influenced the Zohar as well. I refer specifically to the striking examples found in *Midrash Otiyyot de-Rabbi Akiva*, which is utilized quite extensively by the author of the Zohar. But even this text itself is not entirely free of Christian influence (see below n. 72). I have found the following threefold formulations in *Otiyyot de-Rabbi Akiva* (in A. Wertheimer's *Batei Midrashot*, B, Jerusalem 1955, p. 303): "The Holy One Blessed be He is called one and his name is proclaimed with threefold letters. And wherefore is the Holy One Blessed Be He one and his name and his praise are only called before him in a threefold formulation? As it is written (Deut. vi; 4): 'Hear o Israel the Lord our God the Lord is One' [this verse will be dealt with below in my discussion of the Zohar], behold his name is threefold; 'the Lord, the Lord God, merciful' (Ex. xxxiv; 6), behold his name is threefold. 'God of gods and Lord of lords' [Deut. x; 17; here, I think, the verse should be completed: 'a great God, a mighty and a terrible', three aspects determined in daily prayers, as pronounced by Moses, which must not be added to or detracted from, according to the Gemara, Rosh Hashana 32a], behold this is threefold. And wherefore are only threefold praises pronounced before Him? As it is written [Isa. vi; 3; on the use of this verse for these purposes, see below n. 8]: 'Holy, holy, holy, is the Lord of hosts', behold this is threefold...."

In another place in this midrash we found an even more striking threefold formulation (in place of the parallel to p. 404 in the Wertheimer edition): "For all the unity (or unification) of the Holy One Blessed be He is in three." While this formulation does not exist in the printed version (it may have been omitted in most versions because of its Christian connotation), it does appear in a manuscript version at the New York Rabbinical Academy, Mic. 1833 (at the Institute for Manuscript Photocopies in Jerusalem: 10931).

3. The English translation is based on *The Zohar*, transl. H. Sperling and M. Simon, 5 vols. London: Soncino, 1931–49, III,134.

4. This passage is not part of the *Ra'aya Meheimana*, as is indicated in the printed editions, but from the section of *Pikkudin*, written by the author of the main text. See E. Gottlieb, "The *Pikkudin* Passages in the Zohar" (Hebrew), in his *Mehkarim be-Sifrut ha-Kabbala*, Tel Aviv 1976, pp. 215–30.

5. In other words, even though one who recites the *Shema'* says *ehad* (one) at the end of the verse, it nevertheless contains three divine names—a fact that cannot be lightly ignored.

6. This is an allusion to a mystical technique of rolling ones eyes about when they are closed, by which one sees a medley of colors indicating the

unity of the different *sefirot* (divine emanations). This technique is mentioned a number of times in the Zohar (for example, in I, 42a). For a detailed discussion of this, see my "Perakim be-Milon Sefer ha-Zohar" ([Hebrew] Sections of the Zohar Lexicon) (doctoral thesis presented to the Hebrew University, Jerusalem 1977), pp. 291–93, 316–317.

7. In his book, *The Wisdom of the Zohar*, Oxford University Press, 1989 [translated from the Hebrew by David Goldstein], p. III:973. There he also notes the passage in Zohar III,162a, in which the threefold unity is mentioned in the form of a riddle asked by a heavenly voice, underscoring the significance of the issue and its paradoxical nature. "They are two and one is joined to them and when they become three they are one." The solution is: "The two are the names in the *Shema'*, namely Adonai Adonai; Eloheinu is joined to them and it is the seal of the signet, truth, and when they are joined together they are one in a single unification."

The expression "the seal of the signet, truth" alludes to the talmudic passage (Shabbat 55a): "The Holy One Blessed be He's seal is truth." On the possible relationships of this talmudic passage and the Christian ideas (the symbol of the cross and the trinity), see below, end of n. 56. See further A. Jellinek, "Christlicher Einfluss auf die Kabbala," *Der Orient* 12, Leipzig 1851, pp. 580–83. Jellinek also quotes there trinitarian passages from Moses de Leon's *Shekel ha-Kodesh*.

8. R. Martini, *Pugio Fidei*, Leipzig 1687, III:1:3, p. 548 (439). The trinity is also proven there from the verse of the *Kedusha* (i.e., doxology—"Holy Holy Holy"—Isa. vi; 3). The Zohar also attaches trinitarian meaning to this verse (although not for the same purpose): see, for example, Zohar, III, 143b (in the *Idra Rabba*); III, 297a; and the quotation below from the *Shekel ha-Kodesh*. The tripartite formulation from *Midrash Otiyyot de-Rabbi Akiva* (see n. 2) cited above, is also based on this verse, to which were then added others, including the *Shema'*.

9. London 1911, p. 131.

10. The term *hitorerut* is used frequently in the Hebrew writings of R. Moses de Leon as well as appearing in the Aramaic of the Zohar, in such phrases as "the friends awakened" (i.e., were aroused spritually).

11. Earlier in the same work, in the chapter entitled *Sha'ar Helek ha-Yihud*, esp. pp. 99, 104.

12. The use of the term *nishlal* here is unclear. It may refer to that which negates multiplicity, like the negative attributes of the philosophers, or it may be used in the sense of: "naked, without covering" (as in *sholal*, Mic. i; 8), here meaning "simple, unique."

13. Based on Isa. lix; 15.

14. In one of Moses de Leon's explanations of the paradoxical unity of the three upper *sefirot (Hokhma, Bina, Da'at)*, he states: "God is one and is

not three except from our vantage point" (*Shekel ha-Kodesh*, op.cit., p. 132). R. Azriel of Gerona explained the distinction between these three elements in an identical manner (apparently borrowed from the doctrine of the divine attributes found in medieval Jewish philosophy—see Maimonides' *Guide to the Perplexed*, I :61). In his *Perush ha-Aggadot*, Tishby (ed.), Jerusalem 1945, p. 84, he states: "Wisdom, intuition and knowledge are separate qualities only insofar as finite beings perceive them."

15. In the source in *Pirkei de-Rabbi Eliezer*, the text reads "understanding" (*tevuna*) and not "intuition" (*bina*), following the Hebrew wording in Prov. iii; 19 and Ex. xxxi; 3. Moses de Leon apparently chose the term *bina* because of its use in Kabbalistic literature. This section from *Pirkei de-Rabbi Eliezer* is used frequently in the Zohar, and for similar purposes. See, e.g., Zohar, II,14b (where the word *tevuna* is used as in the original. The section belongs to *Midrash ha-Ne'elam*). This section from Pirkei de-Rabbi Eliezer is also alluded to at the beginning of *Idra Rabba* (III,127b–128a), where a meeting of ten companions is described, representing the ten *sefirot* (which, according to the Zohar, are identical with the *asara ma'amarot* [ten sections] of *Pirkei de-Rabbi Eliezer*). Three of the companions (R. Simeon b. Yohai, his son R. Eleazar, and R. Abba) include all of them (they are called *klala de-kula*), and undoubtedly they symbolize *hokhma, tevuna*, and *da'at*. The many implications of this passage are discussed at length in the section on "The Messiah of the Zohar—The Messianic Image of Simeon bar Yohai" [below: "The Messiah"], p. 21. Cf. below, n. 24.

16. In his article, "The Kabbalistic Doctrine in the Christological Teaching of Abner of Burgos" (Hebrew), *Tarbiz*, 27, 1958, p. 281. See below n. 29. Incidentally, a similar trinity, based upon Kabbalistic speculation on lovingkindness, judgment, and mercy (*hesed, din, rahamim*) is found in the writings of a Christian polemicist, quoted in *Sefer Nitahon Yashan* (from the twelfth-thirteenth century), M. Breuer (ed.), Ramat Gan 1978, p. 29. See the editor's note there, and below n. 57.

17. In his article, "Zur Geschichte der Anfange der christlichen Kabbala," *Essays Presented to Leo Baeck*, London 1954, p. 183.

18. The Wisdom of the Zohar (op. cit., n. 6), n. 279.

19. *Spiritus sanctus* in the Latin. However this formulation (as noted by Scholem, op. cit., n. 17) is only quoted by Galatinus. In another version of the text, one finds the variant *Spiritus almus*, meaning "the spirit which nurtures." He may have been acquainted with the Aramaic version, *Ruha de-kelila kolla*—"the spirit which includes all", and this version was distorted by him or a previous editor to *kalkala*—"which nurtures." Possibly the term "Holy Spirit" is not a mistake or Christological "correction" (see below). The phrase in its entirety reads: "Adonai [i.e., the last Adonai in the verse of the *Shema'*], id est deus, hic est Spiritus sanctus qui a duabus procedit, et vocatur mensura vocis."

20. Perhaps his version came about through a mistaken reading of kolla (with the Hebrew letter "kof" = voice) for kolla (with the Hebrew letter "kaf" = all), and the version before him was *etpashtuta de-kholla* (emanation of everything). Compare the commentary on the third name of the tripartite unity in *Shekel ha-Kodesh* (op. cit., n. 13), p. 134: "God, the mystery of knowledge includes the mystery of the emanation. . .for 'Knowledge' includes all the seven lower *sefirot*." This version (if Heredia was familiar with it) appears to be genuine, being corroborated by a parallel in the writings of the author of the Zohar; and no medieval man would have dreamed of using it to forge Zohar passages.

21. As in *Shekel ha-Kodesh*, op.cit., pp. 50, 104, 118.

22. See, e.g., Zohar, I, 50b. Cf. G. Scholem, "Two Tractates by R. Moses de Leon" (Hebrew), *Kovetz al Yad* 8 (18) (1976), pp. 335, 343, 370, 375, 376.

23. *Ibid.*, p. 343.

24. Here, the author is more specific in distinguishing between "voice" (*kol*—symbolizing the *sefira* of *Tiferet* or *Da'at*) and "speech" (*dibbur*), symbolizing *Malkhut*, referred to as "the Holy Spirit." However, on p. 370 he refers to *Malkhut* as an "echo of a voice" (*bat-kol*) and not as itself a voice. (*Bat-kol* serves a similar purpose to the "Holy Spirit," but is normally on a lower level. See BT Yoma 9a: "When the latter prophets, Hagai, Zechariah and Malakhi died, the Holy Spirit disappeared from Israel, but the *bat-kol* was still used.") The "voice" (which is heard, not the inner voice which alludes to the *sefira* of *Bina*) generally denotes the *sefira* of *Tiferet* (or *Da'at*), as noted in the explanation of the trinity cited above (note 15, and see also Zohar, III, 38b). We have, however, also found tripartite formulations in the Zohar, in which the third element is the *sefira* of *Malkhut*. See for instance the symbolism of the three meals eaten on the Sabbath and of the three countenances in the *Idrot*. We likewise found a similar homily on the verse *Shema'* in *Zohar Hadash*, Mosad ha-Rav Kook (ed.), Jerusalem 1978, p. 56d.

25. Heredia cites this passage in the name of R. Yiba and not of R. Yissa, as it is in the printed editions of the Zohar. Recanati in his commentary on the Torah, Deut. vi, 4, also quotes the passage from R. Yiba.

26. See G. Scholem, "A New Passage from the *Midrash ha-Ne'elam* of the Zohar" (Hebrew), *Louis Ginzberg Jubilee Volume* (Hebrew Volume), New York 1946, p. 425ff. In the section, "The Messiah," p. 41, n. 128, I pointed out that even the printed text of the Zohar includes within it different editions of the same work.

27. This is not part of the passage, but a translation of the Hebrew word *Eloheinu*.

28. The version in the Zohar (III, 263a) is: "Our God—depth of rivers and springs." It should be noted however that the expression "the springs

of wisdom" also exists in the Zohar (e.g., I, 117a). The symbols of the river and the spring correspond to the *sefira* of *Bina* (see n. 29), which is alluded to here. This identification is demonstrated both from the course of the extant Zohar homily, and from the parallels above (see above n. 15). Heredia's version also continues with a homily on the name *bina*—see n. 29. From this place onwards there is no parallel between the accepted Zohar version (III, 263a) and the section that Heredia cites in Latin.

29. The word *bina* alluded to here (see n. 28) is associated in the Zohar with *ben* (son), as it is by Abner of Burgos in its Christian connotation (above n. 16). This homily exists in Zohar III, 290a–b (and is noted by Breuer, above n. 16) and in Zohar, II, 123b (both sections belong to the *Idrot*). In addition to the relationship between *bina* and *ben*, both sections contain a description of *bina* in the likeness of a river and spring, just as in Heredia's article. It should be noted, however, that in both the aforesaid sections from the *Idrot* the actual *sefira* of *Bina* is not called *ben*; however, the letters *bet* (ב) and *nun* (נ) contained in it allude to the "son" (*ben*) born from it (i.e., *Tif'eret* or the Small Countenance) and *Bina* is his mother.

30. Verse 9.

31. It follows from many passages in the Zohar that the generation of the Messiah to whom R. Simeon bar Yohai refers in saying that at that time it will be permitted to divulge the mysteries of the Torah is none other than that of Moses de Leon, the true author of the Zohar, to whom these words—uttered at the beginning of the exile, and whose hidden meaning sustained the Jewish people throughout their exile—were purportedly revealed. I discussed this subject at length in the section "The Messiah."

32. *Botsina Kadisha*, the usual designation for R. Simeon bar Yohai. On this term, see my dissertation (op. cit., n. 6), pp. 139–40.

33. *Le-shimusha*—i.e., *tashmish*, sexual intercourse.

34. Gen. ii; 4.

35. Genesis Rabba xii; 9.

36. *Ammuda* (pillar)—the *sefira* of *Yesod*, according to the Kabbalistic interpretation (beginning with *Sefer ha-Bahir*, R. Margoliouth (ed.), Jerusalem 1978, para. 102) of the saying in BT Haggigah 12b: "The world stands upon one pillar, and the Tsaddik is its name, as it is written (Proverbs x; 25), 'The righteous (*tsaddik*) is the foundation of the world.'" These ideas became interchangeable in Kabbalistic literature with the flesh and blood *tsaddik* and it is difficult to differentiate between them. In the Zohar passage cited here, which deals with Abraham, the term *ammud* is also one of the qualities attributed to Abraham—"the pillar of the world" (Exodus Rabba ii, and in Maimonides' *Mishneh Torah, Hilkhot Avodat Kokhavim*, 1:2). See also in my dissertation (op. cit., n. 6), pp. 371–374. The pillar is of course identified with

the male sexual organ—the specific symbol of the *sefira* of *Yesod*—and thus connected with the word *eiver* (organ) which is spelled with the letters of the word *bara* (created) in reverse order, which are also the opening letters of the name Abraham. The Zohar homily subsequently discusses the addition of the letter *heh* to Abraham's name and his circumcision. The two events also refer to the male sexual organ and procreativity (according to the talmudic sages: "Abram does not procreate, Abraham procreates"; in Genesis Rabba xliv; 12, Theodor edition, an alternative version is cited. It is also cited in Zohar, I, 90b). On Abraham as a Kabbalistic symbol and his relation to *Yesod*, see below, n. 42.

37. Genesis Rabba iii; 8.

38. Genesis Rabba xii; 15. Both here and in the Zohar passage, the repair of the condition is alluded to in the same verse, Gen. ii; 4.

39. The Targum Yerushalmi translates the word *bereshit* in Gen. i; 1 as "with wisdom."

40. See, for example, the beginning of *Midrash Aggada*, Buber (ed.), Vienna 1894. There the letters of the word *bereshit* are also discussed in various other combinations.

41. Compare the description in Zohar, II, 103a of the *sitra ahra* (other [i.e., sinister] side) as unable to procreate. See below n. 47.

42. Abraham's main attribute is *hesed* (loving-kindness) which is, however, realized and revealed in the *sefira* of *Yesod*. For this reason Abraham had to be circumcised for his self-completion (see Zohar, III, 142a, in the *Idra Rabba*). See above n. 36.

43. This acknowledgement that the *bara* preceding Abraham is the "son" reminds one of Jesus' (the Christian "son") statement in John ix; 48: "Before Abraham was born, I am." Compare also the Kabbalistic thesis of Picco della Mirandelo based on this verse, on which see H. Wirszubski, *Mekubal Notsri Koreh ba-Torah* ([Hebrew] *A Christian Kabbalist Reads the Torah*) Jerusalem 1977 pp. 19–21.

44. P. 531. A Christological interpretation along these lines was also prevalent in later periods. See the sixteenth-century work by Yair ben Shabbetai, *Herev Pifiyyot*, Jerusalem 1958, 3rd question, p. 18. See also the editor's note there by Y. Rosenthal, which refers to the words of Nicholas de Lyra (thirteenth-fourteenth cent.) and Joshua Lork (fifteenth cent.). Cf. G. Scholem (op. cit., n. 16), p. 187, who cites a similar interpretation in the writings of Galatinus (fifteenth-sixteenth cent.).

45. Ed. Margolioth, sec. 84–86. This passage was also cited by R. Azriel in his *Perush ha-Aggadot* (see n. 14), p. 50, in connection with the idea of redemption.

46. As mentioned above, the period of *tohu* (chaos) is connected with the "kings who ruled in Edom before there ruled a king in Israel" (Gen. xxxvi; 31), which is applied to the Christian rule during Israel's exile (usually referred to as "the Kingdom of Edom"), until "a king reigns in Israel" (i.e., the messianic ruler). I discussed this at length in the section on "The Messiah", pp. 00.

47. On this, see the Zohar passage mentioned above, n. 41, in which one who fails to fulfill the commandment "be fruitful and multiply" is severely criticized. This sin is the cause of all evil, in the view of the author of the Zohar, causing great harm in the supernal realms. He who does not procreate is as though he were devoted to "an other god," the eunuch who does not beget (the "other side" and perhaps also the god of Christian monastic life? Compare Zohar, I, 204b where gentile rule is referred to as "other" and their god as "the other god"). See further, n. 72.

48. The various forms taken by this idea (which lowers the position of the sealed *mem* from the *sefira* of *Bina* to that of *Malkhut*) in Lurianic Kabbala and afterwards in the Sabbateian movement, are discussed at length in my article, "*Tsaddik Yesod Olam*—A Sabbatean Myth" (Hebrew), *Da'at* 1 (1978), pp. 103-5. Subsequently, I have found other sources for the idea which I developed there, which on the contrary state that the letter *mem* will be sealed by the Messiah and will become concealed. See, for example, the interpretation which sees the closed *mem* in Isaiah ix; 6 as the correction of the open *mem* at the end of the word alluding to the destruction of the walls of Jerusalem (Neh. ii; 13): "the walls of Jerusalem which were (הם) broken down." This theme (which, as noted in the article cited above, is alluded to in R. Nathan Shapira's *Sefer Tuv ha-Arets*, and which was greatly developed in Sabbateianism) is also found in *Sefer Herev Pifiyyot* (above n. 44), p. 19. See also editor's note there.

49. For a full discussion of the messianic conceptions associated with the *sefira* of *Yesod* in the Zohar (and in the circle of thirteenth-century Castillian Kabbalists), see the section, "The Messiah", pp. 48–52. On this theme in later Kabbala, see my article "*Tsaddik....*" (op. cit.), esp. pp. 77–78.

50. This idea, which is extremely widespread in the Zohar and in the Kabbala generally, is discussed at length in the section, "The Messiah...", pp. 00. It is also related with the idea of the new Torah to be revealed in the messianic future—on which see below, n. 73.

51. Rosh Hashana 32a: "R. Yohanan said the ten verses of *Malkhiyot*, *Zikhronot* and *Shofarot* are parallel to ten statements with which the world was created. What are they? And he said, and he said in the first chapter of Genesis were nine!? 'In the beginning' (*bereshit*), likewise is a statement, as it is written (Ps. xxxiii; 6): 'By the word of the Lord were the heavens made.' " It is very difficult to interpret and maintain, as R. Yohanan does, that the word "in the beginning" means "and he said", and I think that here,

in the Gemara, there is already an allusion to the philosophy of the *logos* ("word"), through which the heavens were created. There may even be indirect influence here from John's Gospel, in which it is said of the *logos* (i; 3): "Everything was made by it." It should however be noted that the philosophy of the *logos*, associated with the word *bereshit* and *hokhma*, is not necessarily Christian. It has its roots, as is known, in early theological works (in which even the Book of Proverbs played a part) and in Philo's philosophy. It also originates in the beginning of Midrash Genesis Rabba. Sa'adia Gaon (*Emunot ve-Deot*, 2:6) saw in this philosophy, which links the *logos* to *bereshit* and to *hokhma*, a clearly Christian philosophy. On the relationship between the *logos*, the son, *hokhma*, the word *bereshit*, see also *Pugio Fidei* (op. cit., n. 8), p. 629.

52. That is, "On the Nature of Things," London 1863, ed. Thomas Wright.

53. See R. Loewe, "Alexander Neckam's Knowledge of Hebrew," *Medieval and Renaissance Studies* 4, 1958, pp. 17–28.

54. This already follows from the title of the first chapter of his book: "Reductio principii Johannis ad initium Geneseos"—i.e., Matching the beginning (or, principle) of the Gospel of John with the opening of the Book of Genesis.

55. *Ibid.* (op. cit., n. 51), p. 4. Jesus is included in the word *bereshit* also according to the verse in Psalms cxix; 160: "Your word is true from the beginning (*rosh*)". Jesus is *rosh*, which is identical with *reshit* (Gen. i; 1) (in the Vulgate, according to the Septuagint, the two words are translated by the same Latin word: *principium*. Incidentally, the Vulgate, according to the Hebrew, translates the word in Psalms as *caput*); he is also "word" (*davar = logos*), and is also called "truth" (see n. 56)—see op.cit., p. 7.

56. Ibid., p. 9. As regards the letter *tav* indicating the secret of the cross ("*Thau quae crucis exprimit mysterium*) a note was added at the bottom of the page (there were similar notes in the manuscript of the book, and in his preface [p. 77], the editor conjectures that they may have been inscribed by the author—Alexander Neckam). According to the note, only the Greek letter *Thau* is in the form of the cross, and the Hebrew *tav* is in the form of the pillory (*patibulum*). However, he then notes that many Jews think that the form of the Hebrew *tav* was changed at one point to another form. Obviously the author was acquainted with this tradition of the changing of early Hebrew writing (as, for instance, in Sanhedrin 21b) not from a Jewish source, but from the writings of the Church Father Origenes, who heard it from a Judeo-Christian: "A third Jew one of those who believe in Christ said the form of the letter Taw in the old [Hebrew] script resembles the cross." See S. Lieberman, *Greek in Jewish Palestine*, New York 1942, pp. 187–88. (Incidentally, the marginal note in Neckam's book, ibid., also cites another motif associated with the letter tav, which is also from the writings of the Church Fathers. He maintains that the Hebrews painted this sign on their

doorposts prior to the exodus from Egypt. For relevant sources, see Lieberman, op. cit., p. 191, n. 31). Neckam himself (in the event that someone else wrote the notes) also infers that this theme originated in the literature of the Church Fathers, when he says that this secret *in multis locis a sanctis declaratur*; and the expression *a sanctis* can only allude to the Christian saints. Certainly it appears that medieval Jewry was acquainted with the writings of the Church Fathers on this theme (see Lieberman, op. cit., p. 191). In any case, the form of the ancient letter *tav* and its likeness to the cross was known in early Christianity (apparently primarily in Judeo-Christianity), and served as a basis (see Lieberman, op. cit., pp. 185–91) for the story of the *tav* of blood (which was in the form of a cross, the form of the ancient letter *tav*) written on the foreheads of the righteous to seal them for life, and the *tav* of ink written on the foreheads of the wicked to seal them for death (expanding on Ezekiel ix; 4). The Talmud took this story from the Christians, but with the roles of the ink and the blood reversed. In relation to Lieberman's description, I will merely add that he failed to mention the most detailed Jewish version of this story, which is in the *Midrash Otiyot de-R. Akiva* (op. cit., n. 2), pp. 396–97. In one of the manuscripts of this midrash (Vatican ms. 228; 285 in the Institute for Manuscript Photocopies at the National Library in Jerusalem) I found that the *tav* of blood was also placed on the foreheads of the righteous (as well as on the foreheads of the wicked), and this is perhaps a transition stage between the Christian version and the Jewish version (on the connection between this midrash and Christianity, see below n. 73).

The origin of the well-known saying "God's seal is truth" may also be Judeo-Christian, and it may be connected with the Christian symbol of the *tav* as a cross, and as a seal on the forehead. The saying is found in the Gemara (*Shabbat* 55a), at the end of the aforesaid story (concerning Ezekiel's *tav* on the foreheads of the righteous, which is, as already shown, of Christian origin.) In the Gemara version too, the letter *tav* is the basis of God's seal, and not the entire word *emet* (truth), and in this respect the saying is quoted ("*tav* is the end of God's seal, as R. Hanina said: "God's seal is truth'"). The previous homily dealt only with the letter *tav*, which is mentioned in Ezekiel as the seal on the forehead of the righteous. Certainly a whole word, such as *emet*, is not appropriate for a seal, hence a simple form such as that of the letter *tav* is required, and particularly in its ancient form—the form of the cross. This of course is better suited to Christianity, since nothing is more apt for the seal of the god of the Christians than the form of the cross. Furthermore, *emet* as "the seal of God" is expounded by the talmudic sages (Midrash Song of Songs Rabba, on Song of Songs 1; 9: "To a company of horses. . . ." See also JT, Sanhedrin 1:1, and BT, Shabbat 104a, and Rashi's commentary there), as follows: "*Emet* (אמת)—*aleph* (א) is the first letter of the alphabet, *mem* (מ) is in the middle, *tav* (ת) is the last letter. As it is said [Is. 44; 6]: "I am the first, and I am the last, and beside me there is no God.'" The parallel between the idea contained in the verse from Isaiah and letters of the alphabet appears for the first time in the New Testament (Revelation of John, i; 8): "I am the *aleph* and the *tav* (in Greek the *alpha* and the *omega*) says the Lord God, and the present and the past and the future." The three tenses (past, present, and future, and perhaps the middle letter of the alphabet should be mentioned here) may have also been given a trinitarian interpretation (there is perhaps a similar mention in the Zohar—see above n. 7), and the Jewish homily may have become anti-trinitarian (in Song of Songs Rabba, immediately after the passage cited above): "I am the first—I received my kingdom from no other; and I am the last—I transmit it to no other since it is not of this world; and beside me there is no God—there is no second god." When considering the possibility that this saying might be of Christian origin, it should also be remembered that Jesus is sometimes called *emet* (see n. 55). Moreover, this *emet* likewise refers to the gnostic Christian *aletheia* (= truth), which is also composed of the letters of the alphabet, and is parallel to the theme of *Shi'ur Komah* in *Otiyyot de-R. Akiva* (see G. Scholem, *Pirkei Yesod be-Havanat ha-Kabala u-Smaleha,* Jerusalem 1976, p. 163; also M. Idel, "The World of Angels in Human Form" (Hebrew) in *Studies in Jewish Mysticism, Philosophy and Ethical Literature* presented to I. Tishby, Jerusalem 1986 (= Jerusalem Studies in Jewish Thought, vol. 3 [1984], n.5); M. Idel, *Golem,* State University of New York Press 1990, pp. 306–13. In this context, I should like to comment on the saying: "Lie has no legs," which I have found in none of the ancient midrashim other than *Otiyot de-R. Akiva* (pp. 397, 404. A similar expression exists in Gemara, Shabbat 104a: "Truth stands, a lie does not stand," and the interpretation is given there immediately after the discussion of the scattering of the letters "EMeT" in contrast to the bringing together of the letters "SHeKeR" [see preceding paragraph]; it is possible that the saying is also based on this, and not only on the graphic form of the letters ר ק ש (*sheker*) and ת מ א (*emet*) as explicitly stated there). From *Otiyyot de-R. Akiva,* the saying was introduced into the Zohar and into medieval literature. It is interesting to note, nonetheless, that in *Sefer Nitsahon Yashan* (op. cit., n. 16), para. 266, the Christians use the axiom under discussion as anti-Jewish slander.

57. Such as the sentence *Ashit bat be-ashrei* which in his opinion refers to the Virgin Mary (the presence of the word *ashrei* within the letters of *Bereshit* is also mentioned in *Tikkunei Zohar,* sec. 13, while *bat* is found there at the beginning of sec. 19). This method of dividing the word *bereshit* into its separate components is already found in the Midrash Aggada (op. cit., n. 40), and is a set feature of the *Tikkunei Zohar.* (It is also present in R. Isaac ibn Latif. See Wilensky [below n. 59], p. 216).

An interpretation particularly close to that of Neckam's is found in *Sefer ha-Tseruf* (a work contemporary with the Zohar), a Latin translation of which was known to Picco della Mirandola, who himself engaged in such combinations. See H. Wirszubski, *Shelosha Perakim be-Toledot ha-Kabbala ha-Notsrit ([Hebrew] Three Chapters in the History of Christian Kabbala),* Jerusalem 1975, p. 24. In the appendix (p. 53–55), the Hebrew source of the relevant section from *Sefer ha-Tseruf* is printed (as noted there, Moshe Idel copied it at H. Wirszubski's request). In this passage from *Sefer ha-Tseruf* we found several combinations similar to those of Neckam. *Sefer ha-Tseruf* splits the word *bereshit* into the words *av yar* (in his opinion this should be interpreted as *abir* and *shit*, and the word *shit* is also found in the letters *bereshit* by Neckam. Both authors interpret it as derived from the verb שׂ י ת = put. The word *esh* (fire) is also found in both these sources: for Neckam it symbolizes the Holy Spirit, while in *Sefer ha-Tseruf* it symbolizes the Torah. (The word *bereshit* is split up into *berit esh* [covenant of fire] in *Midrash ha-Ne'elam* in Zohar Hadash, Mosad ha-Rav Kook [ed.], p 4d, and in *Tikkunei Zohar*, at the beginning of sec. 23). The word *yesh* is expounded on in both works from the letters of *bereshit* as is the word *bar* meaning *ben* (son). The author of *Sefer ha-Tseruf* interprets the latter word not as Jesus but as God; such an interpretation was obviously designed to contradict the Christians, but he certainly heard the actual homily from a Christian source, as he himself infers (ibid, p. 55): "And many nations erred in their interpretation of the 'son.' " Nonetheless, despite the Christian source of *Sefer ha-Tseruf*, and despite the similarity of certain details with Neckam's work, I do not think that there can be any direct literary link between the two works. (Incidentally, it was my friend Dr. M. Idel who first remarked on the similarity between the two compositions, after seeing several passages from Neckam's work reproduced in R. Loewe's article [above n. 53]. After the article was brought to my attention by Dr. Idel, I began to study Neckam's book and to discover parallels with the Zohar.) I have not found any relation or similarity between *Sefer ha-Tseruf* and the Zohar either. Another Christian interpretation, which finds an allusion to the "trinity" in the letters of the word *bereshit*, is quoted at the beginning of *Sefer Nitsahon Yashan* (op. cit., n. 16). The Christian author notes that he found in the first three letters of the word *bereshit* (i.e., *bara*) the initials of the words *ben* (= son), *ruach* (= spirit), and *av* (= father).

58. These statements of the Church Fathers are collected in an article in the journal *La France Franciscaine*, 12 (1929), pp. 529–37. I wish to thank Fr. Pierre Lenhardt for calling my attention to this article.

59. *Adonai Eloheinu Adonai* in this sentence is also parallel to "I shall be as I shall be" (Ex. iii; 14), interpreted several lines earlier.

60. Such an interpretation is found among all the disciples of R. Isaac the Blind and in Nahmanides. See G. Scholem (*Major Trends in Jewish Mysticism*, New York 1961, p. 55, n. 402. See, e.g., *Ma'arekhet ha-Elohut*, Mantua 1558, chap. 7, pp. 82b–83a, and in Isaac Ibn Latif, *Sha'ar ha-Shamayim*. See Sara O. Heller-Wilensky, "Isaac Ibn Latif—Philosopher or Kabbalist?," in A. Altmann (ed.), *Jewish Medieval and Renaissance Studies*, Cambridge, Mass., 1967, n. 215. Cf. above, n. 57.

61. The letter *nun* is the *Shekhina*, the feminine, while the letter *yod* represents the masculine *sefira* of *Yesod* (which is the "holy covenant", i.e., the covenant of circumcision). From the coupling of these two (as well as from their graphic combination) the letter *tsadi* is produced. However, this coupling and union is not complete, as is explained subsequently.

62. According to Berakhot 61a. The sages' words in the Talmud are borrowed from Plato's *Symposium* and here (in the Zohar) they are interpreted symbolically.

63. According to Moses Cordovero's *Or Yakar* (I, Jerusalem, 1962), p. 23: *lantra* (to guard) rather than *lansra* (to saw).

64. Another version brought by Cordovero (op. cit.) is: *gappin gappin* = organs organs, rather than *appin-be-appin* = face to face.

65. In the section, "The Messiah," pp. 00. In Sabbateianism, discussions of the *tsadi* in the Zohar are explained as referring to Shabbetai Tsvi. Cf. my article, "A Messianic Treatise by R. Wolf the son of R. Jonathan Eybeschuetz" (Hebrew), KS 57 (1982), p. 156, n. 49–50.

66. Cf. Zohar II, 186b.

67. In the section, "The Messiah", I pointed out several other figures who were also incorporated into the Zohar's literary image of R. Simeon b. Yohai. These figures include Jews and non-Jews alike such as: R. Eliezer the Great, R. Akiba, Socrates, Simon Magus, and Simeon Stylites. Now Jesus must be added to the list. I explained at length there why the author of the Zohar chose R. Simeon b. Yohai to be the hero of his story and I showed that the persona of the historical R. Simeon b. Yohai predominated in the creation of the literary image of R. Simeon b. Yohai in the Zohar.

68. In the Zohar we have found R. Simeon b. Yohai described as the son of God in the technical and precise sense of the concept (and not only as an appellation of a mystical character, beloved and intimate in his relation with God, as was the case with several figures such as R. Hanina b. Dosa and Honi ha-Me'aggel). See Zohar, III, 61b: "All the truly virtuous before they come into the world are prepared above and are called by their names. And R. Simeon b. Yohai from the first day of Creation was stationed before the Holy One Blessed be He, and God called him by his name. Happy is his portion, as it is written [Proverbs xxiii; 25]: 'Your father and your mother shall be glad'—your father, this is God, and your mother, this is Knesset Israel." The last phrase is taken from the Gemara (Berakhot 35b), but there it is simply general rhetoric. Various midrashic sources can also be found for other elements of this sentence, which deal with the preexistence of the souls of the righteous, etc. The general sense of the passage we are discussing, however, is quite different, as shown by the contrast expressed in it between R. Simeon b. Yohai and between the other "truly virtuous," and in the according of an exclusive status to R. Simeon b. Yohai.

The description of R. Simeon b. Yohai as being with God on the day the world was created is reminiscent of the description of the *logos*, which is identified with Jesus, at the beginning of John's Gospel, and it seems to me that the author of the Zohar was influenced by this in his description. Very illustrative are the words of the Kabbalist cited in *Nitsotsei Orot* on the page there (this Kabbalist is R. Zevi Hirsch Horowitz. The initials מ " א

stand for his commentary on the Zohar, *Aspaklaria Hame'ira*, Furth 1776, p. 74, as Dr. Zeev Gries has shown me), who finds in the letters of the word *bereshit*, in Genesis i; 1, an allusion to R. Simeon b. Yohai's name (an abbreviation of *Or Torat Rabbi Shimon Bar Yohai*), just as the Christians found in these letters an allusion to Jesus, as I discussed above at length. (In this Zevi Hirsch refers to the allusion that God called R. Simeon b. Yohai by his name. However, this might very well mean the name by which the Holy One called R. Simeon b. Yohai, just as the other righteous "are called by names" before they come to the world, in accordance with the beginning of the passage. Nonetheless, what is unique about R. Simeon b. Yohai is that God himself called R. Simeon b. Yohai that name. The meaning may also be that the Holy One called his own name, i.e., the name of God, over R. Simeon b. Yohai. This also has parallels in the Zohar; see R. Margaliouth's note in *Nitsotsei Zohar*, which is in the margin of the Zohar in his edition, II, 35a; some of the parallels indicated by Rabbi Margaliouth there are valid, if we disregard the general air of vagueness prevailing in all this note. On the subject of the divine status of R. Simeon b. Yohai in the Zohar, see also II, 35a, " 'The face of the Lord' (Ex. xxxiv; 23)—this is R. Simeon b. Yohai." Furthermore, the description at the end of *Idra Zuta* (Zohar, III, 296b) of the erotic union of the divine "Yesod" with the *Shekhina* gives the clear impression that R. Simeon b. Yohai is identified mythically with the *sefira* of *Yesod*; i.e., he is the mate, as though he is the incarnation of this *sefira* (I discussed this issue at length in the section, "The Messiah").

69. In the passage discussed above, whose source is in Zohar, I, 3b, i.e., just one page after our passage. For another parallel, see II, 35a.

70. See, for example, Zohar, III, 135b (which is part of *Idra Rabba*).

71. On the subject of the *Matkela* see my work (op.cit., n. 6), pp. 329–30. There, I discussed the elements of the idea and its development, and even its origins (primarily in the writings of Isaac Sagi Nihor).

72. Cf. above n. 47.

73. The evidence is as follows: (a) The various versions of the Trinity—see above n. 2; (b) The subject of the letter *Tav*—see above n. 56; (c) The subject of Jesus which I explain here; (d) The emphasis on the idea of the New Torah to be revealed by the Messiah. See ibid., p. 346: "The Holy One entrusted two religions to Israel on Mount Sinai, one to Israel and one to the Messiah"; and pp. 367–68: "And the Holy One expounds before you [the righteous in the Garden of Eden] meanings of the new Torah which the Holy One will give to you through the Messiah." This idea also exists in other places, but is little developed (see Ecclesiastes Rabba on Eccles. xi; 8: "The Torah that a man learnt in this world is vanity before the Torah of the Messiah"). Incidentally, this idea is developed again in the Zohar (e.g., III, 130b—which belongs to *Idra Rabba*, and III, 164b), and see above n. 50. My colleague, M. Idel, agrees with me on this issue (some of the above became clear for me

through conversations with him), and he suggests the following additional proofs: (e) Poverty is idealized in *Otiyyot de-R. Akiva* (e.g., p. 361) and thus this midrash is perhaps close in spirit to the Jewish-Christian sect of the Ebionites. (Incidentally, we also found a similar attitude to poverty in the philosophy of the *Tanna de-Vei Eliyahu*, and in the *Kuzari*, and above all in *Tikkunei Zohar* which sees poverty as vital in mysticism. On this, see my work [op. cit., n. 6], p. 48). (f) Numerous passages in *Otiyyot de-R. Akiva* are similar to *Shi'ur Komah* (e.g., p. 370). Such speculations (according to M. Idel) derived from circles with an affinity to Christianity.

74. This passage is found there (according to the Wertheimer edition [cf. above n. 2], pp. 396–406), but concludes before the text with which I am presently dealing, concerning the letter *tsadi*. It seems that the author of the Zohar combined different sections from this midrash in this passage (and perhaps he also had a different version of the midrash).

75. The passage is there, pp. 408–9.

76. The homily in the last sentence ("the son of your mother and not of your father") is found frequently in the polemic literature of the Middle Ages. Cf. *Nitsahon Yashan* (op. cit., n. 16), p. 65: "And of him (= Jesus) Moses said: If your brother, your own mother's son entices you in secret—this is Jesus who denied his father and said he had a mother and not a father, and that he is the son of God." And see Y. Rosenthal's article in *Mehkarim u-Mekorot*, I, Jerusalem 1967, p. 205 which brings several parallels (although he was not aware of the source in the *Midrash Otiyyot de-R. Akiva*). Rosenthal is of the opinion that the rabbis already knew of this homily and therefore they noted that Jesus was judged as an enticer (BT Sanhedrin 43a, according to the uncensored version).

I also found this subject in the polemical book, *Teshuva le-Minim*, in MS Bodleian 2284 (number 20981 in the Institute of Microfilmed Hebrew Manuscripts [below—IMHM]), p. 234: "And it is further written in the Torah of Moses: 'If your brother, your own mother's son entices you in secret', and why is it not written 'the son of your father'? So that you will know that Moses is prophesying that a son will be born in Israel, and the nations of the world will say of him that he has no father, and this is Jesus. And all that it is written in that Torah portion, they did to him and they hung him on a cabbage stalk" (the theme of the "cabbage stalk" is taken from *Das Leben Jesu*, Krauss edition, Berlin 1902, p. 45). In my opinion, *Teshuva le-Minim* is a medieval German reworking of ancient material, which came from Jews who greatly esteemed the personality of Jesus, and denied only his divinity. It should be noted that this homily ("the son of your mother and not the son of your father"), despite its anti-Christian nature (Jesus is an enticer and considered deserving of death), does admit part of the Christian claim: Moses made a prophesy about Jesus, and he is written of in the Torah. Moreover, it is written only "the son of your mother" in the Torah, and not "the son of your father," as if the Torah were admitting that Jesus has no father in Israel.

77. In several manuscripts the entire passage has been deleted. In MS Bodleian 2872 (IMHM 22762) p. 12, instead of the text there appears only, "missing in transcription." The same is true in MS Berlin Tubingen (IMHM 7364), and in MS Escorial 5 5–2c (IMHM 7364).

78. In one contrived explanation (for instance, in MS Munich No. 22, [IMHM 1169], p. 75), the letter *tsadi* is interpreted negatively: "This is an allusion to hunting, for they hunted him down because of the two heads." (Incidentally, the name "Jesus of Nazareth" was changed to "made from the belly" ([ussah mi-beten]—I do not know what this means, it may be a positive epithet in accordance with Jeremiah i; 5.) The term *tsaddik* (righteous) for Jesus is common in Christian writings, and is found already in the New Testament (see Matthew xxvii; 19,24 and parallels).

79. MS Jewish Theological Seminary (New York) mic. 1833 (IMHM 10931).

80. As follows: "Why does the letter *tsadi* have two heads? This is Jesus who was head of Israel and head of the gentiles. And why is the bottom of the *tsadi* bent? Because in the world to come he will not be resurrected and he will fall to Israel. Wherefore do we know this? As it is written: 'For your brother, your own mother's son will entice you in secret', and was not his mother from Israel and his father from Nazarene? And why does the letter *tsadi* at the end of a word stand upright. Because they took him and hanged him on the tree. And why did they sentence him to hanging? From Moses who said [Deut. xxi; 22]: 'And if a man has committed a sin worthy of death, and he is to be put to death, and you will hang him on a tree.' " This homily may well be based on a Christian homily that interpets the said verse positively; namely it is not that Jesus is worthy of death but his death must be related (from the same verb, *tala*, which also means "to hang") to Adam's sin with the tree of knowledge. (A similar homily is attributed to R. Isaac Luria on the subject of R. Moses Cordovero, but it is more apt in the case of Jesus, since the Christians posit that his death came to atone for Adam's sin.) "And why did they sentence him to death? He sinned and caused others to sin, this is why they sentenced him to hanging. Another interpretation: Why does *tsadi* have two forms? . . .", the manuscript then continues as cited above.

81. The verse continues: "And a twig shall sprout from his stock." It seems to me that the "shoot" and the "twig" are the two heads of the letter *tsadi*.

82. I did not understand this explanation.

83. MS Vatican 228 (IMHM 258).

84. Similarly, I have found several manuscripts of *Otiot de-R. Akiva* in which the transcribers infused the passage with a Kabbalistic meaning. In several manuscripts, for instance, they added the homily from *Sefer ha-*

Bahir (Margaliouth, 102) about the pillar called *tsaddik* who is the foundation
of the world (e.g., in MS Bodleian—op.cit., n. 75, just after the scribal symbol
for missing text; and in MS Munich [op.cit., n. 76], next to the passage about
Jesus).

85. Cf. the Kabbalistic commentary on the alphabet found in MS
Columbia University 893 K 12 (IMHM 20669). There (p. 144), the name of
the letter *tsadi* is derived from *tsad* (side); "They were created 'side by side' "
(i.e., male and female). According to the midrash, they are Adam and Eve,
who are the *sefirot* of *Tif'eret* and *Malkut*. The author of this manuscript was
certainly influenced by the Zohar passage under discussion; M. Idel is of the
opinion that the author is R. David b. Yehuda he-Hasid. See Idel's article in
Alei Sefer, 10, 1982, p. 30 (Hebrew).

86. See above, p. 157. This is similar to what we found in the manuscript
of *Otiot de-R. Akiva*—op.cit., n. 83ff.

87. In the commentary "Alfa Beta" in *Kovets Sifrei Stam*, I, Jerusalem
1976, p. 270.

88. Jerusalem 1978, pp. 280–302.

89. See Gershom Scholem: "Tradition and Innovation in Kabbalistic
Ritual" (op.cit., n. 56), chap. 4. See also I. Tishby (op. cit., n. 7), pp. 608–17.
And see E. Gottlieb, "The Theological and Mystical Principle of the Conception
of Man's Destiny in the Kabbala" (Hebrew) in op. cit., n. 4, pp. 29–37.

90. In contrast to the idea of the *tsaddik* who suffers for his generation,
which exists in the writings of the talmudic sages and in the Zohar (see
Shabbat 33b, Zohar, II, 53a, etc.).

91. Incidentally, we also found the opposite of this idea in the Kabbala,
whereby Israel suffers because of God's suffering, because of participation
in the grief, and particularly for rectifying and healing. This idea is not usual
in the Zohar, but its roots can be found there (in the idea of the death of the
Tsaddik so that his soul will serve as "feminine water" for the divine
coupling—see Zohar, I, 245b—I dealt with this idea at length in another section
of this work [n. 15], n. 157. On the explanation of the death of the ten martyrs,
which deals with the divine "catharsis," see Zohar, II, 254b); it is, however,
common in later Kabbala. See, for instance in Lurianic Kabbala (on the
meanings of the reading of the *Shema'*), and the idea of the death of the
sacrifice which was presented as R. Joseph Caro's personal ideal in his *Maggid
Mesharim* (in many places, and as an explicit imitation of King Solomon's
death). The idea also occupies an important place in the philosophy of R.
Nahman of Bratslav (see Y. Weiss: *Kiddush ha-Shem ve-Mitat Korban*, in
Mehkarim be-Hasidut Bratslav, Jerusalem 1975, pp. 172–78). I must add that
I have found the theme of killing for the purpose of rectification in the writings
of R. Nahman of Bratslav not only as a personal aspiration (described in
Weiss's article, above), but also as a rationalization of mass pogroms (see

Likutei Moharan 141, para. 260). Such rationalization of slaughter reached a climax during the Holocaust, in *Esh Kodesh*, a book written by R. Kalonimus Kalamish Shapira, a Hasidic rabbi, in the Warsaw Ghetto, from 1940 to 1943. I think that by this time he had no other explanation (the book was published in Jerusalem in 1960).

92. Quite frequently the Zohar transforms classical rabbinic passages into extremely anti-Christian statements. Thus, in rabbinic teaching the guardian angels of the nations of the world and their lands are actually officers of God; and while they are lower than him in status, they are not negative *per se* (see E. Urbach, *The Sages: Their Concepts and Beliefs*, Jerusalem 1979, p. 138ff). In the Zohar, however, they have generally been turned into emissaries of the *Sitra Ahra*: they themselves are called, at times, *sitrin aharanin* (e.g., Zohar, II, 33a. The use of the plural there is one of the pieces of evidence that the term "Sitra Ahra," which has its origin in the Zohar, at times served there as a technical term and a general appellation for evil forces.)

The gods of the gentiles (identified with their angels) are none other than Satan, who is called *el aher* ("a different God"—for his connection with Jesus, see above, nn. 46–47). The soul of the gentiles has its origin in this god (just as the soul of Israel is part of a transcendant god), and that is why the gentile soul is impure (Zohar, I, 47a) and why the gentiles are a cause of impurity so long as their souls are in their bodies (Zohar, I, 139a).

The change that the Zohar makes in the spirit of rabbinic teaching is especially striking in the discussion of the seventy bullocks sacrificed on Sukkot. According to the sages (Sukkah 55b), it appears that these bulls were offered on behalf of the seventy nations of the world, as the gentile nations were also judged during Sukkot as to whether they would receive rain (see Zech. xiv; 17). While we do find this idea in the Zohar (III, 54b–55a), it is generally understood negatively. First, the bullocks are sacrificed to the gentile ministers so that the latter would deal with the nations and leave Israel alone, not disturbing God's celebration with his children Israel on *Shemini Atseret*, the holiday exclusively for Israel (Zohar, I, 64a in accordance with Numbers xxix; 35: "On the eighth day *you* shall have a solemn assembly"; and on that day there are no longer sacrifices on behalf of the nations of the world. The idea in general is similar to the theme of the goat for Azazel [scapegoat] as it is understood in the Zohar in the wake of *Pirkei de-R. Eliezer*). Moreover, the fact that the number of bullocks offered during the festival decreases each day is seen in the Zohar (III, 24b) as a symbol of the progressive weakening and destruction of the nations. The gift we make to them on the holiday (the bullocks and libation of the water) is in the nature of Proverbs xxv; 21–22: "If your enemy is hungry, give him bread to eat; and if he is thirsty, give him water to drink: For you shall heap coals of fire upon his head. . . ." Our rejoicing on Sukkot is to a great degree rejoicing at their misfortune, and we must rejoice in this even more than on other days of the year, in order to heap more coals of fire on the head of the gentiles (Zohar, III, 259a).

Bibliography

Altmann, A. *Faces of Judaism* (Hebrew). Edited by A. Shapira. Tel Aviv, 1983.

Baer, I. F. "The Historical Background of the *Ra'aya Mehemana*." *Zion* V (1940). 1–44.

Benayahu, M. *Toledoth Ha-Ari* (Hebrew), Jerusalem, 1967.

Catholica Encyclopedia. New York, 1912.

Cohen-Alloro, D. *The Secret of the Garment in the Zohar* (Hebrew), Jerusalem, 1987.

_____. "Magic in the Zohar and Adam's Fall" (Hebrew). *Da'at* 19 (1987). 31–65.

Dan, J. ed. *The Age of the Zohar: Proceedings of the Third International Conference on the History of Jewish Mysticism* (=*Jerusalem Studies in Jewish Thought* 8) (Hebrew). Jerusalem, 1989.

Encyclopedia Judaica. Jerusalem, 1971.

Farber, A. ed. *A Commentary on Ezekiel I, By R. Ya'acov ha-Kohen* (Hebrew). Jerusalem, 1978. Photocopy.

Ginzberg, L. *The Legends of the Jews*, Philadelphia 1968.

Goldreich, A. "Sefer Me'irat Einayim By R. Isaac of Acre." Ph.d. Diss. The Hebrew University of Jerusalem, 1981.

Gottlieb, E. *The Kabbalah in the Writing of R. Bahya ben Asher Ibn Halawa* (Hebrew). Jerusalem, 1970.

_____. *Studies in the Kabbala Literature* (Hebrew). Tel Aviv, 1976.

Idel, M. "The Evil Thought of the Deity" (Hebrew). *Tarbiz* 49 (1980), 356–364.

_____. *Kabbalah: New Perspectives*. Yale University Press, 1988.

———. "Kabbalistic Material from R. David ben Yehuda he-Hasid's School" (Hebrew). *Jerusalem Studies in Jewish Thought* 2 (1983): 169–207.

———. *Studies in Ecstatic Kabbalah*. State University of New York Press, 1988.

———. "The World of Angels in Human Shape" (Hebrew). In *Studies in Jewish Mysticism, Philosophy and Ethical Literature Presented to Isaiah Tishby* (= *Jerusalem Studies in Jewish Thought* 3), edited by J. Dan and J. Hacker, 1–66. Jerusalem, 1966.

———. "The Writings of R. Abraham Abulafia and His Doctrine ([Hebrew] Kitvei R. Avrham Abulafia u-Mishnato)." Ph.D. diss. Hebrew University, Jerusalem, 1976.

Jellinek, A. *Bet ha-Midrasch*, I–IV (Hebrew). Jerusalem, 1967.

Jonas, H. *The Gnostic Religion*. Boston, 1966.

Liebes, Y. "The Angels of the Shofar and Yeshua Sar ha-Panim" (Hebrew). In *Early Jewish Mysticism*, edited by J. Dan, 171–195. Jerusalem, 1987 (= *Jerusalem Studies in Jewish Thought* 6).

———. "The Author of the Book Tsaddik Yesod Olam - the Sabbataian Prophet, Rabbi Leib Prossnitz." *Da'at I* (1978): 73–120.

———. "Criticism on the Book *Between the Lines* by Chaim Wirszubski" (Hebrew). *Tarbiz* 60 (1991), 131–138.

———. "Jones as the Messiah the son of Joseph" (Hebrew). In *Studies in Jewish Mysticism, Philosophy and Ethical Literature Presented to Isaiah Tishby*, edited by J. Dan and J. Hacker, 269–311. Jerusalem, 1986. (= *Jerusalem Studies in Jewish Thought* 3).

———. "The Myth of the Tikkum of the Godhead: The Zohar and Jonathan Ratosh" (Hebrew). Forthcoming.

———. "Myth versus Symbol in the Zohar and Lurianic Kabbala" (Hebrew). *Eshel Be'er Sheva'*. Forthcoming.

———. "New Trends in Kabbala Research" (Hebrew). *Pe'amin*. Forthcoming.

———. "On a Secret Judeo-Christian Sect Originated within Sabbateanism" (Hebrew). *Tarbiz* 57 (1988): 349–384.

———. "Sabbath Meal Songs established by the Holy Ari" (Hebrew). *Molad* IV (1972): 540–555.

———. "Sections of the Zohar Lexicon" (Hebrew). Ph.D. diss. The Hebrew University of Jerusalem, 1986.

———. *Studies in Jewish Myth and Messianism*. State University of New York Press. Forthcoming.

_____. "Who Makes the Horn of Jesus Flourish." *Immanuel* 21 (1987): 55–67.

Macdonald, J. *The Theology of the Samaritans*. London, 1964.

Matt, D. C. *Zohar: The Book of Enlightenment*. New York, 1983.

_____. *The Book of Mirrors by R. David ben Yehuda he-Hasid*. Chico Ca., 1981.

Meier, M. "A Critical Edition of the Sefer Ta'amey ha-Mizwoth by R. Joseph of Hamadan." Ph.D. diss. Brandeis University 1974.

Piekarz, M. *The Beginning of Hasidism*. Jerusalem, 1978.

Scholem, G. G. *Catalogus Codicum Hebracorum. . . Bibliotheca Hierosolymlitana* ([Hebrew] Kitvei Yad be-Kabbala). Jerusalem, 1930.

_____. "The Commentary of R. Issac to Ezekiel's Chariot" (Hebrew). *Tarbiz* II: 188–217.

_____. *Elements of the Kabbalah and its Symbolism* ([Hebrew] Pirqei Yesod be-Havanat ha-Kabbala u-Smaleha). Jerusalem, 1976.

_____. "The Evolution of the Doctrine of the Worlds in the Early Kabbala" (Hebrew). *Tarbiz* II: 415–442; *Tarbiz* III: 33–66.

_____. *Explications and Implications, Writings on Jewish Heritage and Renaissance* ([Hebrew] Devarim be-Go). Tel Aviv, 1975.

_____. "An Inquiry in the Kabbala of R. Issac ben Jacob ha-Cohen" (Hebrew) *Tarbiz* II–V (1931–1934).

_____. *Jewish Gnosticism, Merkabah Mysticism and Talmudic Tradition*. New York, 1960.

_____. *Kabbalah*. Jerusalem, 1974.

_____. "The Kabbala of R. Jacob and R. Isaac, the sons of R. Jacob ha-Kohen' (Hebrew). *Mada'ei ha-Yahadut* II (1927): 165–293.

_____. *Major Trends in Jewish Mysticism*. New York 1961.

_____. *The Messianic Idea in Judaism*. New York 1971.

_____. "R. Moshe of Burgos, the Disciple of R. Issac" (Hebrew). *Tarbiz* III: 258–286; IV: 54–57, 207–225; V: 50–60, 180–198, 305–323.

_____. *Shabbatai Sevi, The Mystical Messiah*. Princeton, New Jersey, 1973.

_____. "Sidrei de-Shimmusha Rabba" (Hebrew). *Tarbiz* XVI (1945): 196–209.

_____. "Two Fragments of R. Moshe de Leon, Fragment from *Shoshan Edut*; *Sod Eser Sefirot Belima* ([Hebrew] Shenei Kuntresim le-R. Moshe de Leon)." Kovets al Yad, VIII (XVIII) Jerusalem 1976, 325–384.

————. *Urspung and Anfänge der Kabbala.* Berlin, 1962.

————. *Zohar: The Book of Splendor.* New York 1974.

Ta-Shma, Israel M. "Rabbi Joseph Karo: Between Spain and Germany" (Hebrew). *Tarbiz* 59 (1990): 153–170.

Tishby I. *Commentarius in Aggadot Auctore R. Azriel Geronensi* (Hebrew). Jerusalem 1945.

————. *The Doctrine of Evil and the Kelippah in Lurianic Kabbalism* (Hebrew). Jerusalem, 1962.

————. *The Wisdom of the Zohar.* Oxford, 1989.

Urbach E. E. "The Traditions about Merkabah Mysticism in the Tannaitic Period" (Hebrew). In *Studies in Mysticism and Religion presented to Gershom Scholem.* Jerusalem, 1967.

Werblowsky, R. J. Z. *Joseph Karo - Lawyer and Mystic.* Oxford, 1962.

Wertheimer S. A. (A. I. Wertheimer - new edition). *Battei Midrashot* (Hebrew). I–II (Jerusalem 1950–1953).

Wilhelm, Y. D. "Sidrei Tikkunim" (Hebrew). In *'Alei 'Ayin - The S. Schoken Jubilee Volume* (Hebrew). Jerusalem 1948–1952, 125–146.

Wolfson, E. R. *The Book of Pomegranate by R. Moses de Leon.* Atlanta, 1988.

————. "Circumcision and the Divine Name: a Study in the Transmission of Esoteric Doctrine." *Jewish Quarterly Review* 78 (1987): 77–112.

————. "Circumcision, Vision of God, and textual Interpretation: From Midrashic Trope to Mystical Symbol." *History of Religion* 27 (1987): 189–215.

————. "The Hermeneutics of Visionary Experience: Revelation and Interpretation in the Zohar." *Religion* 18 (1988): 311–345.

————. "Left Contains the Right: a Study in Zoharic Hermeneutics." *Association for Jewish Studies Review* 2 (1986): 27–52.

————. "Light through Darkness: The Ideal of Human Perfection in the Zohar." *Harvard Theological Review* 81 (1988): 73–95.

Wright, G. R. H. "The Heritage of Stylites." *Australian Journal of Biblical Archaeology* I, Fasc. 3, (1970): 82–107.

Zwelling, J. "Joseph of Hamadan's *Sefer Tashak.*" Ph.D. diss. Brandeis University, 1975.

All footnotes from the *Zohar, Zohar Hadash,* and *Tikunei Zohar* are from Mosad Harav Kook's version.

Sources

Following are the original Hebrew sources of the essays published in this book:

"The Messiah of the Zohar: on R. Simeon bar Yohai as a Messianic Figure." In: S. Re'em, ed., *The Messianic Idea in Jewish Thought: A Study Conference in Honour of the Eightieth Birthday of Gershom Scholem, Held 4–5 December 1977*, Publications of the Israel Academy of Sciences and Humanities, Jerusalem 1982, pp. 87–236.

"How the Zohar was Written." In J. Dan, ed., *The Age of the Zohar: Proceedings of the Third International Conference on the History of Jewish Mysticism*, pp. 1–71. *Jerusalem Studies in Jewish Thought*, 8, Jerusalem, 1989.

"Christian Influences in the Zohar." *Jerusalem Studies in Jewish Thought*, 2, 1982–1983, pp. 43–74.

Index of Subjects, Proper Names, and Classical Works

(prepared by Haggai Rosmarin)

R. Abba, 10, 20, 21, 34, 35, 37, 75, 84, 114, 115, 118, 119, 136, 167, 214, 215, 230

R. Abbahu, 167

Abel, 134

Abner of Burgos, 141, 142, 232

Abraham, 10, 16, 37, 55, 100, 109, 146–149, 165, 166, 171, 173, 181, 188, 196, 210, 232, 233

Abraham bar Hiyya, 217

Abraham ben Azriel, 189

Abraham Ben David, 169, 200, 211

Abulafia, Abraham, 51, 65, 182, 189

Abulafia, Joseph ben Todros, 136, 168

Abulafia, Todros, 18, 19, 47, 93, 130, 135–138, 168, 182, 192, 199

Abulafia, Todros ben Judah, 137, 227

Adam, 30, 70, 113, 158, 242, 243

Adam. See Primordial Man

Aggadat Bereshit, 173

Ahiyah the Shilonite, 165

Akatriel, 65

R. Akiva, 7, 35, 38, 39, 40, 54, 64, 74, 80, 83, 97, 135, 177, 179, 188, 195, 198, 239

Alashqar, Yosef, 198

Albalag, Issac, 137

Aldabi, Meir, 188

Alkabez, Solomon, 81

Altmann, Alexander, 86, 103, 189, 194, 203, 207

Angelet, Joseph, 86, 109, 134, 178, 195, 197, 198, 207, 224, 225

Angelino, Joseph. *See* Angelet Joseph

Angels, 22, 29, 45, 52, 70, 80, 82, 118, 137, 212, 218

Antinomianism, 46, 47

Arikh Anpin, 13, 20, 36, 37, 44, 45, 48, 61, 62, 66, 170, 181. *See also* Large Countenance

Arugat ha-Bosem, 189

Aspaklaria Hame'ira, 240

Attik Yomin, 30, 44, 47, 56, 57

Attika Kaddisha 44–46, 55, 60–62, 75, 186, 187

Avraham of Granada, 225

R. Azriel of Gerona, 54, 55, 142, 175, 181, 182, 189, 221, 230, 233

Babylonian Talmud, 4, 6, 7, 14–16, 18, 21, 22, 24–29, 32–35, 38, 39, 42, 43, 47, 48, 58, 64, 65, 70, 72,

INDEX

Index of References to the Zohar

173080